Ordnance Survey Ireland

City Atlas Series

5th Edition

Dublin

City and District Street

GW00514864

General Travel Information	Route Planner	I
	M50 Map	II
	Outer Orbital Route	III
	Inner Orbital Route	IV
	Dart, Luas and Suburban Rail Network	V
	Dublin Bus Route Network	VI
Dublin City and District Maps		1
City Centre Maps		69
Tourist Information	Places to Visit	73
	Churches and Cathedrals	77
	Libraries	78
	Art Galleries	79
	Museums	80
	Famous People associated with Dublin	81
	Dublin's Parks and Gardens	83
	Embassies	85
	Dublin Bus Information	86
Index to Hospitals		90
Industrial Estates and Business Parks		91
Index to Street Names		93

Compiled and published by Ordnance Survey Ireland, Phoenix Park, Dublin 8, Ireland.
Arna thiomsú agus arna fhoilsiú ag Suirbhéireacht Ordanáis Éireann, Páirc an Fhionnuisce, Baile Átha Cliath 8, Éire.

SPECIAL THANKS TO FÁILTE IRELAND, DUBLIN CITY COUNCIL & DÚN - LAOGHAIRE RATHDOWN COUNTY COUNCIL.

Map data compiled from the OSi Database and validated to April 2004.

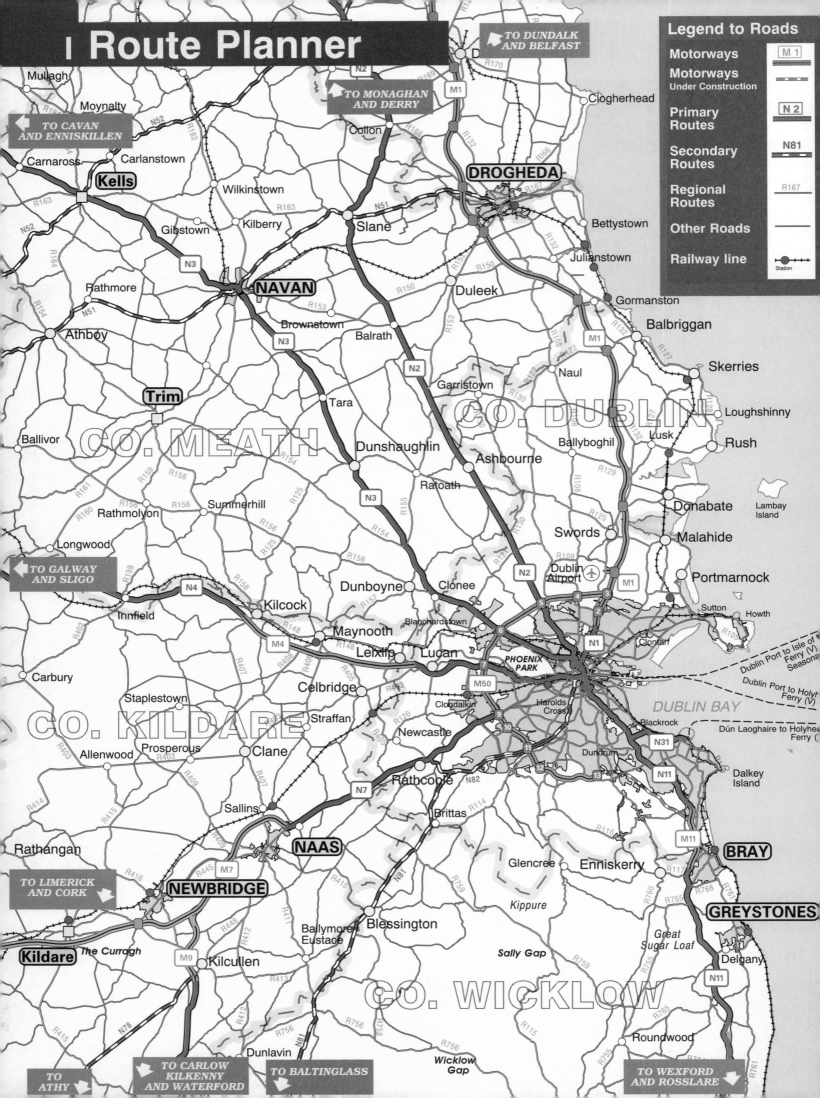

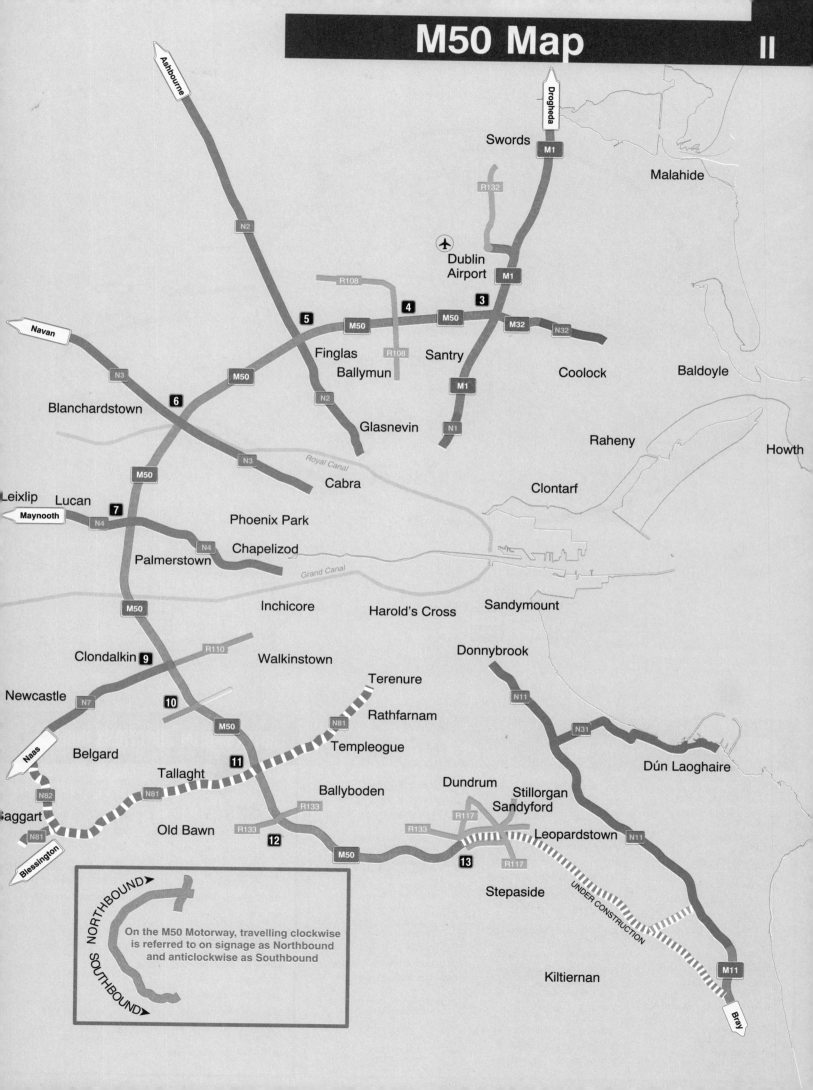

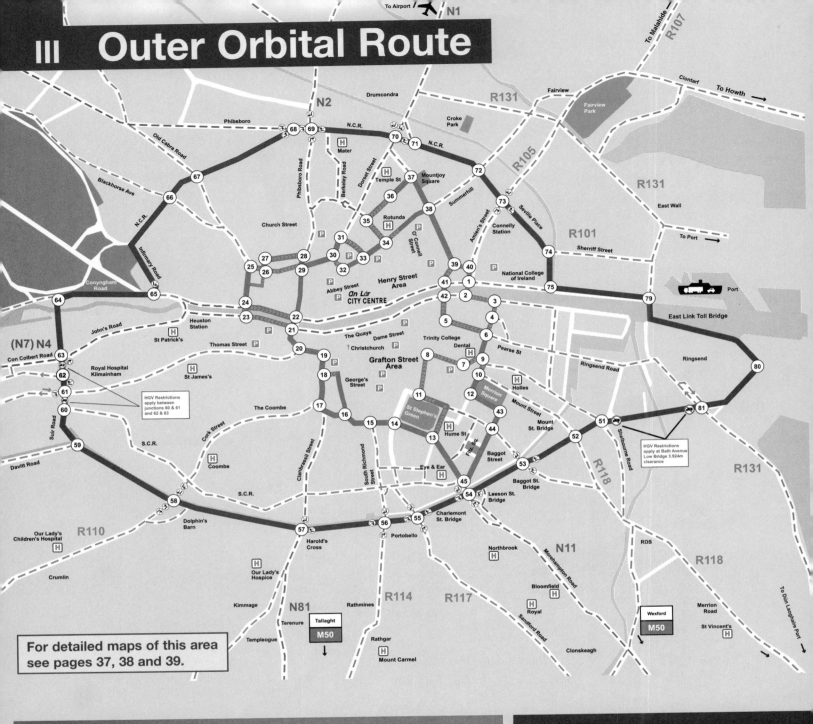

III Outer Orbital Route

For detailed maps of this area see pages 37, 38 and 39.

INNER ORBITAL JUNCTIONS INDEX

J1 Custom House Quay / Talbot Memorial Bridge
J2 Talbot Memorial Bridge / City Quay
J3 City Quay/Lombard St. East
J4 Lombard St. East / Townsend St.
J5 Pearse St. / Tara St.
J6 Pearse St. / Westland Row
J7 Clare St./Lincoln Place
J8 Dawson St. / Nassau St.
J9 Lincoln Place / Westland Row
J10 Clare St. / Merrion Square
J11 St. Stephen's Green / Dawson St.
J12 Merrion St. Upr/Merrion Sq. Sth.
J13 St. Stephen's Green / Leeson St. Lwr.
J14 St. Stephen's Green / Harcourt St.

J15 Wexford St. / Kevin St. Lwr.
J16 Kevin St. / Bride St.
J17 Kevin St. / Patrick St.
J18 Bride Rd. / Patrick St.
J19 Christchurch Place/High St.
J20 High St. / Cornmarket
J21 Bridge St./Merchant's Quay
J22 Inns Quay / Church St.
J23 Ushers Island / Blackhall Place Bridge
J24 Ellis Quay / Blackhall Place Bridge
J25 Blackhall Place / King St.
J26 King St. / George's Lane
J27 George's Lane / Brunswick St. Nth
J28 Brunswick St. Nth. / Church St. Upr
J29 King St. / Church St.
J30 Nth. King St. / Bolton St.
J31 Bolton St. / King's Inns St.

J32 Parnell St. / Ryder's Row
J33 Parnell St. / King's Inns St.
J34 Parnell St. / Parnell Square West
J35 Parnell Square West / Granby Row
J36 Parnell Sq. Nth. / Frederick St. Nth.
J37 Gardiner St. Upr / Mountjoy Square
J38 Summerhill / Gardiner St.
J39 Gardiner St. Lwr. / Beresford Place
J40 Amiens St./Beresford Place
J41 Eden Quay / Butt Bridge
J42 Tara St./Butt Bridge/Burgh Quay
J43 Merrion Sq. Sth. / Fitzwilliam St. Lwr.
J44 Fitzwilliam St. Lwr / Baggot St. Lwr
J45 Fitzwilliam Place / Leeson St. Lwr

OUTER ORBITAL JUNCTIONS INDEX

J51 Shelbourne Rd / Haddington Rd
J52 Mount St. Lwr. / Haddington Rd
J53 Baggot St. Br. / Mespil Rd
J54 Leeson St. Br. /Grand Parade
J55 Charlemont St. Br. / Ranelagh Rd
J56 Portobello / Rathmines Rd
J57 Harold's Cross Br. / Clanbrassil St.
J58 Dolphin's Barn / Crumlin Rd.
J59 Davitt Rd. / Suir Rd.
J60 Suir Rd. / SCR
J61 SCR / Old Kilmainham
J62 SCR / Inchicore Rd.
J63 SCR / St. John's Rd. West
J64 SCR / Conyngham Rd.

J65 Parkgate / Infirmary Rd.
J66 NCR / Blackhorse Ave.
J67 NCR / Prussia St.
J68 NCR / Cabra Rd.
J69 NCR / Phibsboro Rd.
J70 NCR / Dorset St. Lower
J71 NCR / Belvidere Road
J72 NCR / Summerhill
J73 Amiens St. / Seville Pl.
J74 Sheriff St. / Guild St.
J75 Guild St. / North Wall Quay
J79 North Wall Quay / East Link Br.
J80 Sean Moore Rd. / South Bank Rd.
J81 Sean Moore Rd. / Beach Rd.

Legend

- INNER ORBITAL ROUTE
- ONE WAY SYSTEM
- ROUTE TO / FROM O'CONNELL ST.
- PEDESTRIAN STREET
- 38 JUNCTION NUMBER
- COMPULSORY MOVE
- RESTRICTED TURNS
- CAR PARK ROUTE
- DART LINE
- RED LUAS LINE
- GREEN LUAS LINE

J19

Dublin City
Ceantar Shr. Anraí
↑ P HENRY ST. AREA
← N4 - N7 M50 ←
Ceantar Shr. Grafton
GRAFTON ST. AREA P →

You are travelling on the Inner Orbital from junction 17 approaching junction 19. Go straight ahead for Parking if shopping in the Henry Street area.

Turn left to leave the Inner Orbital and head towards the N4, N7 and M50.

Turn Right for Parking if shopping in the Grafton Street area.

For detailed maps of this area see pages 69, 70 and 71.

To help you plan your journeys we have indicated some relevant turn restrictions and compulsory movements on the orbital routes.

Please keep them in mind when you are planning your route.

This information has been supplied by Road and Traffic Department, Dublin City Council

V Dart, Luas and Suburban Rail Network

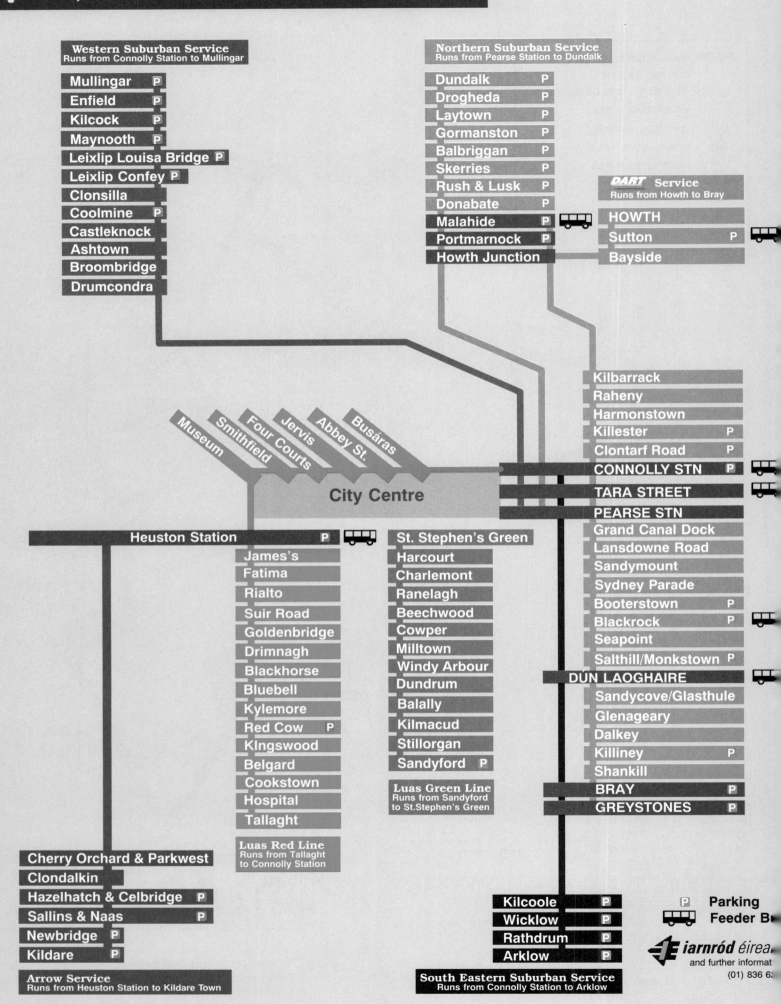

Western Suburban Service
Runs from Connolly Station to Mullingar

- Mullingar P
- Enfield P
- Kilcock P
- Maynooth P
- Leixlip Louisa Bridge P
- Leixlip Confey P
- Clonsilla
- Coolmine P
- Castleknock
- Ashtown
- Broombridge
- Drumcondra

Northern Suburban Service
Runs from Pearse Station to Dundalk

- Dundalk P
- Drogheda P
- Laytown P
- Gormanston P
- Balbriggan P
- Skerries P
- Rush & Lusk P
- Donabate P
- Malahide P
- Portmarnock P
- Howth Junction

DART Service
Runs from Howth to Bray

- HOWTH
- Sutton P
- Bayside
- Kilbarrack
- Raheny
- Harmonstown
- Killester P
- Clontarf Road P
- CONNOLLY STN P
- TARA STREET
- PEARSE STN
- Grand Canal Dock
- Lansdowne Road
- Sandymount
- Sydney Parade
- Booterstown P
- Blackrock P
- Seapoint
- Salthill/Monkstown P
- DÚN LAOGHAIRE
- Sandycove/Glasthule
- Glenageary
- Dalkey
- Killiney P
- Shankill
- BRAY P
- GREYSTONES P

Museum · Smithfield · Four Courts · Jervis · Abbey St. · Busáras

City Centre

Heuston Station P

- James's
- Fatima
- Rialto
- Suir Road
- Goldenbridge
- Drimnagh
- Blackhorse
- Bluebell
- Kylemore
- Red Cow P
- Kingswood
- Belgard
- Cookstown
- Hospital
- Tallaght

Luas Red Line
Runs from Tallaght to Connolly Station

- St. Stephen's Green
- Harcourt
- Charlemont
- Ranelagh
- Beechwood
- Cowper
- Milltown
- Windy Arbour
- Dundrum
- Balally
- Kilmacud
- Stillorgan
- Sandyford P

Luas Green Line
Runs from Sandyford to St.Stephen's Green

- Cherry Orchard & Parkwest
- Clondalkin
- Hazelhatch & Celbridge P
- Sallins & Naas P
- Newbridge P
- Kildare P

Arrow Service
Runs from Heuston Station to Kildare Town

- Kilcoole P
- Wicklow P
- Rathdrum P
- Arklow P

South Eastern Suburban Service
Runs from Connolly Station to Arklow

P Parking
Feeder B

iarnród éirea
and further informat
(01) 836 6

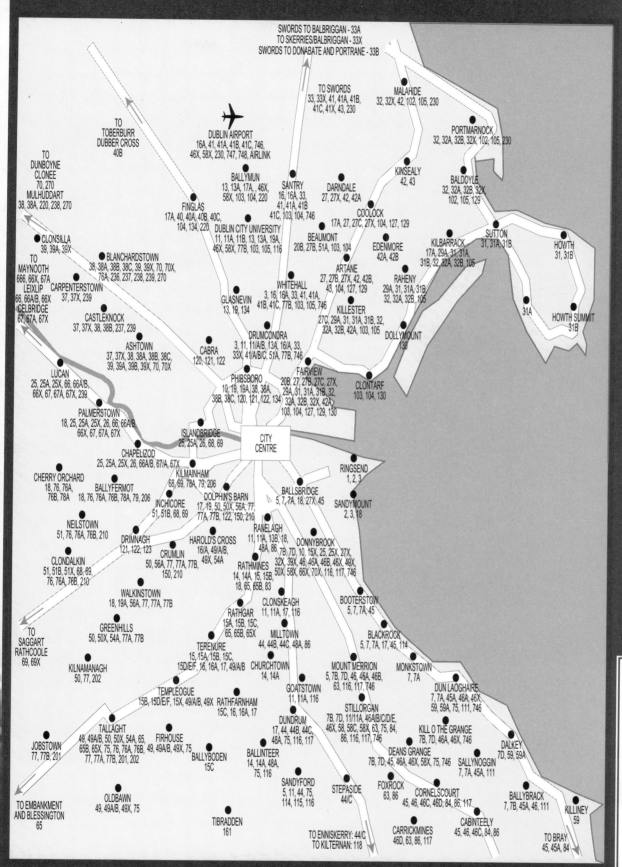

Dublin Bus operates the bus network in the greater Dublin area. This network extends from Balbriggan in North County Dublin to Kilcoole in County Wicklow and westwards as far as Kilcock, County Kildare.

INFORMATION BUREAU AND CUSTOMER SERVICE

Tel. (01) 873 4222 9am to 7pm (Mon - Sat)

Dublin Bus, 59 Upr. O'Connell Street, Dublin 1.

Website: www.dublinbus.ie
e-mail: info@dublinbus.ie

Sept. 2002

Corballis Golf Links

Strand

IRISH   SEA

Biscayne

COAST   ROAD

Castle
Robbswall

The
Lighthouse

THE
CRESCENT

WALK   PATH

The Anchorage
and Spinnaker

THE
CRESCENT

32A
32X
42N
102

105
230

MONKS
MEADOW

32

32B

LIME TREE   AVENUE

CONVENT   LANE

ELMER
COURT

ASHLEY   RISE

HEATHER
GARDENS

Martello
Tower

HATFIELD
GROVE

BRIAR
WALK

WHEATFIELD   ROAD

BRACKEN DRIVE

KELVIN CLOSE

BLACKTHORN
CLOSE

DEWBERRY
PARK

HEATHER
WALK

42N

WENDELL AVENUE

230 102 32X

MARTELLO COURT

WENDELL   AVE

CARRICKHILL

32B
105

CARRICKHILL
WALK

PORTMARNOCK

CARRICKHILL
CLOSE

ROAD

PARK

RISE

STRAND   ROAD

WALK

PARKVIEW

RISE

PORTMARNOCK CRESCENT

AVE

DRIVE

BURROW CT

CARRICKHILL

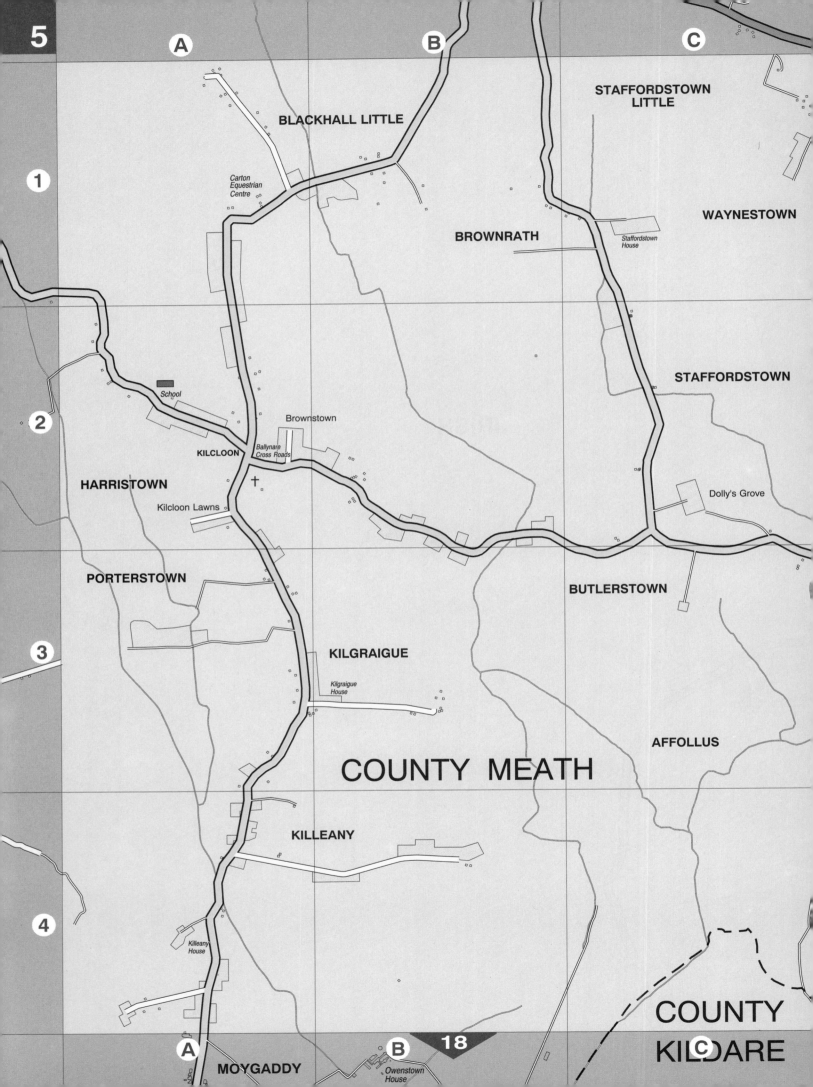

A   B   C

STAFFORDSTOWN
LITTLE

BLACKHALL LITTLE

1

*Carton
Equestrian
Centre*

BROWNRATH

WAYNESTOWN

*Staffordstown
House*

STAFFORDSTOWN

School

2

Brownstown

*Ballynare
Cross Roads*

KILCLOON

Dolly's Grove

HARRISTOWN

Kilcloon Lawns

PORTERSTOWN

BUTLERSTOWN

3

KILGRAIGUE

*Kilgraigue
House*

AFFOLLUS

COUNTY MEATH

4

KILLEANY

*Killeany
House*

A   B   18

MOYGADDY   *Owenstown
House*

COUNTY
KILDARE

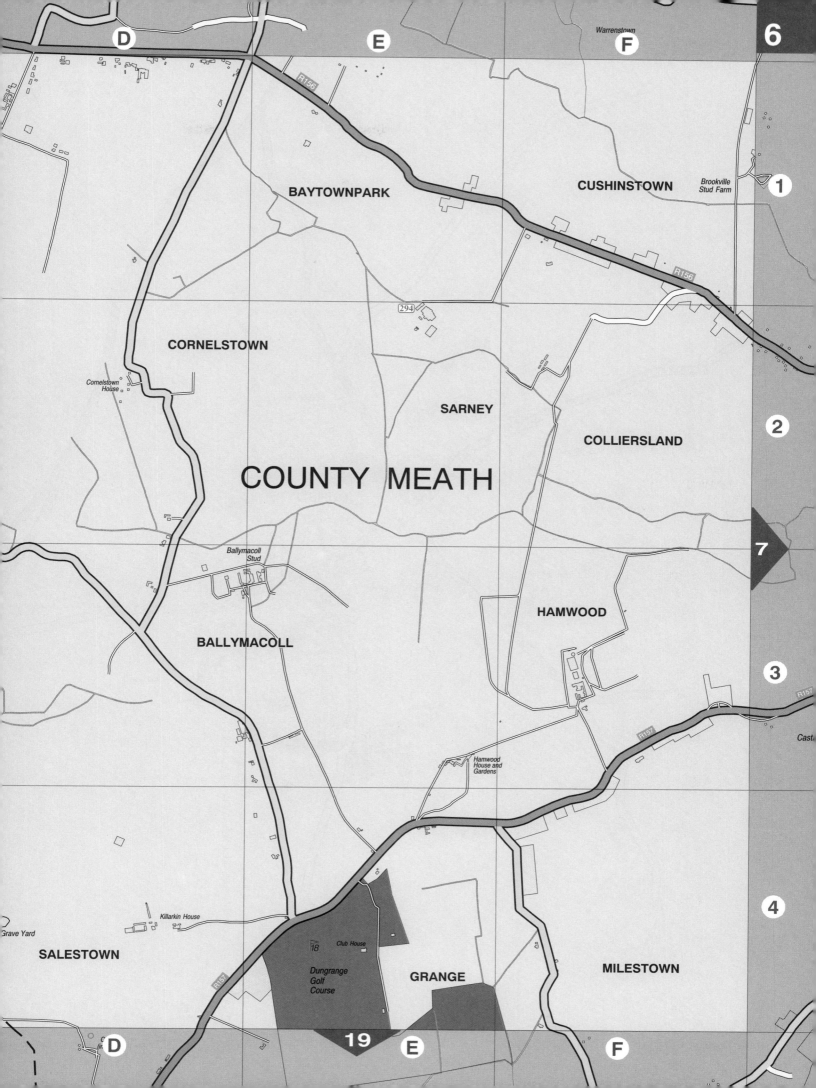

D
E
Warrenstown
F
6

R156

BAYTOWNPARK

CUSHINSTOWN
Brookville
Stud Farm
1

R156

294

CORNELSTOWN

Cornelstown
House

SARNEY

COLLIERSLAND
2

COUNTY MEATH

Ballymacoll
Stud
7

HAMWOOD

BALLYMACOLL
3

R157

Cast

Hamwood
House and
Gardens

Grave Yard
Killarkin House
4

SALESTOWN
R157
18
Club House
Dungrange
Golf
Course
GRANGE
MILESTOWN

D
19
E
F

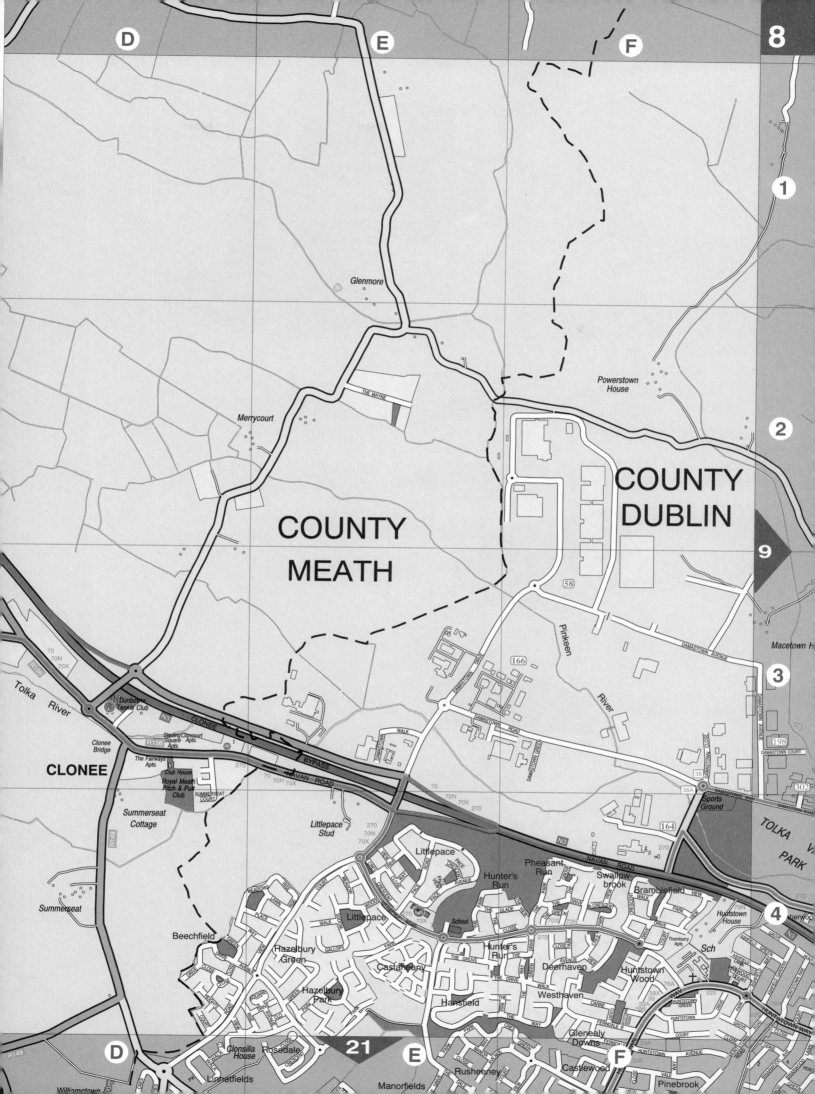

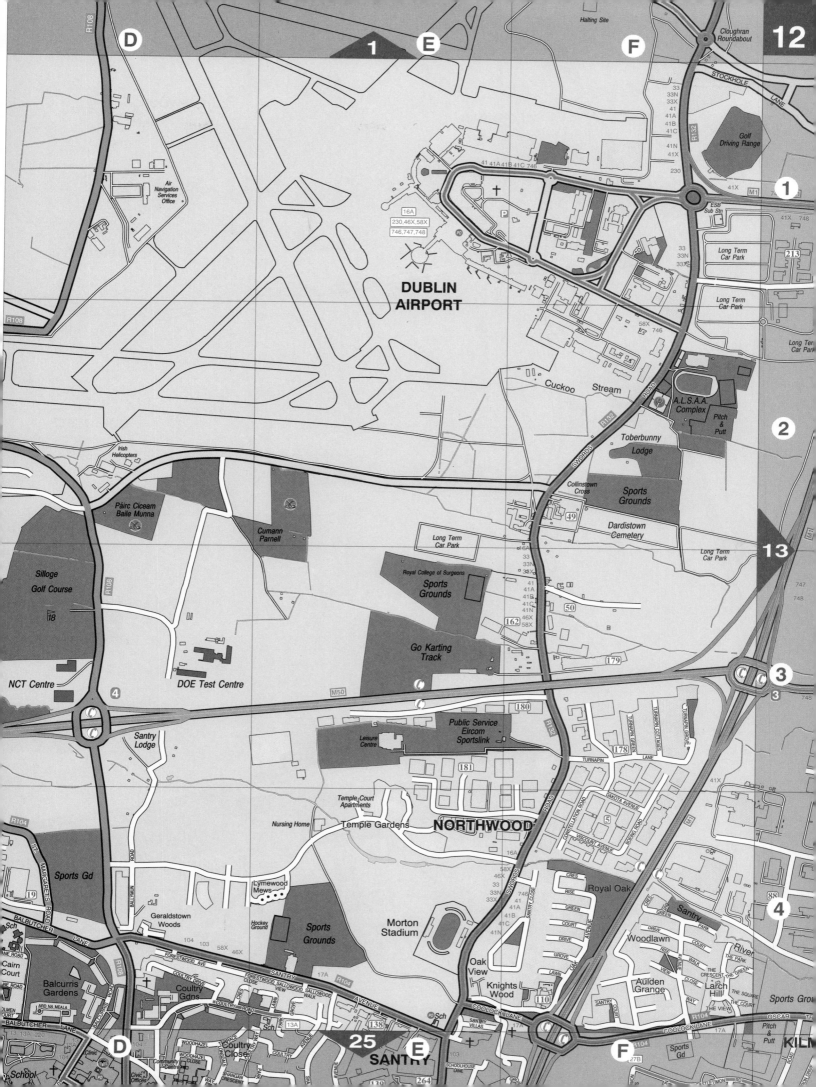

D FELTRIM

Myra
Manor

3 E Eircom

THE
Grange

F

Sports & Leisure
Centre P.S.L.C.
Sports
Gd

230

Portmarnock Stud
Community
School

GRANGE

Club House

PINE
CT

WOODLANDS

102
230

BEECHWOOD

Sports
Ground

KINSALEY

HAZELBROOK

Ardilaun

Malahide Golf Club
27

Kinsaley
Hall

Carrick
Court

1

Kinsaley
Lane

Kinsaley
Bridge

Grave
Yard

Church
(in Ruins)

CHAPEL   ROAD

Church
(in Ruins)

Car
Park

Trotting
Track

Portmarnock
Driving
Range

OLD ROAD

The Links

Sluice River

St PATRICK'S AVE

St MARNOCK'S AVE

102

STRANDMILL AVENUE

School

Teagasc

Research
Centre

Kinsaley
House

Seabrook
Manor

THE FAIRWAYS

GREENFIELD

Seagrave

CADDELL RD

Tennis
Ground

Baldoyle Estuary
Nature Reserve

230

STRAND ROAD

HAZEL GROVE

Pitch
& Putt

School

Station
House

RATHMORE

MILLFIELD

Millbank

42N
230

Portmarnock
Bridge

32X

STATION   ROAD

Car
Park
Portmarnock
Station

Murragh

2

32
32B

Drumnigh
House

Drumnigh
Wood

32A

R124

32X

St Doolagh's Park
Nursing Home

Trinity Gaels

Club
House

Car
Park

DRUMNIGH ROAD

DRUMNIGH

102

15

SAINTDOOLAGHS

Car
Park

MAYNETOWN

BALGRIFFIN

Cemetery

R123

R124

R123   ROAD

Moyne Lodge

MOYNE   ROAD

Wellfield

SNUGBOROUGH

Moyne
Park

Mayne
Bridge

3

BALGRIFFIN
PARK

Balgriffin
Cottages

BALGRIFFIN

Sports
Ground

Mayne   River

32
32A
32B

FATHER COLLINS
PARK

Bridge

32K

R107

THE HOLE IN THE WALL ROAD

Sports Grounds

STAPOLIN

102

Health
Centre

Clare Hall

TEMPLEVIEW
AVENUE

ELMFIELD WAY

Apartments

Grattan
Lodge

Grattan
Hall

127

29A

Trinity
Sports and Leisure
Club

Newgrove
Estate

Sch

DONAGHMEDE

CASTLEROSSE
CRESCENT

School

BALDOY

4

Clare Hall
Shopping Centre

27 27C 127

27.27X 27C

ELMFIELD AVENUE

GRANGE ABBEY ROAD

GRANGE ABBEY DRIVE

Baldoyle Badminton
Club

STAPOLIN

GRANGE   ROAD

29N 129

Youth
Club

D

Sports
Grounds

GRANGEMORE

DRIVE

GRANGEMORE LAWN

Grangemore

27

E

School

GRANGE ABBEY
CRESCENT

GRANGE ABBEY
GROVE

DONAGHMEDE
PARK

GRANGE

29N 129

F

Sc

GRANGE PARK

SEAGRANGE
DRIVE

The Steer

Tower

**Ireland's
Eye**

Carrigeen Bay

Rowan Rocks

Thulla Rocks

Thulla

Lighthouse

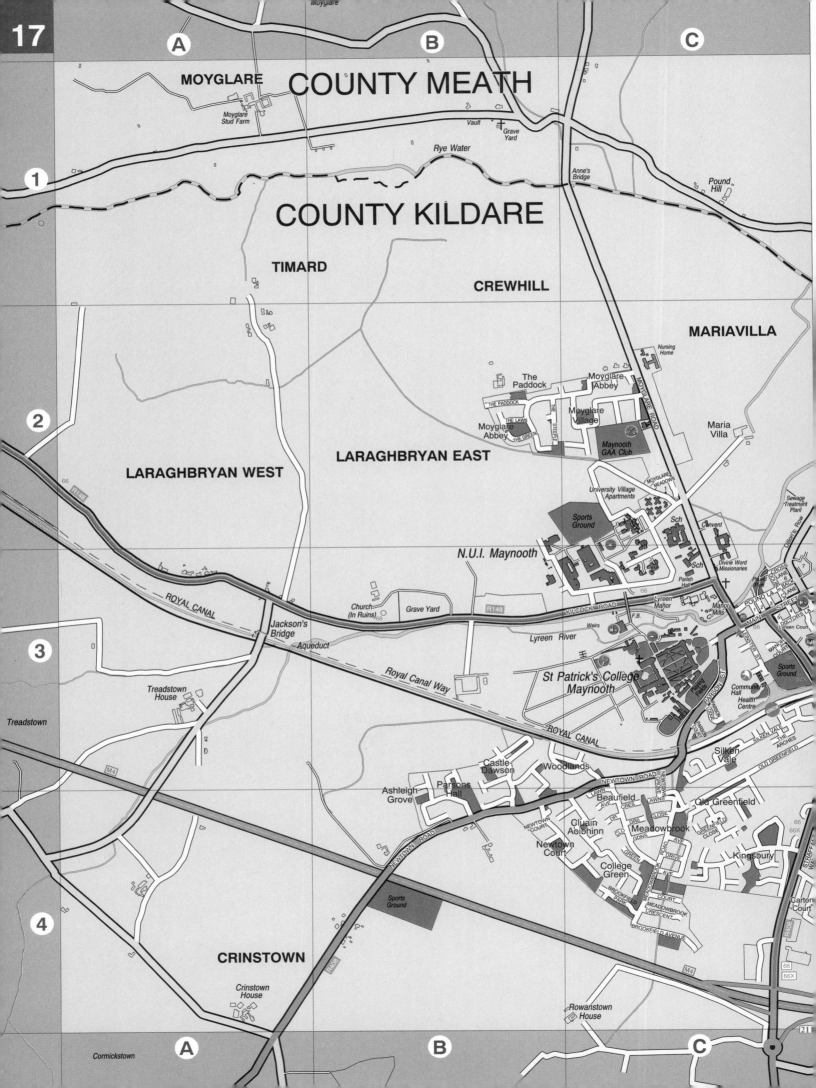

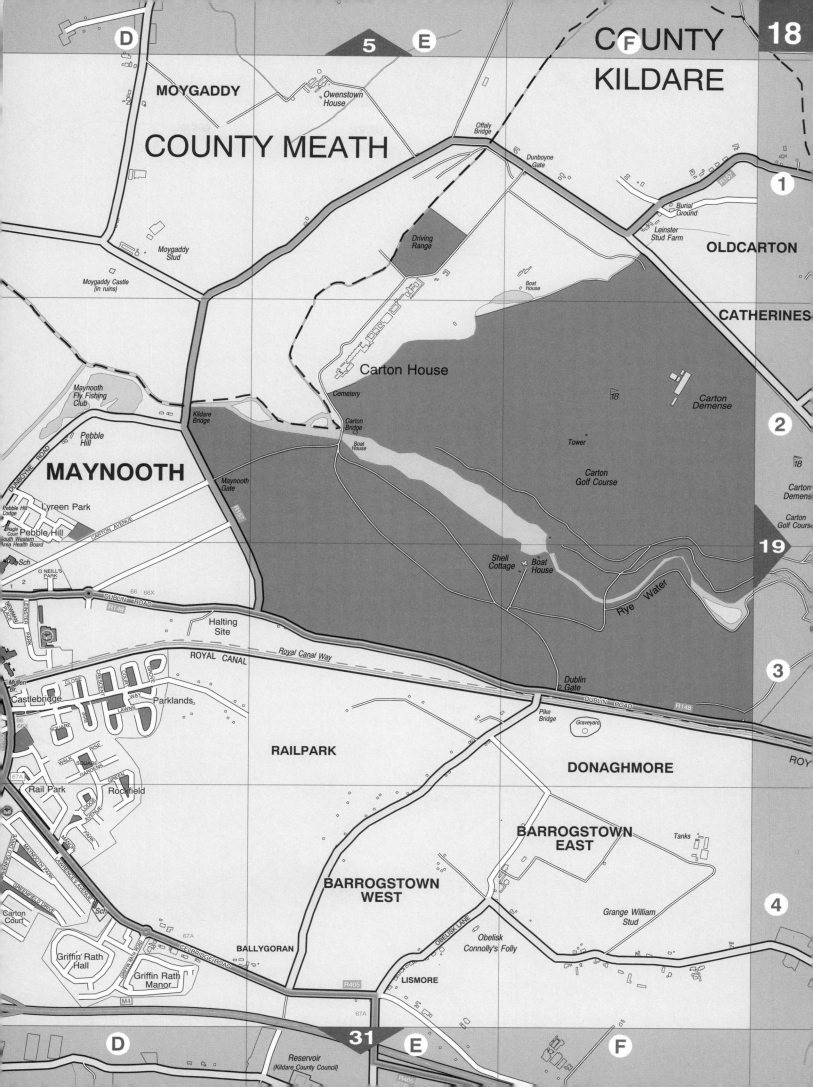

D   5   E   COUNTY
KILDARE

MOYGADDY

COUNTY MEATH

Owenstown
House

Offaly
Bridge

Dunboyne
Gate

R157

Burial
Ground

OLDCARTON

Leinster
Stud Farm

1

CATHERINES

Moygaddy
Stud

Driving
Range

Boat
House

2

Moygaddy Castle
(in ruins)

Carton House

Maynooth
Fly Fishing
Club

Cemetery

18

Carton
Demense

Pebble
Hill

Kildare
Bridge

Carton
Bridge

Tower

Carton
Demense

MAYNOOTH

Maynooth
Gate

Boat
House

Carton
Golf Course

18

Pebble Hill
Lodge

R157

Carton
Golf Course

Lyreen Park

Nagle
Court
South Western
Area Health Board

Pebble Hill

CARTON AVENUE

Sch

Shell
Cottage

Boat
House

19

O NEILL'S
PARK

NEWMAN

LEINSTER PARK

1
2

Sch

66 66X

DUBLIN   ROAD

R148

Rye   Water

PLACE

Halting
Site

Royal Canal Way

3

Mullen
Br.

Castlebridge

ROYAL   CANAL

Dublin
Gate

DUBLIN   ROAD   R148

ROY

66
66X

CLOSE

COURT

CRESCENT

GROVE

WAY

Parklands

Pike
Bridge

Graveyard

SQUARE

LAWNS

RISE.

GARDENS

GREEN

RAILPARK

DONAGHMORE

67A

WALK

SQUARE

LODGE

AVENUE

PARK

Rail Park

Rockfield

BARROGSTOWN
EAST

Tanks

GREENFIELD DRIVE

MAYNOOTH PARK

LAWRENCE'S AVENUE

Sch

Carton
Court

BARROGSTOWN
WEST

Grange William
Stud

4

GREENFIELD DRIVE

GREEN RATH ROAD

67A

CELBRIDGE ROAD

BALLYGORAN

OBELISK LANE

Obelisk
Connolly's Folly

Griffin Rath
Hall

Griffin Rath
Manor

M4

R405

LISMORE

67A

D   31   E   F

Reservoir
(Kildare County Council)

R405

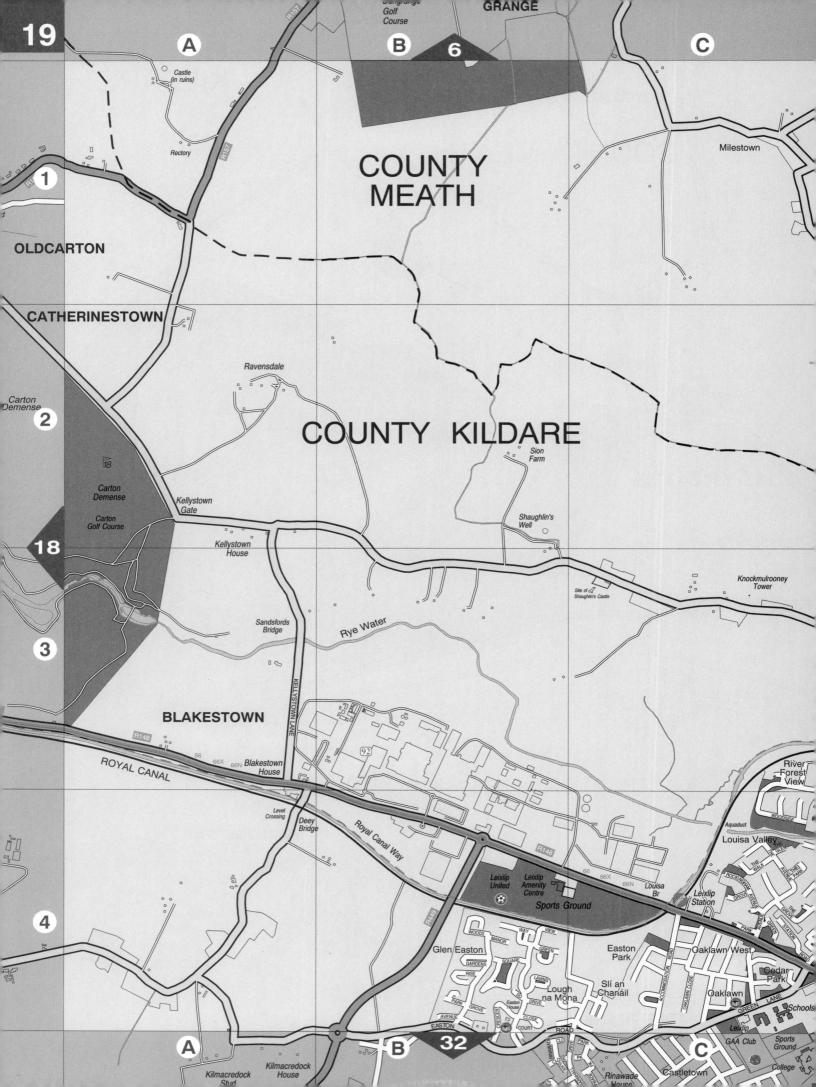

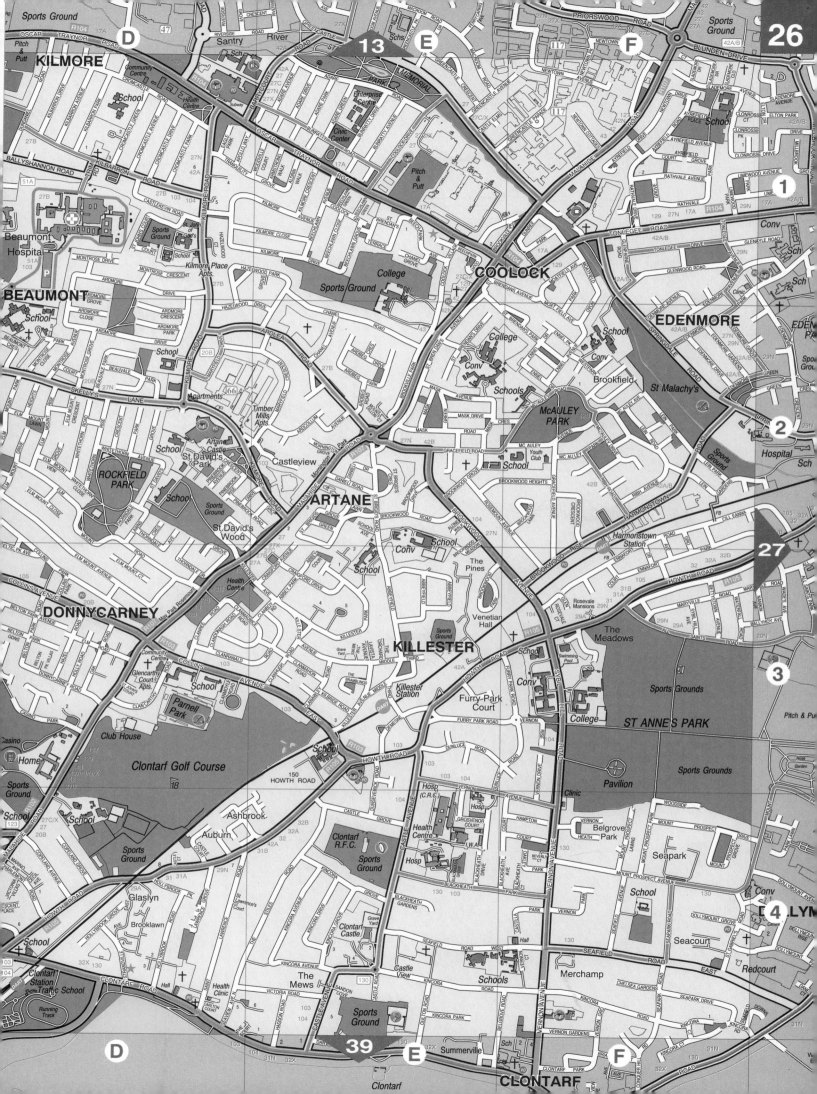

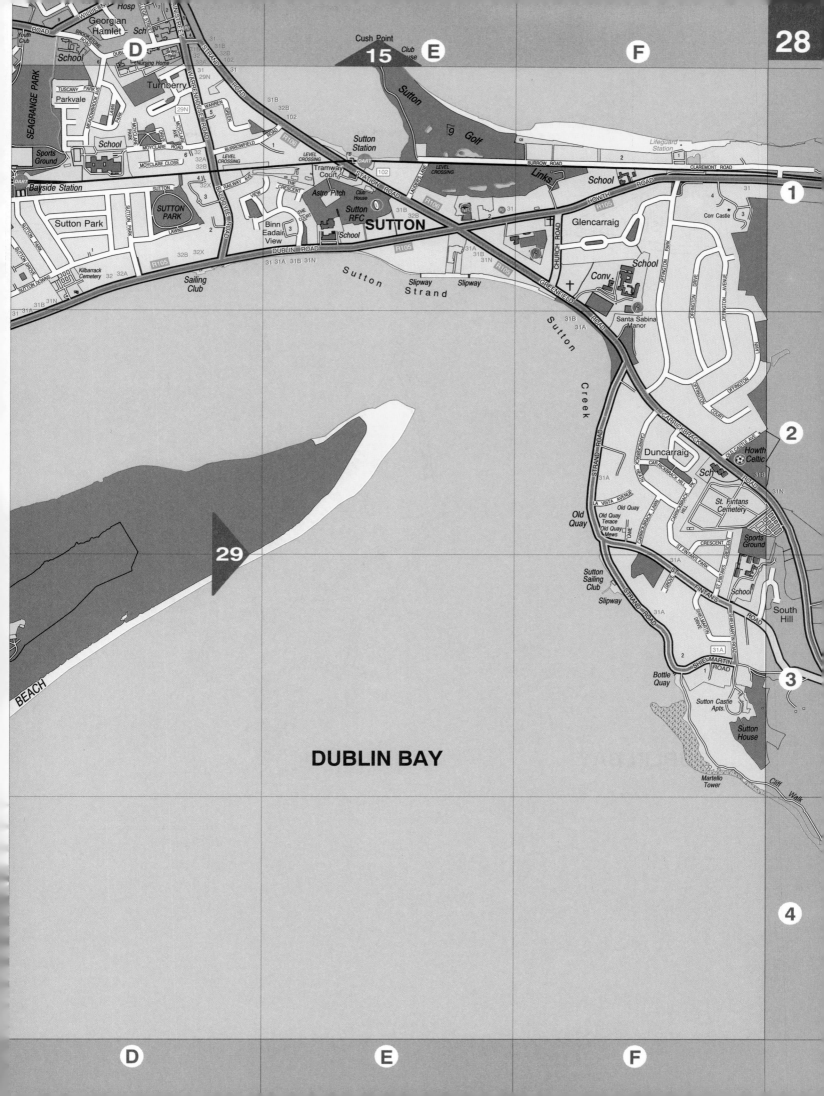

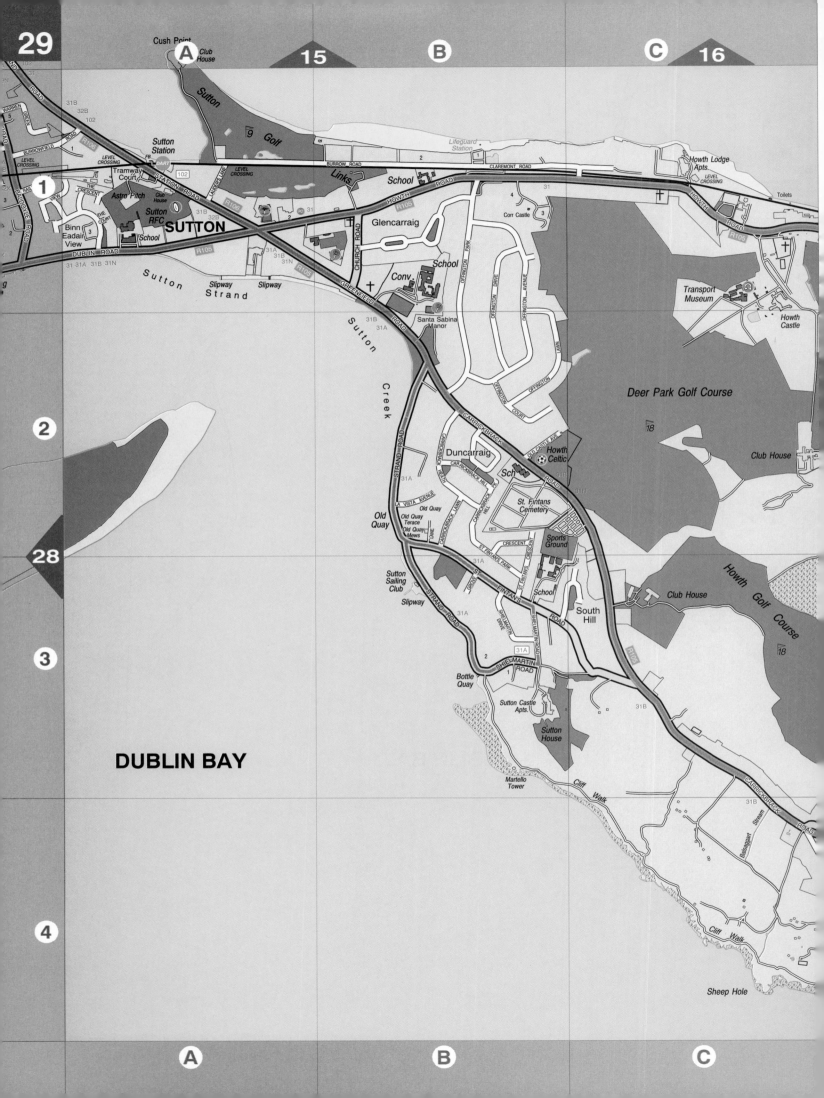

Lighthouse

Slipway

WEST PIER

HOWTH HARBOUR

Slipway

Slipway

EAST PIER

Howth Station

DART

Slipway

Lifeboat Station

Yacht Club

Toilets

7 | 31B | 31N

14   31

HARBOUR

CHURCH   ROAD

10

13   11

Tower

STREET

ABBEY

Asgard Apts.

Balscadden Bay

Baths

Puck's Rocks

EVORA PARK

ST LAURENCE

6

Health Centre

LANE

31B

BALSCADDEN   ROAD

KILROCK   ROAD

ASGARD   PARK

Kilrock

Nose of Howth

Deer

12

GRACE O'MALLEY RD

1

School

HOWTH

NASHVILLE   PARK

Park

TUCKETTS

31

ST PETERS TERRACE

9

12

14

7

2

NASHVILLE   ROAD

R105

LANE

COMBRIDGE

Sch

Kilrock

Golf

27

GRACE O'MALLEY DRIVE

11

MAIN

STREET

RD

13

ASGARD   ROAD

THORMANBY

Cannon Rock

Course

BALKILL PARK

8

31B

Cannon Rock Cottage

BALKILL PARK

BALGLASS   RD

THORMANBY LAWNS

THORMANBY

Gull Cottage

Cannon Rock

Reservoir

BALKILL   ROAD

DUNGRIFFAN

ROAD

2

MARINERS COVE

3

CASANA VIEW

Cliff

Casana Rock

Beann Éadair G.A.A. Club

Club House

WOODCLIFF

GREY'S LANE

WOODCLIFF HEIGHTS

Rockstown

Thormanby Woods

Thormanby Lodge

Walk

Green Ivy

Woodside

BALKILL   ROAD

WINDGATE

Howth Hill Lodge Nursing Home

Piper's Gut

Ben of Howth

Green Hallows Quarries

Blakeney House (Mews)

31

31B

Fox Hole

The Green Hallows

KITESTOWN   RD

The Gate Lodge

Reservoir

NEW RD

WINDGATE RISE

WINDGATE ROAD

31

The Summit

BAILY GREEN ROAD

Tower

Baily Green

Highroom Bed

Reservoir

P

THORMANBY   ROAD

Lough Leven

P

31B 31N

Gaskin's Leap

OLD   CARRICKBRACK   ROAD

31N 31B

CARRICKBRACK

Whitewater Brook

R105

Sisters of Charity Stella Maris

The Great Baily

Webb's Castle Rock

CEANCHOR ROAD

Cliff   Walk

Glenaveena

The Little Baily

Hippy Hole

Doldrum Bay

Lion's Head

Baily Lighthouse

The Needles or Candlesticks

Drumleck Point

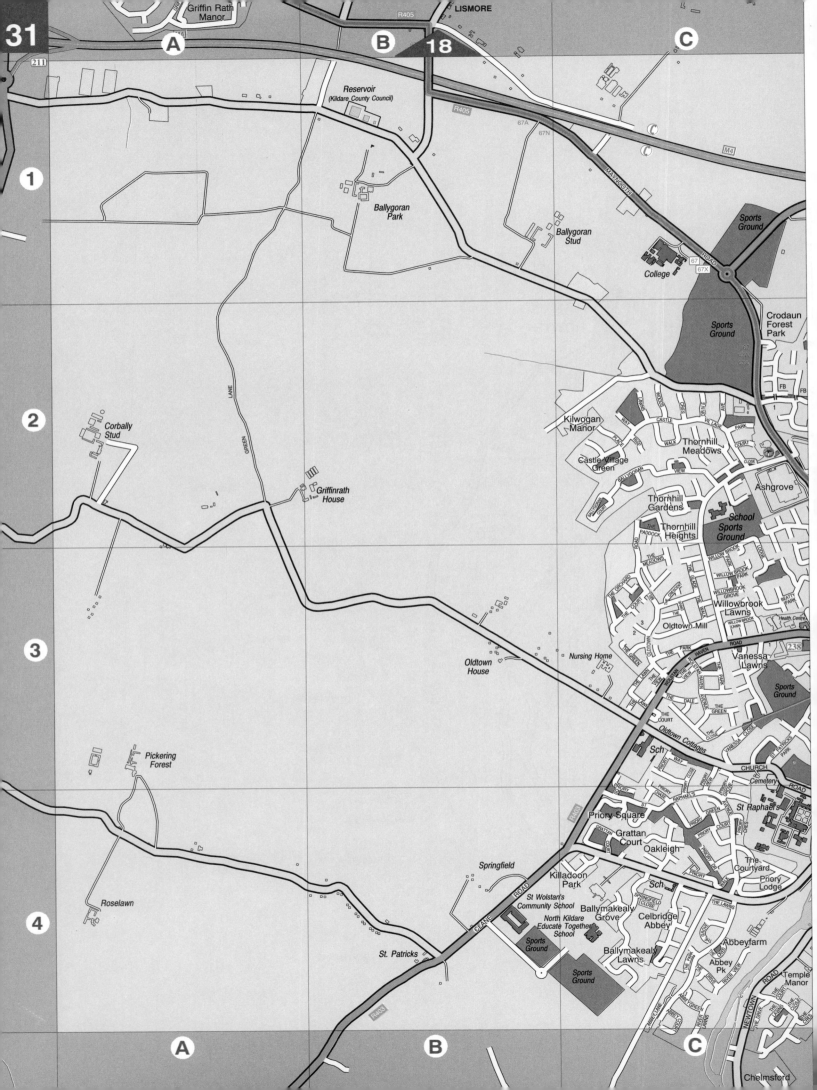

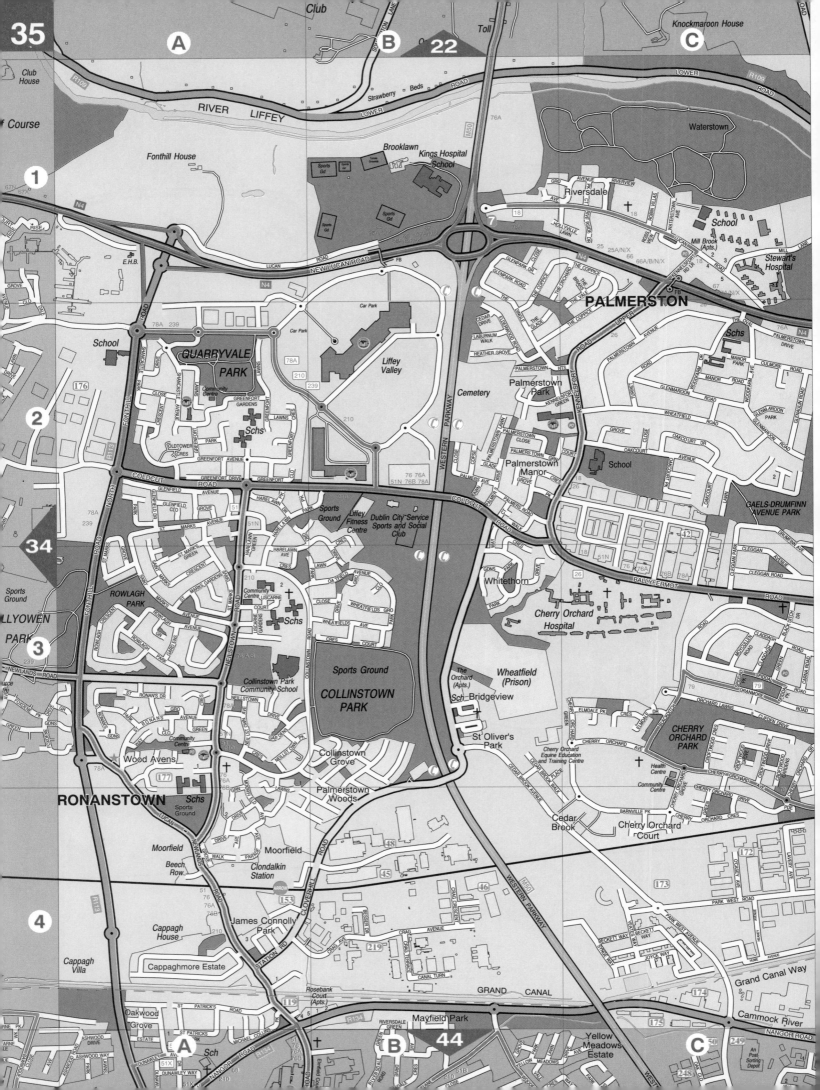

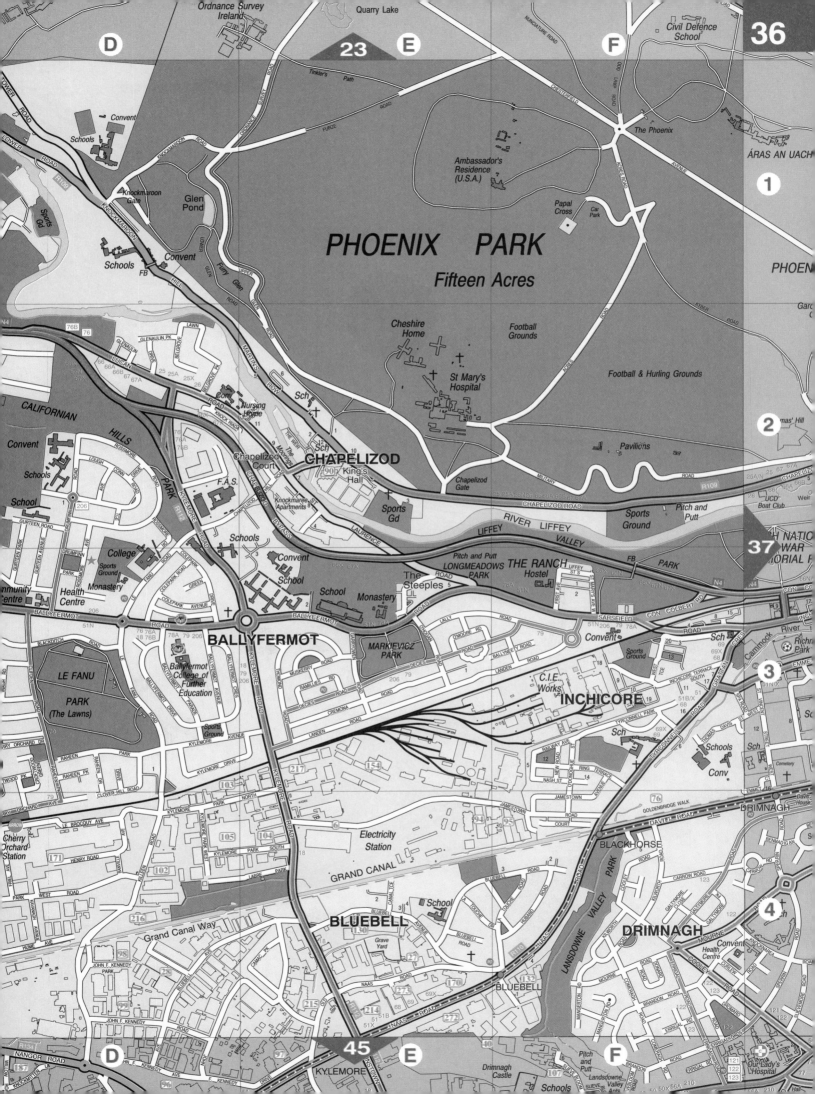

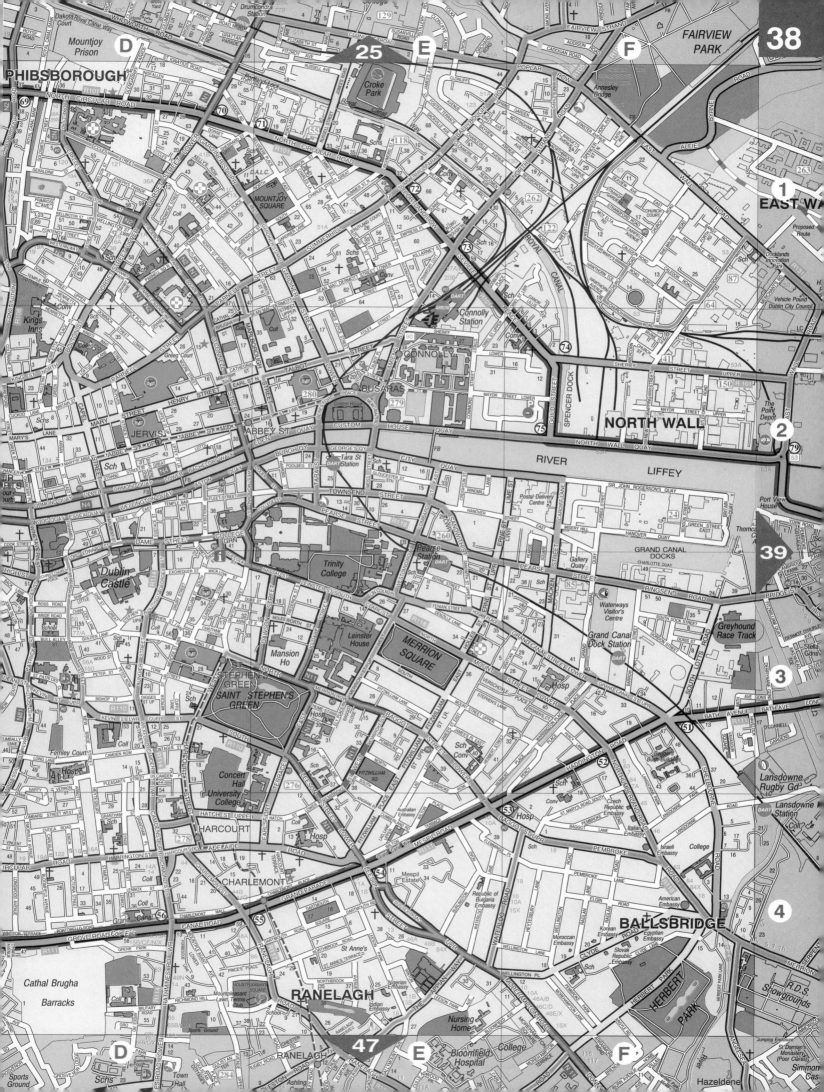

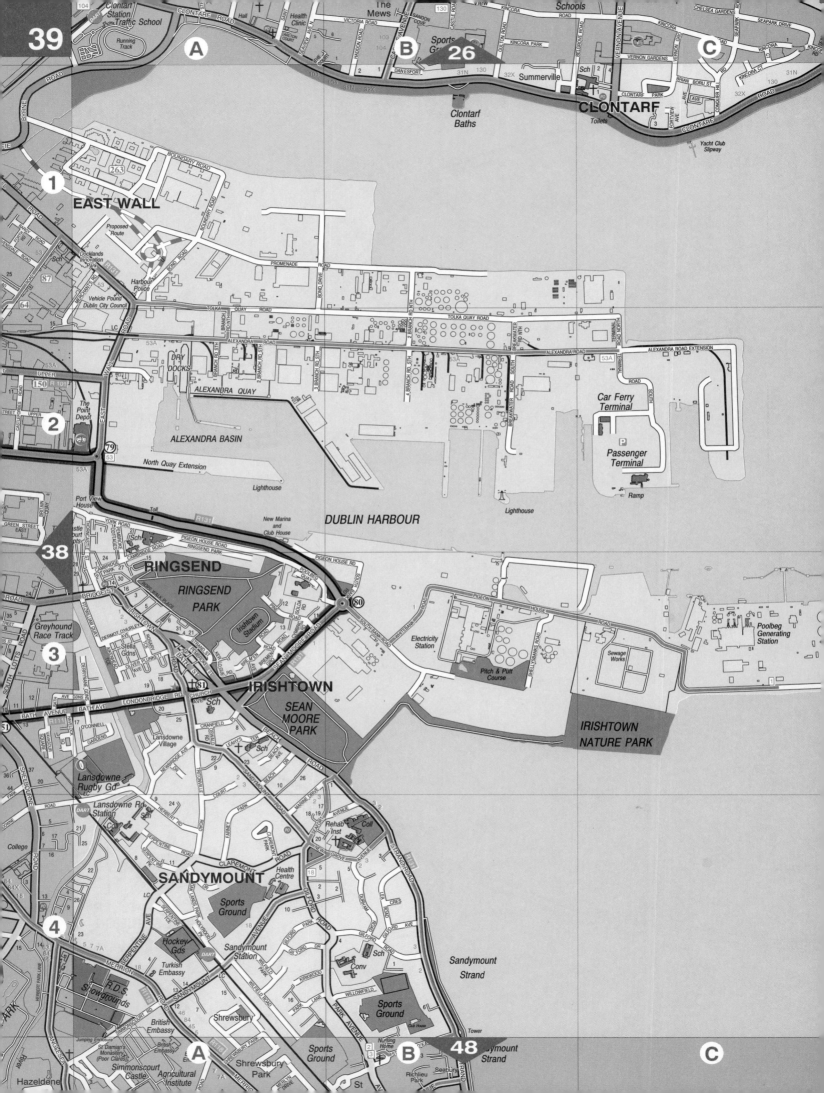

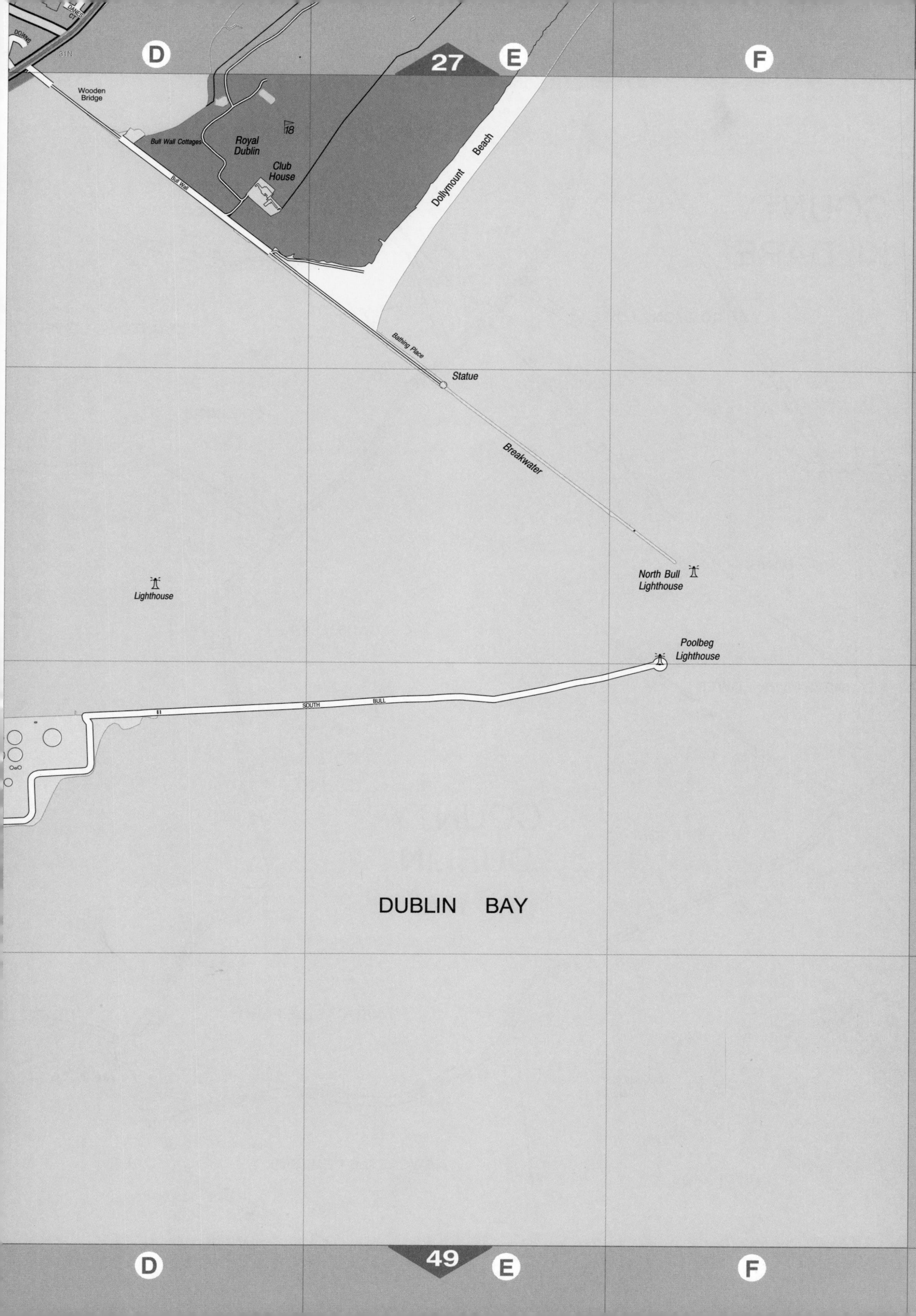
D
27
E
F
Wooden Bridge
Bull Wall Cottages
Royal Dublin
18
Club House
Bull Wall
Dollymount Beach
Bathing Place
Statue
Breakwater
North Bull Lighthouse
Lighthouse
Poolbeg Lighthouse
SOUTH BULL
DUBLIN BAY
1
2
3
4
D
49
E
F

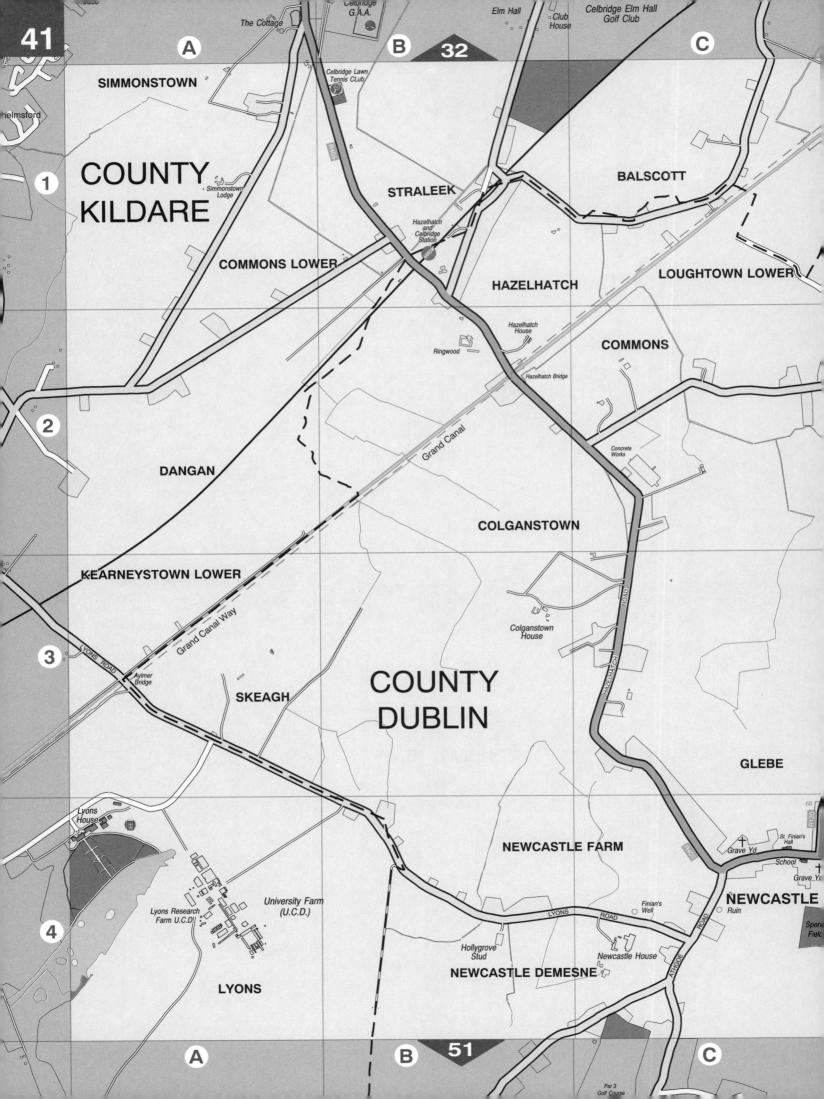

A

B

C

1

SIMMONSTOWN

COUNTY
KILDARE

Simmonstown
Lodge

The Cottage

Celbridge
G.A.A.

Celbridge Lawn
Tennis Club

Elm Hall

Club
House

Celbridge Elm Hall
Golf Club

helmsford

COMMONS LOWER

STRALEEK

Hazelhatch
and
Celbridge Station

BALSCOTT

HAZELHATCH

LOUGHTOWN LOWER

Hazelhatch
House

Ringwood

COMMONS

2

DANGAN

Grand Canal

Hazelhatch Bridge

Concrete
Works

KEARNEYSTOWN LOWER

COLGANSTOWN

3

LYONS ROAD

Grand Canal Way

Aylmer
Bridge

SKEAGH

COUNTY
DUBLIN

Colganstown
House

HAZELHATCH ROAD

GLEBE

Lyons
House

University Farm
(U.C.D.)

NEWCASTLE FARM

St. Finian's
Hall

Grave Yd

School

Grave Yd

4

Lyons Research
Farm U.C.D.

Finian's
Well

NEWCASTLE

Ruin

Sport
Field

LYONS

Hollygrove
Stud

LYONS ROAD

Newcastle House

ATHGOE ROAD

NEWCASTLE DEMESNE

A

B

C

Par 3
Golf Course

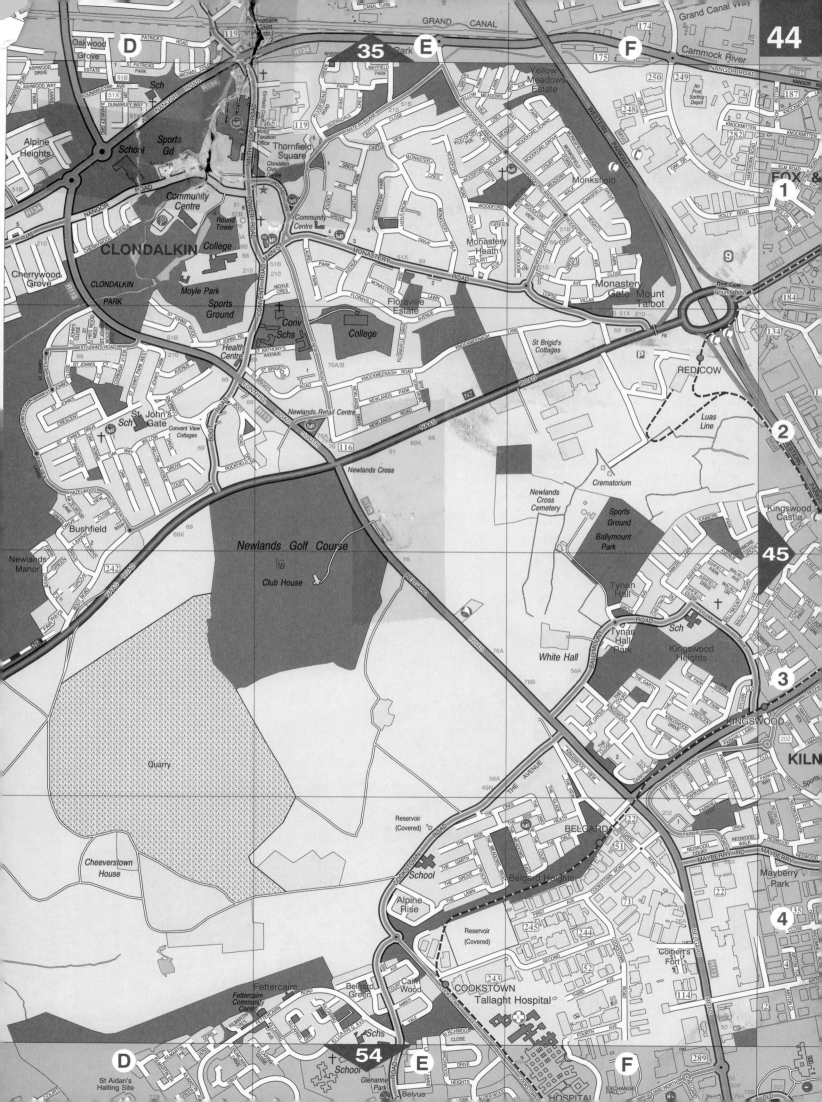

1

2

3

4

Lighthouse

Lighthouse

PIER

Harbour

EAST PIER

Car Ferry
Terminal

7B	746
45A	46A
46X	59
75	111

Yacht Club

Car Ferry
Terminal

Band Stand

Dún Laoghaire
Station

Yacht Club

HARBOUR

CROFTON

ROAD

25

26 27 28

24

GEORGE'S PLACE

QUEEN'S ROAD

Hosp

Dún Laoghaire/Rathdown
Co. Council

Town
Hall

Schs

Yacht Club

Geographical Pointer
Toilets

DÚN LAOGHAIRE

Maritime
Museum

MORAN
PARK

Baths

MARINE RD

GEORGE'S STREET LOWER

Schs

DOMINICK
ST

WOLFE TONE TERRACE N.

Health
Centre

Scotsman's Bay

PEOPLE'S
PARK

Forty Foot
Bathing Place

Harbour

SANDYCOVE AVE WEST

GEORGE'S STREET UPPER

PARK ROAD

WINDSOR TCE

Sandycove/
Glasthule
Station

NEWTOWNSMITH

Tower

Baths

SUMMERHILL ROAD

45A

111

Nursing
Home

MUGRAVE

CORRIG

PATRICK

E.H.B.
Nursing
Home

Children's
Home

Clarinda
Manor

Sch

CLARINDA PARK

GLENAGEARY RD

EDEN RD UPR

EDEN RD LR

Coll

Schs

60

GLASTHULE

EDEN
ROAD

LINK RD

ROAD

BALLYGIHEN

SANDYCOVE

SANDYCOVE ROAD

R119

BREFFNI

Bullock
Harbour

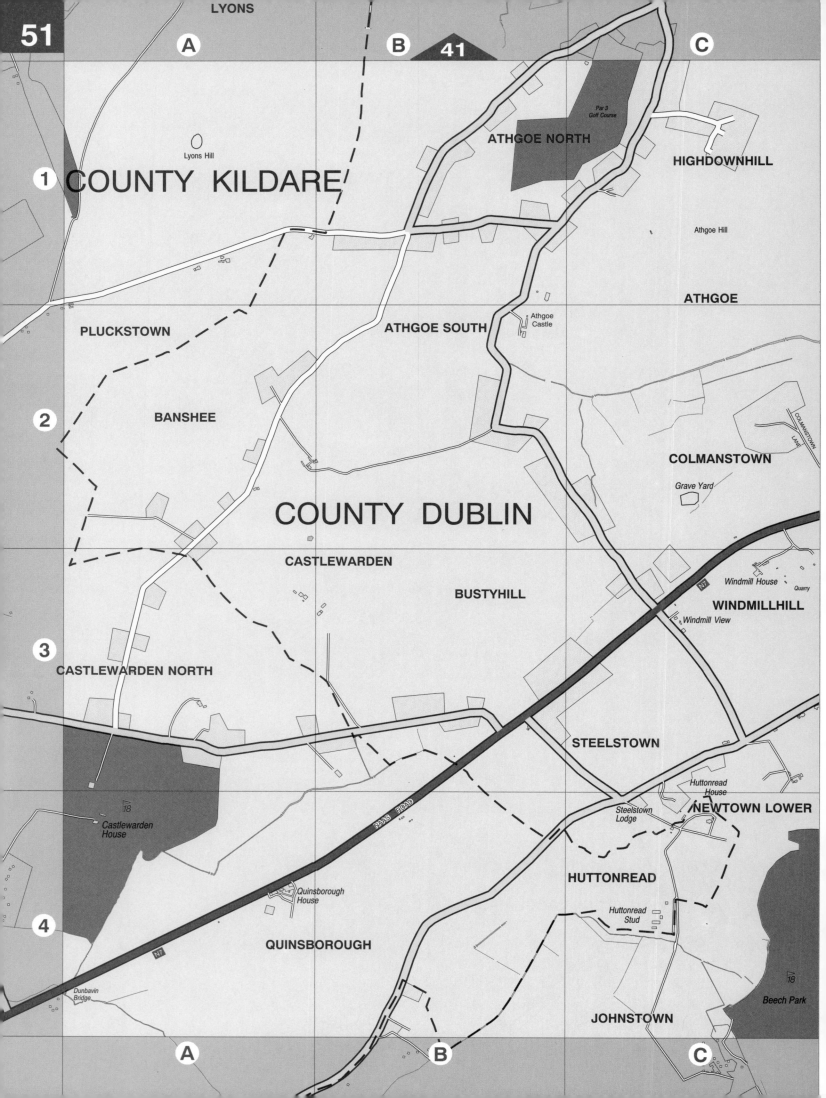

LYONS

A

B 41

C

1 COUNTY KILDARE

Lyons Hill

ATHGOE NORTH

Par 3
Golf Course

HIGHDOWNHILL

Athgoe Hill

ATHGOE

PLUCKSTOWN

ATHGOE SOUTH

Athgoe
Castle

2 BANSHEE

COLMANSTOWN

Grave Yard

COUNTY DUBLIN

CASTLEWARDEN

BUSTYHILL

Windmill House

Quarry

WINDMILLHILL

Windmill View

3 CASTLEWARDEN NORTH

STEELSTOWN

Huttonread
House

NEWTOWN LOWER

Steelstown
Lodge

18

Castlewarden
House

HUTTONREAD

4

NAAS ROAD

Quinsborough
House

Huttonread
Stud

18

Beech Park

N7

Dunbavin
Bridge

QUINSBOROUGH

JOHNSTOWN

A

B

C

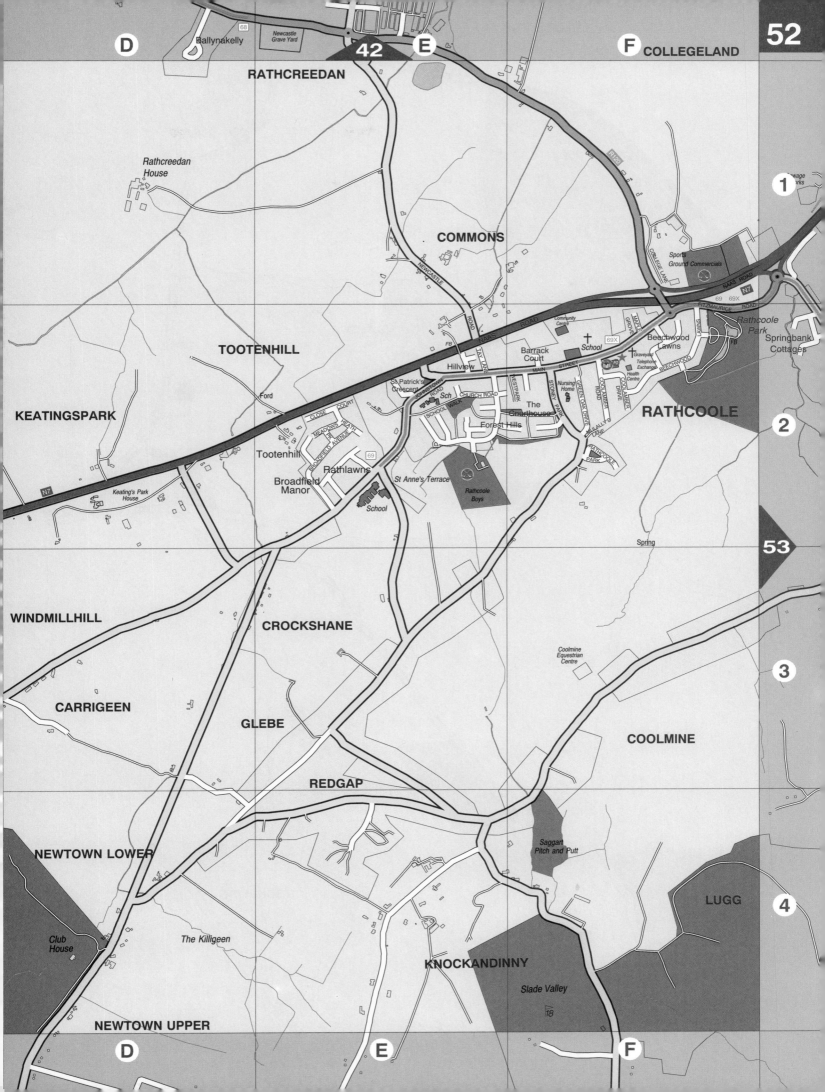

D Ballynakelly Newcastle Grave Yard [68] [42] E F COLLEGELAND

1

RATHCREEDAN

Rathcreedan House

COMMONS

R120

Sewage Works

Sports Ground Commercials

CORBALLY LANE

NAAS ROAD

N7

69 69X FITZMAURICE

Community Centre

Rathcoole Park

Springbank Cottages

TOOTENHILL

Ford

NAAS ROAD

NEWCASTLE ROAD

TAY LANE

Hillview

St Patrick's Crescent

JOHNSTOWN ROAD

Barrack Court

69X

School

Graveyard

Telephone Exchange

Health Centre

Beechwood Lawns

MAPLE GROVE

BEECHWOOD

FB

KEATINGSPARK

Sch

CHURCH ROAD

SCHOOL WALK

MEADOWS HEATH

CLOSE COURT

BROADFIELD AVENUE

Tootenhill

Rathlawns

Broadfield Manor

[69]

School

St Anne's Terrace

Forest Hills

WESTPARK

STONEY PARK

The Courthouse

Nursing Home

GREEN OAK DRIVE

COOLAMBER ROAD

COOLAMBER DRIVE

MULALLY'S LANE

RATHCOOLE PARK

RATHCOOLE

2

N7

Keating's Park House

Rathcoole Boys

Spring

53

WINDMILLHILL

CROCKSHANE

Coolmine Equestrian Centre

3

CARRIGEEN

GLEBE

COOLMINE

REDGAP

NEWTOWN LOWER

Saggart Pitch and Putt

LUGG

4

Club House

The Killigeen

KNOCKANDINNY

Slade Valley

18

NEWTOWN UPPER

D E F

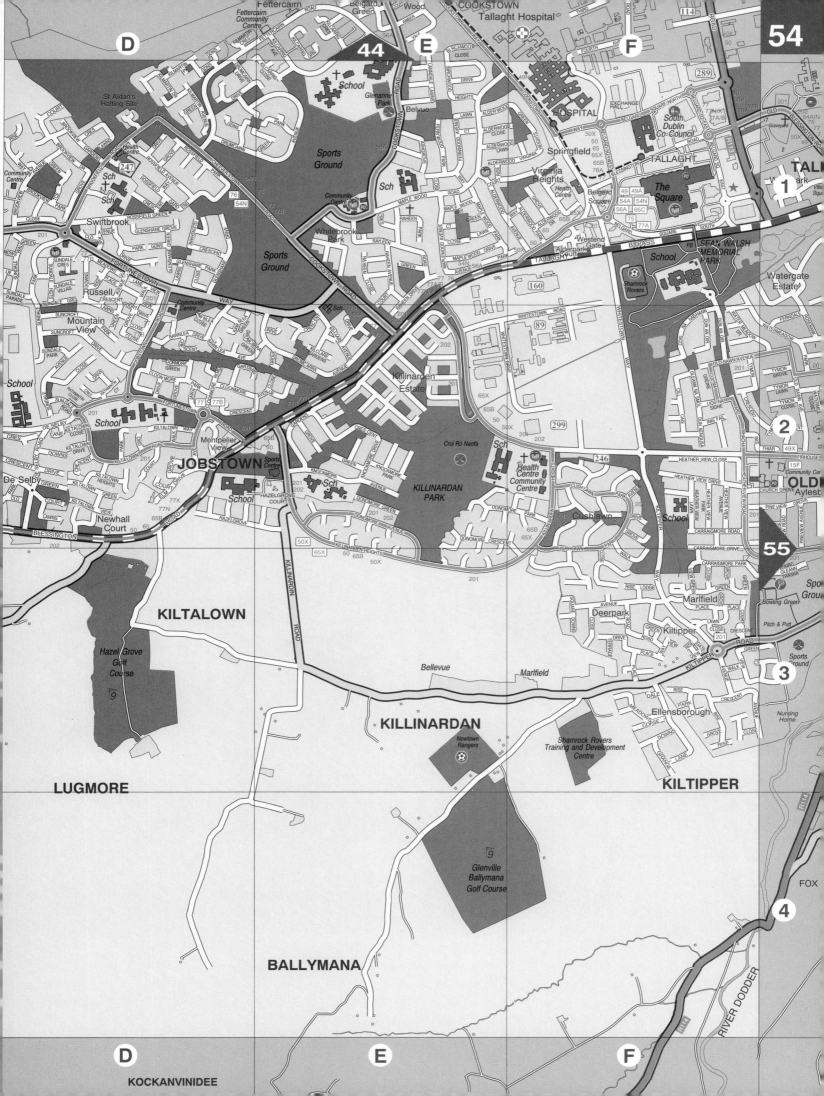

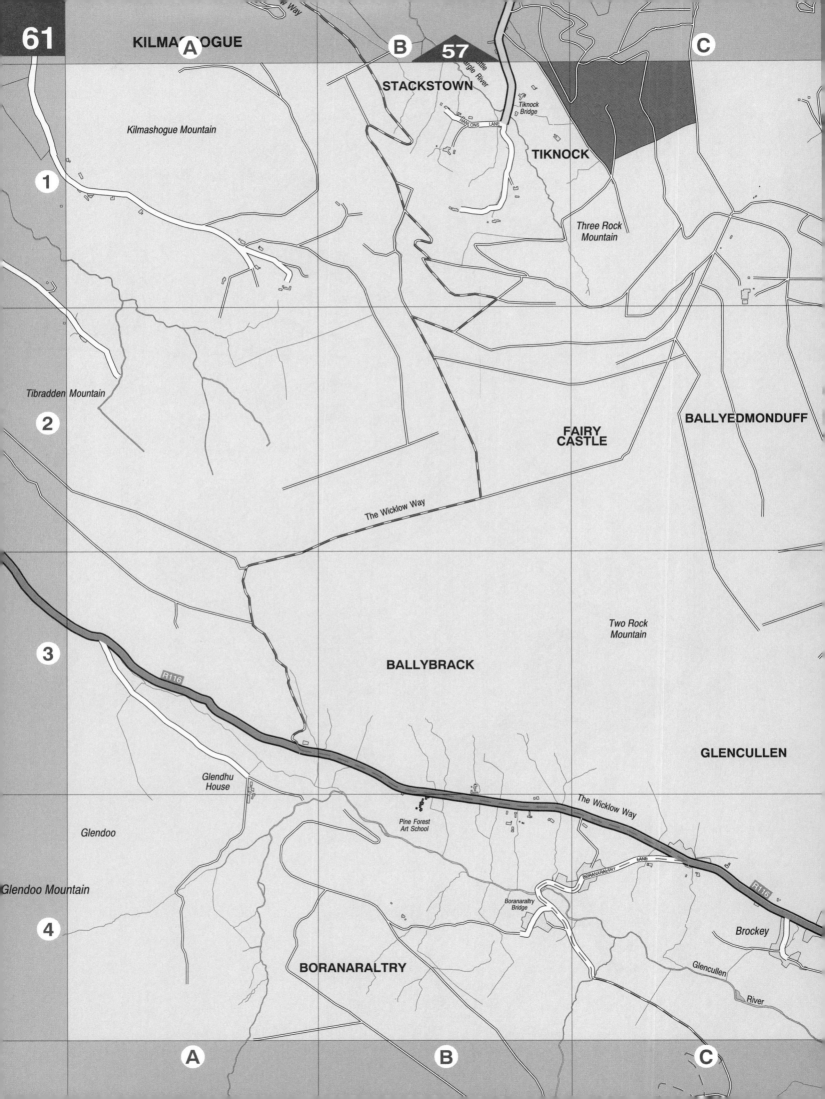

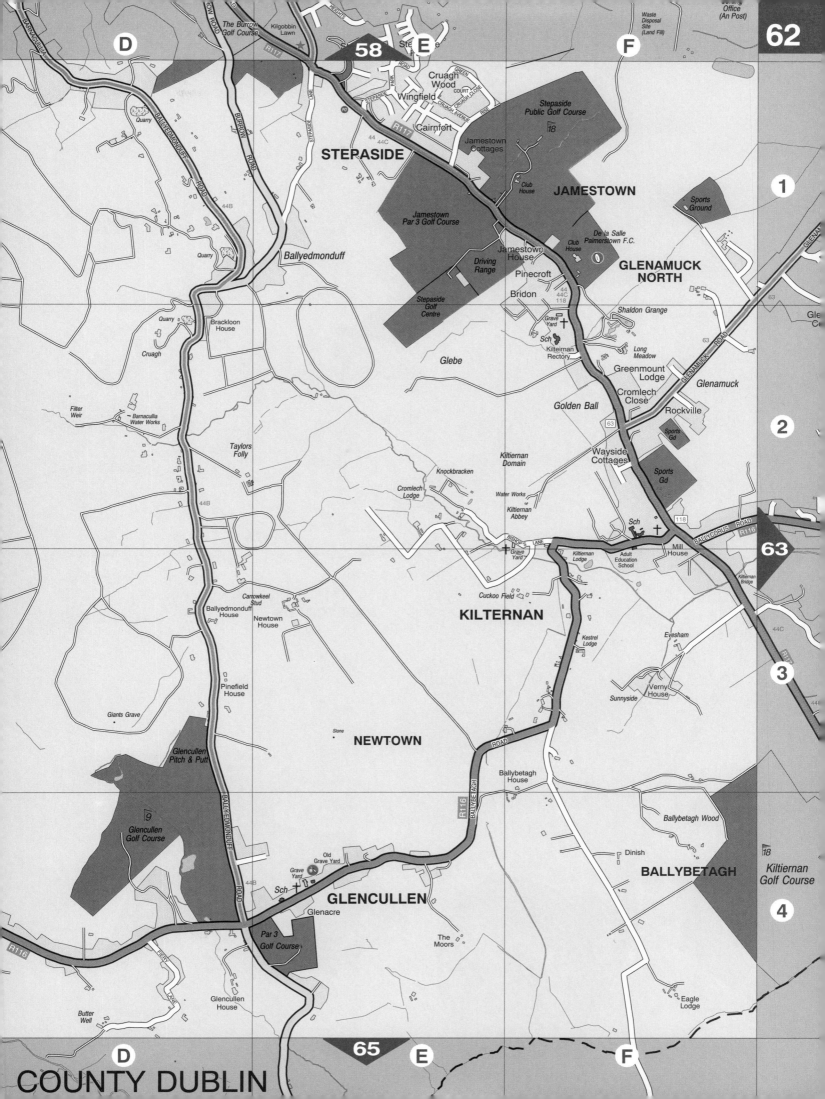

1

2

63

3

Waste Disposal Site (Land Fill)

Office (An Post)

The Burrow Golf Course

Kilgobbin Lawn

Cruagh Wood

Wingfield

Cairnfort

STEPASIDE

Stepaside Public Golf Course

18

Jamestown Cottages

JAMESTOWN

Sports Ground

Quarry

Ballyedmonduff

Jamestown Par 3 Golf Course

Driving Range

Jamestown House

Club House

Club House

De la Salle Palmerstown F.C.

GLENAMUCK NORTH

Quarry

Stepaside Golf Centre

Pinecroft

Bridon

Grave Yard

Sch

Shaldon Grange

Long Meadow

Glenamuck

Quarry

Brackloon House

Glebe

Kilternan Rectory

Greenmount Lodge

Cruagh

Cromlech Close

Rockville

Filter Weir

Barnacullia Water Works

Golden Ball

63

Sports Gd

Taylors Folly

Kiltiernan Domain

Wayside Cottages

Sports Gd

Knockbracken

Water Works

Cromlech Lodge

Kiltiernan Abbey

Sch

118

Mill House

BALLYCORUS ROAD

R116

Kiltiernan Bridge

44C

Bishop's Lane

Grave Yard

Kiltiernan Lodge

Adult Education School

Carrowkeel Stud

Ballyedmonduff House

Newtown House

Cuckoo Field

KILTIERNAN

Kestrel Lodge

Evesham

Pinefield House

Verny House

Sunnyside

Giants Grave

Glencullen Pitch & Putt

Stone

NEWTOWN

Ballybetagh House

Glencullen Golf Course

9

R116

BALLYBETAGH ROAD

Ballybetagh Wood

Old Grave Yard

Dinish

BALLYBETAGH

18

Kiltiernan Golf Course

Grave Yard

Sch

GLENCULLEN

Glenacre

The Moors

4

R116

Par 3 Golf Course

Butter Well

Glencullen House

Eagle Lodge

COUNTY DUBLIN

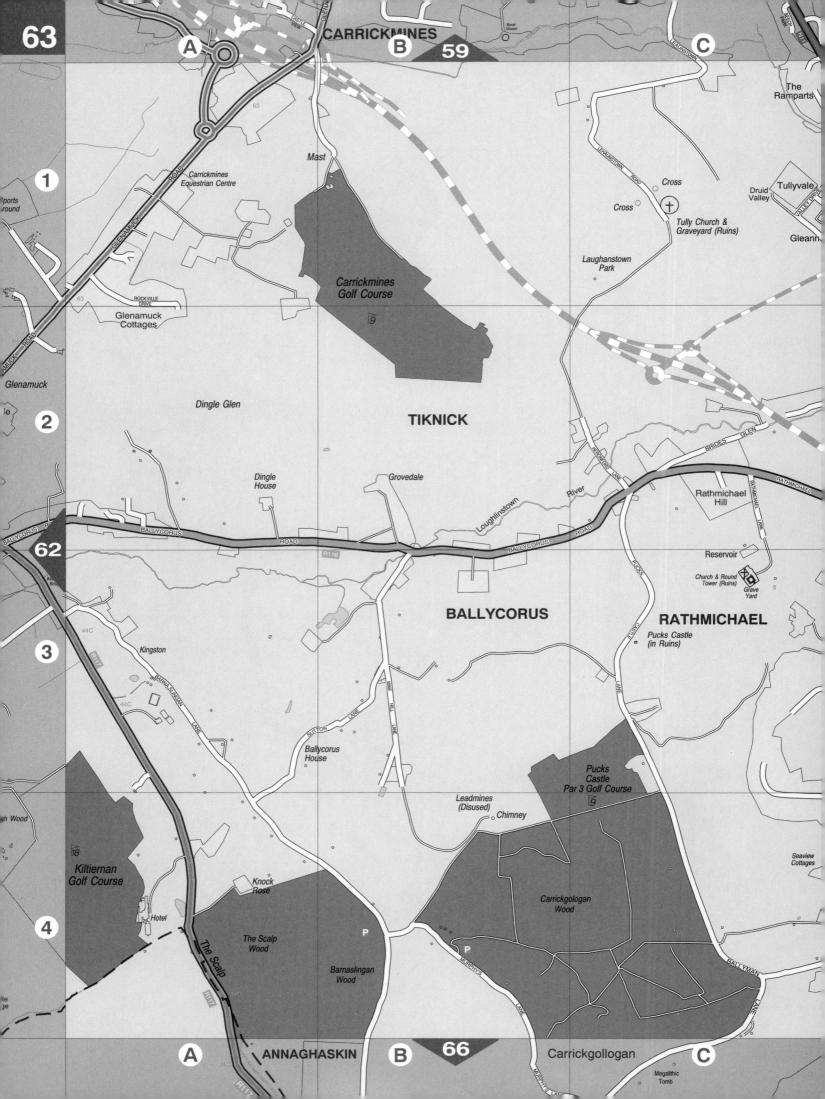

A

B

C

The Ramparts

BEECH PARK

N11

Burial Ground

1

Carrickmines Equestrian Centre

Mast

Cross

Cross

Druid Valley

Tullyvale

VALLEY DRIVE

GLENAMUCK ROAD

ROCKVILLE DRIVE

Glenamuck Cottages

Carrickmines Golf Course

9

LEHAUNSTOWN ROAD

Tully Church & Graveyard (Ruins)

Gleann

Laughanstown Park

Glenamuck

2

Dingle Glen

TIKNICK

BRIDES GLEN

Dingle House

Grovedale

Loughlinstown River

LEHAUNSTOWN LANE

Rathmichael Hill

RATHMICHAEL LANE

RATHMICHAEL

BALLYCORUS ROAD

BALLYCORUS ROAD

R116

BALLYCORUS ROAD

62

Reservoir

Church & Round Tower (Ruins)

Grave Yard

44C

R117

Kingston

BARNASLINGAN LANE

3

BALLYCORUS

PUCKS CASTLE LANE

Pucks Castle (in Ruins)

44C

SUTTON LANE

MINE HILL LANE

Ballycorus House

Pucks Castle Par 3 Golf Course

9

Leadmines (Disused)

Chimney

18

Kiltiernan Golf Course

Knock Rose

Carrickgologan Wood

Seaview Cottages

Hotel

The Scalp Wood

P

P

4

The Scalp

R117

MC

Barnaslingan Wood

MURPHYS LANE

BALLYMAN

MURPHY'S LANE

Carrickgollogan

Megalithic Tomb

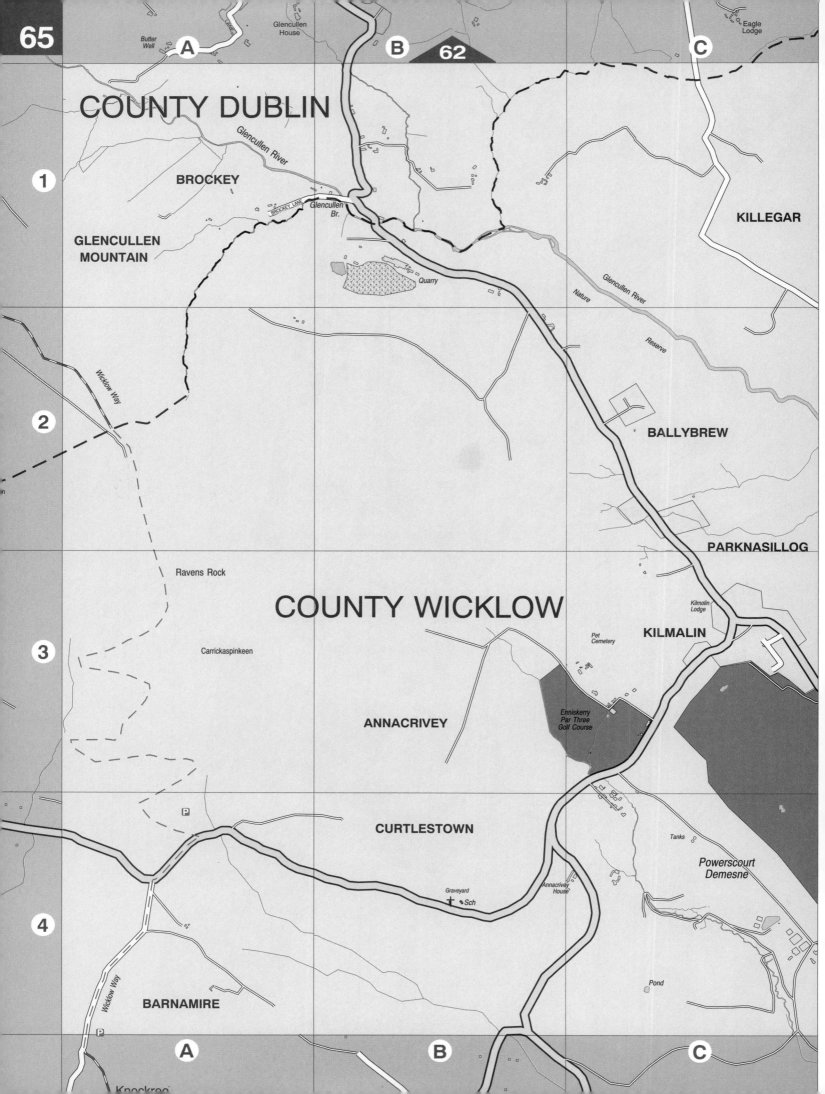

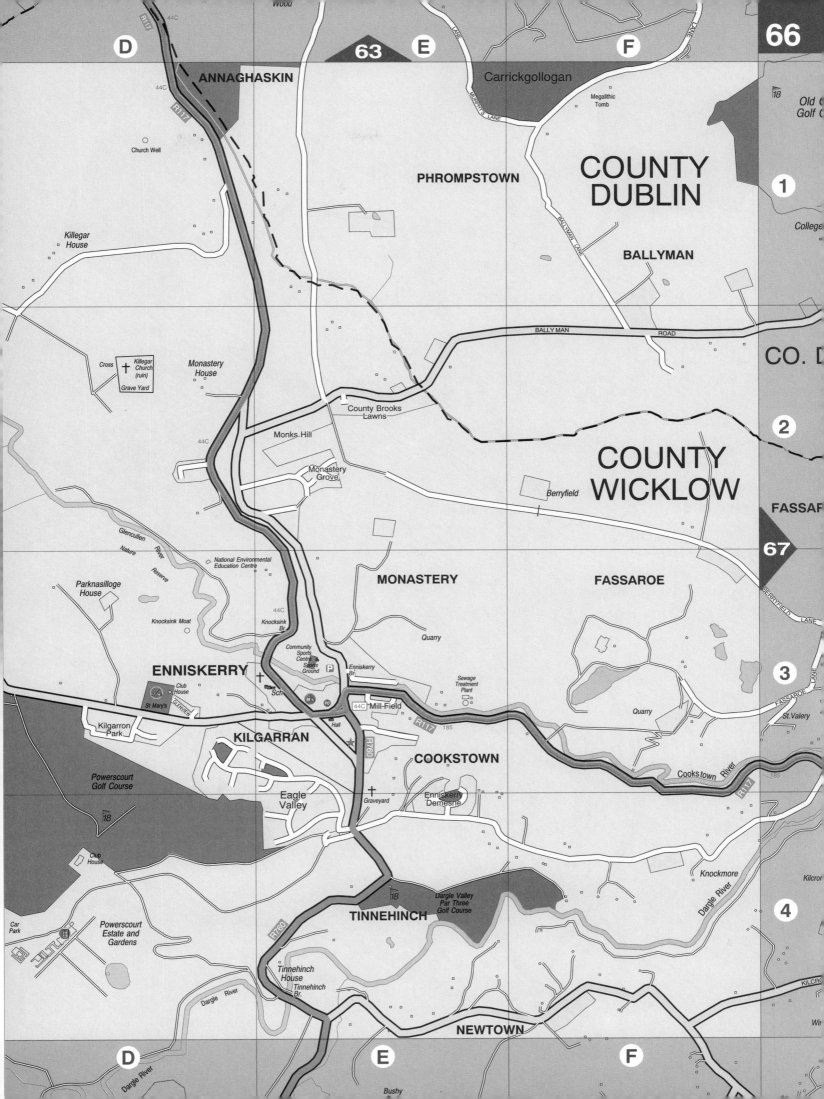

D E F

1

BRAY

17
16
15
*National
Sea Life
Aquarium*
ALBERT AVE
14
6
7 18
SIDMONTON AVE
8
11
12
9
MEATH
10
ARAVON
CT
SOUTH STRAND ROAD
45
VICTORIA
AVE
13

2

3
CONVENT AVENUE
Hall
R766
ROAD
19
20
45
23
SIDMONTON
2
4
5
STONEHAM
MEWS
PUTLAND
ROAD
CUALA LA
CAMABERRY RD
EDWARD RD
NEWCOURT
ROAD
*Fontenoy
Terrace*
RAHEEN PARK
NEWCOURT
ROAD
AVENUE
CUALA
GROVE
Naylor's Cove

3
*Raheenacluig Church
(in Ruins)*
Golf Course
NEWCOURT
ROAD
1

*Briar
Wood*
Tunnel *Bray
Head*

NEWCOURT

R761

COUNTY WICKLOW

4
84X
84
184
Tunnel

*Tunnel
Tunnel*

D E F

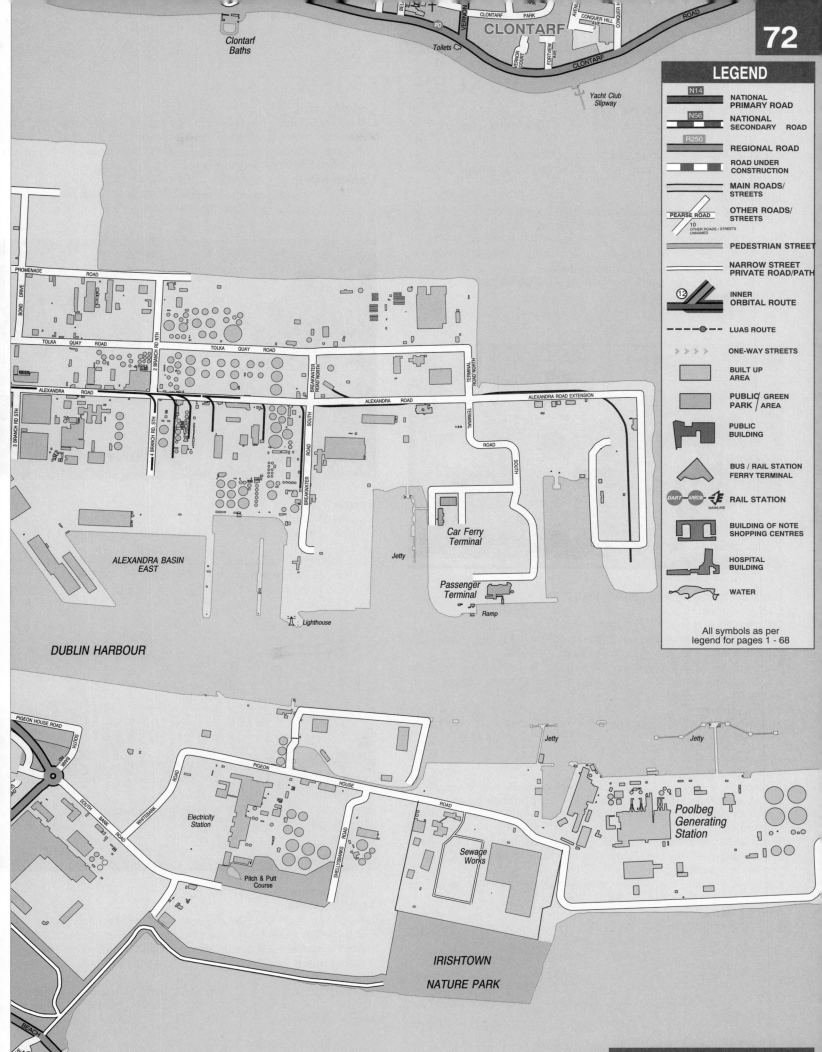

Clontarf
Baths

CLONTARF

Toilets

PO

VERNON
CLONTARF PARK
VERNON COURT
FORTVIEW AVE
CONQUER HILL AVE
CONQUER
ROAD

Yacht Club
Slipway

LEGEND

N14	**NATIONAL PRIMARY ROAD**
N56	**NATIONAL SECONDARY ROAD**
R250	**REGIONAL ROAD**
	ROAD UNDER CONSTRUCTION
	MAIN ROADS/ STREETS
PEARSE ROAD / 10 OTHER ROADS / STREETS UNNAMED	**OTHER ROADS/ STREETS**
	PEDESTRIAN STREET
	NARROW STREET PRIVATE ROAD/PATH
⑫	**INNER ORBITAL ROUTE**
•–––•	**LUAS ROUTE**
> > > >	**ONE-WAY STREETS**
	BUILT UP AREA
	PUBLIC GREEN PARK / AREA
	PUBLIC BUILDING
	BUS / RAIL STATION FERRY TERMINAL
DART ARROW MAINLINE	**RAIL STATION**
	BUILDING OF NOTE SHOPPING CENTRES
	HOSPITAL BUILDING
	WATER

All symbols as per
legend for pages 1 - 68

PROMENADE   ROAD

BOND   DRIVE

TOLKA   QUAY   ROAD

2 BRANCH RD NTH

TOLKA   QUAY   ROAD

BREAKWATER ROAD NORTH

TERMINAL ROAD NORTH

ALEXANDRA   ROAD

ALEXANDRA   ROAD

ALEXANDRA ROAD EXTENSION

3 BRANCH RD STH

4 BRANCH RD STH

BREAKWATER   ROAD   SOUTH

TERMINAL   ROAD   SOUTH

ALEXANDRA BASIN
EAST

Car Ferry
Terminal

Jetty

Passenger
Terminal

Ramp

Lighthouse

DUBLIN HARBOUR

PIGEON HOUSE ROAD

SOUTH BANK RD

SOUTH   BANK   ROAD

WHITEBANK   ROAD

PIGEON

HOUSE

ROAD

SHELLYBANKS   ROAD

Electricity
Station

Pitch & Putt
Course

Sewage
Works

Jetty

Jetty

Poolbeg
Generating
Station

BEACH

DROMARD TER

AVENUE

DRIVE

ROAD

IRISHTOWN

NATURE PARK

PLACES TO VISIT

Phoenix Park Visitor Centre

Located in the Phoenix Park, 5kms from the City Centre. The Tower House possibly dates from the 17th Century, and nearby is the visitor centre. There are exhibitions, a film show, and visitors can view a colourful and realistic historical interpretation of the past.

Visiting times:

Mid March - end of March: daily		10.00 a.m. - 5.30 p.m.
April - September:	daily	10.00 a.m. - 6.00 p.m.
October:	daily	10.00 a.m. - 5.00 p.m.
November - Mid March:	Sat. - Sun.	10.00 a.m. - 5.00 p.m.

Last admission 45 minutes before closing.
Free guided tours to Áras an Uachtaráin Saturdays only.
Phone 670 9155.

23 C4

Phoenix Park Visitor Centre

Bank of Ireland: (former Parliament House)
College Green.
Origins: Built between 1729 and 1739.
Designed by Sir Edward Lovatt Pearce (1699-1733) and enlarged by James Gandon and Robert Parke between 1785 and 1794.
The Bank of Ireland took over this building in 1804. It had been the scene of many dramatic events in Irish politics up to the passing of the Act of Union in 1800.
Visiting times:
Monday, Tuesday, Wednesday and Friday. 10.00 a.m. – 4.00 p.m.
Thursday   10.00 a.m. – 5.00 p.m.

38 D2

Castletown House
Located in Celbridge, Co. Kildare. Castletown House, designed by Italian architect Alessandro Galilei and Irish architect Sir Edward Lovett Pearce for the speaker of the Irish House of Commons, William Connolly.
Building commenced in 1722, and Castletown House was continuously used by the Connolly family until 1965 when the house and lands were sold.
Castletown House came into state ownership in 1979 under the management of the Office of Public Works.
Visiting times:

April to September:	Monday to Friday	10.00 a.m. – 6.00 p.m.
	Saturday/Sunday/	
	Bank Holidays	1.00 p.m. – 6.00 p.m.
October:	Monday to Friday	10.00 a.m. – 5.00 p.m.
	Sunday/	
	Bank Holidays	1.00 p.m. – 5.00 p.m.
November:	Sundays only	1.00 p.m. – 5.00 p.m.

Last admission one hour before closing.

32 D2

Celbridge Abbey
Located 12 miles from Dublin, Celbridge Abbey was built by Bartholomew Van Homrigh, Lord Mayor of Dublin in 1697.
The Abbey grounds contain many colourful attractions and are open to the public at the following times.
Visiting times:

Monday to Saturday	10.00 a.m. - 6.00 p.m.
Sunday/Bank Holidays	11.00 a.m. - 6.00 p.m.

31 C4

Castletown House

Custom House
Custom House Quay
Origins: Designed by James Gandon and built between 1781 and 1791.
The building was reduced to a shell when it was gutted by fire during the War of Independence. It was restored by the Office of Public Works after the Irish Free State was established.

38 E2

Custom House

Casino Marino
Malahide Road
Located just 4kms from the city centre, off the Malahide Road, Dublin 3. The Casino, has been described as one of the finest 18th century classical buildings in Ireland. Access is by Guided Tour only.
Visiting times:

January Closed		
February / March	Saturday / Sunday 12 noon	- 4.00 p.m.
April	Saturday / Sunday 12 noon	- 5.00 p.m.
May and October	daily	10.00 a.m. - 5.00 p.m.
June - September	daily	10.00 a.m. - 6.00 p.m.
November / December	Saturday / Sunday 12 noon	- 4.00 p.m.

26 D3

Casino Marino

City Hall
Cork Hill, Dame Street.
Origins: Formerly the Royal Exchange, designed by Thomas Cooley (1740 – 1784) and completed between 1769 and 1779.
This is the headquarters of Dublin's municipal government. Archives dating back to the twelfth century are stored in the Muniment Room. It also houses the mace and sword of the city, along with 102 Royal Charters, including the original charter of 1171 by which Dublin was granted to the men of Bristol by Henry II.

38 D2

Dublinia – Christ Church,
St. Michael's Hill, Dublin 8.
The realistic and novel exhibition that is Dublinia is situated in the old Synod Hall on St. Michael's Hill, alongside of Christ Church Cathedral, to which it is connected by an ornate pedestrian archway over St. Michael's Hill.
The exhibition heralds the arrival of the Anglo-Normans in 1170 through a broad spectrum of Dublin life to the closure of the Monasteries in 1540.
Visiting times:
April - September: daily — 10.00 a.m. - 5.00 p.m.
October - March: Monday to Saturday — 11.00 a.m. - 4.00 p.m.
Sunday/Bank Holiday — 10.00 a.m. - 4.30 p.m.

38 D3

Dublin Castle
The main entrance is located at the junction of Cork Hill and Castle Street. Dating from the 13th Century, the site, once a Viking stronghold, has served as a military fortress, prison, courts of law, and the core of British Administration in Ireland until 1922. Dublin Castle is now used for State functions. Guided tours of State Apartments, Chapel Royal and Undercroft.

Visiting times:
Monday/Friday — 10.00 a.m. - 5.00 p.m.
Saturday,Sunday and Public Holidays — 2.00 p.m. - 5.00 p.m.

38 D3

Dublin Castle

The Throne Room, Dublin Castle

St. Patrick's Hall, Dublin Castle

Dunsink Observatory
Dunsink Lane, near Castleknock.
Origins: Founded in 1783, this is one of the world's oldest observatories. It formerly belonged to Trinity College but is now the centre of the school of Astronomical Physics of the Dublin Institute for Advanced Studies.
Visiting times: Open to the public on the first and third Wednesday of each month from October to March, at 8.00 p.m.
Admission free on written application to the secretary enclosing stamp-addressed envelope.

23 B2

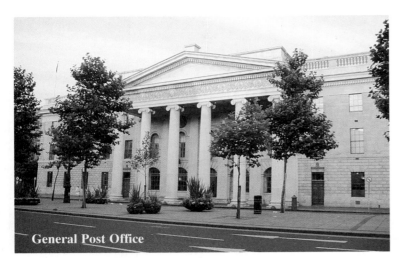
General Post Office

Leinster House

General Post Office
O'Connell Street.
Origins: Designed by Francis Johnston and built between 1814 and 1818.
The GPO became the focal point of the 1916 Insurrection and the Proclamation of the Irish Republic took place there. Destroyed by fire, it was restored in 1929. In the public office is a noteworthy statue representing the Death of Cuchulainn, the work of Oliver Sheppard R.H.A.

38 D2

Kilmainham Jail
Inchicore Road, Dublin 8.
One of the largest decommissioned jails in Europe, it played its part in some of the most patriotic and tragic episodes that light the path of Ireland's journey to modern nationhood, from the 1780's to 1924. Featuring many exhibitions and a multi-lingual audio-visual show. Access by guided tour only.
Visiting times:

October - March:	Monday to Friday	9.30 a.m. - 4.00 p.m.
	Sunday	10.00 a.m. - 4.45 p.m.
April - September:	daily	9.30 a.m. - 4.45 p.m.

Last admission one hour before closing.

37 A3

Leinster House
Kildare Street.
Origins: Designed by Richard Cassells, building commenced on this fine Georgian mansion in 1745. Originally the residence of the Duke of Leinster, the building became the property of the Royal Dublin Society in 1815. In 1922 it was purchased by the first Irish Free State Government to serve as a Parliament House. Presently it is the meeting place of the Dail (Chamber of Deputies) and Seanad (Senate).

38 E3

Waterways Visitor Centre
Grand Canal Quay, Dublin 2
Located at Grand Canal Docks, beside McMahon Bridge, Pearse Street.
The centre houses an exhibition outlining the history of Ireland's Inland Waterways and the activities and experiences currently available.
Featuring an audio-visual show and working models of various engineering features.
Visiting times:

| October - May: | Wednesday to Sunday 12.30 p.m. - 5.00 p.m |
| June - September: | daily 9.30 a.m. - 6.30 p.m |

Last admission 45 minutes before closing

38 F3

Four Courts

Royal Hospital and Irish Museum of Modern Ar

Four Courts
Inns Quay.
Origins: Designed by James Gandon and built between 1785 and 1802. This building, dominated by a great domed central mass, is one of Gandon's masterpieces. The Irish Law Courts and Law Library are housed here. Like the Custom House, Gandon's other great building, it was also destroyed by fire during the struggle for Irish independence. Although significantly altered, the building was completely restored by 1932.

38 D2

Royal Hospital and Irish Museum of Modern Art
Military Road, Kilmainham.
The most important 17th century building in Ireland has been restored. Guided tours available of the Master's Quarters, the Great Hall with the portrait collection, and the chapel which contains outstanding woodcarving by Tabary and a magnificent Baroque ceiling.

Visiting times:	Tuesday to Saturday	10.00 a.m. - 5.30 p.m.
	Sunday and Bank Holidays 12 noon - 5.30 p.m
	Closed Monday

37 B3

Trinity College

Trinity College

Main entrance, College Green.
Origins: Trinity College is the sole college of the University of Dublin. Founded by Queen Elizabeth I in 1592, it is built on the site of the Augustinian priory of All Hallows which was founded by Dermot McMurrough. The oldest buildings now surviving are the Rubrics, a range of brick apartments dating from 1700. The Palladian facade was added in 1759. In the same year the Provost's house (facing the northern end of Grafton Street) was built. This is the only great Georgian house in Dublin still being used for its original purpose. Many world-famous men have attended this college over the centuries.
Visiting Times: Monday to Saturday   10.00 a.m. - 5.00 p.m.
                   See also 'Trinity College Library'.

38 E2

Mansion House

Dawson Street.
Origins: This Queen Anne house was built in 1705, the round room having been added in 1821 as the venue for a function to honour King George IV. Built in brick, the building underwent changes during the Victorian era.
Since 1715 the Mansion House has been the residence of Dublin's Lord Mayor. In 1919 the Declaration of Independence was adopted here and here also was signed the truce which ended Anglo-Irish hostilities in 1921.

38 E3

Swords Castle

Built in 1183 as a summer palace for the first Norman Archbishop of Dublin, Swords Castle was designed both as a residence and as a place of defence. In 1324 Archbishop de Bicknor left Swords and the castle fell into disrepair. Despite many attempts at renovation over the centuries, it has remained so. Currently in the ownership of Fingal Council, and now in the process of being restored.
Visiting times:
          Monday, Wednesday and Thursday 10.00 a.m. - 4.00 p.m.
          Friday   10.00 a.m. - 3.00 p.m.

2 D2

Howth Castle

The great English architect Sir Edwin Lutyens restyled this 14th century castle overlooking Dublin Bay. The grounds are also noted for its wild rhododendron gardens. The grounds are open daily from 8.00 a.m. to sunset.

29 C1

Howth Transport Museum

This Museum is located in the grounds of Howth Castle. It features lorries, trucks, fire engines and tractors. Also exhibited is the restored Hill of Howth No.9 Tram.
Visiting times:
June - August: Monday to Saturday   10.00 a.m. - 5.00 p.m.
September - May: Sat., Sun. and Bank Holiday 2.00 p.m. - 5.00 p.m.
          26th.Dec. to 1st. Jan.   2.00 p.m. - 5.00 p.m.

29 C1

Malahide Castle

Built by Sir Richard de Talbot about 1200 and developed over the centuries into the imposing architectural achievement that it is today. The castle houses part of the National Portrait Collection in the Great Hall.
The extensive grounds are open from 9 a.m. - 9 p.m.daily and incorporate the 20 acre Talbot Botanic Garden, which is open to all from 2 p.m. to 5 p.m. daily.
Visiting times:
   All year: Monday to Friday   10.00 a.m. - 5.00 p.m.
   April - October: Sat./Sun./B.Holiday 11.00 a.m. - 6.00 p.m.
   November - March: Sat./Sun./B.Holiday 2.00 p.m. - 5.00 p.m.
                        Closed daily from 12.45 p.m. - 2.00 p.m.
Also included is the Fry Model Railway Museum, which contains a unique collection of hand-made models showing the history of Irish railways from its inception to the modern day period.

3 A3

Bray Courthouse

Located on Main Street between Quinsborough Road and Seapoint Road, this building was designed by William Murray, and built in 1841. It is now the location of Bray Heritage Museum, and Bray Tourist Office.
Visiting times: daily   10.00 a.m. – 5.00 p.m.

67 C2

Bray Town Hall

Located on Main Street at the junction of Killarney Road and Vevay Road is the jewel in Bray's architectural crown. Designed by Edward G. Dawber for architects Thomas Newenham Deane & Son, it was built in 1884 at the request of Lord and Lady Brabazon for the people of Bray. Currently the seat of Bray Urban District Council.

67 C2

St Patrick's College, Maynooth

St Patrick's College, Maynooth was founded in 1795 as the National Seminary for Ireland. In 1896, it was granted a Pontifical Charter which empowered it to confer degrees in Theology, Philosophy and Canon Law. The Universities Act (1997) resulted in the creation of a new university, National University of Ireland, Maynooth. St. Patrick's College, which consists of the Pontifical University and the National Seminary, continues to exist side by side with NUI Maynooth. The two institutions share the same campus and work in close co-operation with each other.
Visiting times:
May - September: Monday to Friday   11.00 a.m. - 5.00 p.m.
                    Saturday and Sunday   2.00 p.m. - 6.00 p.m.
Groups welcome.

17 C3

Powerscourt Gardens

Powerscourt Gardens, situated 12 miles south of Dublin is a blend of formal gardens, sweeping terraces, statuary and ornamental lakes together with secret hollows, rambling walks, walled gardens and over 200 variations of trees and shrubs. Facilities include tea rooms, craft shop, garden centre, play area and riverside picnic spots.
Visiting times:
          9.30 a.m. - 5.30 p.m.
   Waterfall open daily 9.30 a.m. - 7.00 p.m.
          Closes Winter at dusk

66 D4

CHURCHES AND CATHEDRALS

Christ Church Cathedral
Main entrance, Christchurch Place.
Origins: The original church was built about 1030 by Sigtryggr Silkenbeard, Norse King of Dublin. A new church was built in 1173 by Strongbow. The present structure dates mainly from the nineteenth century, although the wonderful medieval crypt still remains. Christ Church contains many interesting historical remains.
Visiting times:

Monday to Friday	9.45 a.m. - 5.00 p.m.
Saturday/Sunday	10.00 a.m. - 5.00 p.m.
Group tours available on request / application.	

38 D3

St. Audoen's Church
High Street
Origins: St. Audoen's dates from medieval times and is the oldest of Dublin's parish churches. The tower houses Ireland's three most ancient bells, dating from 1423. There's a font in the nave dating from 1124. St. Audoen's Arch stands nearby. This is Dublin's only surviving city gate. Built in 1240 it originally led to a strand on the River Liffey.
Visiting times: June - September: 9.30 a.m. - 5.30 p.m.

37 C3

St. Mary's Church
Mary Street.
Origins: Dating from 1627, this was the first Dublin church to be built with galleries. Theobald Wolfe Tone was baptised here in 1763 and Sean O'Casey the playwright in 1880. The Church is now a retail outlet.

38 D2

St. Michan's Church
Church Street
Origins: Founded by the Norse in 1096, the present building dates from 1685-6, having been much restored in 1828. The Church's Harris organ is said to have been used by Handel during his visit to Dublin. Dry magnesium limestone vaults beneath the church contain mummified corpses which may be seen by the public.
Visiting times: Church and Vaults:

March - October	Monday to Friday	10.00 a.m. - 4.30 p.m.
	Closed 12.30 p.m. - 2.00 p.m.	
November - March	Monday to Friday	12.30 p.m. - 3.30 p.m.
	Saturday	10.00 a.m. - 12.45 p.m.
	Vaults closed on Sundays.	

37 C2

St. Mary's Pro-Cathedral
Marlborough Street.
Origins: Designed by John Sweetman and built between 1815 and 1825. Originally intended for O'Connell Street but erected on this less suitable site to satisfy Protestant opposition at the time. The interior reveals the inspiration of Chalgin's Church of St. Philippe de Roule, Paris. Some interesting monuments may be seen inside. The metropolitan church of the diocese, it is used for State functions. A Latin Mass is sung each Sunday at 11 a.m. by the Palestrina Choir of which the famous tenor John McCormack was once a member.
Visiting times:

Monday to Friday	7.30 a.m. - 6.45 p.m.
Saturday	7.30 a.m. - 7.15 p.m.
Sunday	9.00 a.m. - 1.45 p.m.
and	5.30 p.m. - 7.45 p.m.

38 D2

St. Werburgh's Church
Werburgh Street, off Christchurch Place.
Origins: Erected in 1715 on the site of the medieval successor to pre-Norman St. Werburgh's. Destroyed by fire in 1754, the church was re-opened in 1759. A spire was added in 1768 but removed in the early nineteenth century by the fearful authorities of Dublin castle, which it overlooked. Until 1790 St. Werburgh's was the Chapel Royal. In the vaults beneath is buried Lord Edward Fitzgerald. His captor Town Major Sirr, is buried in the nearby churchyard.
This fine Georgian building, now well restored, contains many interesting features including an attractive pulpit designed by Francis Johnston and carved by Richard Stewart, as well as a sixteenth-century Fitzgerald tomb located in the porch.
Visiting times: By appointment only. Tel. 478 3710

Monday to Friday	10.00 a.m. - 4.00 p.m.
Entrance: North Door, 8 Castle Street.	
Main Sunday Service:	10.00 a.m.

38 D3

St. Patrick's Cathedral
Patrick Street.
Origins: St. Patrick's, Ireland's largest church, was built on the site of the pre-Norman parish church of St. Patrick. The church was rebuilt in 1191 by Archbishop Comyn. In 1213 it gained cathedral status, but later, in 1300 a papal decree gave Christ Church precedence. At the Reformation it became a parish church, but under the Catholic restoration of Philip and Mary it once again became a cathedral.
A university was established there in 1320 but was suppressed later by Henry VIII. The square tower dates from the fourteenth century.
During the wars of the seventeenth century the Cromwellians used the ruinous cathedral as a stable for their horses. But the future saw a great improvement in the fabric of the building. A spire was added by the architect John Semple in 1749 and a general restoration was undertaken between 1844 and 1869 being financed by Sir Benjamin Lee Guinness. Jonathan Swift was Dean of St. Patrick's from 1713 to 1745. His pulpit may still be seen and his tomb, with its famous epitaph is in the south aisle. Buried nearby is Esther (Stella) Johnston one of Swift's two great lovers.
Visiting times:

Monday to Friday		9.00 a.m. - 6.00 p.m.
Saturday	March - October:	9.00 a.m. - 5.00 p.m.
	November - February:	9.00 a.m. - 5.00 p.m.
Sunday	March - October:	9.00 a.m. - 11.00 p.m
	12.45 a.m. - 3.00 p.m.	4.15 p.m. - 6.00 p.m.
Sunday	November - February:	10.00 a.m. - 11.00 a.m
	12.45 p.m. - 3.00 p.m.	

38 D3

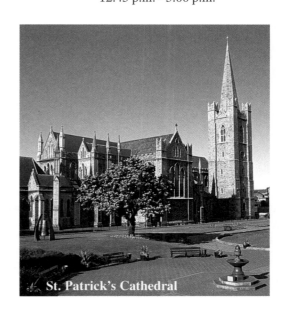
St. Patrick's Cathedral

LIBRARIES

Chester Beatty Library
Dublin Castle.

One of the world's most valuable private collections of oriental manuscripts and miniatures can be seen here. There are manuscripts of the New Testament, Manichean papyri and Eastern miniatures, as well as picture scrolls, albums and jades from the Far East.
The library is located in the Clock Tower building and is open daily. Admisson free.

Visiting Times:

May - September:	Monday to Friday	10.00 a.m. - 5.00 p.m.
October - April:	Tuesday to Friday	10.00 a.m. - 5.00 p.m.
	Saturday	11.00 a.m. - 5.00 p.m.
	Sunday	1.00 p.m. - 5.00 p.m.

Closed Jan 1st./ Good Friday/24,25,26 Dec/Monday Public Holidays
For guided tours phone 407 0750.

48 D1

Trinity College Library

Trinity College Library
Main entrance to college from College Green.

Dating from the late sixteenth century, Trinity College Library is Ireland's oldest library. It contains over 1,000,000 volumes and Ireland's most extensive collection of manuscripts and early printed books. Its greatest treasure is the Book of Kells (probably eighth century). This is considered to be the most beautiful illuminated manuscript in existence today. Manuscripts in the library include State letters of Queen Elizabeth I, diaries of Wolfe Tone and manuscripts of the Irish dramatist, John Millington Synge.
The library is housed in two buildings – the Old Library (completed in 1732) and the New Library (1967). Trinity College Library has the right to a copy of any book printed in Ireland or Britain.

Visiting hours:	Monday to Saturday	9.30 a.m. - 5.00 p.m.
June - September:	Sunday	9.30 a.m. - 4.30 p.m.
October - May:	Sunday	12 noon - 4.30 p.m.

38 E2

Royal Irish Academy Library
19 Dawson Street.

A very extensive collection of ancient Irish manuscripts can be seen in this library. These include the 'Book of the Dun Cow', the 'Book of Ballymote', the 'Speckled Book' and the 'Stowe Missal'. Also to be seen is the Cathach or Battle Book, believed to be the actual copy of the Psalms made in the sixth century by St. Colmcille. An autograph copy of the Annals of the Four Masters made in Donegal between 1632 and 1636 is also there.

Visiting hours:	Monday to Thursday 10.00 a.m. - 5.30 p.m.
	Friday 10.00 a.m. - 5.00 p.m.
	Closed Bank Holidays and during the last three weeks in August.
	Admission free.

38 E3

Marsh's Library
St. Patrick's Close.

This is Ireland's oldest public library, founded in 1701 by Archbishop Narcissus Marsh. The collection consists mainly of theological, medical, ancient historical, Hebrew, Syriac, Greek, French and Latin literature. Still to be seen are the original carved bookcases and the cages into which readers were locked to prevent theft.

Visiting Hours:

Weekdays 10.00 a.m. - 1.00 p.m. and 2.00 p.m. - 5.00 p.m.
Saturday 10.30 a.m. - 1.00 p.m.
Closed Tuesdays, Sundays and Bank Holidays.

38 D3

National Library
Kildare Street.

Founded in 1877, the National Library is the largest public library in Ireland. Over 500,000 books as well as maps, prints and manuscripts are housed there. Its huge newspaper collection provides a rich source of historical reference. An extensive collection of historical and literary manuscripts relating to Ireland and microfilms of documents from overseas libraries and archives are available for reference. The public service counter is manned by helpful officials.

Visiting hours:	Monday to Wednesday 10.00 a.m. - 9.00 p.m.
	Thursday / Friday 10.00 a.m. - 5.00 p.m.
	Saturday 10.00 a.m. - 1.00 p.m.

38 E3

National Library

Dublin City Libraries

There are twenty-eight public libraries maintained by the Corporation of Dublin.
The administrative headquarters for the Dublin Public Libraries is at Fenian Street. It houses special reference collections, including the Gilbert Library of manuscripts and books relating to Dublin. And there are extensive collections of books on Ireland. A collection of W. B. Yeats material contains a full edition of Mosada.

Other Dublin Libraries

Other libraries of note are the King's Inn Library, Henrietta Street; University College Library, Belfield; the Worth Library, Steeven's Hospital; the Franciscan Library, Franciscan House of Studies, Killiney; the Central Catholic Library at 74 Merrion Square; the Royal Dublin Society's Library at Ballsbridge and the library in the Ilac Centre, Henry Street.

ART GALLERIES

Hugh Lane Municipal Gallery of Modern Art.

Charlemont House, Parnell Square.

This building, dating from 1762, was formerly the residence of Lord Charlemont. The collection was originally housed in Harcourt Street, the present gallery dating from 1908. It was Sir Hugh Lane who contributed the nucleus of this collection of pictures. Lane was drowned in the sinking of the Lusitania in 1915. Before his death he left his continental collection to the National Gallery in London but had stipulated in his will that they should return to Dublin. Unfortunately an unwitnessed codicil of his will caused complications and his intentions were declared invalid.

After many years it was agreed in 1959 to divide the pictures between Dublin and London in two groups. The two groups are exchanged every five years. This gallery has an interesting collection of works by nineteenth and twentieth-century artists.

National Gallery

Merrion Lawn, Merrion Square West.

The gallery was officially opened in 1864. It then consisted of only 100 pictures donated by William Dargan and George Mulvany. Dargan was a railway entrepreneur who died in 1867. His statue may be seen on the lawn outside the gallery.

There are now over 2000 pictures in the gallery, representing all the European schools. Donors of pictures include Lady Milltown, Sir Hugh Lane, Edward Martyn, the Friends of the National Collections and Sir Alfred Chester Beatty. Famous works by Poussin, Goya and Gainsborough, may be seen. Irish artists are well represented, in a comprehensive collection which includes works by Ashford, Barry Barrett, John Butler Yeats, Hone, Osborne, Lavery and Orpen. Part of the National Portrait Gallery provides an interesting survey of personalities spanning 300 years. This is housed under the same roof.

National Gallery

Hugh Lane Municipal Gallery of Modern Art.

Visiting times:		
Monday to Saturday	9.30 a.m. - 5.30 p.m.	
Thursday	9.30 a.m. - 8.30 p.m.	
Sunday	12 noon - 5.30 p.m.	
Closed Good Friday and 24th - 26th December		
Restaurant open during gallery hours.		

Art Reference Library open Monday to Friday: 10.00 a.m. - 5.00 p.m. Free public lectures Sundays at 3.00 p.m. and Tuesdays at 10.30 a.m. Conducted tours of gallery on Saturdays at 3.00 p.m. and Sundays at 2.00 p.m., 3.00 p.m. and 4.00 p.m. Admission free.

38 E3

Visiting times:	Tuesday to Thursday	9.30 a.m. to 6.00 p.m.
	Friday and Saturday	9.30 a.m. to 5.00 p.m.
	Sunday	11.00 a.m. to 5.00 p.m.
	Closed Monday.	Admission free.

38 D1

Royal Hospital and Irish Museum of Modern Art
Military Road, Kilmainham.
The Irish Museum of Modern Art was established in 1991 and exhibits Irish and International Art of the 20th century

Visiting times:	Tuesday to Saturday	10.00 a.m. – 5.30 p.m.
	Sunday	12 noon – 5.30 p.m.
	Closed Monday.	

37 B3

MUSEUMS

National Museum of Ireland
Kildare Street/Merrion Street.

The contents of this museum comes under three headings – Irish Antiquities, Art and Industrial and Natural History. The Irish Antiquities division holds one of Europe's most impressive collections of antiquities. Items displayed cover every age from the Stone Age to medieval times. Gold lunulae, torques and fibulae from the Bronze Age are of particular interest, as well as famous items like the Tara Brooch, the Cross of Cong and the Ardagh Chalice from the early Christian period.

The main entrance is from Kildare Street but part of the Natural History division is approached from Merrion Street.

Visiting times: Tuesday to Saturday   10.00 a.m. - 5.00 p.m.
             Sunday   2.00 p.m. - 5.00 p.m.
             Closed Monday.   *38 E3*

National Museum of Ireland
Collins Barracks, Benburb Street.

Collins Barracks which was acquired by the National Museum in 1994 is Europe's oldest military barracks and the world's oldest continuously occupied barracks .

It houses exhibits of the decorative arts and of the economic, social, political and military history of the state.

Among the exhibits are: Etruscan vases; a pocket book carried by Wolfe Tone during his imprisonment in the barracks in 1798; gauntlets worn by King William at the Battle of the Boyne and a life-belt and oar from the wreckage of the Lusitania.

Visiting Times: Tuesday to Saturday   10.00 a.m. - 5.00 p.m.
              Sunday   2.00 p.m. - 5.00 p.m.
              Closed Mondays, Christmas Day and Good Friday.
                                          37 C2

Dublin Civic Museum
South William Street.

Occupying the former City Assembly House, this museum was opened in 1953. It contains a permanent collection of exhibits of antiquarian and historical interest, pertaining to Dublin city. Newspapers and cuttings, as well as maps, prints, and various unique items provide a vivid record of Dublin's past.

Visiting times:

             Closed until further notice.
             For information Tel 6794260.   *38 D3*

The Writer's Museum

The Writer's Museum
18/19 Parnell Square North.

Opened in 1991 in two restored Georgian houses. It features a display of paintings, photographs, manuscripts and other memorabilia relating to Irish writers such as Shaw, Yeats, Beckett, Wilde, O'Casey, Joyce, Behan and Swift.

Opening hours: Monday to Saturday   10.00 a.m. - 5.00 p.m.
              Sundays and Bank Holidays   11.30 a.m. - 5.00 p.m.
              Closed 24th - 26th December

                                           38 D1

Genealogical Office and Heraldic Museum
2 Kildare St. Dublin 2.

The oldest office of state in Ireland, founded in 1552. It contains the unique Heraldic Museum with its colourful display of coats of arms, banners and facility.

The Consultancy Service on ancestry tracing is designed to enable you to undertake on your own the task of uncovering your Irish roots.

Opening Hours: Monday to Wednesday   10.00 a.m. - 8.30 p.m.
              Thursday to Friday   10.00 a.m. - 4.30 p.m.
              Saturday   10.00 a.m. - 12.30 p.m.
                                          38 E3

Genealogical Office and Heraldic Museum

National Print Museum
Garrison Chapel, Beggars Bush, Dublin 4.

This Museum houses a unique collection of implements, artefacts and machines from all sectors of the printing industry in Ireland. Many of them are still in full working order.

Visiting times:
May - September:
Monday to Friday   10.00 a.m. - 12.30 p.m. and 2.30 p.m. - 5.00 p.m.
Saturday, Sunday and Bank Holidays   12 noon - 5.00 p.m.
October - April:
Tuesday, Thursday, Saturday and Sunday   2.00 p.m. - 5.00 p.m.
Guided tours and audio visual show.
                                           38 F3

National Wax Museum
Granby Row.

On display are life-size figures of prominent Irish historical, political, theatrical, literary and sporting personalities. Taped narrations on each scene, guide one along. The Chamber of Horrors is a must for all the family.

Visiting times: Monday to Saturday   10.00 a.m. - 5.30 p.m.
              Sunday   12 noon - 5.30 p.m.
                                           38 D1

FAMOUS PEOPLE ASSOCIATED WITH DUBLIN

Dublin has produced an amazing number of well-known writers, scientists and scholars. Many of these personalities not only distinguished themselves in their native city, but through their work established their names world - wide. The following is a brief guide to some of the most famous people who were born in Dublin and/or lived there for a considerable period of time.

THE WORLD OF LETTERS

Samuel Beckett, (1906-1989). Novelist and dramatist, born in Dublin. Novels include 'Murphy','Mollag and Malone Dies'. Plays include 'Waiting for Godot', 'Va et Vient', and 'Silence'. Awarded the Nobel Prize for Literature in 1969.

Brendan Behan, (1923-1964). Dublin-born dramatist. Plays include 'The Quare Fellow' and 'The Hostage'.

Edmund Burke, (1729-1797). Son of a Dublin attorney. Orator, political philosopher and champion of American liberties.

Anna Maria Hall (née Fielding) (1800 - 1881).Author, born Dublin. Published Sketches of Irish Character (1829); further Sketches followed, and nine novels. She had four plays produced successfully. With her husband, published Ireland, its Scenery, Characters, etc. (1840), her best-known work and a valuable record of pre-Famine conditions.

James Joyce, (1882-1941). Poet and writer, born and educated in Dublin. Works include 'A Portrait of the Artist as a Young Man', 'Ulysses' and 'Finnegan's Wake'. The Martello Tower where Joyce lived outside Dublin is now a museum in his memory.

Mary Lavin (1912 - 1996). Writer, born 1912, Massachusetts of Irish parents. She was educated at Loreto College, St Stephen's Green, Dublin, and UCD. Amongst her achievements are the Katherine Mansfield Prize, the Éire Society Gold Medal (1974), and two Guggenheim fellowships. She was elected MIAL, was president 1972-74, and received its Gregory Medal in 1975.

William E.H. Lecky, (1838 - 1903). Famous Dublin-born historian.

Joseph Sheridan Le Fanu, (1814-1873). Nineteenth-century Dublin novelist, author of 'The House by the Churchyard', among others.

Charles Jones Lever, (1806-1872). A native of Dublin. His novels include 'Harry Lorrequer' and 'Charles O'Malley'.

Edmund Malone, (1741-1812). This great scholar specialised in the study of Shakespeare.

James Clarence Mangan, (1803-1849). Son of a Dublin grocer. His poetry includes 'Dark Rosaleen', 'O'Hussey's Ode to the Maguire' and the autobiographic ballad 'The Nameless One'.

Annie M P Smithson (1873 - 1948). Nurse and writer, Born in Dublin. Secretary and organiser of the Irish Nurses' Organisation between 1929 and 1942. In 1917 she published her first novel, Her Irish Heritage. It became a best-seller. In 1944 she published her autobiography, Myself-and Others. One of the earliest members of the Old Dublin Society.

Lady Jane Francesca Wilde (née Elgee) 'Speranza', (1826 - 1896). Writer, born in Dublin. As an ardent nationalist, she contributed verse and prose to the 'Nation' under the pen-name Speranza. In 1851 she married Dr (afterwards Sir) William Wilde. She published a volume of poems in 1864 under her pen-name Speranza, and as Lady Wilde she published a number of works on folklore. She was the mother of Oscar Wilde.

Katharine Tynan (1859 - 1931). Novelist and poet. Born in Dublin. Educated at the Siena Convent, Drogheda, she wrote over a hundred novels, many poems, and an autobiography in five volumes.

Ethna Carbery (pen-name of Anna MacManus, née Johnston) (1866 - 1911). Writer, Born Ballymena, County Antrim. She wrote many poems for the Nation, United Ireland and other papers.

Theodora Fitzgibbon (née Rosling) (1916 - 1991). Cookery expert, author, and lecturer, born in London of Irish parents.. She specialised in cookery and published more than thirty books. From 1960 to 1976 she worked on her encyclopaedia, The Food of the Western World (1976). Her novel Flight of the Kingfisher (1968) was turned into a play and broadcast by the BBC.

Thomas Moore, (1779-1852). Like Mangan this poet was also a grocer's son. He distinguished himself as an adaptor of traditional airs and as a writer of biographies. Works include 'Moore's Melodies', 'The Twopenny Post Bag' and 'Lalla Rookh'.

Sean O'Casey, (1880-1964). Originally a labourer, O'Casey became one of Ireland's most famous dramatists. Plays include 'The Shadow of a Gunman', 'Juno and the Paycock', 'The Plough and the Stars', 'The Silver Tassie' and 'Purple Dust'.

George Bernard Shaw, (1856-1950). Shaw, a world-famous playwright and wit spent the first twenty years of his life in Dublin, his birthplace. Works include 'John's Bull's Other Island', 'Candida', 'The Doctor's Dilemma', 'Man and Superman', 'Pygmalion', 'Heartbreak House' and 'Saint Joan'. In 1925 he won the Nobel Prize for Literature.

Richard Brinsley Sheridan, (1751-1816). Dramatist and distinguished parliamentary orator. Born in Upper Dorset Street. His three great comedies were 'The Rivals', 'The School for Scandal' and 'The Critic'.

James Stephens, (1882-1950). Novelist and poet. His novels include 'The Crock of Gold', 'The Charwoman's Daughter', 'The Demigods' and 'In the Land of Youth'. Poems include 'The Goat Paths' and 'The Snare'.

Jonathan Swift, (1667-1745). Known mainly as a satirist. Became Dean of St. Patrick's in 1713. Probably best known for 'The Tale of a Tub', the 'Drapier's Letters' and 'Gulliver's Travels'.

John Millington Synge, (1871-1909). Although a Dubliner, this dramatist's first love was the West of Ireland. This is reflected in his work. Best known are 'Playboy of the Western World', 'Riders to the Sea' and 'Deirdre of the Sorrows'.

Sir James Ware, (1594-1666). As an historian and antiquary, Ware is one of Dublin's most distinguished great scholars.

Oscar Wilde, (1854-1900). Born in Dublin and educated at Trinity College, Wilde moved to London when he was twenty-five. His outstanding works are the novel 'The Picture of Dorian Gray', and 'The Importance of being Earnest', his dramatic masterpiece. Also of note is his long letter 'De Profundis' and 'The Ballad of Reading Gaol'.

William Butler Yeats, (1865-1939). Born in London and educated in Dublin, Yeats contributed much to the cultural life of Dublin. He was awarded the Nobel Prize for Literature in 1923. Published works include 'Responsibilities', 'The Tower' and 'The Winding Stair'. This great literary personality played a major part in the establishment of the Abbey Theatre in 1904.

THE WORLD OF MUSIC

Michael William Balfe, (1808-1870). Balfe was famous as a conductor and composer of operas. Works include 'The Bohemian Girl' and 'Il Talismano'.

Michele Esposito (1855 - 1929). Composer, pianist, teacher, conductor, editor and music publisher. Born Naples. Came to Dublin 1882. Senior Professor of Piano at the RIAM for 46 years. He died in Florence in 1929.

John Field, (1782-1837). Outstanding as a pianist and romantic composer. His nocturnes are said to have inspired Chopin. Glinka, founder of the Russian school, was taught by Field.

Catherine Hayes (1825 - 1861). Soprano, born Patrick Street, Limerick. She studied under Antonio Sapio in Dublin and then in Paris and Milan under Felici Ronconi. She appeared at La Scala, in 1845, and successfully toured the world.

Margaret Sheridan (1889 - 1958). Soprano, born, Castlebar, Co. Mayo, educated at Dominican Convent, Eccles Street, Dublin. Studied at the Royal Academy of Music, London and in Rome. In 1936 she retired and returned to Ireland.

Sir Charles Villiers Stanford, (1852-1924). Composer of opera, songs, symphonies and chamber music.

THE WORLD OF VISUAL ARTS

Beatrice Behan (1925 - 1993). Artist, widow of Brendan Behan, Born Dublin. She studied painting in Italy and her work was exhibited at the RHA. In 1974 she published her memoirs, My Life With Brendan Behan.

Muriel Brandt (1909 - 1981). Painter, Born Belfast. Her first important commission was a set of panels in the Church of the Immaculate Conception ('Adam and Eve's'), Merchants' Quay, Dublin. She painted portraits of Sir Alfred Chester Beatty, George O'Brien, and other notables. Her picture of Micheál Mac Liammóir, Christine Longford and Hilton Edwards, directors of the Gate hangs in the foyer of the theatre.

Máire de Paor (neé MacDermott) (1925 - 1994). Archaeologist and activist in the contemporary arts, born Buncrana, Co. Donegal. Elected MRIA in 1960 and represented the academy on the Board of Visitors of the National Museum. Founder-member of Cumann Merriman in 1967. Member of the Arts Council between 1973 and 1993. Early in 1994 she was appointed to the Cultural Relations Committee of the Department of Foreign Affairs.

Willhelmina Geddes (1888 - 1955). Stained-glass artist, born Drumreilly, County Leitrim. Her stained glass is on view in the Hugh Lane Municipal Gallery, Dublin, and the Victoria and Albert Museum, London, and over thirty of her designs are in the National Gallery, Dublin.

Evie Hone (1894 - 1955). Artist. Her best-known works are My Four Green Fields for the CIE offices, Upper O'Connell Street, Dublin (now in Government Buildings), five windows for the Jesuit college of Tullabeg at Rahan, County Offaly, and a large window depicting the Last Supper and the Crucifixion for the chapel of Eton College.

Nathaniel Hone I, (1718-1784). Portrait painter and a founder member of the Royal Academy, London.

Nathaniel Hone II, (1831-1917). Painter of landscapes and seascapes. Hone II was a member of the Barbizon Group. He was also a founder of the modern school of Irish painting.

Mary Harriet (Mainie) Jellett (1897 - 1944). artist, born 36 Fitzwilliam Square, Dublin. In 1943 with Evie Hone and others she founded the Irish Exhibition of Living Art. Examples of her austere abstract paintings are in the Municipal Gallery of Modern Art, Dublin. Died in Dublin.

James Arthur O'Connor, (1791 - 1841). Landscape painter.

Sir. William Orpen, (1870 - 1931). Orpen specialised in portrait painting.

Sarah Purser (1848-1943). Sarah Purser established herself as a portrait painter. In 1923, Purser was the first woman to be admitted as an associate member of the Royal Hibernian Academy, Dublin, and the following year she was elected a member.

Jack Butler Yeats, (1871-1957). This modern artist painted in a highly original style, his work distinguished by a heavy, unmistakeable texture. His brother was William Butler Yeats.

John Butler Yeats, (1839-1922). Well known as a portrait painter. Father of Jack and William Butler Yeats.

Harry Clarke, (1889-1931) **Michael Healy**, (1893-1941), Renowned for their Stained Glass creations.

John Henry Foley, (1818-1874). **Thomas Kirk**, (1777-1845).

Andrew O'Connor, (1874-1941). **Edward Smyth,**(1749-1812). Well known for their sculptures.

THE WORLD OF MEDICINE AND SCIENCE

Sir Robert Stawell Ball, (1840-1913). Noted astronomer and mathematician.

Abraham Colles, (1773-1843). In the medical world Colles is remembered for 'Colles' Law', 'Colles' fracture' and 'Colles' Fuchsia'.

Sir Dominic Corrigan, (1802-1880). Corrigan specialised in diseases of the aorta. Remembered for 'Corrigan's Disease', 'Corrigan's Pulse'. He also invented 'Corrigan's Button'.

Sir Philip Crampton, (1778-1858). This famous Dublin surgeon played an important role in establishing the fame of the Dublin medical school in the early nineteenth century. He was co-author of a book on bedside teaching with Robert Graves.

George Francis Fitzgerald, (1851-1901). Fitzgerald made a valuable contribution to the study of physics.

Robert Graves, (1796-1853). The concept of bedside teaching was introduced in medical education by Robert Graves. His book 'Clinical Lectures' became an international textbook for medical students.

Sir William Rowan Hamilton, (1805-1865). Hamilton was the discoverer of quaternions. Through his pioneering work he achieved international fame by foreshadowing the quantum theory and later important discoveries in nuclear physics.

Richard Kirwan, (1735-1812). The first systematic textbook in English on mineralogy was written by Kirwan.

Francis Rynd, (1801-1861). A major contribution was made to medical science by Rynd, through his invention of the hypodermic syringe.

George Salmon, (1819-1904). Dublin-born mathematician.

William Stokes, (1804-1878). Stokes is remembered for 'Stokes-Adams-Syndrome' and 'Cheyne-Stokes Respiration'. He was the author of 'Diseases of the Chest and Diseases of the Heart and Aorta'.

Sir William Wilde, (1815–1876). Wilde was noted as an ophalmologist, -otologist, and archaeologist. In the medical field he is associated with 'Wilde's Incision' and 'Wilde's Cord'. He was Oscar Wilde's father.

Ellen Hutchins (1785-1815). Botanist, born in Ballylickey, Co.Cork. The major part of her botanical collection lies in Kew Botanical Gardens, London.

Mary Ward (1827-1869). Microscopist, artist, entomologist and author. Born in Ballylin, Co Offaly. Two of her books were selected to be displayed at the international exhibition at the Crystal Palace in 1862.

THE WORLD OF HUMANITIES

Louie Bennett (1870 - 1956). Irish trade unionist. Born in Dublin. She helped to start the Irishwomen's Suffrage Federation in 1913 and co-founded the Irish Women's Reform League. She was the first woman President of the Irish Trades Union Congress in 1931-2 and again in 1947-8.

Leslie de Barra (née Price) (1893 - 1984). Revolutionary and Red Cross official. After marriage, she devoted the rest of her life to the relief of human suffering at home and abroad. Chairwoman of the Irish Red Cross from 1950.

Catherine McAuley (1778 - 1841). Founded the Order of Mercy which became one of the largest religious congregations ever founded, is buried at the convent in Baggot Street.

Helena Molony (1884 - 1967). Actress and trade unionist. She became secretary of the Irish Women Workers' Union in 1915 and was subsequently honoured with presidency of the Irish Trade Union Congress.

DUBLIN'S PARKS AND GARDENS

Garden of Remembrance
Parnell Square East Dublin 1.
The Garden of Remembrance was designed by Daithí Hanly and is dedicated to the memory of those who died in the cause of Irish freedom. The central theme is peaceful remembrance and reflection, and the sculpture by Oisen Kelly, "Children of Lir" reflects this.

Opening Hours:	March - April/October:	11.00 a.m. - 7.00 p.m.
	May - September:	9.30 a.m. - 8.00 p.m.
	November - February:	11.00 a.m. - 4.00 p.m.

38 D1

St. Anne's Park and Gardens
Mount Prospect Avenue, Clontarf.
In a pleasant setting adjacent to Dollymount Strand, the rose gardens in this park cover over three acres alone. The Park and Gardens are open all year round. Admission free. Entrance Howth Road/All Saints Road .

27 A3

Marlay Park
Rathfarnham.
This is the largest park on the south side of Dublin. It covers three hundred acres in a highly picturesque setting at the foot of the Dublin mountains. It is the starting point of the 'Wicklow Way' long distance signposted walk. A craft centre, including workshops, is situated within the area of the park.

57 A2

Merrion Square Park
Merrion Square.
Formerly only for the use of the residents of Merrion Square, this public park is surrounded on all sides by some of Dublin's finest Georgian architecture. Open all year, daylight hours.

38 E3

National Botanic Gardens

National Botanic Gardens
Botanic Road, Glasnevin.
Covering 19.5 hectares, these beautiful gardens contain a huge assortment of trees, plants and shrubs. Rare blooms and palms are housed in the huge Victorian conservatories. These gardens were founded in 1795 when the estate, on which the gardens now stand, was purchased from the Ticknell family by the Royal Dublin Society.
Open all year except Christmas Day.

Visiting times:	Summer: Monday - Saturday	9.00 a.m. – 6.00 p.m.
	Sunday	10.00 a.m. – 6.00 p.m.
	Winter : Monday - Sunday	10.00 a.m. – 4.30 p.m.
	Admission free.	

25 A3

Herbert Park
Ballsbridge.
A charming mature park, well laid out with interesting trees, shrubs and flower beds. An attractive feature is the large pond on the eastern side of the park.

38 F4

St. Enda's Park

St. Enda's Park
Grange Road, Rathfarnham.
One of Dublin's most attractive suburban public parks. The park occupies the grounds of St. Enda's, the former school where the patriot Padraic Pearse once taught. The well-restored estate house has been opened as a museum to Pearse's memory.
Visiting hours:

November - January:	10.00 a.m. – 4.00 p.m.
February - April, September - October:	10.00 a.m. – 5.00 p.m.
May - August:	10.00 a.m. – 5.30 p.m.

56 F1

St. Stephen's Green
Covering twenty-two acres at the top of Grafton Street, St. Stephen's Green is right in the heart of the city. The varied landscaping of this delightful park includes trees, flower beds, a waterfall and an artificial lake. Several notable monuments and sculptures may also be seen.

Opening Times:	During daylight hours.	
	Monday to Saturday	8.00 a.m. - Dusk.
	Sundays and Bank Holidays	10.00 a.m. - Dusk.
	Christmas Day	10.00 a.m. - 1.00 p.m.

38 D3

Irish National War Memorial Park.
Islandbridge.
Designed by the English architect Sir Edward Lutyens, these gardens are dedicated to the memory of 49,400 Irish soldiers who died in the First World War.

Opening Times:	During daylight hours only.	
	Monday - Friday from	8.00 a.m.
	Saturday and Sunday from	10.00 a.m.

37 A2

National War Memorial Gardens,

Phoenix Park

North-western edge of city.

Acknowledged as one of the largest enclosed urban parks in the world, it covers 1,760 acres, with a circumference of seven miles.

Close to the main entrance at Parkgate Street are the People's Gardens and the Zoological Gardens (see separate entry). Within the park are the residence of the President of Ireland (Aras an Uachtarain), the American Ambassador's residence and the Ordnance Survey Office. In the south-western part of the park is 'The Fifteen Acres', an area of playing fields actually covering two hundred acres. In eighteenth-century Dublin this was used as a duelling ground. During the visit of Pope John Paul II in 1979 it was the site of an outdoor Mass.

Visiting times: Phoenix Park is open to the public at all times but the People's Gardens have their own opening times.

Monday to Friday	8.30 a.m. - 9.00 p.m. in summer.
	8.30 a.m. - 4.00 p.m. in winter.
Saturday/Sunday	10.00 a.m. - 9.00 p.m. in summer.
	10.30 a.m. - 4.00 p.m. in winter.

Admission free.

37 B2

Zoological Gardens

Phoenix Park

In these outstanding attractive gardens may be seen a large collection of wild animals and birds from all over the world. Spacious houses and outdoor enclosures add to the total effect. Lion breeding has a long and distinguished history at Dublin Zoo. Two natural lakes house pelicans, flamingos, ducks and geese.

Visiting hours:	Weekday	9.30 a.m. - 6.00 p.m.
	Sunday	10.30 a.m. - 6.00 p.m.

Last admission 1 Hour before closing.
Gardens close at dusk in winter.

37 A1

Other public parks

Most notable are Corkagh Demesne in Clondalkin, Palmerston Park Dartry, Bushy Park, Terenure, Mountjoy Square Park, Griffeen Valley Park in Lucan and Ward River Valley Park, Swords.

Furry Glen, Phoenix Park

Phoenix Monument, Phoenix Park

Apostolic Nunciature
183 Navan Road
Dublin
Tel: 838 0577

24 D4

Argentine Embassy
15 Ailesbury Drive
Dublin 4
Tel: 269 1546 / 269 1713

48 D1

Australian Embassy
2nd Floor,
Fitzwilton House
Wilton Terrace, Dublin 2
Tel: 664 5300

38 E4

Austrian Embassy
15 Ailesbury Court Apts.
93 Ailesbury Road
Dublin 4
Tel: 269 4577 / 269 1451
48 D1

Belgian Embassy
2 Shrewsbury Road
Dublin 4
Tel: 269 2082 / 269 1588
48 D1

**Embassy of the
Federative Republic
of Brazil**
Europa House
Block 9. Harcourt Centre
41-49 Harcourt House,
Dublin 2.
Tel: 475 6000 / 416 1202
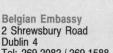
38 D4

British Embassy
29 Merrion Road
Dublin 4
Tel: 205 3700
48 D1

Bulgarian Embassy
22 Burlington Road
Dublin 4
Tel: 660 3293

38 E4

Canadian Embassy
4th Floor
65/68 St.Stephen's Green South
Dublin 2
Tel: 417 4100
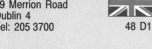
38 E3

Chilean Embassy
44 Wellington Road
Ballsbridge
Dublin 4
Tel: 667 5094

38 F4

**Embassy of the
People's Republic
of China**
40 and 77 Ailesbury Road
Dublin 4
Tel: 269 1707 / 269 6756
48 D1

**Embassy of the
Republic of Croatia**
Adelaide Chambers
Peter Street
Dublin 8
Tel: 476 7181
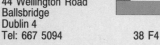
38 D3

**Embassy of the
Republic of Cuba**
2 Adelaide Court,
Adelaide Road,
Dublin 2
Tel: 475 0899 / 475 2999
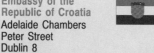
38 E4

Embassy of Cyprus
71 Lower Leeson Street
Dublin 2
Tel: 676 3060
38 E3

Czech Embassy
57 Northumberland Road
Dublin 4
Tel: 668 1135 / 668 1343

38 F4

**Royal Danish
Embassy**
121/122
St. Stephen's Green West,
Dublin 2
Tel: 475 6404 / 475 6405
38 D3

**Embassy of the
Arab Republic
of Egypt**
12 Clyde Road
Ballsbridge, Dublin 4
Tel: 660 6566 / 660 6718 /
667 6150 (Visas)
38 F4

**Embassy of the
Federated Democratic
Republic of Ethiopia**
Suite 2
1-3 Merrion House,
Fitzwilliam Street Lower,
Dublin 2
Tel: 678 7062 / 678 7063
38 E3

Estonia Embassy
Ailesbury Road
Dublin 4
Tel: 219 6730
48 D1

Finnish Embassy
Russell House
Stokes Place
St. Stephen's Green South
Dublin 2
Tel: 478 1344
38 D3

French Embassy
36 Ailesbury Road
Dublin 4
Tel: 277 5000
48 D1

**Embassy of the
Federal Republic
of Germany**
31 Trimleston Avenue
Booterstown, Co. Dublin
Tel: 269 3011 / 269 3123
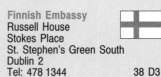
48 E2

Greek Embassy
1 Upper
Pembroke Street
Dublin 2
Tel: 676 7254 / 676 7255
38 E3

**Embassy of the
Republic of Hungary**
2 Fitzwilliam Place
Dublin 2
Tel: 661 2902 / 661 2905
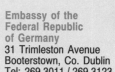
38 E4

Indian Embassy
6 Leeson Park
Dublin 6
Tel: 496 6792 /497 0959
38 E4

**Embassy of the
Islamic Republic
of Iran**
72 Mount Merrion Avenue
Blackrock, Co. Dublin
Tel: 288 0252 / 288 2967
/ 288 5881
48 F3

Israel Embassy
122 Pembroke Road
Dublin 4
Tel: 2309400
38 F4

Italian Embassy
63/65 Northumberland Road
Ballsbridge, Dublin 4
Dublin 4
Tel: 660 1744 / 664 2300
/664 2301

38 F4

Japanese Embassy
Nutley Building
Merrion Centre
Nutley Lane, Dublin 4
Tel: 202 8300 / 269 4033
48 E1

**Embassy of the
Republic of Korea**
15 Clyde Road
Ballsbridge, Dublin 4
Tel: 660 8800
38 F4

**Embassy of the
Republic of Latvia**
14 Lower Leeson Street,
Dublin 2
Tel: 662 1610
38 E3

Embassy of Lesotho
2 Clanwilliam Square,
Grand Canal Quay,
Dublin 2.
Tel: 676 2233

38 F3[41]

**Embassy of the
Republic of Lithuania**
90 Merrion Road,
Ballsbridge,
Dublin 4.
Tel: 668 8292
48 E1

Embassy of Malaysia
Level 3A-5A
Shelbourne House
Shelbourne Road
Ballsbridge
Dublin 4.
Tel: 667 7280
38 F3

Mexican Embassy
43 Ailesbury Road
Dublin 4
Tel: 260 0699
48 D1

**Embassy of the
Kingdom of Morocco**
39 Raglan Road
Dublin 4
Tel: 660 9449
38 F4

Netherlands Embassy
160 Merrion Road
Dublin 4
Tel: 269 3444
48 D1

**Embassy of the
Federal Republic
of Nigeria**
56 Leeson Park
Dublin 6
Tel: 660 4366 / 660 4051
38 E4

**Royal Norwegian
Embassy**
Hainault House
34 Molesworth Street,
Dublin 2
Tel: 662 1800

38 E3

**Embassy of the
Islamic Republic
of Pakistan**
Ailsbury Villa
Ailsbury Road
Ballsbridge
Dublin 4.
Tel: 261 3032 / 261 3033 / 260 6938
48 D1

**Embassy of the
Republic of Poland**
5 Ailesbury Road
Dublin 4
Tel: 283 0855
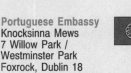
48 D1

Portuguese Embassy
Knocksinna Mews
7 Willow Park /
Westminster Park
Foxrock, Dublin 18
Tel: 289 4416 / 289 3375

59 A2

Embassy of Romania
26 Waterloo Road
Dublin 4
Tel: 668 1085
48 D1

**Embassy of the
Russian Federation**
184/186 Orwell Road
Rathgar, Dublin 14
Tel: 492 2048(Embassy)
492 3492 (Consular Section)

47 B3

**Embassy of the
Slovak Republic**
20 Clyde Road
Dublin 4
Tel: 660 0012 / 660 0008
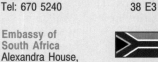
38 F4

**Embassy of the
Republic of Slovenia**
Morrison Chambers
2nd Floor,
32 Nassau Street
Dublin 2
Tel: 670 5240
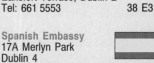
38 E3

**Embassy of
South Africa**
Alexandra House,
Earlsfort Centre,
Earlsfort Terrace, Dublin 2
Tel: 661 5553
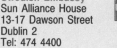
38 E3

Spanish Embassy
17A Merlyn Park
Dublin 4
Tel: 283 9900 / 269 1640

48 E1

Swedish Embassy
Sun Alliance House
13-17 Dawson Street
Dublin 2
Tel: 474 4400
38 E3

Swiss Embassy
6 Ailesbury Road
Ballsbridge
Dublin 4
Tel: 218 6382
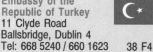
48 D1

**Embassy of the
Republic of Turkey**
11 Clyde Road
Ballsbridge, Dublin 4
Tel: 668 5240 / 660 1623

38 F4

Embassy of Ukraine
16 Elgin Road,
Ballsbridge,
Dublin 4.
Tel: 668 8601 / 668 5189
38 F4

**Embassy of the
United States of America**
42 Elgin Road
Ballsbridge, Dublin 4
Tel: 668 8777

38 F4

For further information contact:
Dept of Foreign Affairs,
80 St. Stephen's Green, Dublin 2.
Tel: 478 0822 / www.foreignaffairs.gov.ie

Route Network

Dublin Bus operates the bus network in the greater Dublin area. This network extends from Balbriggan in North County Dublin to Kilcoole in County Wicklow and westwards as far as Kilcock, County Kildare.

Other Services:

In addition to the network described above, Dublin Bus operates the following additional services:

Nitelink –a network of 22 routes radiating from the City Centre which operate every Monday - Wednesday at 0.30 a.m.and 2.00 a.m., Thursday - Saturday at 0.30 a.m. and every twenty minutes thereafter until the last bus at 4.30 a.m. - Price €4. Additional services to Balbriggan, Portrane, Maynooth, Dunboyne, and Ashbourne operates Monday - Wednesday at 0.30 a.m.and 2.00 a.m. and Thursday - Saturday at 0.30 a.m., 2.00 a.m. and 3.30 a.m.. Price €6.

Airlink – an Express Bus Service connecting Dublin Airport with Dublin City Centre. The 747 service links Dublin Airport with Bus Aras - Price €4.50. The 748 links Dublin Airport with Heuston Station - Price €4.50.

Private Hire – Double Deck, Single Deck or Minibuses can be hired for group Outings, Parties, Weddings etc.

Sightseeing Tours – Dublin Bus operate a range of tours – see Tours Information section for more details.

Hours of operation

Scheduled services operate from 6.00 a.m. throughout the day with last buses departing the City Centre at around 11.30p.m. In addition to these services a special **Nitelink Network** operates Monday - Saturday nights.

Dublin Bus's Head Office is located at 59 Upper O'Connell Street. Opening hours are from 9.00 a.m. until 5.30 p.m. Monday to Friday and up to 1.00 p.m. on Saturdays. A telephone information service is available on 01-8734222 between 9.00 a.m. and 7.00 p.m. Monday to Saturday.

Timetables are provided on most of the bus stops in the City. In addition, guides and timetables for local areas are available from our Head Offices at 59 Upper O'Connell Street, Dublin 1.

Cash Fares / Autofare System

Fares are charged on the basis of distance travelled and range from €0.75 to €1.65 for single journeys. On some longer distance routes, fares of up €4.05 are applicable. Cash fares are paid on entry to the bus. Dublin Bus operates an **exact fares** system; bank notes cannot be accepted.

Autofare - an exact fare system -*how does it work?* Having established the appropriate fare for the journey you propose to take, you insert the exact fare **in coins only** **(bank notes cannot be accepted)** into the top of the fare box. A ticket will then be issued by the ticket machine once the driver is satisfied that the correct fare has been deposited. If you have to deposit more than the exact fare, the driver will issue a passenger refund ticket for the overpayment. This passenger refund ticket, together with your travel ticket, must be presented at Dublin Bus, 59 Upper O'Connell Street in order to claim a refund of the overpayment.

Prepaid Tickets

Dublin Bus prepaid tickets are available from the Head Office in O'Connell Street as well as from a network of over 270 Ticket Agents throughout the Greater Dublin Area.

2 Easy tickets offer two journeys within 1 month of first validation and are available for adults and school children.

Rambler tickets are also available and offer unlimited bus travel for 1, 3, 5 or 7 days. These Rambler tickets are also valid on the Airlink service.

Transfer 90 Ticket - valid for travel on two bus journeys within 90 minutes of each other inside the Citizone area.

Nitelink tickets - available for single journeys on Dublin Bus Nitelink services.

Bus/Rail Long, Medium and Short Hop Tickets - allows the user to unlimited Bus and Rail/Dart travel within zone.

Tours

Dublin City Hop On Hop Off Tour

The Dublin Tour has been carefully designed to give you the freedom to explore and experience the history and culture of Dublin at your leisure. The complete tour lasts one hour and twenty minutes, but tour "all day" tickets will allow you to hop on and off as often as you wish through the day at any of the 16 stops. Each stop is conveniently located and all display the distinctive green and cream open-top bus sign. Most of the city's major attractions can be reached on the tour and buses operate frequently throughout the day.

Coast & Castle Tour

Visit the magnificent Malahide Castle set in 250 acres of parkland. View the majestic splendour of Dublin Bay set against the landscape of the Dublin & Wicklow Mountains from the idyllic setting of Howth Summit.

South Coast Tour

Enjoy the elegance of Dun Laoghaires promenade and bustling yacht-filled harbour, the charm of Dalkey, panoramic views of Killiney Bay and even more! Return through scenic Dublin and Wicklow Mountains and villages - breathtakingly beautiful.

Ghost Bus Tour

This tour introduces you to the dark romance of a city of gaslight ghosts and chilling legends. You will see haunted houses, learn of Dracula's Dublin origins and even a crash course in body snatching. Near journey's end, the lights go out and darkness invites the macabre traditions of the Irish wake. Your host will conclude the tour by explaining the meaning of life and death! Irish style. All tours depart from Dublin Bus's Head Office in 59 O'Connell Street. Prices range from €8.89 to €15.24 for adults for the above Sightseeing Tours.

CONTACT DETAILS:
For further information on any of the above,
please contact:- Information Bureau and Customer Service
phone: (01) 873 4222 **or** visit our Web Site:www.dublinbus.ie

PLACE NAME	SERVED BY BUS NO.
Abbey Pk. (Baldoyle)	32B
Abbotstown Ave.	40/A, 220
Adelaide Rd.	14, 15A, 15B, 44, 44N, 48A, 48N
Ailesbury Rd.	3, 5, 7, 7A
Airport (Dublin)	16, 16A, 41, 41A, 41B, 41C, 46X, 58X, 230, 746, 747, 748
Albert Rd.	59, 59A
Alexandra Basin (Ext. Gates)	53A
Alexandra Rd.	53A
All Saints' Rd.	29A
Allenton Estate	49A
Amiens St.	20B, 90, 130
Angelsea Rd.	46, 63, 84
Annamoe Rd.	10, 10A
Anne Devlin Pk.	15B
Appian Way	10, 10A, 11/A/B,13B, 18, 46A, 46X, 84X
Ardee St.	50, 56A, 150
Ardlea Rd.	20B, 27B
Artane Shopping Centre	20B
Artane	27, 27N, 42, 42B, 127, 129
Arthur Griffith Pk. (Lucan)	25A, 239
Ashbourne	88N
Ashington	122
Ashtown	37, 38/A, 39, 39N, 70, 70N
Auburn Avenue	37X, 38
Aughrim St.	10, 10A, 37, 38, 39,
Aungier St.	16, 16A, 19, 19A, 83
Aylesbury	15D/F, 49X, 75, 201
Baggot St.	10, 15X, 18, 25X, 49X, 50X, 51X, 66X, 67X, 77X
Bakers Corner	46A, 46X, 58, 58C, 58X, 75, 746
Balbriggan	33,33A, 33N
Balbutcher	13A, 104, 220
Baldonnel	68
Baldoyle	29N, 32, 32A, 32B, 32X, 102, 105, 129
Balgaddy	78A, 239
Balgriffin	42, 43
Ballinclea Rd.	7, 45A, 86
Ballinteer	14, 14A, 48A, 48N, 75, 116, 161
Ballsbridge	5, 7, 7A, 7N, 18, 27X, 45, 46
Ballybrack	7, 7N, 45A, 46, 111
Ballyboden	15C, 15N, 15X
Ballybough	27N, 51A, 123
Ballycoolin Road	220, 236
Ballycullen Drive	15N, 49B, 49X
Ballydowd	25, 66, 66A/B, 67, 67A
Ballyfermot	18, 51N, 76/A/B, 78A, 79, 206
Ballygall Parade	134
Ballygall Rd. E.	19, 40A, 134
Ballygall Rd. W.	17A, 19A, 134
Ballyknockan	65
Ballymore Eustace	65
Ballymount Rd.	56A
Ballymun	13, 13A, 17A, 40N, 220
Ballymun Rd.	11, 11A, 11B, 13/A, 19A, 46X, 58X, 77X, 103
Ballymun Shopping Centre	13, 13A, 17A, 103, 104, 220
Ballyogan	44C, 63, 86, 115, 117
Ballyroan	15B
Ballyshannon	27B

PLACE NAME	SERVED BY BUS NO.
Ballywaltrim	145, 146
Balrothery (Tallaght)	54N, 65, 77X
Baltiboys	65 (Ballyknockan)
Bangor Rd.	17, 18, 63, 121
Barnaculla	44B
Barry's Bridge	84, 184
Bawnogue	51B, 51N, 210
Bawnville Rd.	76B, 77A
Beaumont Ave. (Churchtown)	14, 14A, 16A
Beaumont Rd. (Whitehall)	16, 16A, 20B, 27N, 51A, 103
Beaumont Hospital	27B, 42A, 51A, 103, 104
Beechwood Ave.	11, 11A, 11B, 13B, 48A
Belcamp Rd.	42
Belfield (U.C.D.)	2, 3, 10, 10A, 11/B, 15X, 17, 25X, 27X, 32X, 33X, 39X, 41X, 46/A/B/D/X, 46N, 49X, 50X, 58X, 65X, 70X, 77X, 84X
Belgard Rd.	50, 50X, 76, 76A, 76B
Belgrave Square	13B, 18
Berkeley Rd.	10, 10A, 38/A, 120
Binn's Bridge	11, 11A, 13/A,16, 16A, 40, 40A, 40B
Bird Ave.	11, 11A, 48A
Biscayne (Malahide)	32A, 32X, 42, 102, 230
Blackhall Place	37, 39, 70, 70N
Blackhorse Ave.	10, 10A, 37, 172
Blackrock	7, 7A, 7N, 17, 45, 114, 115
Blakestown	39, 39N, 39X, 76A, 220
Blanchardstown	38/A, 39/N/X, 70/N/X, 76A, 236, 237, 239, 270
Blessington	65
Blessington St.	10, 10A, 38/A,120
Bluebell	51, 51B, 38, 69
Blunden Drive	27N, 42A/B
Bohernabreena	49A
Bolbrook	76B, 77A/X
Booterstown	5, 7, 7A, 45
Botanic Gardens	13/A, 19, 134
Botanic Rd.	13/A, 19/A, 134
Braemor Rd.	14
Brandon Rd.	123
Bray	45, 45A, 84, 145, 146, 184, 185
Brewery Rd.	46/A/X, 63, 84/X, 86, 118
Brittas	65
Broadford	48A, 75, 116
Broadstone	19, 19A, 134
Brookfield	56A, 77, 202
Brookwood Ave.	42A/B, 104
Broombridge Rd.	120
Bulfin Rd.	19
Bull Wall	130
Burgage	65
Busáras (Central Bus Station)	20B,27, 27B, 29A, 31/A/B, 32/A/B, 42, 43, 53, 90, 130, 747, 748
Bushy Pk.	15B
Bushy Pk. Rd.	16, 16A
Butterfield Ave.	15B, 16, 16A, 17, 75
Cabinteely	45, 46/C, 84, 86
Cabra	39N, 120, 121, 122
Cabra Rd.	38/A, 120, 121, 122
Cabra West	120
Camden St.	15N, 16, 16A, 19, 19A, 49N, 65/B, 65X, 83
Cappagh Hosp.	40A, 104, 220

PLACE NAME	SERVED BY BUS NO.
Cappagh Rd.	40, 40A, 104, 220
Cappaghmore	51, 76/A/B, 210
Captain's Rd.	54A, 83
Captain's Hill	66A, 66X
Cardiff Bridge Rd.	40, 220
Carnlough Rd.	120
Carpenterstown	37, 37X, 70N, 239
Carrickbrack Road	31B, 31N
Carrickhill Road	32X, 42N, 102
Carrickmines	44N, 46D, 63, 86, 117
Carysfort Ave.	7A, 17, 114, 115
Casement Pk.	40
Cashel Rd.	17, 18, 83
Castle Ave.	29A, 31, 103, 104, 130
Castleknock	37, 37X, 38, 39N, 70N, 237
Castle Lawns	65, 65B, 77A, 77X
Castletimon Rd.	27B
Cathal Brugha Street	51A, 123
Cedarwood Rd.	19, 19A
Celbridge	67, 67A, 67N, 67X
Chapelizod	25, 25A, 26, 66, 66A, 66B, 66N, 67, 67A
Charlemont St.	44, 48A
Cheeverstown Road	54N, 56A, 76, 76A, 77, 77X, 202
Chelmsford Rd.	11, 11A, 13B 18, 44, 48A
Cherry Orchard	18, 76, 76A, 76B, 78A
Cherrywood Villas	51B, 51N, 51X
Christchurch Place	49X, 50/X, 51B, 54A, 77X, 78A, 123, 206
Churchtown	14, 14A, 48N
Church St.	134
Churchview Road	7, 7X, 45A, 46, 58, 111
Citywest	50, 65B, 77X
Clanbrassil St.	49/X, 54A, 54N
Clare Hall	27, 27X, 42, 43, 127
Clogher Rd.	121
Cloghran	33, 41, 41/A/B, 41C, 230, 746
Clondalkin	51, 51B, 51N, 51X, 68, 69, 76, 76A, 76B, 210
Clonburris	51, 68, 76, 76A, 76B, 210
Clonee	70, 270
Clonliffe Rd.	3, 11, 11A, 16, 51A
Clonkeen Rd.	45, 46D
Clonsilla	39, 39N, 39X, 220, 237
Clonskea	11, 11A/B, 17, 44N, 116
Clontarf Castle	130
Clontarf Rd.	103, 104, 130
Cloverhill Rd.	79
Colberts Rd.	50
Coldcut	18, 26, 76, 76A/B, 78A
Collinstown	33, 41, 41B, 41C, 746
Collins Ave.	3, 16/A, 20B, 42A, 103, 105
Collin's Museum	172
Connolly Station	20B, 27X, 90, 127, 129, 130, 748
Conyngham Rd.	25/A, 26, 66/A/B, 67/A
Cookstown Road	49N, 56A
Cooldrinagh Rd.	66, 67
Cooley Rd.	18, 50, 56A, 123, 150
Coolmine Cross Rd.	39, 76A
Coolock	17A, 27/N/X, 42A/B
Coolock Lane	16A, 17A, 41, 41B, 746
Corduff	38, 39N, 220, 238
Cornelscourt Centre	44N, 45, 46, 84/X, 86, 117
Cowper Rd.	13B
Croke Park	3, 11, 11A, 16/A, 51A

PLACE NAME	SERVED BY BUS NO.
Cromcastle Dr.	27B, 103, 104
Cromwellsfort Rd.	19A
Crooksling	65
Cross Chapel	65
Crumlin Village	17, 18, 150
Crumlin (Shopping Centre)	50, 56A, 77/A/N, 150, 210
Cushlawn	65B, 201
Custom Hse. Quay	53A
Dalkey	59, 59A
Dalymount Pk.	10, 10A, 19/A, 38, 120, 134
Danieli Rd.	27, 42, 42B
Darndale	27/N/X, 42, 43, 42A/B
Dartry Rd.	14A
Deansgrange	45, 46A/D/X,58X, 75, 746
Deanstown Ave.	40A/C, 220
Delgany	184
Distillery Rd.	51A
Dodsboro'	25, 66/A/B, 67/A
Dollymount	31N, 130
Dolphin's Barn	17, 19, 50/X, 56A, 77N/X 122, 150, 210
Donabate	33B
Donaghies	29A
Donaghmede	29A/N, 127
Donaghmede Shopping Centre	29A
Donaghmore	65
Donnybrook	10, 10A, 32X, 33X, 41X, 46/A/B/X, 58/C/X, 84X, 118, 746
Donnycarney	20B, 27/B/X, 42/B/N, 43
Donore Ave.	19, 121
Dorset St.	3, 11/A, 13/A, 16, 40C, 46X, 58X, 77B, 746
Drimnagh	121, 122, 123
Drimnagh Rd.	18, 50, 56A, 77, 122, 150
Drumcondra	3, 11/A,13A, 16/A, 33N/X, 41A/N, 46X, 58X, 77B, 746
Drumcondra Road Upr.	3, 11/A,13A, 16/A, 33N/X, 41A/N, 46X, 58X, 77B/X, 746
Drumfin Rd.	18, 76/A/B, 78A, 79, 206
Dubber Cross	40B
Dublin Airport	16/A, 33N, 41/A/B/C/N, 46X, 58X, 230, 746, 747, 748
D.C.U.	11/A/B, 13/A, 19A, 46X, 58X, 77B, 103, 105, 116
Dublin Zoo	10, 10A
Dunard Estate	37, 172
Dunawley	51B, 51N, 51X, 210
Dunboyne	70, 70N, 70X, 270
Dundrum	17, 44, 48A/N, 75
Dungriffin Rd.	31B
Dun Laoghaire	7/A/N, 45A, 46A/N/X, 59/A, 75, 111, 746
Dun Laoghaire (Shopping Centre)	7, 7A, 45A, 46A, 59/A, 75, 111
Dunsink Drive	40C
Earlsfort Terrace	14/A, 15/A/B/C, 44, 48A, 127, 129
East Wall Rd.	53
Eccles Street	3, 11/A/B, 13/A, 16/A, 121
Edenmore	27N, 42A/B
Embankment (Tallaght)	65
Enniskerry	44, 185
Errigal Rd.	56A, 123
Exchequer St.	16, 19, 83

PLACE NAME	SERVED BY BUS N0
Fairview	20B, 27/B/N/X, 29A/N, 31, 32, 42/A/B/N, 127, 129, 130
Faussagh Rd.	120
Feltrim Road	42N, 43
Fettercairn	56A, 65, 65B, 76, 77, 202
Finglas	17A, 40/A/B/C, 88N, 104, 134, 220
Finglas East	17A, 104, 134
Finglas West	40, 40A/N, 104
Finglas South	40, 40A/B/C/N, 220
Firhouse	49, 49A/N,75
Firhouse Road	15X, 49X
Fitzwilliam Place	11, 11A, 11B, 13B
Fitzwilliam Sq.	11, 11A, 13B, 46A
Fortfield Rd.	54A
Foster Ave.	11A, 17, 46B
Four Courts	25, 26, 66/A/B,67/A
Fox & Geese	51, 51B, 68, 69, 210
Foxrock	46N, 63, 86
Foxrock Church	46/A/D/N/X, 58/C/X, 63, 75, 84, 84X, 746
Galtymore Rd.	123
Gardiner St.	3,11,16, 33X, 40/A, 41/C, 746
Georges St. Sth.	15D/E/F,16,19, 65/B, 83
Gilford Rd.	3
Glasanaon Rd.	19, 134
Glassmore	41, 41A, 41X
Glasnevin	13, 19, 134
Glasnevin Ave.	13/A, 17A, 19/A, 40N
Glasnevin Cemetery	40/A/B/C
Glasthule	59, 59A
Glenageary Rd. Lr.	7, 7A, 45A, 111
Glenamuck	63
Glencullen	44B
Glen Ellan	41A
Glen O'The Downs	184 (Willow Gr.)
Glenview	54A, 65, 65B, 76B
Goatstown	11, 11A, 44N
Gracefield Rd.	42B, 104
Gracepark Rd.	27N, 51A
Grand Canal St.	7, 7A, 45
Grange Rd. (Rathfarnham)	16, 75, 116
Grange X Rd. (Raheny)	29A
Granville Pk.	46A, 114
Greencastle Rd.	27
Greenhills Rd.	50, 77, 77N/X
Greenpark (Walkinstown)	15A, 77, 77A
Greystones	84, 84X, 184
Griffith Ave. (Glasnevin)	11, 11A, 13A,19A
Griffith Ave. (Extension)	220
Griffith Ave. (Whitehall)	3, 13A, 16/A, 41, 746
Griffith Ave. (Marino)	20B, 27N, 123
Grove Rd. (Finglas)	17A, 19, 19A
Guild St.	53A
Haddington Rd.	7, 7A, 45
Haddon Rd.	130
Halfway Hse. (Walkinstown)	18, 50, 77, 77A, 210
Hanlon's Corner	10,10A, 37/X, 39, 70/X
Harcourt St.	14, 14A, 15/A/B/C, 48A
Harrington St.	16, 16A, 19/A
Hatch St.	14, 14A, 15/A/B/C, 48A
Harmonstown	42A, 42B
Harmonstown Road	42A, 42B
Harold's Cross	16, 16A, 49/A/B, 19A
Hartstown	39/N/X, 220
Hazelbrook Rd.	15A, 17, 54A, 19A
Hempstown	65
Herbert Pk.	7A, 10, 46A
Herbert Rd.	3
Heuston Stn.	25X, 26,46A/X, 51/X, 66/A/B/X, 67/A/X, 69/X, 79, 90, 748, 90A
Highfield Rd.	14A, 15A, 15B
High St.	123
Holles St.	5, 7/A, 45, 46
Hollybank Rd.	3, 11, 11A,13A, 16/A, 41, 41C,746
Home Farm Rd.	3, 11, 11A, 13A, 16/A, 41, 41C, 746
Howth	31, 31B, 31N
Howth Rd.	29A/N, 31, 31A, 32/A/B, 42A, 105
Howth Summitt	31B/N
Hume St. (Off Stephen's Green)	14, 14A, 15/A/B/C, 44/B/C,48A
Huntstown	39/N/X, 76A, 220
Iona Rd.	13, 13A, 19, 19A, 134
Inchicore	51, 51B/N, 68, 69
Inchicore Rd.	68, 69, 79
Irishtown	1, 2, 3
Islandbridge	25, 25A, 26, 51, 66/A/B 68, 69
James' St.	51B/N, 78A, 123, 206
Jamestown Rd (Finglas)	19/A, 40B, 104, 134, 220
Jamestown Rd. (Inchicore)	51, 51B, 68, 69
Jobstown	50, 65, 65B, 77/B/X, 201
Jones Rd.	51A
Kenilworth Pk.	16, 16A, 18, 49/A, 83
Kennelsfort Rd.	26
Kilbarrack	17A, 29A, 31/A, 32/A/B
Kilbarrack Shopping Centre	29A
Kilbarron	27B, 103, 104
Kilcock	66
Kilcoole	84/X
Kilcross	44, 114, 115, 117
Kilcroney	44, 185
Kildare Rd.	121
Kildonan Rd.	17A, 40/A
Kill Avenue	46A/D
Killester	29A/N, 31/A/B, 32/A/B, 42A, 103, 105
Killester Ave.	27, 27B
Killinardan	50/X, 65, 65B, 77, 201
Killincarrick	84/X, 184
Killiney	59
Killiney Camp Site	45A
Killiney Shop. Centre	7, 45A, 46, 58, 86, 111
Kill O'The Grange	46A, 46N
Kilmacud	5,11/A, 44N, 46B,75, 86
Kilmainham	51B, 78A, 206
Kilmainham Jail	68, 69, 79
Kilmore	27B/N, 103
Kilnamanagh	49N, 50
Kilternan	44, 63, 118
Kimmage Rd. Lr.	54A/N,19A
Kimmage Rd. West.	15A, 17, 19A, 54N
Kingswood Heights	56A, 76, 76A, 76B
Kinsealy	42/N, 43
Kinvara Pk.	37, 38, 39, 70
Kinsealy Court	43
Knockmore	65B, 77, 201
Kylemore Rd.	18, 51/X, 68, 69/X, 79, 206
Lady's Well	38, 220, 238
Lakelands Pk.	15, 15B, 49, 65, 65B
Lamb The	65
Lambert Estate	14A
Lamb's Cross	44, 44B, 44C, 115, 117
Landscape Rd.	14
Lansdowne Rd.	5, 7, 7A, 46
Larkhill	3, 16/A, 41/B/C
Larkfield Gdns.	18, 19A, 54A, 83
Laurel Lodge	37, 237, 239
Leeson St.	11/A, 13B, 32X, 33X, 39X, 41X, 46A/B/X, 58/X, 70X, 84X, 118, 127, 129, 746
Leixlip	66, 66A, 66B, 66X
Leonard's Corner	16/A, 19/A, 49X
Leopardstown Road	46/A/X, 63, 75, 84/X, 86, 118
Liam Mellowes Road	17A, 40/A
Liffey Valley S.C.	78A, 210, 239
Limekiln Ave.	15A, 54A, 150
Lissenhall Bridge	33, 33A, 33B, 33X
Little Pace	70/N/X, 270
Londonbridge Rd.	3
Long Mile Rd.	18, 56A, 210
Lord Edward St.	46X, 50/X, 54A, 56A, 77X, 150
Loughlinstown	7X, 45, 84/X, 111
Loughshinney	33, 33A
Lucan	25/A/X, 66/A/B/X, 67/A/X, 239
Lusk	33/N/X, 33A
Macken St.	1, 2, 3
Macroom Rd.	27
Malahide	32A/X, 42/N, 102, 230
Malahide Rd.	20B, 27/N, 42/B/N, 43, 103, 127, 129
Manor St.	37, 39/X, 70/X, 172
Marian Pk (Baldoyle)	32B
Marian Pk. (Templeogue)	15B
Marine Road	45A, 46A/X, 59, 75, 111
Marino	27N, 123
Mather Rd. Nth.	11A
Maynooth	66/X, 67A/N/X
Meadow Grove (Churchtown)	14, 14A
Mellowes Rd.	17A, 40/A, 104
Merchant's Quay	25, 26, 51B, 69, 79, 90
Merrion Rd.	5, 7, 7A, 45
Merrion Row	10, 10A, 11, 13B, 51X
Merrion St. Upr	48A
Merrion Sq.	5, 7, 7A, 27X, 44, 45, 46, 49X, 50X, 77X
Milltown	44, 44B, 48A/N, 86
Milltown Cross	68
Mobhi Rd.	11, 11A, 19A
Monkstown	7A
Monkstown Farm	46A, 46X
Monkstown Road	7, 7A
Morehampton Road	10,10A, 15X, 39X, 46A/B, 46X, 65X,70X, 77X, 84X
Mount Jerome Cemetery	16, 16A, 54A, 19A
Mount Merrion	5, 46, 46A, 46B, 63
Mount Merrion Avenue	5, 17
Mount Prospect Avenue	130
Mountown	46A, 746
Mount St.	5, 7/A, 27X, 45,46
Mulhuddart	38, 220, 238, 270
Murphystown	44, 115, 117, 118
McKee Ave.	134
McKee Rd.	19A
McKelvey Ave.	134
Naas Rd.	18, 51, 51B, 68, 69, 210
Nangor Road	51/B/N/X, 68, 76/A/B
Nassau Street	7X, 25X, 27X, 32X, 46X, 51X, 66X, 67X, 84X
National Stadium	19
Navan Rd.	37, 38, 39, 70, 122
Neilstown	51/N, 76/A/B, 78A, 210
Newcastle (Co. Dublin)	68
Newcastle (Co. Wicklow)	84
Newcomen Bridge	20,27/B, 29A, 31/A/B, 32/A/B, 42/A/B, 43, 53, 130
Newgrove Cross	29A
Newlands Cross	51, 69X, 76, 76A, 76B
Newtown Pk. Ave	45, 46/A/X, 58, 63, 75, 84/X, 114
Nth. Circular Rd.	10, 38, 120
Ninth Lock Road	51/B/N, 76/A/B
Nth. Frederick Street	3, 10, 10A, 11, 13, 13A, 16, 19
North Rd.(Finglas)	40A, 134
Northside S.C	17A, 27, 27B, 42A
North Strand Rd.	20B, 27/B, 29A, 31/A/B, 32/A/B, 42/A/B, 53, 130
North Wall	53A
Nutgrove S.C	16A, 17, 75, 161
Nutgrove Way	16, 48N, 75
Nutley Lane	2, 3, 5, 7, 7A, 27X, 46, 46A, 46B, 58, 63
Old Bawn Rd.	15D/N, 49/A/N/X, 75, 77X
Old Cabra Rd.	39, 70
Oldcourt (Bray)	45, 145, 146
Omni Park Shop. Cent.	16A, 103, 104
Orwell Pk. Estate	54A, 150
Orwell Rd.	14, 14A
Oscar Traynor Road	17A, 27B, 104
Oxmantown Road	10, 10A, 172
Palmerston Pk.	13B
Palmerston Rd.	13B
Palmerstown	18, 25, 25A, 26, 66, 67, 76A
Parkgate St.	25, 26, 51,66,67, 68, 69
Patrick St.	49/X, 50/X, 54A, 56A, 77X, 150
Peamount	68
Peck's Lane	37
Pelican Hse. (Mespil Rd)	10, 10A, 11/A/B
Pembroke Pk.	10, 10A, 46A
Pembroke Rd.	5, 7, 7A, 10, 18
Pembroke St.	10, 10A, 11/A,13B, 46A/B, 58, 127, 129, 746
Phibsboro	10, 19/A, 38/A, 39N, 120, 121, 122, 134
Philipsburgh Ave.	27N, 123
Phoenix Pk. (N.C.Rd.)	10, 10A
Phoenix Pk. (Parkgate St.)	25, 25A, 26, 66/A, 67/A, 68, 69
Pigeon Hse. Rd.	1
Plunkett Rd.	40/A
Poppintree (Ballymun)	13, 13A, 40N,104, 220
Portmarnock	32/A/X, 42N,102,105, 230
Portrane	33B
Powerscourt	44, 185
Priorswood	7, 42A
Quarry Rd.	120, 121
Quarryvale	78A, 239
Raheen (Tallaght)	56A, 65, 76, 77
Raheny	29A/N, 31/A/B/N, 32/A/B, 105, 129
Ranelagh	11, 11A, 13B, 18, 44/N, 48A/N, 86

PLACE NAME	SERVED BY BUS NO.
Rathbeale	41B
Rathcoole	69, 69X
Rathfarnham	15A/B/C/N, 16/A/C, 17, 48N
Rathfarnham Shopping Centre	15B, 16, 75
Rathgar	15A/B/C/N, 49N
Rathmines	14/A, 15A/B/C/N, 18, 49N, 65C/X, 83
Rathmines Rd. Upr.	14, 14A
Ratoath Rd.	40C, 120
R.D.S. (Ballsbridge)	7, 7A, 18, 45
Rialto	17, 19
Richmond Rd.	3, 11, 11A, 13A, 16/A, 746
Ringsend	1, 2, 3
Riverside (Coolock)	27
River Valley (Swords)	33N, 41C/N, 230
Robinhood	51, 51B, 68, 69, 210
Rochestown Ave.	7, 45A,46, 58/C/X, 86, 111
Rockbrook	161
Roebuck Rd.	11, 11A, 17
Rolestown	41B
Rowlagh	51, 76/A/B,78A, 210, 239
Rush	33, 33A, 33N, 33X
St. Anne's Est.	29A
St. Assam's Ave.	31/A/B, 32/A/B
St. Maelruan's Pk.	49/A/B, 75
St. Margaret's Rd.	134
St. Pappin's Rd.	11
St. Patrick's College (Drumcondra)	3, 11/A, 13A, 16/A, 41/A/B/C, 46X, 58X, 77X
St. Peter's Rd. (Walkinstown)	19
St. Stephen's Green	10, 10A, 11, 13B, 15/A/B/C, 20B, 25X, 32X, 33X, 39X, 46N, 46X, 58X, 66X, 67X, 70X, 84X

PLACE NAME	SERVED BY BUS NO.
Saggart	69/X
Sallynoggin	7, 7A/N, 45A, 58C, 111
Sandford Rd.	11, 11A, 44, 84A
Sandycove	59, 59A
Sandyford	44, 44B/C/N
Sandyford Ind. Est.	5, 11, 75, 114, 115, 116
Sandymount Ave.	5, 7, 7A, 18
Sandymount Gn.	2, 3, 18
Sandymount Tower	2, 3, 18 (Sun.)
Santry	16/A, 33, 41/C, 41B, 746
Santry Ave.	17A, 41/A, 103, 104
Sarsfield Rd.	51N, 78A, 79, 206
Scalp, The	44
Scholarstown Road	15/E/N
Seabury	32X, 42N, 102, 105, 230
Seamount	42
Seskin View Rd.	76B, 77A/X
Shankill	7N, 45, 45A, 46, 58X,84
Shanard Rd.	16
Shanboley Rd.	16/A, 103, 104
Shangan	13A
Shanganagh Cliffs Est.	45A
Shanowen Rd.	16
Sheepmoor	39, 76A, 220
Shop River (Enniskerry)	185
Sillogue	13/A
Skerries	33/N/X
Spawell	54A, 54N, 65/B
Spiddal Pk.	79
Springfield Est. (Tallaght)	50/X, 65, 76, 77/X, 201
Stannaway Rd.	18, 83
Stepaside	44, 118
Stillorgan	11/A, 46/A/C/E/N/X, 63, 75, 84/X, 86, 115, 116, 118, 746

PLACE NAME	SERVED BY BUS NO.
Stillorgan Shopping Centre	11/A, 46/A/C/E, 63, 75, 84/X, 86, 115, 116, 118, 746
Stoneybatter	37, 39, 70/N/X, 172
Stradbrook	45
Strand Rd. (Sutton)	31A, 31B
Strand Rd. (Sandymount)	2, 3
Sth. Circular Rd.	16, 16A, 19/A, 122
Sth. Richmond Street	14, 15/A/B/C, 83
Suir Rd.	123
Sundrive Road	17, 18, 50, 54A, 56A, 83, 150
Sutton Cross	31, 31A, 31B, 31N
Swords	33A, 33/B/N/X, 41/A/B/C, 230
Swords Manor	33N, 41/A/N/X
Swords Rd. (Whitehall)	3, 16/A, 33, 41A/B/C, 104, 103 746
Swords Rd. (Drumcondra)	3, 16/A, 33, 41/A/B/C, 746
Sycamore Rd.	19A, 104, 220
Sylvan Drive	56A
Tallaght	49/A/N, 50/X/N, 54N, 56A, 65/X, 75, 76/B, 77/A/N/X, 201, 202
Templeogue	15B/D/X, 49/N/X, 65/X
Templeville Rd.	54A
Terenure	15A/B/D/E/F/N, 16, 16A, 17, 49/A
The Rise (Mt. Merrion)	46A, 46B, 746
Thomas St.	51B/N, 78A, 123, 206
Tinode	65
Tolka Est.	19
Tonlegee Rd.	17A, 29A
Trees Road	5, 46/A/X, 58X, 63, 84/X
Tritonville Rd.	2, 3
Tymon North	77A

PLACE NAME	SERVED BY BUS NO.
U.C.D.	2, 3, 10, 10A, 11/B, 15X, 17, 25X, 27X, 32X, 33X, 39X, 41X, 46/A/B/N/X, 49X, 50X, 58X, 66X, 70X, 84X
Valleymount	65 (Ballyknockan)
Vernon Ave.	103, 104, 130
Villa Pk.	37, 38, 39, 70, 122
Wadelai Est.	11
Walkinstown Ave.	18, 56A
Walkinstown Cross	50, 56A, 77, 77A,155
Waterloo Rd.	10, 10A, 18, 15X, 25X, 49X, 50X, 51X, 65X, 66X, 67X, 77X
Wellmount Road	40/A/B
Wendell Avenue	32X, 42N
Willington	54A, 150
Werburg St.	50/X, 56A, 150
Westland Row Stn. (Pearse Stn.)	1, 2, 3, 48A
Weston Ave.	14A
West Rd.	53
Wexford St.	16, 16A, 19, 19A, 83, 122
Whitechurch	15C, 116, 161
Whitehall (Drumcondra)	3, 16/A, 33, 41/B/C, 746
Whitehall Rd. (Terenure)	15A, 54N
Whitestown	39
Whitworth Rd.	13, 40/A/B/C
Willbrook	15C/N
Willow Grove	184
Windgates	184
Woodford	51B, 51N, 210
Woodbrook	45, 45A, 58X, 84
Woodlawn (Firhouse)	49, 75
Wyattville Rd.	7, 46, 58X, 46X, 111
Yellow Walls Rd.	32X, 42, 102, 105, 230
Zion Rd.	15C

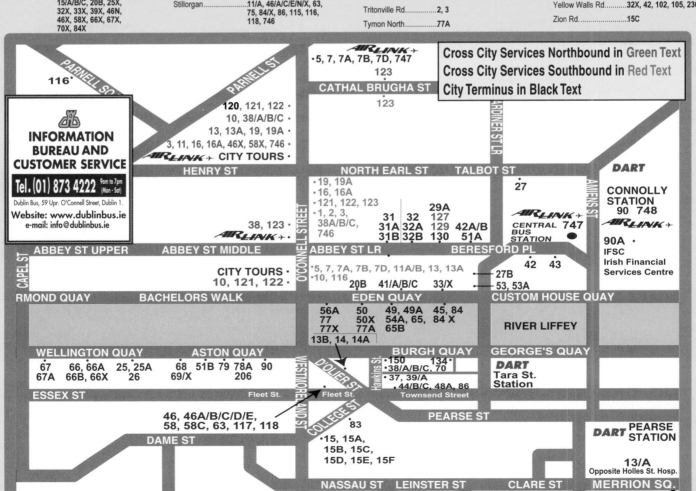

Name	Phone Number	Page	Grid Ref.
Beaumont Hospital	809 3000	**26**	D1
Blackrock Clinic	283 2222	**48**	F3
Bloomfield Hospital (Donnybrook)	668 3815	**47**	B1
Bon Secours Private (St. Joseph's Glasnevin)	837 5111	**25**	A3
Cappagh National Orthopaedic (Finglas)	834 1211	**23**	C1
Central Mental Hospital (Dundrum)	298 9266	**47**	C3
Cheeverstown (Templeogue)	499 3700	**46**	D4
Cheery Orchard (Ballyfermot)	620 6000	**35**	C3
Children's University Hospital (Temple Street)	878 4200	**38**	D1
City of Dublin Skin and Cancer (Hume Street)	676 6935	**38**	E3
Clonskeagh (Vergemount)	268 0500	**47**	C2
Coombe Women's Hospital (Dolphin's Barn)	408 5200	**37**	C4
Dublin Dental School & Hospital (Lincoln Place)	612 7200	**38**	E3
Gascoigne Home (Camden Row)	496 9399	**38**	D4
Highfield Private Hospital (Whitehall)	837 4444	**25**	B3
James Connolly Memorial Hospital (Blanchardstown)	821 3844	**22**	F1
Leopardstown Park (Foxrock)	295 5055	**58**	E3
Mater Misericordiae University Hospital Ltd (Eccles Street)	803 2000	**38**	D1
Mount Carmel (Braemor Park)	492 2211	**47**	A3
National Maternity (Holles Street)	637 3100	**38**	E3
National Rehabilitation Hospital (Dun Laoighaire)	285 4777	**59**	C2
Orthopaedic Hospital of Ireland (Clontarf)	833 2521	**26**	E4
Our Lady's Hospital for Sick Children (Crumlin)	409 6100	**46**	D1
Our Lady's Hospice (Harold's Cross)	406 8700	**37**	C4
Rotunda (Maternity), (Parnell Street)	873 0700	**38**	D1
Royal City of Dublin (Baggot Street)	668 1577	**38**	F4
Royal Hospital (Donnybrook)	497 2844	**47**	B1
Royal Victoria Eye and Ear (Adelaide Road)	664 4600	**38**	E4
St. Bricin's Military (Infirmary Road)	804 6990	**37**	B2
St. Brigid's Home (Crooksling)	458 2123	**53**	A4
St. Clare's Home (Griffith Avenue)	837 3619	**25**	A2
St. Edmundsbury Hospital (Lucan)	628 0221	**34**	E1
St. James Hospital (James's Street)	410 3000	**37**	B3
St. John of God (Stillorgan)	288 1781	**58**	F1
St. Joseph's (Clonsilla)	821 7177	**21**	B2
St. Joseph's (Raheny)	847 8433	**27**	A2
St. Luke's (Oakland, Highfield Road)	406 5000	**47**	A2
St. Mary's Orthopaedic (Baldoyle)	832 3056	**15**	A4
St. Mary's Hospital (Phoenix Park)	677 8132	**36**	E2
St. Michael's Public Hospital (Dun Laoighaire)	280 6901	**50**	D4
St. Patrick's (James Street)	249 3200	**37**	B3
St. Paul's (Beaumont)	837 7673	**25**	C1
St. Vincent's University Hospital (Elm Park, Merrion Road)	277 4000	**48**	E1
St. Vincent's (Richmond Road)	884 2400	**25**	B4
Simpson's Hospital (Dundrum)	298 4322	**57**	B2
Stewart's Hospital (Palmerston)	626 4444	**35**	C1
Tallaght Hospital	414 2000	**54**	F1
Verville Retreat (Vernon Avenue)	833 2598	**26**	E4

Name	Page	Grid Ref.	No.
Advance Business Park	12	F3	179
Airport Business Park	13	A1	213
Airport Business Campus	12	E4	1
Airside Business Park Swords	2	D3	266
Airside Retail Park	1	C3	295
Airton Business Park	45	A4	2
Airton Business Park	45	A4	3
Airton Business Park	45	A4	4
Airways Ind Est	12	F4	5
Allied Ind Est	36	E4	6
Alltech Technology Park	6	E2	294
Ardee Court	67	B2	7
Ashgrove Ind Est Dun Laoghaire	59	C1	8
Aughrim Lane Ind Est	37	C1	268
Avonbeg Ind Est	45	B2	9
Avondale	49	A4	167
Baldonnel Business Park	43	A4	241
Baldoyle Ind Est	27	C1	10
Balfe Road Ind Est	45	C1	196
Balheary Ind Park	2	D1	1
Ballyboggan Ind Est	24	D3	12
Ballycoolin Business Park	10	D4	13
Ballymount Business Centre	45	B2	14
Ballymount Cross Ind Est	45	A2	15
Ballymount Ind Est	45	B2	16
Ballymount Road Ind Est	45	B2	17
Ballymount Trading Centre	45	B2	18
Ballymun Ind Est	12	D4	19
Barbeque Poultry Business Pk	64	E3	300
Base Park Ind Est	9	A3	301
Beech Hill Office Campus Clonskeagh	47	C2	228
Beechlawn Ind Complex	45	B2	20
Beechwood Close Ind Est	67	C4	21
Belfield Office Park	47	C2	229
Belgard Ind Est	44	F4	22
Benson St. Enterprise Centre	38	F2	24
Blackhorse Ind Est	37	B1	25
Blackrock Business Park	49	A3	169
Blanchardstown Corporate Park	9	C3	165
Blanchardstown Corporate Park No. 2	9	C3	210
Blanchardstown Ind Park (off Snugborough)	9	C4	26
Bluebell Business Centre	36	E4	273
Bluebell Business Park	36	E4	27
Bluebell Ind Est	36	D4	28
Bracetown Business Park	7	C1	29
Bray Business Park Kilruddery	67	C4	255
Bray Ind Est	67	C4	30
Bridges Ind Est	45	A1	32
Bridgewater Business Centre	37	A1	31
Brookfield Enterprise Centre	54	D1	247
Broombridge Ind Est	24	E3	33
Broomfield Business Park Malahide	3	B3	271
Broomhill Business Pk Close	45	A4	35
Broomhill Business Pk Drive	45	A4	36
Broomhill Business Pk Road	45	A4	37
Broomhill Business Pk Tce	45	A4	38
Burton Hall Campus	58	E2	39
Butterly Business Park	26	D2	66
Calmount Business Park	45	B2	197
Carrigalea Ind Est	45	B1	40
Cashel Business Centre	46	E2	293
Castleforbes Business Park	38	F2	41
Cedar Ind Park Bray	67	B4	258
Celbridge Ind Est	29	C3	238
Central Park Business Park	58	E2	253
Century Business Park	11	B4	206
Chapelizod Ind Est	36	E2	90
Cherry Orchard Ind Est	35	C2	42
Cherrywood Business Park	64	D1	251
Churchtown Business Park	47	B4	225
Cian Park Ind Est	25	B4	43
City Junction Business Park	13	C4	212
City Link Business Park	36	E4	215
City West Business Campus	53	B1	44
Clondalkin Business Centre	35	B4	46
Clondalkin Commercial Park	35	B4	45
Clondalkin Enterprise Centre	35	A3	177
Clonshaugh Ind Est	13	A4	47
Clonskeagh House Office Pk	47	C2	226
Clonskeagh Square Office Pk	47	C2	227
Cloverhill Ind Est	35	B4	48
College Business and Technology Park	9	C4	200
Collinstown Ind Est	12	F3	50
Collinstown Ind Park (Intel)	19	B3	92
Collinstown Cross Ind Est Cloghran	12	F2	49
Concord Ind Est Naas Road	36	E4	272
Cookstown Business Centre	44	F4	245
Cookstown Enterprise Park	44	F4	51
Cookstown Ind Est	44	F4	52
Cookstown Ind Est The Extension	44	E4	243
Cookstown Square	44	F4	244
Coolmine Industrial Est	22	D2	53
Courtyard Business Park, The Nangor Rd	43	B2	269
Crag Avenue Ind Centre	35	B4	219
Cranford Centre Stillorgan	48	D2	274
Croke Park Ind Est	38	E1	55
Crosbie Business Centre	38	F1	262
Crossbeg Ind Est	45	A2	56
Crosslands Ind Park	45	A2	57
Cruiserath Business Park	9	C3	199
Crumlin Business Park Stanaway Drive	46	E1	292
Damastown Business Centre	9	A3	302
Damastown Ind Est	8	F3	58
Damastown Ind Park	8	F4	166
Dartmouth House Ind Centre	36	E3	217
Deansgrange Business Park	59	B2	59
Donnelly Centre, The Cork Street	37	C3	275
Dublin Ind Est /Glasnevin/Broombridge	24	E3	61
Dun Laoghaire Ind Est	59	B2	63
Dunboyne Business Park	7	B2	62
Dundrum Business Park	47	C3	231
Earls Court Business Park	47	B4	224
Earlsfort Centre	38	E3	276
East Point Business Park	39	A1	263
East Road Ind Est	38	F1	64
Elmfield Ind Est Ninth Lock Rd	44	E1	65
Feltrim Ind Park Swords	2	E3	67
Finches Industrial Park	45	B1	68
Finglas Business Park	24	E3	23
Fonthill Retail Park Clondalkin	35	A2	176
Frank Fahey Centre Naas Road	45	B1	277
Furry Park Ind Est Santry	12	E3	181
Gaywood Ind Est Mulhuddart	9	B3	70
Glasnevin Business Centre	24	D3	220
Glasnevin Business Park	32	D3	221
Glen Abbey Complex	44	F4	71
Glen Ind Est	24	E3	73
Glenageary Office Park	60	D2	291
Glenview Ind Est	37	B4	74
Glenville Ind Est Mount Merrion	48	E3	75
Goldenbridge Ind Est	36	F4	76
Grange Castle International Business Park	43	B1	239
Green Isle Business Park	44	D3	242
Greenhills Business Centre Greenhills Rd	45	B4	193
Greenhills Business Park	45	B4	192
Greenhills Centre	45	B4	191
Greenhills Ind Est	45	C1	77
Greenmount Ind Est	37	C4	78
Greenogue Ind Est	42	E4	235
Grove Ind Est Dubber Cross	11	B3	79
Grove Ind Est Finglas	24	E1	80
Harbour Ind Est	67	C1	81
Harcourt Centre, The	38	D4	278
Henley Ind Park	36	D4	216
Hewlett Packard Ind Park	32	F2	234
Hibernian Insurance Ind Est	45	A4	82
Hills Ind Est	34	D1	83
Hollywood Business Park	9	C3	303
Horizon Logistics	11	B2	204
Howth Junction Business Pk	27	B1	270
I.D.A. Enterprise Centre (Pearse Street Enterprise Centre)	38	F3	85
I.D.A. Ind Centre	37	C1	86
I.D.A. Small Ind Centre	13	A4	88
I.D.A. Small Ind Centre	38	F1	87
I.D.A. Tallaght Business Park	54	F2	89
Industrial Yarns Complex	67	C1	91
International Financial Services Centre (IFSC)	38	E2	279
Irish Life Centre	38	E2	280
J.F.K. Ave	45	A1	96
J.F.K. Park	36	D3	98
J.F.K. Road	36	D3	99
Jamestown Business Park	11	B4	208
Jamestown Little Ind Est	11	A4	298
Jamestown Ind Centre	36	E4	95
KCR Ind Est	46	E2	100
Kilbarrack Ind Est	27	B1	101

Name	Page	Grid Ref.	No.
Kilcarberry Ind Park Clondalkin	43	A1	283
Killarney Road Business Pk	67	B3	257
Killinardin Enterprise Park	54	F2	246
Kinsealy Business Park	14	D1	281
Knockmitten Business Park	44	F1	282
Kylemore Ind Est	36	D4	102
Kylemore Park North	36	D3	103
Kylemore Park South	36	E4	104
Kylemore Park West	36	D4	105
Landys Ind Est	56	D1	106
Lansdown Valley	45	C1	107
Leopardstown Office Park	58	E2	261
Leopardstown Retail Park	58	E2	108
Liberties Craft & Small Industries Centre	37	C3	109
Liffey Trust Enterprise Centre, The	38	F2	150
Lilmar Ind Est	12	F4	110
Loughlinstown Ind Est	64	D1	111
Maltings Business Park, The Marrowbone Lane	37	C3	259
Maynooth Business Campus	17	A4	211
Merrywell Business Park	45	A2	182
Merrywell Ind Est	45	A2	188
Metropolitan Ind Est	37	A3	113
Mill Lane Business Park Leixlip	33	B1	232
Millennium Business Park	10	E3	202
Monarch Ind Est	44	F4	114
Montone Business Park Oak Road	44	F1	248
Mount Pleasant Ind Est	47	A1	284
Mulcahy Keane Est	45	C2	115
Mygan Business Park	11	B4	207
Naas Road Business Park	36	E4	132
Naas Road Ind Park	36	E4	170
Nangor Road Business Centre	35	C4	174
Newcastle Business Centre	42	E1	297
Newcourt Business Park	11	A2	205
Newlands Business Centre	44	E2	116
Newtown Ind Est	13	C4	117
North Park & Northern Cross Business Park	11	A4	209
North Richmond Ind Est	38	E1	118
North Ring Business Park Santry	12	F3	180
North West Business Park	10	D3	201
Northern Cross Business Park	11	A4	209
Nutgrove Enterprise Park	57	A1	252
Nutgrove Office Park	47	A4	223
Oak Road Business Park	44	F1	250
Oakfield Ind Est	44	E1	119
Old Court Ind Est	67	B4	120
Old Sawmills Ind Est	45	B2	121
Ossory Ind Est	38	F1	122
Palmgrove Ind Est	25	B2	265
Park West Enterprise Centre	35	C4	172
Park West Ind Park	36	D4	171
Parkmore Ind Est	45	B1	123
Parkway Business Centre	45	A1	183
Pearse Street Enterprise Centre	38	F3	85
Phoenix Ind Est	23	B3	124
Pineview Ind Est Firhouse Road	55	C1	125
Pinewood Close Ind Est	67	C4	126
Plato Business Park	9	A3	198
Poppintree Ind Est	11	C4	127
Red Cow Business Park	45	A1	184
Richmond Road Ind Est	25	B4	129
Richview Office Park	47	C2	230
Riversdale Ind Est	36	E4	130
Riverview Business Centre Clondalkin	35	C4	175
Robinhood Ind Est	45	B1	131
Rock Enterprise Centre	43	B3	240
Rosemount Business Park	10	D4	133
Royal Liver Retail Park	36	E4	214
S.P.A.D.E. Unemployment Enterprise Centre	37	C3	287
Sandyford Business Centre	58	E2	137
Sandyford Ind Est	58	E2	135
Sandyford Office Park	58	E2	136
Sandyford Park	58	E2	163
Santry Avenue Ind Est	12	E4	138
Santry Hall Ind Est	25	B1	139
Shankhill Business Centre	64	E2	141
Shanowen Ind Est Santry	25	B1	142
Sitecast Ind Est	45	B4	194
Solus Tower Estate	67	C1	254
South City Business Park	54	F2	299
South City Executive Park	46	E1	288
South County Business Park	58	F2	143
Southern Cross Business Park	67	B4	256
Square Ind Complex, The	54	F1	289
St Joans Ind Est	45	A2	134
St John's Court Office Park	25	B1	264
St Margaret's Business Park	11	A4	286
Stables Office Park, The	15	A1	304
Stadium Ind Est	10	E4	203
Stillorgan Ind Park	58	D2	144
Sunbury Ind Est	45	B2	145
Sunshine Ind Est	37	A4	146
Swanward Business Centre	45	A2	185
Swiftbrook Ind Est	53	A2	147
Swords Business Campus	2	D1	267
Swords Business Park	2	E2	148
Tallaght Enterprise Centre	55	A1	149
Taurus Business Park Greenhills Road	45	B4	195
Terenure Business Park	46	F2	290
Terenure Enterprise Centre	46	F2	296
Tolka Ind Park	24	D3	34
Tolka Valley Business Park	24	D3	222
Turnpike Ind Est see Ballymount Cross	45	A2	151
Unidare/Jamestown Business Pk	24	E1	152
Weatherwell Ind Est	35	B4	153
West Pier Business Campus Dun Laoghaire	49	C4	168
Western Business Park	44	F1	249
Western Ind Est	45	A1	156
Western Office Park	22	E2	236
Western Parkway Business Centre Ballymount Rd	45	B2	157
Western Parkway Business Park	45	B2	190
Western Retail Park	22	E2	237
Westgate Business Park	45	A3	186
Westland Sq Business Park	38	E2	260
Westlink Ind Est	36	E3	154
Westpoint Business Park	8	F4	164
Westway Centre	45	B2	189
White Heather Ind Est	37	B4	158
White Swan Business Park	37	C4	159
Whitestown Ind Est	54	F1	160
Willow Business Park Knockmitten Lane	45	A1	187
Woodford Business Park Santry	12	F3	178
Woodlawn Ind Est	12	F3	162

Due to the limitations imposed by scale it has not been possible to include all street names on the maps. Unnamed streets have been given small numbers which appear after their grid reference in this index. A list of such streets, by grid reference, is given on page 130.
Streets not named or indicated by number on map pages are prefixed by * and are given their approximate location and grid reference.

STREET NAME	PAGE/GRID REFERENCE		STREET NAME	PAGE/GRID REFERENCE		STREET NAME	PAGE/GRID REFERENCE		STREET NAME	PAGE/GRID REFERENCE	
A			*Adam Court (off Grafton Street)	38	D3	Alden Road	27	C1	Annaly Road	24	F4
			Adamstown Road	34	D2	Alder Court	4	D4 [1]	Annamoe Drive	37	C1
1 Branch Road North	39	A2	Adare Avenue	26	E1	Alderpark Court	54	F1	Annamoe Parade	37	C1 [2]
1 Branch Road South	39	A2	Adare Drive	26	E1	Alderwood Avenue	54	E1	Annamoe Park	37	C1
150 Howth Road	26	E3	Adare Green	26	E1	Alderwood Close	54	E1	Annamoe Road	37	B1
2 Branch Road North	39	B2	Adare Park	26	E1	Alderwood Court	54	E1	Annamoe Terrace	37	C1
2 Branch Road North Extension	39	B1	Adare Road	26	E1	Alderwood Drive	54	F1	Annaville Avenue	59	A1
2 Branch Road South	39	A2	Addison Drive	24	F3	Alderwood Green	54	E1	Annaville Close	47	C4
3 Branch Road South	39	A2	Addison Lane	24	F3	Alderwood Grove	54	F1	Annaville Grove	47	C3 [1]
4 Branch Road South	39	B2	Addison Place	25	A3 [9]	Alderwood Lawn	54	E1	Annaville Lodge	47	C3
Abberley	64	E1	Addison Road	25	C4	Alderwood Park	54	F1	Annaville Park	47	C3
Abbey Cottages	38	D2 [43]	Adelaide Court	38	D4 [57]	Alderwood Rise	54	E1	Annaville Terrace	47	C4
Abbey Court	26	E3	Adelaide Court	38	D4	Alderwood Way	54	F1	Anne Street North	38	D2 [5]
Abbey Court	31	C4	Adelaide Mews	48	E1	Aldrin Walk	26	E1	Anne Street South	38	D3
Abbey Court (Monkstown)	59	B1 [7]	Adelaide Road	67	C2	Alexander Terrace	67	C2 [43]	Anner Road	37	A3
Abbey Drive	24	D3	Adelaide Road (Dun Laoghaire)	60	E1	Alexander Terrace (North Wall)	38	F2 [11]	Anne's Lane	38	D3 [33]
Abbey Green	31	C4	Adelaide Road (Leeson Street)	38	D4	Alexandra Quay	39	A2 [2]	Annesley Avenue	38	F1 [1]
Abbey Lane	31	C4	Adelaide Street	50	D4	Alexandra Quay	39	A2	Annesley Bridge Road	38	F1
Abbey Park	31	C4	Adelaide Terrace (Dun Laoghaire)	60	E1 [28]	Alexandra Road	39	A2	Annesley Park	47	B1
Abbey Park (Baldoyle)	27	C1	*Adelaide Terrace (off Brookfield Road)	37	B3	Alexandra Road Extension	39	C2	Annesley Place	38	F1
Abbey Park (Kill o' the Grange)	59	B1	Adelaide Villas	60	E1 [27]	Alexandra Terrace (Dundrum)	47	C4	Annfield	22	D3
Abbey Park (Killester)	26	E3	Adelaide Villas	67	C2	Alexandra Terrace (Portobello)	38	D4 [45]	Annfield Court	22	D3
Abbey Road	59	B1 [8]	Admiral Court	15	A4 [9]	Alexandra Terrace (Terenure)	46	F2	Annfield Crescent	22	D3
Abbey Road	59	B1	Admiral Park	15	A4	Alexandra Villas	47	C4 [3]	Annfield Drive	22	D3
Abbey Street (Howth)	30	D1	Adrian Avenue	46	F1	Alfie Byrne Road	38	F1	Annfield Lawn	22	D3
Abbey Street Lower	38	E2	Affollus	5	C3	All Hallows Garden	25	B3	Annsbrook	47	C2
Abbey Street Middle	38	D2	Aideen Avenue	46	E2	All Hallows Square	25	B3 [7]	Annville Drive	58	E1
Abbey Street Old	38	E2 [19]	Aideen Drive	46	E2	All Saints Drive	27	A3	Apollo Way	26	D1
Abbey Street Upper	38	D2	Aideen Place	46	E2	All Saints Park	27	A3	*Appian Close (on Leeson Park)	38	E4
Abbey Terrace	30	D1 [11]	Aikenhead Terrace	39	A3	All Saints Road	26	F3	Apples Road	58	D2
Abbey View	59	B1	Aiken's Village	58	D3	Allen Park Drive	58	E1	Aran Avenue	64	E1
Abbeydale	34	F3	Ailesbury	25	B1 [1]	Allen Park Road	58	E1	Aran Close	64	E1
Abbeydale Close	34	F3	Ailesbury Drive	48	D1	*Allen Terrace (off Avondale Avenue)	37	C1	Aran Drive	64	E1
Abbeydale Crescent	34	F3	Ailesbury Gardens	48	E1	Allendale Square	21	B2	Aranleigh Court	56	F1
Abbeydale Gardens	34	F3	Ailesbury Grove (Donnybrook)	48	D1	Allenton Avenue	55	A3	Aranleigh Dell	57	A1
Abbeydale Park	34	F3	Ailesbury Grove (Dundrum)	57	B1	Allenton Crescent	55	A2 [3]	Aranleigh Gardens	56	F1
Abbeydale Rise	34	F3	*Ailesbury Lane (off Ailesbury Road)	48	D1	Allenton Drive	55	A3	Aranleigh Mount	56	F1
Abbeydale Walk	34	F3	Ailesbury Lawn	57	B1	Allenton Gardens	55	A3	Aranleigh Park	57	A1
Abbeyfarm	31	C4	Ailesbury Mews	48	E1	Allenton Green	55	A3	Aranleigh Vale	56	F1
Abbeyfield	26	E3	Ailesbury Park	48	E1	Allenton Lawns	55	A2	Aravon Court	68	D2
Abbeyfield	47	B2	Ailesbury Road	48	D1	Allenton Park	55	A2	Arbour Hill	37	C2
Abbeylea Avenue	1	C1	Ailesbury Wood	48	D1	Allenton Road	55	A1 [1]	Arbour Place	37	C2
Abbeylea Close	1	C1	Airfield Court	48	D2	Allenton Way	55	A3	Arbour Terrace	37	B2 [6]
Abbeylea Drive	1	C1	Airfield Drive	47	B4 [13]	Allies River Road	67	A1	Arbutus Avenue	37	C4 [8]
Abbeylea Green	1	C1	Airfield Park	48	D2	Allingham Street	37	C3 [15]	Arbutus Grove	67	B1 [4]
Abbeyvale Avenue	1	B1	Airfield Road	46	F2	Alma Park	49	C4 [30]	Arbutus Place	38	D4 [51]
Abbeyvale Close	1	B1	Airlie Heights	33	B2	Alma Place	49	C4 [14]	Ard Lorcain	58	F1
Abbeyvale Court	1	B1	Airton Close	45	A4	Alma Road	49	B4	Ard Lorcain Villas	58	F1 [2]
Abbeyvale Crescent	1	B1	Airton Road	45	A4	Alma Terrace	47	A1 [13]	Ard Mhacha	54	F2
Abbeyvale Drive	1	B2	Airton Terrace (off Greenhills Rd)	45	A4	Almeida Avenue	37	B3 [26]	Ard Mhuire Park	60	E2
Abbeyvale Green	1	B2	Albany Avenue	49	B4	Almeida Terrace	37	B3 [27]	Ard Mor Avenue	53	C1
Abbeyvale Grove	1	B1	Albany Court	64	E1	Alone Walk	26	E2	Ard Mor Close	53	C1
Abbeyvale Lawn	1	B1	Albany Road	47	B1	Alpine Heights	44	D1	Ard Mor Court	53	C1
Abbeyvale Place	1	B1	Albert Avenue	68	D2	Alpine Rise	44	E4	Ard Mor Crescent	53	C1
Abbeyvale Rise	1	B1	Albert College Avenue	25	A2	Altadore	60	D2	Ard Mor Dale	53	C1
Abbeyvale View	1	B2	Albert College Court	25	A2	Alton Terrace	60	F2	Ard Mor Drive	53	C1
Abbeyvale Way	1	B2	Albert College Crescent	25	A2	Alverno	39	B1 [1]	Ard Mor Green	53	C1
Abbeywood	34	F3	Albert College Drive	25	A2	Amber Vale	44	E4	Ard Mor Lawn	53	C1
Abbeywood Avenue	34	E3	Albert College Grove	25	A2	Amberwood	9	A4	Ard Mor Park	53	C1
Abbeywood Close	34	F3	Albert College Lawn	25	A2	Amiens Street	38	E2	Ard Mor Walk	53	C1
Abbeywood Court	34	F3	Albert College Park	25	A2	Anastasia Lane	60	F2 [3]	Ard Na Greine	47	A3 [11]
Abbeywood Crescent	34	F3	Albert Court	38	F3 [30]	Anglers Rest	47	C1	Ard na Mara	3	A3
Abbeywood Park	34	F3	Albert Court	38	F4	Anglesea Avenue	49	A3	Ard na Meala	12	D4
Abbeywood Way	34	F3	Albert Court	60	E1	Anglesea Lane	50	D4 [20]	Ard Ri Road	37	C2
Abbots Hill	3	C3	*Albert Court (off Grand Canal St)	38	F4	Anglesea Park	60	E2	Ard Righ Place	37	C2 [27]
Abbotstown Avenue	23	C2	Albert Park	60	E1 [3]	Anglesea Road	47	C1	Ardagh Avenue	59	A1
Abbotstown Drive	24	D2	Albert Place East	38	F3 [14]	Anglesea Row	38	D2 [7]	Ardagh Close	59	A1 [6]
Abbotstown Road	24	D2	Albert Place West	38	D4 [15]	Anglesea Street	38	D2	Ardagh Court	58	F1
Abercorn Road	38	F2	Albert Road Lower	60	E1	Anley Court	34	E1	Ardagh Crescent	59	A1
Abercorn Square	36	F3 [19]	Albert Road Upper	60	E2	Ann Devlin Avenue	46	E4	Ardagh Drive	59	A1
Abercorn Terrace	36	F3 [10]	Albert Terrace	38	D4 [18]	Ann Devlin Drive	46	E4	Ardagh Grove	59	A1
Aberdeen Street	37	B2	Albert Terrace	50	D4 [27]	Ann Devlin Park	56	E1	Ardagh Park	59	A1
Abington	2	F3	Albert Walk	67	C2	Ann Devlin Road	46	E4	Ardagh Park Road	59	A1
Abington	3	A3	Aldborough Parade	38	E1 [17]	Anna Villa	47	B1	Ardagh Road	37	B4
Accommodation Road	19	C4	Aldborough Place	38	E1	Annabeg	60	D4 [1]	Ardara Avenue	14	D4
Achill Road	25	B3	*Aldborough Square (off Aldborough Place)	38	E1	Annacrivey	65	B3	Ardbeg Crescent	26	E2
Achill Road	64	E1	Aldemere	21	B2	Annadale	47	B4 [16]	Ardbeg Drive	26	E2
Acorn Drive	57	B1	Alden Drive	27	C1	Annadale Avenue	25	C4 [1]	Ardbeg Park	26	E2
Acorn Road	57	B1	Alden Park	27	C1	Annadale Crescent	25	C3	Ardbeg Road	26	E2
Acres Road	36	F2				Annadale Drive	25	C3	Ardbrugh Close	60	F2 [31]
Adair	39	A4 [14]				Annaghaskin	66	D1	Ardbrugh Road	60	F2
*Adair Lane (Dorset Street)	38	D1				Annally Court	21	B1	Ardbrugh Villas	60	F2 [21]
*Adair Terrace (on St Joseph's Parade)	38	D1				Annally Drive	21	B1	Ardcian Park	1	C1
						Annally Terrace	21	B1	Ardcollum Avenue	26	E2
									Ardee Road	38	D4

STREET NAME	PAGE/GRID REFERENCE	STREET NAME	PAGE/GRID REFERENCE	STREET NAME	PAGE/GRID REFERENCE	STREET NAME	PAGE/GRID REFERENCE
Ardee Row	37 C3 [34]	Ashdale Avenue	46 F2	Ashwood Park	44 D1	Avondale Park	67 B3
Ardee Street	37 C3	Ashdale Close	2 E3	Ashwood Road	44 D1	Avondale Park (Dalkey)	60 E2
Ardee Street	67 B2	Ashdale Gardens	46 F2	Ashwood Way	44 D1	Avondale Park (Dun Laoghaire)	49 A4 [1]
Ardeen	33 C2	Ashdale Park	46 F2 [1]	*Ashworth Place	37 C4	Avondale Park (Raheny)	27 A2
Ardeevin Avenue	33 C2	Ashdale Road	46 F2	(off Mount Drumond Avenue)		Avondale Road (Dalkey)	60 D2
Ardeevin Court	33 C2	Ashdale Road (Swords)	2 E3	Aspen Drive	2 E3	Avondale Road (Phibsborough)	37 C1
Ardeevin Drive	33 C2	Ashfield	46 D4	Aspen Park	2 E3	Avondale Square	7 B2 [2]
Ardeevin Road	60 F2	Ashfield Avenue (Clondalkin)	44 F3	Aspen Park	59 C1 [11]	Avondale Terrace	45 C2
*Ardeevin Terrace	60 F2	Ashfield Avenue (Ranelagh)	47 B1	Aspen Road	2 E3	Avonmore	59 A2
(off Ardeevin Road)		Ashfield Close (Clondalkin)	44 F3	Aspen Wood	22 D2	Avonmore Avenue	55 B1 [5]
Ardenza Park	49 B3 [3]	Ashfield Close (Templeogue)	46 D4	Assumpta Park	64 E3	Avonmore Close	55 B1
Ardenza Terrace	49 B3 [1]	Ashfield Court	9 A4	Aston Place	38 D2 [39]	Avonmore Drive	55 B1
Ardglas Estate	57 C1	Ashfield Drive	44 F3	Aston Quay	38 D2	Avonmore Grove	55 B1
Ardilaun	14 F1	Ashfield Gardens	9 A4	Astro Park Sports Club	45 A4	Avonmore Park	55 B1
Ardilaun Road	38 E1 [3]	Ashfield Green	8 F4	Athgoe	51 C1	Avonmore Road	55 B1
*Ardilaun Square	38 E1	Ashfield Grove	9 A4	Athgoe Drive	64 E2 [4]	Aylesbury (Estate)	55 A2
(off Sackville Avenue)		Ashfield Lawn	8 F4	Athgoe North	51 B1	Aylmer Ave	42 D4
Ardilea Downs	48 D4	Ashfield Park (Booterstown)	48 D4	Athgoe Road	41 C4	Aylmer Road	42 D4
Ardilea Wood	48 D4	Ashfield Park (Clondalkin)	44 F3	Athgoe Road	64 E2	Ayrefield Avenue	26 F1
Ardlea Road	26 E2	Ashfield Park (Mulhuddart)	9 A4 [2]	Athgoe South	51 B2	Ayrefield Court	26 F1
Ardlui Park	59 A1	Ashfield Park (Templeogue)	46 D4	Athletic Union League Sports	13 A2	Ayrefield Drive	26 F1
Ardmeen Park	59 A1	Ashfield Park (Terenure)	46 F2	Ground		Ayrefield Grove	26 F1
Ardmore Avenue	37 B1 [4]	Ashfield Road (Ranelagh)	47 B1	Atlumney Villas	38 D4 [12]	Ayrefield Park	26 F1 [2]
Ardmore Close	26 D2	Ashfield Way	8 F4	Atmospheric Road	60 E1 [29]	Ayrefield Place	26 F1
Ardmore Crescent	26 D2	Ashford Cottages	37 B1 [17]	Aubrey Grove	64 E3	Ayrefield Road	26 F1
Ardmore Crescent	67 B2	*Ashford Cottages	37 B1	Aubrey Park	64 E3		
Ardmore Drive	26 D1	(off Ross Street)		Auburn	26 D4	**B**	
Ardmore Grove	26 D1	Ashford Place	37 B1 [16]	Auburn Avenue (Cabinteely)	60 D3		
Ardmore Lawn	67 B3	*Ashford Place (off Ross Street)	37 B1	Auburn Avenue (Castleknock)	23 A3	Bachelor's Walk	38 D2
Ardmore Park	67 B2	Ashford Street	37 B1 [10]	Auburn Avenue (Donnybrook)	47 C1	Bachelors Way	38 D2 [30]
Ardmore Park (Artane)	26 D2	Ashgrove	31 C2	Auburn Close	23 A3	Back Lane (Baldoyle)	15 A4 [3]
Ardmore Park	59 C1	Ashgrove (Kill o' the Grange)	59 C1	Auburn Close	60 D3	Back Lane (High Street)	38 D3
(Kill o' the Grange)		Ashgrove (Tallaght)	54 E1	Auburn Drive (Cabinteely)	60 D3	*Back Lane (off Sandwith St Upr)	38 E3
Ardmore Wood	67 B3	Ashgrove Court	57 C1 [8]	Auburn Drive (Castleknock)	23 A3	Back Road	3 B4
Ardpatrick Road	24 D4	Ashgrove Terrace	57 C1 [2]	Auburn Green	23 A3	Baggot Close	38 E3
Ardtona Avenue	47 B4 [6]	*Ash-Hurst	60 E4	Auburn Grove	3 A3	Baggot Court	38 E3 [9]
Arena Road	58 E2	Ashington Avenue	24 D3	Auburn Road	60 D3	Baggot Lane	38 F4
Argus House	37 C4 [4]	Ashington Close	24 D3	Auburn Road (Cabinteely)	60 D3 [1]	Baggot Road	23 C4
Argyle Road	38 F4	Ashington Court	24 D3	Auburn Road (Donnybrook)	47 C1 [11]	Baggot Street Lower	38 E3
Arkendale Court	60 E1 [26]	Ashington Crescent	23 C3	Auburn Street	38 D1	Baggot Street Upper	38 E4
Arkendale Road	60 E1	Ashington Dale	24 D3	*Auburn Terrace	37 B3	Baggot Terrace	23 C4 [1]
Arkendale Woods	60 E1 [25]	Ashington Gardens	24 D3	(Old Kilmainham)		Baggotrath Place	38 E3 [28]
Arkle Road	58 E2	Ashington Green	24 D3	Auburn Villas	47 A2	Bailey Green Road	30 E3
Arkle Square	58 F2 [6]	Ashington Grove	24 D3	Auburn Villas	67 B2 [1]	Bailey View	60 F1 [15]
Arklow Street	37 B1 [13]	Ashington Heath	24 D3	Auburn Walk	37 B1 [18]	Bailey's Row	38 E1 [11]
Armagh Road	46 D1	Ashington Mews	24 D3	Aughavannagh Road	37 C4	Balally Avenue	58 D1
Armstrong Street	37 C4 [37]	Ashington Park	24 D3	Aughrim Court	37 C1 [21]	Balally Close	58 D1
*Armstrong Street	37 C4	Ashington Rise	23 C3	Aughrim Lane	37 C1 [1]	Balally Drive	58 D1
(off Harold's Cross Road)		Ashlawn	57 C1	Aughrim Place	37 B1 [8]	Balally Grove	58 D2
Armstrong Walk	26 E1	Ashlawn Court	67 B2	Aughrim Street	37 B1	Balally Hill	58 D2
Army Road	37 A2	Ashlawn Park	60 D4	Aughrim Villas	37 B1 [12]	Balally Park	58 D1
Arnold Grove	60 D2	Ashleigh Green	22 F3	Augustine Villas	67 C2 [30]	Balally Road	57 C1
Arnold Park	60 D2	Ashleigh Grove	17 B4	Aulden Grange	12 F4	Balally Terrace	58 D2 [1]
Arnott Street	38 D3	Ashleigh Grove	22 F3	Aungier Lane	38 D3 [23]	Balbutcher Drive	11 C4
Arran Green	67 C2	Ashleigh Lawn	3 B3	Aungier Place	38 D3 [10]	Balbutcher Lane	11 C4
Arran Quay	37 C2	Ashley Avenue	2 D2	Aungier Street	38 D3	Balbutcher Way	11 C4
Arran Quay Terrace	37 C2 [10]	Ashley Drive	2 D2	Austin's Cottages	38 F1 [23]	Balcurris Gardens	12 D4
Arran Road	25 B3	Ashley Grove	2 D2	Avalon	59 A3 [3]	Balcurris Road	12 D4
Arran Street East	38 D2	Ashley Heights	67 B2 [4]	Avalon Apts.	29 B1 [2]	Baldoyle	15 A4
Arran Street West	37 C2 [17]	Ashley Rise	4 D4	Ave Maria Road	37 B3 [18]	Baldoyle Badminton Club	14 F4
Arranmore Avenue	38 D1 [36]	Ashling Close	37 B4	Avenue Road	38 D4 [26]	Baldoyle Road	28 D1
Arranmore Road	47 C1	Ashling Court	47 B1	Avila Apts	59 A1 [10]	Balfe Avenue	45 C1
Artane	26 E2	Ashling Heights	22 E1	Avila Park	23 C1	Balfe Gardens	32 D4 [1]
Artane Cottages Lower	26 E2 [2]	Ashmount	9 A4 [1]	Avila Park Gardens	23 C1	Balfe Road	45 C1
Artane Cottages Upper	26 E2 [3]	Ashmount	9 A41	Avoca Apartments	32 D3	Balfe Road East	46 D1
Arthur Griffith Park	34 D3	Ashmount Court	37 A3 [23]	Avoca Avenue	48 F4	Balfe Street	38 D3 [29]
Arundel	49 B4 [19]	Ashton Avenue	56 D1	Avoca Avenue	67 C3	Balgaddy Road	34 F3
*Asdill's Row (off Temple Bar)	38 D2	Ashton Close	56 D1	Avoca Hall	49 A4 [10]	Balglass Road	30 D2
Asgard (Apts.)	30 D1	Ashton Grove	56 D1	Avoca Park	48 F4	Balgriffin	14 D3
Asgard Park	30 D2	Ashton Lawn	56 D1	Avoca Place	49 A3	Balgriffin Cottages	14 D3
Asgard Road	30 D2	Ashton Park	49 B4	Avoca Road	48 F4	Balgriffin Road	14 D3
*Ash Grove (Meath Street)	37 C3	Ashton Wood	67 A4	Avoca Terrace	48 F4	Balheary Road	2 D1
Ash Park Avenue	34 E3	Ashtown	23 C3	Avoca Wood	48 F4	Balkill Park	30 D2
Ash Park Court	34 E3	Ashtown Gate Road	23 B4	Avondale	20 D4	Balkill Road	30 D2
Ash Park Grove	34 E2	Ashtown Grove	23 C4	Avondale Avenue	37 C1	Ballawley Court	57 C2
Ash Park Heath	34 E2	Ashtown Lodge	23 C4 [4]	Avondale Court	49 A4	Ballentree	9 B2
Ash Street	37 C3	Ashtown Road	23 B3	Avondale Court	60 E1 [31]	Ballentree Avenue	9 B2
Ashberry	34 D3	Ashtowngate	23 C3	Avondale Crescent	60 E2	Ballentree Close	9 B2
Ashbrook	23 C3	Ashurst	48 E4 [3]	Avondale House	38 E1 [63]	Ballentree Crescent	9 B2
Ashbrook	26 D4	Ashurst	60 E4	Avondale Lawn	49 A4	Ballentree Drive	9 B2
*Ashbrook Terrace (Ranelagh)	47 B1	Ashville Close	34 E1			Ballentree Grove	9 B3
*Ashbrook Villas (Ranelagh)	47 B1	Ashwood Avenue	43 C1			Ballentree Lodge (Apts.)	9 B2
Ashbury Park	67 C2	Ashwood Close	43 C1			Ballentree Villa	9 B3
Ashcroft	27 A2	Ashwood Drive	44 D1			Ballinclea Heights	60 E3
Ashcroft Grove	22 D1 [5]	Ashwood Lawns	44 D1				

STREET NAME	PAGE/GRID REFERENCE
Ballinclea Road	60 D3
Ballinteer	57 B2
Ballinteer Avenue	57 B2
Ballinteer Close	57 B2
Ballinteer Court	57 B2 [2]
Ballinteer Crescent	57 B2
Ballinteer Drive	57 B2
Ballinteer Gardens	57 C2
Ballinteer Grove	57 B2
Ballinteer Park	57 B2 [3]
Ballinteer Park	57 B2
Ballinteer Road	57 C1
Ballinteer St. John's G.A.A. Club	57 A2
Ballintrane Wood	1 C2
Ball's Lane	38 D2 [23]
Ballsbridge	38 F4
Ballsbridge Avenue	39 A4 [26]
Ballsbridge Gardens	39 A4 [25]
Ballsbridge Park	39 A4 [23]
Ballsbridge Terrace	38 F4 [14]
Ballsbridge Wood	38 F4
Ballybetagh	62 F4
Ballybetagh Road	62 E4
Ballyboden	56 E1
Ballyboden Crescent	56 E1
Ballyboden Road	56 E1
Ballyboggan Road	24 E3
Ballybough Avenue	38 E1 [42]
Ballybough Court	38 E1 [43]
Ballybough Lane	38 E1 [4]
Ballybough Road	38 E1
Ballybrack	60 E4
Ballybrack	61 B3
Ballybrew	65 C2
Ballybride	64 D3
Ballybride Road	64 D3
Ballycoolin Road	10 D4
Ballycorus	63 A3
Ballycorus Road	62 F2
Ballycorus Road	63 A2
Ballycullen Avenue	55 B2
Ballycullen Drive	55 B2
Ballycullen Road	55 C1
Ballycullen View	55 B2
Ballycullen View	55 C2
Ballydowd Grove	34 E1
Ballydowd Manor	34 E2
Ballyedmonduff	61 C2
Ballyedmonduff Road	62 D1
Ballyfermot	36 D3
Ballyfermot Avenue	36 D3
Ballyfermot Crescent	36 D3
Ballyfermot Drive	36 D3
Ballyfermot Parade	36 D3
Ballyfermot Road	35 C3
Ballyfermot Road	36 D3
Ballygall Avenue	24 E1
Ballygall Crescent	24 E1
Ballygall Parade	24 E2
Ballygall Place	24 E2 [1]
Ballygall Road	24 E2
Ballygall Road East	24 F2
Ballygall Road West	24 E1
Ballygihen Avenue	60 E1
Ballygihen Villas	60 E1 [20]
Ballygoran	18 E4
Ballygoran Court	31 C2
Ballygoran View	31 C2
Ballygorten	31 C2
Ballyhoy Avenue	27 A3
Ballymace Green	46 E4
Ballymacoll	6 D3
Ballymadrough Road	2 F1
Ballymakeally Lawns	31 C1
Ballymakealy Crescent	34 F1
Ballymakealy Grove	31 C4
Ballyman	66 F1
Ballyman Lane	63 C4
Ballyman Lane	66 F1
Ballyman Road	67 A1
Ballymana	54 E4
Ballymanagin Lane	35 A4 [1]
Ballymorris	67 B4 [2]
Ballymorris	67 B4
Ballymoss Parade	58 F2 [5]
Ballymoss Road	58 E2
Ballymount Avenue	45 B2
Ballymount Cottages	45 A2
Ballymount Drive	45 B2
Ballymount Road	44 F3
Ballymount Road Lower	45 B2
Ballymount Road Upper	45 A2
Ballymount Square	45 B2
Ballymun	25 A1
Ballymun Road	25 A1
Ballynakelly	42 D4
Ballyneety Road	36 F3
Ballynoe Court	67 B3 [1]
Ballyogan Avenue	58 F4
Ballyogan Close	58 F4
Ballyogan Court	58 F4
Ballyogan Crescent	58 F4
Ballyogan Drive	58 F4
Ballyogan Estate	58 F4
Ballyogan Green	58 F4
Ballyogan Lawn	58 F4
Ballyogan Park	58 F4
Ballyogan Road	58 F4
Ballyogan Vale	59 A4
Ballyogan Wood	59 A4
Ballyolaf Manor	57 C1 [6]
Ballyoulster Park	32 E3
Ballyowen Avenue	34 F1
Ballyowen Court	34 F1
Ballyowen Crescent	34 F1
Ballyowen Drive	34 F1
Ballyowen Green	34 F1
Ballyowen Grove	34 F1
Ballyowen Lane	34 F1
Ballyowen Lane	34 F2
Ballyowen Lawn	34 F1
Ballyowen View	34 F1
Ballyowen Way	34 F1
Ballyroan Court	56 D1 [3]
Ballyroan Crescent	56 E1
Ballyroan Heights	56 E1
Ballyroan Park	56 D1
Ballyroan Road	56 E1
Ballyshannon Avenue	25 C1
Ballyshannon Road	26 D1
Ballytore Road	46 F3
Ballywaltrim Cottages	67 B4 [1]
Ballywaltrim Heights	67 B3
Ballywaltrim Road	67 A4
Balnagowan	47 B2 [4]
Balrothery Cottages	55 C1 [5]
Balrothery Estate	45 B4
Balscadden Road	30 E1
Balscott	41 C1
Bancroft Avenue	55 A1
Bancroft Close	55 B1
Bancroft Crescent	45 B4
Bancroft Downs	45 A4
Bancroft Grove	55 B1
Bancroft Park	55 A1
Bancroft Road	55 B1
Bangor Drive	37 B4
Bangor Road	46 E1
Bankside Cottages	47 B2
Bann Road	24 E3
Bannaville	38 D4 [41]
Bannow Road	24 E4
Banshee	51 A2
Bantry Road	25 A3
Banville Avenue	36 D4
Barberstown Lane	1 A4
Barclay Court	49 A3
Bargy Road	38 F1
Barnacoille Park	60 E1
Barnamire	65 A4
Barnamore Crescent	24 D3
Barnamore Grove	24 D3
Barnamore Park	24 D3
Barnaslingan Lane	63 A3
Barnhall Drive	32 F1
Barnhill Avenue	60 E2
Barnhill Cross Road	34 D1
Barnhill Grove	60 F2 [7]
Barnhill Lawn	60 E2 [1]
Barnhill Park	60 E2 [3]
Barnhill Road	60 E2
*Barnhill Villas (on Barnhill Road)	60 F2
Barnville Park	35 C4
Barrack Court	52 E2
*Barrack Lane (off Irishtown Road)	39 A3
Barrett Street	49 C4 [2]
Barrogstown East	18 F4
Barrogstown West	18 E4
Barron Place	25 A3 [4]
Barrow Road	24 E3
Barrow Street	38 F3
Barry Avenue	24 D1
*Barry Close (off Barry Drive)	24 D1
Barry Drive	24 D1
Barry Green	24 D1
Barry Park	24 D1
Barry Road	24 D1
Barryscourt Road	26 E1
Barton Avenue	56 F1
Barton Court	57 A1 [3]
Barton Drive	56 F1
Barton Road East	57 B1
Barton Road East Extension	57 A1
Barton Road Extension	57 A1
Barton Road West	56 F1
Bartra Rock (Apts.)	60 F1 [18]
Basin Street Lower	37 B3
Basin Street Upper	37 B3
*Basin View (off Basin Street Upper)	37 B3
Baskin Cottages	13 C1
Baskin Lane	13 B1
Bass Place	38 E3 [3]
Bath Avenue (Malahide)	3 C2
Bath Avenue (Sandymount)	38 F3
Bath Avenue Gardens	38 F3
Bath Avenue Place	38 F3 [10]
Bath Lane	38 D1 [42]
Bath Place	49 A3 [8]
Bath Street	39 A3
Bawnlea Avenue	54 D2
Bawnlea Close	54 D2
Bawnlea Crescent	54 D2
Bawnlea Drive	54 D2
Bawnlea Green	54 D2
Bawnogue Cottages	43 C1 [1]
Bawnogue Road	43 C1
Bawnville Avenue	55 A2
Bawnville Close	55 A2
Bawnville Drive	55 B2
Bawnville Park	55 B2
Bawnville Road	55 A2
Baymount Park	27 A4
Bayshore Lane	64 E1
Bayside Boulevard North	27 C1
Bayside Boulevard South	27 C1
Bayside Crescent	27 C1 [1]
Bayside Park	27 C1
Bayside Square East	27 C1
Bayside Square North	27 C1
Bayside Square South	27 C1
Bayside Square West	27 C1
Bayside Walk	27 C1
Bayswater Terrace	60 F1 [7]
Baytownpark	6 E1
Bayview	64 E1
Bayview	67 C2 [51]
*Bayview (On Seapoint Road)	67 C2
Bayview Avenue	38 E1
Bayview Close	64 E1
Bayview Court	64 E1
Bayview Crescent	64 E1
Bayview Drive	64 E1
Bayview Glade	64 E1 [12]
Bayview Glen	64 E1
Bayview Grove	64 E1
Bayview Lawns	64 E1
Bayview Park	64 E1
Bayview Rise	64 E1
Beach Avenue	39 A3
Beach Drive	39 A3
Beach Park	15 A1
Beach Road	39 A3
Beach View	27 C2
Beacon Court	58 D2
*Beacon Hill (off Nerano Road)	60 F2
Beaconsfield Court	37 A3 [18]
Bealing	9 B2
Bealing Avenue	9 B2
Bealing Close	9 B2
Bealing Crescent	9 B2
Bealing Grove	9 B2
Bealing Mews	9 B2
Bealing View	9 B2
Bealing Walk	9 B2
Bealing Wood	9 B2
Beann Éadair G.A.A. Club	30 D2
Bearna Park	58 D3
Beatty Grove	32 D2
Beatty Park	32 D3
Beatty's Avenue	38 F4 [8]
Beaucourt	25 B3 [4]
Beaufield	17 C4
Beaufield Ave	17 C4
Beaufield Close	17 C4
Beaufield Crescent	17 C4
Beaufield Drive	17 C4
Beaufield Gardens	17 C4
Beaufield Green	17 C4
Beaufield Grove	17 C4
Beaufield Lawn	17 C4
Beaufield Manor	48 E4
Beaufield Mews	48 E4 [2]
Beaufield Park	48 E4
Beaufort	60 E1 [19]
Beaufort Court	46 F4 [10]
Beaufort Downs	46 F4
Beaufort Villas	46 F4 [3]
Beaumont	26 D1
Beaumont Avenue	47 B4
Beaumont Avenue	57 B1
Beaumont Close	47 B4 [3]
Beaumont Cottages	34 D2
Beaumont Crescent	26 D2
Beaumont Drive	47 B4
Beaumont Gardens	48 F4
Beaumont Grove	25 C2
Beaumont Road	25 C2
Beaumount Hall	25 C2 [7]
Beaupark Downs	49 B4 [15]
Beauvale Park	26 D2
Beaver Close	38 E1 [51]
Beaver Row	47 C1
Beaver Street	38 E1
Beckett Hall	59 B4
Beckett Way	35 C4
Bedford Court	46 E1 [5]
*Bedford Lane (off Aston Quay)	38 D2
*Bedford Row (off Aston Quay)	38 D2
Beech Drive	57 B1
Beech Grove (Blackrock)	48 F2
Beech Grove (Lucan)	34 E2
Beech Hill	47 C2
Beech Hill Avenue	47 C2
Beech Hill Court	47 C1
Beech Hill Crescent	47 C2 [3]
Beech Hill Drive	47 C2
Beech Hill Office Campus	47 C2
Beech Hill Road	47 C2
Beech Hill Terrace	47 C2 [4]
Beech Hill Villas	47 C2 [2]
Beech Lawn	57 B1
Beech Park (Cabinteely)	59 C4
Beech Park (Castleknock)	22 F3
Beech Park (Lucan)	34 E1
Beech Park Avenue (Blanchardstown)	23 A3
Beech Park Avenue (Deans Grange)	59 B2
Beech Park Crescent	23 A3 [1]
Beech Park Drive	59 B2
Beech Park Grove	59 B2
Beech Park Lawn	23 A3
Beech Park Road	59 B2
Beech Road	45 A1
Beech Road	67 B2
Beech Row	35 A4
Beech Row	44 D1 [1]

STREET NAME	PAGE/GRID REFERENCE	STREET NAME	PAGE/GRID REFERENCE	STREET NAME	PAGE/GRID REFERENCE	STREET NAME	PAGE/GRID REFERENCE
Beech Walk	56 E2 [4]	Belfry Avenue	53 C3	Belmont	59 A1	Beverly Drive	56 D2
Beechbrook Grove	14 D4 [4]	Belfry Close	53 C3	Belmont	67 C4	Beverly Green	55 C2
Beechcourt	60 D3	Belfry Dale	53 C3	Belmont Avenue	47 C1	Beverly Grove	56 D1
Beechdale	7 B3	Belfry Gardens	53 C3	*Belmont Court	47 C1	Beverly Heights	56 D2
Beechdale Avenue	55 B3	Belfry Green	53 C3	(off Belmont Ave)		Beverly Lawns	56 D2
Beechdale Court	55 B3	Belfry Lawn	53 C3	Belmont Gardens	47 C1	Beverly Park	55 C1
Beechdale Crescent	55 B3	Belfry Meadows	53 C3	Belmont Green	58 F1	Beverly Rise	55 C2
Beechdale Lawn	55 B3	Belfry Park	53 C3	Belmont Green	59 A1	Bewley	34 E2
Beechdale Mews	47 B1 [19]	Belfry Place	53 C3	Belmont Grove	58 F1	Bewley Avenue	34 E2
Beechdale Park	55 B3	Belfry Rise	53 C3	Belmont Lawn	58 F1	Bewley Drive	34 E2
Beechdale Place	55 C3	Belfry Square	53 C3	Belmont Park	27 A2	Bewley Grove	34 E2
Beechdale Road	55 C3	Belfry Terrace	53 C3	Belmont Park	47 C1 [3]	Bewley Lawn	34 E2
Beechdale Way	55 B3	Belfry Walk	53 C3	*Belmont Place	38 E1	Bianconi Avenue	53 B1
Beeches Park	60 E1	Belfry Way	53 C3	(off Gardiner St Middle)		Big Lane	32 D3
Beeches Road	58 D1	Belgard Close	44 F3 [2]	*Belmont Terrace	58 F1	Bigger Road	45 C2
Beechfield	8 E4	Belgard Green	44 E4	(off Stillorgan Road)		Binn Eadair View	29 A1
Beechfield Avenue	8 D4	Belgard Heights	44 F4	Belmont Villas	47 C1	Birch Avenue	58 D2
Beechfield Avenue	45 C2	Belgard Road	44 E3	Belton Park Avenue	26 D3	Birch Dale	59 A2 [9]
Beechfield Close	8 D4	Belgard Square	54 F1	Belton Park Gardens	26 D3	Birch Dale	59 C1 [12]
Beechfield Close	46 D2	Belgard Square East	54 F1	Belton Park Road	26 D3	Birch Grove	59 C1
Beechfield Court	8 D4	Belgard Square North	54 F1	Belton Park Villas	26 D3	Birchdale Close	2 E3
Beechfield Drive	8 D4	Belgard Square South	54 F1	Belton Terrace	67 C2 [44]	Birchdale Drive	2 E3
Beechfield Green	8 D4	Belgard Square West	54 F1	Belvidere Avenue	38 E1 [19]	Birchdale Park	2 F3
Beechfield Haven	64 E2 [3]	Belgrave Avenue	47 B1	Belvidere Court	38 D1 [11]	Birchdale Road	2 E3
Beechfield Heights	8 D4	Belgrave Place (Monkstown)	49 B4 [10]	Belvidere Place	38 D1	Birches Road	58 D1
Beechfield Lawn	8 E4	Belgrave Place (Rathmines)	47 A1 [15]	Belvidere Road	38 E1	Birchfield Avenue	47 C4
Beechfield Manor	64 E2	Belgrave Road (Monkstown)	49 B4	Ben Edar Road	37 B1	Birchfield Court	47 C4
Beechfield Meadows	8 E4	Belgrave Road (Rathmines)	47 A1	Ben Inagh Park	49 A3 [3]	Birchfield Heights	47 C4
Beechfield Mews	46 D2 [4]	Belgrave Square (Monkstown)	49 B4	Benbulbin Avenue	37 A4	Birchfield Lawn	47 C4
Beechfield Place	8 E4	Belgrave Square (Rathmines)	47 A1	Benbulbin Road	37 A4	Birchfield Park	47 C4
Beechfield Rise	8 E4	Belgrave Square East	47 A1	Benburb Street	37 C2	Birch's Lane	47 C4
Beechfield Road	8 D4	Belgrave Square East (Monkstown)	49 B4	Beneavin Court	24 F2	Birchview Avenue	45 A4
Beechfield Road	45 C2			Beneavin Drive	24 F2	Birchview Close	45 A4
Beechfield View	8 E4	Belgrave Square North	47 A1	Beneavin Park	24 F1	Birchview Court	45 A4
Beechfield Way	8 E4	Belgrave Square North (Monkstown)	49 B4	Beneavin Road	24 F1	Birchview Drive	45 A4
Beechlawn	48 F3			Bengal Terrace	24 F4 [4]	Birchview Heights	45 A4
Beechlawn Avenue	26 E1	Belgrave Square South	47 A1	Benmadigan Road	37 A4	Birchview Lawn	45 A4
Beechlawn Avenue (Ballinteer)	57 B1	Belgrave Square South (Monkstown)	49 B4	Benson Street	38 F2	Birchview Rise	45 A4
Beechlawn Close	26 E1			Bentley Avenue	67 C4 [3]	Birchwood Close	44 E4
Beechlawn Green	26 E1	Belgrave Square West	47 A1	Bentley Park	67 C4	Birchwood Drive	54 E1
Beechlawn Grove	26 E1	Belgrave Square West (Monkstown)	49 B4	Bentley Road	67 C4	Birchwood Heights	54 E1
Beechlawn Manor	46 F2 [20]	Belgrave Terrace	68 D2 [10]	Bentley Villas	49 C4 [17]	Bird Avenue	47 C3
Beechlawn Mews	46 F2 [21]	Belgrave Terrace (Monkstown)	49 B4 [11]	Beresford	25 B3	Biscayne	3 C3
Beechmount Drive (Windy Arbour)	47 C3	*Belgrave Terrace (On Meath Road)	67 C2	Beresford Avenue	25 B3	Bishop Street	38 D3
Beechpark Avenue	26 E1	*Belgrave Villas	68 D2 [9]	Beresford Green	25 B3	Bishops Lane	62 F2
Beechpark Close	23 A3 [3]	*Belgrave Villas (On Meath Road)	67 C2	Beresford Lane	38 E2 [9]	Bishop's Orchard	9 B2
Beechpark Court	26 E1			Beresford Lawn	25 B3	Bishop's Orchard Boulevard	9 B2
Beechurst	67 B2	Belgrave Villas (Rathmines)	47 B1 [16]	Beresford Place	38 E2	Bishop's Orchard House (Apts.)	9 B2
Beechview	56 E2 [1]	Belgree	9 B2	Beresford Street	38 D2	Bisset's Strand	3 B2
Beechwood Avenue Lower	47 B1	Belgree Avenue	9 B2	Berkeley Avenue	38 D1 [55]	Black Street	37 B2 [9]
Beechwood Avenue Upper	47 B1	Belgree Close	9 B2	Berkeley Place	38 D1 [57]	Blackberry Lane	15 A1
Beechwood Close	21 C1	Belgree Court	9 B2	Berkeley Road	38 D1	Blackberry Lane	38 D4 [8]
Beechwood Close	67 C4	Belgree Drive	9 B2	Berkeley Street	38 D1	Blackberry Rise	15 A1
Beechwood Downs	21 C1	Belgree Green	9 B2	Berkeley Terrace	38 F3 [36]	Blackburn Square	46 F4 [15]
Beechwood Grove	60 D1 [11]	Belgree Grove	9 B2	Bernard Curtis House	36 F4 [2]	Blackcourt Road	22 E1
Beechwood Lawn	60 D2	Belgree Heights	9 B2	Berryfield	34 D3	Blackditch Drive	35 C3
Beechwood Lawns	52 F2	Belgree Lawns	9 B2	Berryfield Crescent	24 D2	Blackditch Road	35 C3
Beechwood Park (Dun Laoghaire)	60 D1	Belgree Rise	9 B2	Berryfield Drive	24 D2	Blackglen Court	58 D3
		Belgree Square	9 B2	Berryfield Lane	67 A3	Blackglen Road	57 C3
Beechwood Park (Rathmines)	47 B1 [7]	Belgree Walk	9 B2	Berryfield Road	24 D2	Blackhall Green	37 C2
Beechwood Road	47 B1	Belgree Woods	9 B2	Berwick Avenue	1 B2	Blackhall Little	5 B1
Beggar's Bush Buildings	38 F3	Belgrove Lawn	36 D2	Berwick Court	1 B1	Blackhall Parade	37 C2 [4]
Beggars Bush Court	38 F3 [48]	Belgrove Park	26 F4	Berwick Crescent	1 B1	Blackhall Place	37 C2
Belarmine Park	58 D4	Belgrove Park	36 D2	Berwick Drive	1 B1	Blackhall Street	37 C2 [13]
Belarmine Way	58 D4	Belgrove Road	26 F4	Berwick Grove	1 B1	Blackheath Avenue	26 F4
Belcamp Avenue	13 B4	*Bella Avenue (off Bella St)	38 E1	Berwick Hall	47 A4	Blackheath Court	26 F4
Belcamp Crescent	13 B4	*Bella Place (off Bella St)	38 E1	Berwick Lawn	1 B1	Blackheath Drive	26 E4
Belcamp Gardens	13 B4	Bella Street	38 E1 [27]	Berwick Place	1 B1	Blackheath Gardens	26 E4
Belcamp Green	13 B4	Belleview Maltings	37 A2	Berwick Rise	1 B2	Blackheath Grove	26 E4
Belcamp Grove	13 B4	Belleville Apts	23 C4	Berwick View	1 B1	Blackheath Park	26 E4
Belcamp Lane	13 C4	Belleville Avenue	47 A2	Berwick Walk	1 B2	Blackhorse Avenue	37 B1
Belclare Avenue	11 C4	Bellevue	37 C3	Berwick Way	1 B1	Blackhorse Grove	37 B1
Belclare Crescent	11 C4	Bellevue Ave (Merrion)	48 E2	Berystede	38 E4 [25]	Blackpitts	37 C3
Belclare Drive	11 C4	Bellevue Avenue (Dalkey)	60 E2	Bessborough Avenue	38 F1	Blackrock	49 A3
Belclare Green	11 C4	Bellevue Copse	48 E2	Bessborough Parade	38 D4 [9]	Blackthorn Avenue	58 E2
Belclare Grove	11 C4	Bellevue Cottages	24 F3 [4]	Besser Drive	35 B4	Blackthorn Close	4 D4
Belclare Lawns	11 C4	Bellevue Court	48 E2 [2]	Bethany House	39 B4 [4]	Blackthorn Close	58 D2 [7]
Belclare Park	11 C4	Bellevue Park	48 E2	Bethesda Place	38 D1 [58]	Blackthorn Court	58 D2 [4]
Belclare Terrace	11 C4	Bellevue Park Avenue	48 E2	Bettyglen	27 B2	Blackthorn Drive	58 D2
Belclare Way	11 C4	Bellevue Road	60 D2	Bettysford	44 E1 [3]	Blackthorn Green	58 D2 [6]
Belfield Close	47 C3 [8]	Bellman's Walk	38 F2 [2]	Bettystown Avenue	26 F3	Blackthorn Grove	58 D2 [3]
Belfield Court	48 D2	Bell's Lane	38 E3 [30]	Beverly Avenue	56 D1	Blackthorn Road	58 D2
Belfield Downs	47 C4	*Belmont	58 F1	Beverly Court	26 F4	Blackwater Road	24 E3
Belfield Park (Apts)	48 E3			Beverly Crescent	55 C2	Blackwood Close	21 A1
				Beverly Downs	55 C2	Blackwood Crescent	21 A1

STREET NAME	PAGE/GRID REFERENCE
Blackwood Drive	21 A1
Blackwood Lane	3 C4
Blackwood Lawn	21 A1
Blackwood Mews	21 A1
Blackwood Park	21 A1
Blackwood Place	21 A1
Blakeney House (Mews)	30 E3
*Blakes Villas (on Grangegorman Lower)	37 C1
Blakesfield	21 C1
Blakestown Cottages	22 D1
Blakestown Drive	22 D1
Blakestown Road	22 D1
Blakestown Way	22 D1
Blanchardstown	22 F2
Blanchardstown ByPass	22 F2
Blanchardstown Road North	9 B4
Blanchardstown Road South	22 D2
Blarney Park	46 E1
Blessington Court	38 D1 [56]
Blessington Lane	38 D1 [53]
*Blessington Place (off St Joseph's Parade)	38 D1
Blessington Road	53 C2
Blessington Road (Tallaght)	54 D2
Blessington Street	38 D1
Bloomfield Avenue (Donnybrook)	38 E4
Bloomfield Avenue (Portobello)	38 D4
Bloomfield Cottages	38 D4 [49]
Bloomfield Park	38 D4 [46]
Bluebell	36 E4
Bluebell Avenue	36 E4
Bluebell Road	36 E4
Blundelstown	42 E3
Blunden Drive	13 C4
Blythe Avenue	38 F2 [4]
*Boardman's Lane (off Cork Street)	37 C3
Boden Dale	56 F1
Boden Mill	56 E2
Boden Park	56 E1
Boden Wood	46 F4
Boeing Road	12 F4
Boghall Road	67 B4
Bohernabreena Road	55 A3
Bolbrook Avenue	55 B1 [3]
Bolbrook Close	55 B1 [4]
Bolbrook Drive	55 B1 [1]
Bolbrook Grove	55 B1
Bolbrook Park	55 B1
Bolbrook Villas	55 B1
Bolton Green	1 A2
Bolton Street	38 D2
Bond Drive	39 A1
Bond Road	39 A1
Bond Street	37 C3
Bonham Street	37 C2
Boolavogue Road	38 F1 [13]
Boot Road	44 D2
Booterstown	48 E2
Booterstown Avenue	48 F3
*Booterstown Grove (off Booterstown Avenue)	48 F2
Booterstown Park	48 F3
Boranaraltry	61 B4
Boranaraltry Bridge	61 B4
Boranaraltry Lane	61 C4
Boroimhe Alder	1 C3
Boroimhe Ash	1 C3
Boroimhe Aspen	1 C3
Boroimhe Beech	1 C3
Boroimhe Birches	1 C3
Boroimhe Blackthorn	1 C3
Boroimhe Cedars	1 C3
Boroimhe Cherry	1 C3
Boroimhe Elms	1 C3
Boroimhe Hawthorn	1 C3
Boroimhe Laurels	1 C3
Boroimhe Maples	1 C3
Boroimhe Oaks	1 C3
Boroimhe Pines	1 C3
Boroimhe Poplars	1 C3
Boroimhe Willows	1 C3
Botanic Avenue	25 A4
Botanic Hall	24 F3
Botanic Park	25 A4 [14]
Botanic Road	25 A4
Botanic Villas	25 A4 [10]
Boulevard Bealing Village	9 B2
Boulevard Mount Eustace	9 B2
Boundary Road	39 A1
Bow Bridge	37 B3
Bow Bridge Place	37 B3
Bow Lane East	38 D3 [37]
Bow Lane West	37 B3
Bow Street	37 C2
Boyne Court	37 C4 [31]
Boyne Lane	38 E3 [2]
Boyne Road	24 E3
Boyne Street	38 E3
Brabazon Cottages	67 C2 [16]
Brabazon Place	37 C3 [35]
Brabazon Row	37 C3 [18]
Brabazon Square	37 C3 [40]
Brabazon Street	37 C3 [17]
Bracken Drive	4 D4
Bracken Hill	57 C3
Bracken Road	58 D2
Brackenbush Park	60 D4
Brackenbush Road	60 D4
Bracken's Lane	38 E2 [28]
Brackenstown Avenue	1 C2
Brackenstown Road	1 C2
Braemor Avenue	47 A3
Braemor Drive	47 A3
Braemor Grove	47 A3
Braemor Park	47 A3
Braemor Road	47 A3
Braithwaite Street	37 C3
Bramblefield Court	8 F4
Bramblefield Crescent	8 F4
Bramblefield Drive	8 F4
Bramblefield Park	8 F4
Bramblefield View	8 F4
Bramblefield Walk	8 F4
Bramley Avenue	22 E3
Bramley Court	22 E3
Bramley Crescent	22 E3
Bramley Garth	22 E3
Bramley Green	22 E3
Bramley Grove	22 E3
Bramley Heath	22 E3
Bramley Park	22 E3
Bramley Road	22 E3
Bramley View	22 E3
Bramley Walk	22 E3
Bramley Way	22 E3
Brandon Road	36 F4
Brandon Road	45 C1
Brandon Terrace	37 B3 [32]
Bray	68 D1
Bray Commons	67 B2
Bray Head Terrace	67 C3 [20]
Bray Road	59 B2
Bray Road	59 C4
Bray Southern Cross Route	67 B4
Breakwater Road North	39 B2
Breakwater Road South	39 B2
Breffini Terrace	60 E1
Breffni Gardens	15 A4 [5]
Breffni Road	60 E1
Bregia Road	24 F4
Brehon Field Road	57 B2
Brehons Chair	57 A3
Bremen Avenue	39 A3
Bremen Grove	39 A3
Bremen Road	39 A3
Brendan Behan Court	38 E1 [33]
Brendan Road	47 C1
Brennan's Cottages (Synge Street)	38 D4
Brennans Parade	68 D2 [14]
Brennans Terrace	68 D2 [4]
Brennanstown Avenue	59 C4
Brennanstown Road	59 B4
Brennanstown Square	59 C4
Brennanstown Vale	59 B4
Brewery Road	58 F2
Brian Avenue	25 C4
Brian Boru Avenue	39 C1
Brian Boru Street	39 C1
Brian Road	25 C4
Brian Terrace	25 C4
Briansboro Terrace	37 C4 [23]
Briar Walk	4 D4
Briar Wood	68 D3
Briarfield Grove	27 B1
Briarfield Road	27 B2
Briarfield Villas	27 B1 [5]
Briarly Court	47 B4 [4]
Briarsfield Walk	27 B1 [4]
Briarwood Avenue	22 D1
Briarwood Close	9 A4
Briarwood Gardens	22 D1
Briarwood Green	22 D1
Briarwood Lawn	22 D1
Briarwood Park	22 D1 [2]
Briarwood Road	22 D1 [4]
Brickfield	67 B3
Brickfield Drive	37 B4
Brickfield Lane	37 C3 [48]
Bride Close	38 D3 [55]
Bride Road	38 D3
Bride Street	38 D3
Bride Street New	38 D3
Brides Glen	1 B1
Brides Glen	63 C2
Bridge Street	2 D2
Bridge Street	39 A3
Bridge Street Lower	37 C2
Bridge Street Upper	37 C3
Bridgefoot Street	37 C2
Bridgewater Quay	37 A2
Bridon	62 F1
Brighton Avenue	59 A4
Brighton Avenue (Clontarf)	26 D4 [1]
Brighton Avenue (Monkstown)	49 B4
Brighton Avenue (Rathgar)	46 F2
Brighton Cottages	59 A3 [1]
Brighton Court	59 A4
Brighton Gardens	46 F2
Brighton Green	46 F2 [13]
Brighton Hall	59 A4
Brighton Lane	49 B4 [22]
Brighton Lodge	59 A3 [4]
Brighton Place	59 A4
Brighton Road (Foxrock)	59 A4
Brighton Road (Terenure)	46 F2
Brighton Square	46 F2
Brighton Terrace	49 B4 [9]
Brighton Terrace (Dun Laoghaire)	60 E1 [13]
Brighton Vale	49 B3
Britain Place	38 D1 [47]
Britain Quay	38 F2
Broadfield Avenue	52 E2
Broadfield Close	52 E2
Broadfield Court	52 E2
Broadfield Heath	52 E2
Broadfield Manor	52 E2
Broadfield Meadows	52 E2
Broadfield View	52 E2
Broadford Avenue	57 B2
Broadford Close	57 B2
Broadford Crescent	57 B2
Broadford Drive	57 B2
Broadford Hill	57 B2
Broadford Lawn	57 B2
Broadford Park	57 B2
Broadford Rise	57 B2
Broadford Road	57 B2
Broadford Rovers F.C.	57 A2
Broadford Walk	57 B2
Broadmeadow	1 C1
Broadstone Avenue	38 D1 [68]
*Broadstone Avenue (off Royal Canal Bank)	38 D1
*Broadstone Place (off Royal Canal Bank)	38 D1
Broadway Drive	22 E2
Broadway Grove	22 E2
Broadway Park	22 E2
Broadway Road	22 E2
Brockey	61 C4
Brockey	65 A1
Brockey Lane	65 A1
Brodin Row	37 B2 [15]
Brompton Court	22 E3
Brompton Grove	22 E2
Brompton Grove	22 E3
Brompton Lawn	22 E2
Brook Court	49 B4
Brookdale	55 A2
Brookdale Avenue	1 B3
Brookdale Close	1 B2
Brookdale Court	1 B3
Brookdale Drive	1 B2
Brookdale Green	1 B2
Brookdale Grove	1 B2
Brookdale Lawns	1 B2
Brookdale Park	1 B2
Brookdale Road	1 B2
Brookdale Walk	1 B2
Brookdale Way	1 B2
Brookdene	64 E2
Brookfield	34 D3
Brookfield	47 C1 [19]
Brookfield (Blackrock)	48 F3
Brookfield (Coolock)	26 F2
Brookfield (Milltown)	47 B2
Brookfield Avenue	17 C4
Brookfield Avenue	49 A4
Brookfield Avenue	68 D3 [4]
Brookfield Court	46 E2 [6]
Brookfield Court	49 A4 [12]
Brookfield Court	54 D1 [1]
Brookfield Estate	46 E2
Brookfield Green	46 E2 [5]
Brookfield Grove	49 A4 [11]
Brookfield Park	17 C4
Brookfield Place	49 A4
Brookfield Road (Kilmainham)	37 B3
Brookfield Road (Tallaght)	54 D1
Brookfield Street	37 B3
Brookfield Terrace	49 A4
Brookhaven Drive	22 E1
Brookhaven Grove	22 E1
Brookhaven Lawn	22 E1
Brookhaven Park	22 E1
Brookhaven Rise	22 E1
Brooklands	48 E1
Brooklawn	34 D3
Brooklawn (Blackrock)	48 F3
Brooklawn (Clontarf)	26 D4
Brooklawn Avenue	49 B4 [12]
Brooklawn Wood	49 B4 [13]
Brookmount Avenue	55 C1
Brookmount Lawns	55 C1 [1]
Brookpark	34 D3
Brookstone Lane	15 A4 [6]
Brookstone Road	15 A4
Brookvale	34 D1 [8]
Brookvale Downs	46 F3
Brookvale Road (Donnybrook)	47 C1 [8]
Brookvale Road (Rathfarnham)	46 F3
Brookview Avenue	54 D1
Brookview Close	54 D1
Brookview Court	54 D1
Brookview Crescent	54 D1
Brookview Drive	54 D1
Brookview Gardens	54 D1
Brookview Green	54 D1
Brookview Grove	54 D1
Brookview Lawns	54 D1
Brookview Park	54 D1
Brookview Rise	54 D1
Brookview Terrace	54 D1
Brookview Way	54 D1
Brookville	24 D1
Brookville Crescent	26 E1 [2]
Brookville Park (Artane)	26 E2
Brookville Park (Coolock)	26 E1
Brookville Park (Dean's Grange)	59 B1
Brookwood	56 E2
Brookwood Avenue	26 E2
Brookwood Crescent	26 F2
Brookwood Drive	26 E2
Brookwood Glen	26 F3
Brookwood Grove	26 E2

STREET NAME	PAGE/GRID REFERENCE
Brookwood Heights	26 F2
Brookwood Lawn	26 F2
Brookwood Meadow	26 E2
Brookwood Park	26 E3
Brookwood Rise	26 F3
Brookwood Road	26 E2
Broombridge Road	24 E4
Broomfield	3 B4
Broomfield Court	64 E2
Broomfield Mews	3 C4
Broomhill Close	45 A4
Broomhill Drive	45 A4
Broomhill Road	45 A4
Broomhill Terrace (Off Broomhill Road)	45 A4
Brown Street North	37 C2 [5]
Brown Street South	37 C3
Brownrath	5 B1
Brownstown	5 B2
Brownstown	42 D1
Brunswick Place	38 F3 [22]
Brunswick Street North	37 C2
Brunswick Villas (Pearse Street)	38 E2 [30]
Brusna Cottages	49 A3 [12]
Buckingham St Lower	38 E1
Buckingham St Upper	38 E1
Buckingham Village	38 E1 [56]
Buckleys Lane	33 A1
Bulfin Gardens	37 A3
Bulfin Road	37 A3
Bull Alley Street	38 D3
*Bull Lane (Off Main Street)	67 C2
Bull Wall Cottages	40 W1
Bullock Steps	60 F1 [8]
Bunratty Avenue	26 E1
Bunratty Drive	26 E1
Bunratty Road	26 E1
Bunting Road	45 C1
Burdett Avenue	60 E1
Burg an Rí Glen	34 F3
Burg an Rí Terrace	34 F3
Burgess Lane	37 C2 [18]
Burgh Quay	38 E2
Burke Place	37 B3 [42]
*Burke Place (off Mount Brown)	37 B3
Burleigh Court	38 E4 [34]
Burlington Gardens	38 E4 [33]
Burlington Road	38 E4
Burmah Close	60 F2 [22]
Burnell Park Avenue	22 E4
Burnell Park Green	22 E4
Burren Court	11 C4
*Burris Court (off High Street)	38 D3
Burrow Court	15 A1
Burrow Road	62 D1
Burrow Road (Stepaside)	58 D4
Burrow Road (Sutton)	29 B1
Burrowfield Road	28 D1
Burton Hall Avenue	58 E2
Burton Hall Road	58 E2
Burton Road	60 F2
Bushfield	44 D2
Bushfield Avenue	47 B1 [8]
Bushfield Drive	44 D2
Bushfield Green	44 D2
Bushfield Grove	44 D3
Bushfield Lawns	44 D2
Bushfield Park	44 D3
Bushfield Place	47 B1 [17]
Bushfield Square	25 C4 [15]
Bushfield Terrace	47 B1
Bushypark House	46 E3
Bushy Park Gardens	46 F3
Bushy Park Road	46 F3
Bustyhill	51 B3
Butlerstown	5 C3
Buttercup Close	13 C4
Buttercup Drive	13 C4
Buttercup Park	13 C4
Buttercup Square	13 C4
Butterfield Avenue	46 E4
Butterfield Close	46 E4
Butterfield Court	46 F4
Butterfield Crescent	46 F4
Butterfield Drive	46 F4

STREET NAME	PAGE/GRID REFERENCE
Butterfield Grove	46 E4
Butterfield Meadow	46 E4 [1]
Butterfield Orchard	46 E4
Butterfield Park	46 E4
Butterly Business Park	26 D2
*Byrne's Cottages (Francis Street)	37 C3
Byrne's Lane (Jervis St)	38 D2 [31]
*Byrne's Lane (Pearse Sq West)	38 F2

C

STREET NAME	PAGE/GRID REFERENCE
Cabinteely	59 C4
Cabinteely Avenue	59 C3
Cabinteely Bypass	59 C3
Cabinteely Close	59 C3
Cabinteely Court	59 C3 [5]
Cabinteely Crescent	59 C3
Cabinteely Drive	59 C3
Cabinteely Green	59 C3
Cabinteely Park	59 C3 [3]
Cabinteely Way	59 C3
Cabra Drive	37 B1
Cabra Grove	37 B1
Cabra Park	24 F4
Cabra Road	37 B1
Caddell	14 F2
Cadogan Road	25 C4
Cairn Court	12 D4
Cairn Hill	59 B2
Cairnfort	62 E1
Cairnwood Avenue	44 E4
Cairnwood Court	44 E4
Cairnwood Green	44 E4
Calderwood Avenue	25 C3
Calderwood Grove	25 C3 [3]
Calderwood Road	25 C3
Caledon Court	38 F1 [25]
Caledon Road	38 F1
Callary Road	48 D3
Calmount Avenue	45 B2
Calmount Road	45 B2
Camac Close	37 A3 [6]
Camac Court	37 A3 [10]
Camac Park	36 E4
Camac Terrace	37 B3
Camac View (Bow Bridge)	37 B3
Camaderry Road	68 D3
Camberley	47 B4
Camberley Oaks	47 B4
Cambridge Avenue	39 A3 [7]
Cambridge Court	39 A3 [24]
Cambridge Park	39 A3
Cambridge Road (Rathmines)	47 A1
Cambridge Road (Ringsend)	39 A3
*Cambridge Square (off Thorncastle St.)	39 A3
Cambridge Street	39 A3 [1]
Cambridge Terrace (Dun Laoghaire)	49 C4 [24]
Cambridge Terrace (Ranelagh)	38 E4 [7]
Cambridge Villas	47 A1 [16]
Camden Avenue	23 C3
Camden Buildings	38 D3 [54]
Camden Court	38 D4 [30]
Camden Lock	38 F3 [39]
Camden Market	38 D4 [28]
Camden Place	38 D3
Camden Row	38 D3
Camden Street Lower	38 D3
Camden Street Upper	38 D4
Camden Villas	38 D3 [22]
Cameron Square	37 B3 [5]
Cameron Street	37 C3
Camogie Road	37 A2
Campbell's Court	38 D2 [34]
Campbell's Lane (off Belvidere Ave)	38 E1 [71]
Campbell's Row (off Portland Street N)	38 E1 [69]
Campfield Terrace	57 C1
Canal Road	38 D4
Canal Terrace	36 E4
Canal Turn	35 B4
Cannon Mews East	38 F3 [47]
Cannon Rock View	30 E2 [1]
Cannonbrook	34 D2

STREET NAME	PAGE/GRID REFERENCE
Cannonbrook Lawn	34 D2
Cannonbrook Park	34 D2
Canon Lillis Avenue	38 F1
Canon Mooney Gardens	39 A3 [15]
Canonbrook Avenue	34 D2
Canonbrook Court	34 D2
Capel Street	38 D2
Cappagh Avenue	24 D1
Cappagh Drive	24 D2
Cappagh Green	24 D1
Cappagh Road	24 D1
Cappaghmore Estate	35 A4
Cappoge	10 F4
Cappoge Cottages	10 E4
Captain's Avenue	46 D1
Captain's Drive	46 D2
Captain's Hill	20 D4
Captain's Road	46 D2
Cara Park	13 B3
Caragh Court	25 C4 [12]
Caragh Road	37 B1
Carberry Road	25 C3
Carbury Place	49 A3 [20]
Carbury Terrace	38 F2 [9]
Cardiff Castle Road	24 D2
Cardiff Lane	38 F2
Cardiffs Bridge	24 D3
Cardiffsbridge Avenue	24 D2
Cardiffsbridge Grove	24 D1 [1]
Cardiffsbridge Road	24 D2
Card's Lane (Pearse St)	38 E2 [13]
Careys Lane	2 F4
Carfdiff Castle Road	24 D1
Carleton Road	25 C4
Carlingford Parade	38 F3 [4]
Carlingford Road	25 A4
Carlisle Avenue	47 B1
Carlisle Court	46 F2 [23]
Carlisle Street	38 D4
Carlisle Terrace	60 D1 [17]
Carlisle Terrace (Malahide)	3 B3
*Carlisle Terrace (Off N C Rd)	37 C1
*Carlisle Terrace (On Seymour Road)	67 C2
*Carlisle Terrace (on Tivoli Road)	60 D1
Carlton Court	2 D2
Carlton Court	26 D4
Carlton Terrace	67 C2 [41]
Carlton Villas	38 F4 [6]
Carlton Villas	67 C2 [42]
Carmanhall Road	58 E2
Carman's Hall	37 C3
Carna Road	35 C3
Carndonagh Drive	27 B1
Carndonagh Lawn	27 B1
Carndonagh Park	27 B1
Carndonagh Road	27 B1
Carne Court	8 F4
Carnegie Court	2 D1
Carnew Street	37 B1 [9]
Carnlough Road	24 E4
Caroline Row	39 A3 [16]
Carpenterstown	22 D3
Carpenterstown Avenue	22 E3
Carpenterstown Park East	22 E3
Carpenterstown Road	22 E4
Carraig Glen	59 C4
Carraig Grennane	60 E4
Carraroe Avenue	27 A1
Carrick Court	14 F1
Carrick Lawn	58 D1 [2]
Carrick Terrace	37 B3 [29]
Carrickaspinkeen	65 A3
Carrickbrack Heath	29 B2
Carrickbrack Hill	29 B2
Carrickbrack Lawn	29 B2
Carrickbrack Park	29 B2
Carrickbrack Road	29 B2
Carrickbrennan Lawn	49 C4
Carrickbrennan Road	49 C4
Carrickfoyle Terrace	37 A3 [15]
Carrickhill Close	4 D4
Carrickhill Drive	15 A1
Carrickhill Heights	15 A1

STREET NAME	PAGE/GRID REFERENCE
Carrickhill Rise	4 D4
Carrickhill Road	15 A1
Carrickhill Road Middle	15 A1
Carrickhill Road Upper	3 C4
Carrickhill Walk	4 D4
Carrickmines	59 B4
Carrickmines Avenue	59 B4
Carrickmines Chase	59 B4
Carrickmines Dale	59 B4
Carrickmines Garth	59 B4
Carrickmines Little	59 A4
Carrickmines Oaks	59 B4
Carrickmount Avenue	57 B1
Carrickmount Drive	57 A1
Carrig Road	11 C4
Carrigallen Drive	24 E3
Carrigallen Park	24 E3
Carrigallen Road	24 E3
Carrigeen	52 D3
Carriglea Avenue	55 B2
Carriglea Avenue	59 C2
Carriglea Court	55 B2
Carriglea Court	59 C1 [14]
Carriglea Downs	59 C2
Carriglea Drive	55 B2
Carriglea Gardens	59 C1
Carriglea Grove	55 B2
Carriglea Rise	55 B2
Carriglea View	55 B2
Carriglea Walk	55 B2
Carrigmore	53 B2
Carrigmore Close	53 B2
Carrigmore Court	53 C2
Carrigmore Downs	53 B1
Carrigmore Drive	54 F2
Carrigmore Elms	53 B2
Carrigmore Grove	53 B2
Carrigmore Lawns	53 B1
Carrigmore Manor	53 B2
Carrigmore Park	54 F3
Carrigmore Place	53 B2
Carrigmore Road	54 F2
Carrigmore Terrace	53 B2
Carrigmore Way	53 C2
Carrigwood	55 C2
Carrow Road	36 F4
Carton Avenue	18 D2
Carton Court	17 C4
Carton Court	18 D4
Carysfort Avenue	49 A4
Carysfort Downs	58 F1
Carysfort Drive	60 F1 [1]
Carysfort Grove	59 A1
Carysfort Hall	49 A4
Carysfort Park	49 A4
Carysfort Road	60 F1
Carysfort Wood	59 A1
Casana View	30 E2
*Casement Close (off Barry Road)	24 D1
Casement Drive	24 D1
Casement Green	24 D1
Casement Grove	24 D1
Casement Park	24 D1
Casement Road	24 D1
Casement Road	24 D2
Casement Villas	59 B1
Cashel Avenue	46 E2
Cashel Road	46 D1
Casimir Avenue	46 F1
*Casimir Court (off Casimir Avenue)	46 F1
Casimir Road	46 F1
Casino Park	26 D3
Casino Road	25 C4
Cassian Court	24 D3 [2]
Castaheany	8 E4
Castilla Park	26 F4
Castle Avenue (Clondalkin)	44 E1
Castle Avenue (Clontarf)	26 E4
Castle Avenue (Swords)	2 D2
Castle Close (Clondalkin)	44 E1
Castle Close (Dalkey)	60 F1
Castle Court	46 F4
Castle Court	47 A4 [1]

STREET NAME	PAGE/GRID REFERENCE	STREET NAME	PAGE/GRID REFERENCE	STREET NAME	PAGE/GRID REFERENCE	STREET NAME	PAGE/GRID REFERENCE
Castle Court	64 E1	Castlefield Orchard	55 C1	Castlewood Park	47 A1	Charlemont Place	38 E4
Castle Court (Booterstown)	48 F2	Castlefield Park	21 C2	Castlewood Place	47 A1 [6]	Charlemont Road	26 D4
Castle Court (Clontarf)	26 D4	Castlefield Park	55 C2	Castlewood Terrace	47 A1 [5]	Charlemont Street	38 D4
Castle Court (Dundrum)	57 C1 [4]	Castlefield Way	55 C2	Cathal Brugha Street	38 D2	Charlemont Terrace	50 D4 [18]
*Castle Court (off Cypress Lawn)	46 D4	Castlefield Woods	21 C2	Cathedral	38 D2	Charles Lane	38 E1
Castle Cove	3 A2	Castleforbes Road	38 F2	Cathedral Lane	38 D3 [5]	*Charles Sheils Houses	58 F2
Castle Cove	60 F2 [32]	Castlegate	64 D3	Cathedral View Court	38 D3 [43]	*Charles Street Great	38 E1
Castle Crescent	44 E1 [4]	Castlegrange	43 C1	Cathedral View Walk	38 D3 [44]	*Charles Street West	38 D2
Castle Dawson	17 B3	Castlegrange Avenue	2 D1	*Catherine Court	38 E1	(off Ormond Quay Upper)	
Castle Down Croft	2 F2	Castlegrange Close	2 D1	(off William Street N)		Charleston Avenue	47 B1
Castle Down Grove	2 F2	Castlegrange Close	43 B1	Catherine Lane	37 C2 [22]	Charleston Court Flats	47 B1 [9]
Castle Down Road	2 F2	Castlegrange Court	43 C1	Catherine Street (Swift's Alley)	37 C3 [45]	Charleston Road	47 B1
Castle Drive	44 E1	Castlegrange Drive	43 B1	Cats Ladder	60 F2 [5]	Charlestown Avenue	11 B4
Castle Drive (Swords)	2 D2	Castlegrange Green	43 B1	Causeway Road	27 B3	Charlestown Court	11 B4
Castle Elms	26 E1	Castlegrange Heights	2 D1	Cavendish Row	38 D1 [21]	Charlestown Drive	11 B4
Castle Farm Wood	64 E3	Castlegrange Hill	2 D1	Cave's Strand	3 A2	Charlestown Green	11 B4
Castle Grove	58 E4	Castlegrange Lawn	43 C1	Ceanchor Road	30 D4	Charlestown Park	11 B4
Castle Grove (Clondalkin)	44 E1	Castlegrange Road	43 C1	*Ceannt Fort (off Mount Brown)	37 B3	Charlestown Road	11 B4
Castle Grove (Clontarf)	26 E4	Castlegrange Road	2 D1	Cecil Avenue	26 D4	Charlestown Way	11 B4
Castle Grove (Swords)	2 D2	Castlegrange Square	43 C1	*Cecilia Street (off Temple Bar)	38 D2	Charleville	47 B4
Castle Heath	3 A3	Castlegrange Way	2 D1	Cedar Avenue	45 A3	Charleville Avenue	38 E1
Castle Lawn	58 E4	Castlekevin Road	26 D1	Cedar Brook Avenue	35 B3	Charleville Close	47 A1
Castle Lawns	2 F2	Castleknock	22 F3	Cedar Brook Place	35 B3	Charleville Mall	38 E1
Castle Lawns	45 B4	Castleknock Avenue	22 F3	Cedar Brook Walk	35 B3	*Charleville Road (Phibsborough)	37 C1
*Castle Market (off Drury Street)	38 D3	Castleknock Brook	22 F3	Cedar Court	46 F2	Charleville Road (Rathmines)	47 A1
Castle Park	33 A1	Castleknock Close	22 E3	Cedar Court	64 D1	Charleville Square	46 E4
Castle Park	45 B4	Castleknock Court	22 F3 [2]	Cedar Drive	7 B2	Charleville Terrace	37 C1
Castle Park (Clondalkin)	44 E1	Castleknock Crescent	22 F3	Cedar Drive	35 B2	(on Charleville Rd)	
Castle Park (Monkstown)	49 C4	Castleknock Dale	22 F3	Cedar Grove	21 C2 [2]	Charlotte Quay	38 F3
Castle Park (Swords)	2 D2	Castleknock Downs	22 E3	Cedar Hall	47 C1 [16]	Charlotte Terrace	60 F2 [18]
Castle Park Estate (Tallaght)	55 B1	Castleknock Drive	22 F3	Cedar Lodge Apts	56 E2	Charlotte Way	38 D4 [32]
Castle Place	31 C2	Castleknock Elms	22 F3	Cedar Park	19 C4	Charlton Lawn	48 D4
*Castle Place (on Breffni Road)	60 F1	Castleknock Gate	23 B4 [1]	Cedar Park	27 A1	Charnwood	21 C2
Castle Riada Avenue	34 E3	Castleknock Glade	22 F3	Cedar Square	48 F4 [4]	Charnwood	67 C3
Castle Riada Crescent	34 E2	Castleknock Golf and		Cedar Walk	27 B2	Charnwood Avenue	21 C2
Castle Riada Drive	34 E3	Country Club	22 F3	Cedarmount Road	48 E4	Charnwood Courts	21 C2
Castle Riada Grove	34 E2	Castleknock Grange	22 F3	Cedarwood	32 D3	Charnwood Dale	21 C2
Castle Road	26 E4	Castleknock Green	23 A3	Cedarwood Avenue	24 F1	Charnwood Gardens	21 C2
Castle Road	34 E2	Castleknock Grove	22 F3	Cedarwood Close	24 F1	Charnwood Green	21 C2
Castle Rosse	14 F4	Castleknock Laurels	22 F3	Cedarwood Green	24 F1	Charnwood Grove	21 C2
*Castle Steps (off Castle St)	38 D3	Castleknock Lodge	23 A4	Cedarwood Grove	24 F1	Charnwood Heath	21 C2
Castle Street	67 C2	Castleknock Manor	23 A3 [5]	Cedarwood Park	24 F1	Charnwood Meadows	21 C2
Castle Street (Cork Hill)	38 D3 [3]	Castleknock Meadows	22 F3	Cedarwood Rise	24 F1	Charnwood Park	21 C2
Castle Street (Dalkey)	60 F2	Castleknock Oaks	22 F3	Cedarwood Road	24 F1	*Chatham Court	38 D3
Castle Terrace	3 B2	Castleknock Park	23 A3	Ceder Park	1 B3	(on Chatham Street)	
*Castle Terrace	60 F1	Castleknock Rise	22 E3	Ceder View	1 B3	*Chatham Lane	38 D3
(off Ulverton Road)		Castleknock Road	22 F3	Celbridge	32 D3	(off Chatham Street)	
Castle Terrace	37 C1 [17]	Castleknock Road	23 A4	Celbridge Abbey	31 C4	Chatham Row	38 D3 [35]
(Phibsborough Ave)		Castleknock Vale	22 F3	Celbridge Road	18 D4	Chatham Street	38 D3
*Castle Terrace (off Castle Street)	67 C2	Castleknock View	22 F3	Celbridge Road (Leixlip)	32 F2	*Chaworth Terrace	37 C3
Castle View	44 E1	Castleknock Walk	22 E3	Celbridge Road (Lucan)	33 A2	(Hanbury Lane)	
Castle View	59 A4	Castleknock Way	22 F3	*Celestine Avenue	39 A3	Cheeverstown Road	54 D1
Castle Village	31 C2	Castleknock Wood	22 F3	(off Dermot O'Hurley Ave)		Chelmsford Avenue	38 E4 [8]
Castle Village Avenue	31 C2	Castlelands	60 F1 [16]	Celtic Park Avenue	25 C2	Chelmsford Lane	47 B1 [15]
Castle Village Close	31 C2	Castlelands Grove	60 F1 [12]	Celtic Park Road	25 C2	Chelmsford Road	47 B1
Castle Village Court	31 C2	Castlepark Road	60 E1	Chalet Gardens	34 E1	Chelsea Gardens	26 F4
Castle Village Crescent	31 C2	Castlerosse Crescent	14 F4	Chalfont Avenue	3 B2	Cheltenham Place	38 D4 [13]
Castle Village Drive	31 C2	Castlerosse Drive	14 F4	Chalfont Park	3 B2	Cherbury Court	48 F3
Castle Village Green	31 C2	Castlerosse View	14 F4	Chalfont Place	3 B2	Cherbury Gardens	48 F3
Castle Village Lawns	31 C2	Castleside Drive	46 F3	Chalfont Road	3 A2	Cherbury Mews	48 F3 [4]
Castle Village Park	31 C2	Castletimon Avenue	25 C1	*Chamber Court (Chamber St)	37 C3	Cherbury Park Avenue	34 D2
Castle Village Rise	31 C2	Castletimon Drive	25 C1	Chamber Street	37 C3	Cherbury Park Road	34 D2
Castle Village Walk	31 C2	Castletimon Gardens	25 C1	Champions Avenue	38 E2 [32]	Cherries Road	58 D2
Castle Village Way	31 C2	Castletimon Green	25 C1	Chancery Lane	38 D3	Cherrington Close	64 E3
Castle Village Woods	31 C2	Castletimon Park	25 C1	Chancery Place	38 D2	Cherrington Drive	64 E3
Castle Villas	60 F2	Castletimon Road	25 C1	Chancery Street	38 D2	Cherrington Road	64 E3
Castlebridge	18 D3	Castletown	32 F1	Chanel Avenue	26 E2	Cherry Avenue	22 E3
Castlebrook	57 C1	Castletown Court	32 D3	Chanel Grove	26 E1	Cherry Avenue (Swords)	1 C3
Castlebyrne Park	49 A4	Castletown Drive	32 D3	Chanel Mews	24 D4	Cherry Court	46 F2
Castlecurragh Heath	9 A4	Castletown Grove	32 D3	Chanel Road	26 E2	Cherry Court	64 D1 [2]
Castlecurragh Park	9 B4	Castletown Lawn	32 D3	*Chapel Avenue (off Bath St)	39 A3	Cherry Drive	22 E3
Castlecurragh Vale	9 B4	Castletymon Court	45 B4	Chapel Lane	67 B1	Cherry Garth	48 E4
Castledawson Avenue	48 F3	Castletymon Gardens	45 B4	Chapel Lane (Parnell Street)	38 D2 [13]	Cherry Garth (Swords)	1 B2
Castlefarm	1 C1	Castletymon Green	45 B4	Chapel Lane (Swords)	2 D2	Cherry Grove	45 C2
Castlefarm	64 E3	Castleview	7 B3	Chapel Road	14 D1	Cherry Grove (Swords)	1 B3
Castlefield	55 C2	Castleview	26 E2	Chapelizod	36 E2	Cherry Lawn	22 E3
Castlefield Avenue	55 C1	Castleview	57 C1 [7]	Chapelizod Bypass	36 E2	Cherry Lawns	33 C2
Castlefield Court	21 C2	Castleview Park	3 A3	Chapelizod Court	36 E2	Cherry Orchard Avenue	35 C3
Castlefield Court	55 C1	Castlewarden	51 A	Chapelizod Hill Road	36 E2	Cherry Orchard Court	35 C4
Castlefield Drive	55 C2	Castlewarden North	51 A3	Chapelizod Road	36 F2	Cherry Orchard Crescent	35 C4
Castlefield Green	55 C2	Castlewood	21 C1	Charlemont	25 C3	Cherry Orchard Drive	35 C4
Castlefield Grove	55 C2	Castlewood Avenue	47 A1	Charlemont Avenue	50 D4 [5]	Cherry Orchard Drive	36 D3
Castlefield Lawn	55 C1	Castlewood Close	47 A1 [24]	Charlemont Gardens	38 D4 [20]	Cherry Orchard Green	35 C3
Castlefield Manor	3 B3	*Castlewood Close	47 A1	Charlemont Mall	38 D4	Cherry Orchard Grove	35 C4
Castlefield Manor (Firhouse)	55 C1	(on Castlewood Ave)		Charlemont Parade	38 E1 [5]	Cherry Orchard Parade	35 C4

STREET NAME	PAGE/GRID REFERENCE
Cherry Orchard Way	35 C4 [1]
Cherry Orchard Way	35 C3
Cherry Park	22 E3
Cherry Park (Swords)	1 B3
Cherry Tree Drive	67 C3 [1]
Cherry Wood	64 D1
Cherryfield Avenue	45 C2
Cherryfield Avenue Lr	47 B1
Cherryfield Avenue Upr	47 B1
Cherryfield Close	21 B1
Cherryfield Court	21 B1
Cherryfield Drive	45 C2
Cherryfield Lawn	21 C1
Cherryfield Park	21 C1
Cherryfield Road	45 C2
Cherryfield View	21 B1
Cherryfield Walk	21 B1
Cherryfield Way	46 D4
Cherrymount Crescent	26 D3 [1]
Cherrymount Grove	26 D3 [2]
Cherrymount Park	37 C1 [3]
Cherrywood	32 D3
Cherrywood Avenue	44 D1
Cherrywood Crescent	43 C1
Cherrywood Drive	43 C1
Cherrywood Grove	44 D1
Cherrywood Lawn	43 C2
Cherrywood Park	43 C2
Cherrywood Park	64 D1
Cherrywood Road	64 D2
Cherrywood Villas	44 D1 [6]
Cherrywood Villas	44 D1
Chester Downs	60 D1
Chester Road	47 B1
Chester Square	60 E1 [23]
Chesterfield Avenue	23 B4
Chesterfield Avenue (Phoenix Park)	36 F1
Chesterfield Close	23 B4
Chesterfield Copse	23 B3
Chesterfield Grove	23 B4
Chesterfield Park	23 B3
Chesterfield View	23 B3
Chestnut Court	25 C1 [1]
Chestnut Grove (Ballinteer)	57 B2
Chestnut Grove (Celbridge)	32 D3
Chestnut Grove (Clondalkin)	44 F3
Chestnut Grove (Dunboyne)	7 B3
Chestnut Park	59 A2 [5]
Chestnut Road (Clondalkin)	45 A1
Chestnut Road (Mount Merrion)	48 E3
Christchurch Place	38 D3
Christchurch Square	38 D3 [51]
Church Avenue	25 B3
Church Avenue	14 F2 [2]
Church Avenue (Blanchardstown)	22 F2
Church Avenue (Glasnevin)	25 A3 [2]
Church Avenue (Irishtown)	39 A3
Church Avenue (Killiney)	60 E4
Church Avenue (Rathmines)	47 A1
Church Avenue North (Drumcondra)	25 B3
Church Avenue South (Dolphin's Barn)	37 B3 [22]
Church Avenue West (Church Street)	37 C2 [25]
*Church Avenue (off Irvine Street)	38 F2
Church Court	22 F3
Church Gardens	47 A1
Church Green	46 F1
Church Grove	55 A2
Church Lands	67 C3
Church Lane	25 B3
Church Lane (College Green)	38 D2 [41]
Church Lane (Rathfarnham)	46 F3
Church Lane South	38 D3 [53]
*Church Lane South (off Kevin Street)	38 D3
Church Park	46 F1
Church Park Avenue	46 F1
Church Park Court	46 F1
Church Park Drive	46 F1
Church Park Lawn	46 F1

STREET NAME	PAGE/GRID REFERENCE
Church Park Way	46 F1
*Church Place (off Irvine Terrace)	38 F2
Church Road	2 D2
Church Road	52 E2
Church Road (Bray)	67 C3
Church Road (Celbridge)	32 D4
Church Road (Dalkey)	60 F1
Church Road (East Wall)	38 F1
Church Road (Finglas)	24 D2
Church Road (Killiney)	60 D3
Church Road (Malahide)	3 B3
Church Road (Mulhuddart)	9 A4
Church Road (Sutton)	29 B1
Church Street	37 C2
Church Street (Finglas)	24 E2
Church Street (Howth)	30 D1
Church Street East	38 F2
Church Street New	37 C2 [11]
Church Street Upper	37 C2
Church Terrace	67 C2 [45]
*Church Terrace (off Church Street)	37 C2
Church View (Clondalkin)	44 D2 [1]
Church View (Finglas)	24 D2 [7]
Church View (Harold's Cross)	46 F1
Church Walk	24 D4
Churchfields	47 C2
Churchgate Avenue	39 C1 [1]
Churchill Mews	60 F1 [17]
Churchill Terrace	39 A4 [6]
Churchland's	58 D3
Churchtown	47 B4
Churchtown Avenue	47 B3
Churchtown Close	47 B3
Churchtown Drive	47 B3
Churchtown Road Lower	47 B3
Churchtown Road Upper	47 A4
Churchtown Road Upper	47 B4
Churchview Avenue	60 D3
Churchview Drive	60 D3
Churchview Park	60 D3
Churchview Road	60 D3
Cian Park	25 B4
Cianlea	1 B1
Cill Cais	54 F2
Cill Eanna	26 F2
Cill Manntan Park	67 C2 [9]
Cill Sarain	67 B3
City Quay	38 E2
Citywest Avenue	53 C1
Citywest Road	53 C1
Claddagh Green	35 C3
Claddagh Road	35 C3
Claddagh Terrace	68 D2 [15]
*Claddagh Terrace (On Albert Avenue)	67 C2
Clanawley Road	26 E3
Clanboy Road	26 E3
Clanbrassil Close	37 C4 [17]
Clanbrassil Street Lower	37 C4
Clanbrassil Street Upper	37 C4
Clancarthy Road	26 D3
Clancy Avenue	24 E1
Clancy Road	24 E1
Clandonagh Road	26 D3
Clane Road	31 B4
Clanfadda Wood	48 F3
Clanhugh Road	26 E3
Clanmahon Road	26 E3
Clanmaurice Road	26 D3
Clanmawr	64 E2
Clanmoyle Road	26 D3
Clanranald Road	26 D3
Clanree Road	26 D3
Clanwilliam Place	38 F3
Clanwilliam Square	38 F3 [41]
Clanwilliam Terrace	38 F3 [40]
Clare Hall	14 D4
Clare Lane	38 E3 [14]
Clare Park Villas	25 B3 [3]
Clare Road	25 B3
Clare Street	38 E3
Claremont Avenue	25 A3 [1]
Claremont Close	24 F4

STREET NAME	PAGE/GRID REFERENCE
Claremont Court	24 F4
Claremont Court	39 A4 [21]
Claremont Crescent	24 F4
Claremont Drive	24 F2
Claremont Grove	60 E3
Claremont Lawn	24 F4
Claremont Park	39 A4
Claremont Road (Killiney)	60 E3
Claremont Road (Sandymount)	39 A4
Claremont Road (Sutton)	29 B1
Claremont Terrace	47 C4 [7]
Claremont Villas	60 E1 [4]
Claremount	64 E3
Claremount Pines	59 B4
Claremount Terrace	68 D2 [11]
Clarence Mangan Road	37 C3
*Clarence Mangan Square (off John Dillon St)	38 D3
Clarence Place Great	38 F3 [1]
Clarence St Great North	38 E1 [67]
Clarence St Great Nth	38 E1
*Clarendon Market (off William St)	38 E1
*Clarendon Row (off King St South)	38 D3
Clarendon Street	38 D3
Clareville Court	24 F4 [7]
Clareville Grove	24 F4
Clareville Road	46 F1
Clarinda Manor	50 D4 [22]
Clarinda Manor	60 D1
Clarinda Park East	60 D1
Clarinda Park North	50 D4
Clarinda Road	50 D4
Clarinda Park West	50 D4
Clarke Terrace	37 B3 [16]
Clarkeville Terrace	35 C1 [3]
Claude Road	25 A4
Clayton Terrace	36 E2 [8]
Clearwater Court	24 D3 [1]
Clearwater Cove	49 C4 [31]
Cleggan Avenue	35 C3
Cleggan Park	35 C3
Cleggan Road	35 C3
Clifden Drive	35 C3
Clifden Road	36 D3
Cliff Terrace	60 E1 [18]
Clifton Avenue	49 C4 [11]
Clifton Lane	49 C4 [10]
Clifton Park	64 E2
Clifton Terrace	49 C4 [13]
Cliftonville Road	25 A4
Clinch's Court	38 E1 [7]
Clogher Road	46 E1
Cloghran	1 C4
Cloister Avenue	49 A4
Cloister Court	24 D3
Cloister Gate	49 A4
Cloister Green	49 A4
Cloister Grove	49 A4
Cloister Square	49 A4
Cloister Way	49 A4
Clonard Avenue	57 C2
Clonard Close	57 C2
Clonard Drive	57 C2
Clonard Grove	57 C2
Clonard Lawn	57 C2
Clonard Park	57 C2
Clonard Road (Crumlin)	46 D1
Clonard Road (Sandyford)	57 C2
Clonasleigh	64 E2 [2]
Cloncourt Apts.	8 D3
Clondalkin	44 D1
Clonee	8 D3
Clonfert Road	46 E1
Clonkeen Crescent	59 B2
Clonkeen Drive	59 B2
Clonkeen Grove	59 B2
Clonkeen Lawn	59 B2 [5]
Clonkeen Road	59 B2
Clonlara Road	39 A3 [12]
Clonlea	57 C2
Clonlea Wood	57 C2 [1]
Clonliffe Avenue	38 E1
Clonliffe Gardens	25 B4
Clonliffe Road	25 B4

STREET NAME	PAGE/GRID REFERENCE
Clonmacnoise Grove	46 E1 [4]
Clonmacnoise Road	46 E1
Clonmel Road	25 A2
Clonmel Street	38 D3 [18]
Clonmellon Grove	14 D4 [3]
Clonmore Court	25 A3 [11]
Clonmore Road (Ballybough)	38 E1
Clonmore Road (Goatstown)	48 E4
Clonmore Terrace	38 E1 [6]
Clonmore Villas	38 E1 [39]
Clonrosse Court	26 F1
Clonrosse Drive	26 F1
Clonrosse Park	26 F1
Clonshaugh Avenue	13 A4
Clonshaugh Close	13 B4
Clonshaugh Court	13 B4 [4]
Clonshaugh Court	13 B4
Clonshaugh Crescent	13 A4
Clonshaugh Drive	13 B4
Clonshaugh Glen	13 B4
Clonshaugh Green	13 B4
Clonshaugh Grove	13 B4
Clonshaugh Heights	13 A4
Clonshaugh Lawns	13 B4
Clonshaugh Meadow	13 A4
Clonshaugh Park	13 B4
Clonshaugh Rise	13 B4 [2]
Clonshaugh Road	13 A4
Clonshaugh Walk	13 B4
Clonsilla	21 C2
Clonsilla Close	22 E2
Clonsilla Park	22 E2
Clonsilla Road	22 E2
Clonskeagh	47 C2
Clonskeagh Drive	47 C2 [6]
Clonskeagh Road	47 C2
Clonskeagh Square	47 C2 [7]
Clontarf	39 C1
Clontarf Park	39 C1
Clontarf Road	26 D4
Clonturk Avenue	25 B3 [1]
Clonturk Court	25 B3 [6]
Clonturk Gardens	25 B4 [3]
Clonturk Park	25 B4
Cloonlara Crescent	24 E3
Cloonlara Drive	24 E2
Cloonlara Road	24 E2
Cloonmore Avenue	54 D2
Cloonmore Close	54 E2
Cloonmore Crescent	54 D2
Cloonmore Drive	54 D2
Cloonmore Gardens	54 D2
Cloonmore Green	54 D2
Cloonmore Grove	54 D2
Cloonmore Lawn	54 D2
Cloonmore Park	54 D2
Cloonmore Road	54 D2
Cloragh Road	56 E4
Clover Hill	67 A3
Clover Hill Drive	36 D3
Clover Hill Road	36 D4
Cloverhill Road	35 A4
Cloyne Road	46 E1 [2]
Cluain Aoibhinn	17 C4
Cluain Mhuire	60 D1
Cluain Mhuire (Newtown Park Avenue)	49 B4
Cluain R	34 F2
Club Road	45 A1
Clune Road	24 E1
Cluny Grove	60 D3
Cluny Park	60 E2
Clutterland	42 F1
Clyde Court	38 F4 [19]
Clyde Lane	38 F4
Clyde Road	38 F4
Cnoc Aoibhean	33 B2
Co. Wicklow Lawn Tennis Club	67 C3
Coast Road	15 A4
Coast Road (Malahide)	3 C2
Coates Lane	17 C3 [3]
Coburg Place	38 E1
*Coghill's Court (off Dame Street)	38 D2
Cois Coillte	64 D1 [3]

STREET NAME	PAGE/GRID REFERENCE
Cois Eala	38 D4
Cois Na hAbhann	54 F2
Cois Sleibhe	67 B4
Coke Lane	37 C2 [42]
*Coke Lane (off Arran Quay)	37 C2
Colbert's Fort	44 F4
*Colbert's Fort (off St James Walk)	37 B3
Coldcut Road	35 B2
Coldwell Street	60 D1
Colepark Avenue	36 D3
Colepark Drive	36 D3
Colepark Green	36 D3
Colepark Road	36 D3
Coleraine Street	38 D2
Colganstown	41 B2
Coliemore Road	60 F2
Coliemore Villas	60 F2 [14]
College Crescent	46 D3
College Drive	46 E3
College Fort	22 F4
College Gate	22 F3
College Green	17 C4
College Green	38 D2
College Grove	22 F4
College Lane	38 E3 [19]
College Lane	52 F1
College Manor	25 B4 [8]
College Mews	25 B4 [11]
College Park (Castleknock)	23 A4
College Park (Kimmage)	46 E3
College Park Avenue	57 C2
College Park Close	57 C2
College Park Court	57 C2 [2]
College Park Drive	57 C2 [3]
College Park Grove	57 C2
College Park Way	57 C2
College Road (Castleknock)	22 F4
College Road (Whitechurch Road)	57 A3
College Street	15 A4 [8]
College Street	38 E2
College Street (Baldoyle)	15 A4
College View	55 A1 [6]
College Wood	22 F3
Collegeland	42 F4
Collegeland	52 F1
Collier's Avenue	47 B1 [3]
Colliersland	6 F2
Collins Avenue	25 C2
Collins Avenue East	26 D3
Collins Avenue Extension	25 A2
Collins Avenue West	25 B2
Collins Court	25 C3 [6]
Collins Court	49 A3 [13]
Collins Drive	24 E1
Collins Green	24 E1
Collins Park	26 D3
Collins Place	24 E1
Collins Row	24 E2 [6]
Collinstown Crescent	35 B3 [1]
Collinstown Grove	35 B3
Collinstown Park Community School	35 A3
Collinstown Road	35 A3
Collinswood	25 C2
Colmanstown	51 C2
Colmanstown Lane	51 C2
Colthurst Close	34 F2
Colthurst Crescent	34 F2
Colthurst Gardens	34 F2
Colthurst Green	34 F2
Colthurst Mews	34 F2
Colthurst Park	34 F2
Colthurst Rise	34 F2
Colthurst Road	34 F2
Colthurst Way	34 F2
Comeragh Road	36 F4
Common Little	42 D4
Commons	41 C2
Commons	52 E1
Commons East	2 D2
Commons Little	42 D4
Commons Lower	41 A1
Commons Road	44 D2
Commons Road	64 E2
Commons Street	38 E2
Compass Court	23 C3 [1]
Comyn Place	25 A3 [5]
Con Colbert Road	37 A3
Confey	20 D4
Congress Gardens	60 E1 [2]
Congress Hall	7 B3
Congress Park	7 B31
Connaught Parade	24 F4 [6]
Connaught Place	50 D4 [26]
*Connaught Place (Crofton Road)	50 D4
Connaught Street	24 F4
Connawood Copse	67 B1
Connawood Crescent	67 B1
Connawood Drive	67 B1
Connawood Green	67 B1
Connawood Grove	67 B1
Connawood Lawn	67 B1
Connawood Walk	67 B1
Connawood Way	67 B1
Connolly Avenue	3 A4
Connolly Avenue	37 A3
Connolly Gardens	37 A3 [3]
Connolly's Folly	18 E4
Conor Clune Road	23 C4
Conquer Hill Avenue	39 C1
Conquer Hill Road	39 C1
Constellation Road	12 F4
Constitution Hill	38 D2
Convent Avenue	25 B4
Convent Avenue	68 D3
Convent Close	38 E3 [40]
Convent Court	58 E1 [4]
Convent Lane	4 D4
Convent Lane	46 F4
Convent Place	38 E4 [12]
Convent Road (Blackrock)	49 A4
Convent Road (Clondalkin)	44 E2
Convent Road (Dalkey)	60 F2
Convent Road (Dun Laoghaire)	50 D4
Convent View	68 D2 [23]
Convent View Cottages	24 D4 [2]
Convent View Cottages	44 D2
Convent View Crescent	24 D4 [3]
Convey Way	24 D4
Conway Court	38 F3 [23]
Conyngham Road	37 B2
Cook Street	38 D2
Cooks Road	1 A4
Cookstown	66 E3
Cookstown Estate Road	44 F4
Cookstown Road	44 E4
Cookstown Way	44 E4
Coolamber Court	56 D1 [1]
Coolamber Drive	52 F2
Coolamber Park	56 D1
Coolamber Road	52 F2
Coolatree Close	25 C2
Coolatree Park	25 C2
Coolatree Road	25 C2
Cooldrinagh Lane	33 B1
Cooldrinagh Terrace	33 B1
Cooleen Avenue	25 C1
Coolevin (Ballybrack)	60 D4
Coolevin Road	38 D3 [49]
Cooley Road	36 F4
Coolgariff Road	25 C1
Coolgreena Close	25 C2
Coolgreena Road	25 C1
Coolkill	58 D3
Coolmine	52 F3
Coolmine Boulevard	22 D2
Coolmine Close	22 D2
Coolmine Cottages	9 A4
Coolmine Court	22 E2
Coolmine Green	22 D3
Coolmine Lawn	22 D2
Coolmine Mews	22 D2 [1]
Coolmine Park	22 E2
Coolmine Road	22 E3
Coolmine Woods	22 E2
Coolnevaun	58 E1
Coolock	26 E1
Coolock Drive	26 E1
Coolock Green	26 E1
Coolock Lane (Santry)	12 F4
Coolock Village	26 E1
Coolock Village Close	26 E1
Coolrua Drive	25 C1
Coolwater Lake	53 B2
Coombe Court	37 C3 [62]
Cope Street	38 D2 [22]
Copeland Avenue	26 D4
Copeland Grove	26 D4
Copper Alley (off Lord Edward St)	38 D2 [49]
Copper Beech Grove	67 B2 [6]
Coppinger	49 A4
Coppinger Close	48 F4
Coppinger Glade	48 F4
Coppinger Row	38 D3 [34]
Coppinger Walk	49 A4
Coppinger Wood	48 F4
Corbally Avenue	53 C2
Corbally Close	53 C2
Corbally Down	53 C2
Corbally Drive	53 C2
Corbally Glade	53 C2
Corbally Green	53 C2
Corbally Heath	53 C2
Corbally Lawn	53 C2
Corbally Park	53 C2
Corbally Rise	53 C2
Corbally Square	53 C2
Corbally Vale	53 C2
Corbally Way	53 C2
Corbawn Avenue	64 E2
Corbawn Close	64 F2
Corbawn Court	64 F2
Corbawn Dale	64 F2
Corbawn Drive	64 F2
Corbawn Glade	64 E3
Corbawn Grove	64 F2
Corbawn Lane	64 E2
Corbawn Lawn	64 E3
Corbawn Wood	64 E2
Corduff	22 F1
Corduff Avenue	22 F1
Corduff Close	22 F1
Corduff Cottages	22 E1
Corduff Crescent	22 F1
Corduff Gardens	22 F1
Corduff Green	22 F1
Corduff Grove	9 B4
Corduff Park	9 B4
Corduff Place	22 F1
Corduff Way	22 F1
*Cork Hill (off Dame St)	38 D2
Cork Street	37 C3
Corkagh View	44 D2
Corke Abbey	67 C1
Corke Abbey Avenue	67 B1
Cormac Terrace	46 F2
Corn Exchange Place	38 E2 [24]
Cornelscourt	59 B3
Cornelscourt Hill Road	59 B3
Cornelstown	6 D2
Cornerpark	42 D3
Cornmarket	37 C3
Corr Castle	29 B1
Corr Castle Apts	29 B1 [3]
Corrbridge Terrace (off Claremont Road)	29 B1 [1]
Corrib Road	46 E2
Corrib Road	46 F2
Corrig Avenue	50 D4
Corrig Close	45 B3
Corrig Park	50 D4
Corrig Road (Dalkey)	60 F1
Corrig Road (Dun Laoghaire)	60 D1
Corrig Road (Stillorgan)	58 E2
Corrybeg	46 D4
Cosy Lodge	47 A1 [26]
Coulson Avenue	46 F2
Coultry Avenue	25 B1
Coultry Close	25 A1
Coultry Crescent	12 D4
Coultry Drive	12 D4
Coultry Gardens	12 D4
Coultry Grove	12 E4
Coultry Lawn	12 E4
Coultry Park	12 E4
Coultry Road	12 D4
Coultry Way	25 B1
Coundon Court	60 E4
County Brooks Lawns	66 E2
Court House Square	17 C3 [5]
Courthill Drive	7 B2
Courtlands	59 C3
Courtney Place	38 F1 [8]
Cow Parlour	37 C3 [24]
Cowbooter Lane	30 E2
Cowper Downs	47 A1
Cowper Drive	47 B2
Cowper Gardens	47 B2
Cowper Mews	47 A2 [4]
Cowper Road	47 B2
Cowper Street	37 B1
Cowper Village	47 A2
Cows Lane	38 D2 [48]
Crag Avenue	35 B4
Crag Avenue Business Park	35 B4
Crag Crescent	35 B4
Crag Terrace	35 B4
Craigford Avenue	26 E3
Craigford Drive	26 E3
Craiglands	60 F2 [26]
Craigmore Gardens	49 A3 [5]
Crampton Avenue	38 F4 [16]
*Crampton Court (off Dame St)	38 D2
Crampton Quay	38 D2 [40]
*Crane Lane (off Dame Street)	38 D2
Crane Street	37 C3
Cranfield Place	39 A3
Cranford Court	48 D2
Cranmer Lane	38 F3 [19]
Crannagh	47 C2 [9]
Crannagh Castle	46 F3
Crannagh Court	46 F3
Crannagh Grove	47 A3
Crannagh Park	46 F3
Crannagh Road	46 F3
Crannagh Way	47 A3 [8]
Crannogue Close	11 C4
Crannogue Road	11 C4
Crawford Avenue	25 A4
*Crawford Terrace (off Kings Avenue)	38 E1
Creighton Street	38 E2
Cremona Road	36 E3
Cremore Avenue	24 F3
Cremore Crescent	24 F3
Cremore Drive	24 F3
Cremore Heights	24 F2
Cremore Lawn	24 F3
Cremore Park	25 A3
Cremore Road	24 F3
Cremore Villas	24 F3 [5]
Cremorne	56 D1
Cremorne (Terenure Road East)	46 F2
Crescent Gardens	38 F1 [11]
Crescent House	26 D4 [6]
Crescent Place	26 D4
Crescent Villas	25 A4
Crestfield Avenue	25 B2
Crestfield Close	25 B2
Crestfield Drive	25 B2
Crestfield Park	25 B2
Crestfield Road	25 B2
Crewhill	17 B1
Crinan Strand	38 E2 [31]
Crinken Glen	64 E3
Crinken Lane	64 D4
Crinstown	17 A4
Croaghpatrick Road	24 D4
Crockaunadreenagh	52 E4
Crockshane	52 E3
Crodaun Court	31 C2 [1]
Crodaun Forest Park	32 D2
Crofton Avenue	50 D4
Crofton Mansions	50 D4
*Crofton Mansions (Crofton Rd Dun Laoghaire)	50 D4
Crofton Road	50 D4

STREET NAME	PAGE/GRID REFERENCE		STREET NAME	PAGE/GRID REFERENCE		STREET NAME	PAGE/GRID REFERENCE		STREET NAME	PAGE/GRID REFERENCE	
Crofton Terrace	49	C4 [6]	Curragh Hall Mews	9	B3	Dargle Drive	57	A1	Deerpark Avenue	54	F3
Crofton Terrace	50	D4 [25]	Curragh Hall Road	9	B3	Dargle Heights	67	B2	Deerpark Close	23	A3
Croftwood Crescent	35	C3	Curragh Hall View	9	B3	Dargle Road (Dean's Grange)	59	A1	Deerpark Close	54	F3
Croftwood Drive	35	C3	Curragh Hall Way	9	B3	Dargle Road (Drumcondra)	25	A4	Deerpark Downs	54	F3
Croftwood Gardens	35	C3	Curtlestown	65	B4	*Dargle Terrace	67	B2	Deerpark Drive	23	A3
Croftwood Green	36	D3	Curzon Street	38	D4	(On Lower Dargle Road)			Deerpark Drive	54	F3
Croftwood Grove	35	C3	Cushinstown	6	F1	Dargle Valley	57	A1	Deerpark Green	54	F3
Croftwood Park	36	D3	Cushlawn Avenue	54	F2	Dargle View	57	A1	Deerpark Lawn	23	B3
Croke Villas	38	E1 [68]	Cushlawn Close	54	F3	Dargle View Golf Course	67	C1	Deerpark Lodge	54	F3
Cromcastle Avenue	26	D1	Cushlawn Drive	54	F2	Dargle Wood	56	D1	Deerpark Place	54	F3
Cromcastle Close	26	D1 [2]	Cushlawn Grove	54	F2	Darley Cottages	67	C2 [15]	Deerpark Rise	54	F3
Cromcastle Court	26	D1 [6]	Cushlawn Park	54	F2	Darley Street	37	C4 [40]	Deerpark Road	48	D4
Cromcastle Drive	26	D1	Cushlawn Walk	54	F3	Darley Street	38	D4	Deerpark Road	54	F3
Cromcastle Green	26	D1	Custom House Harbour	38	E2 [27]	Darley's Terrace	37	C3 [9]	Deerpark Road	23	A3
Cromcastle Park	26	D1	Custom House Quay	38	E2	Darling Estate	23	C4	(Castleknock Road)		
Cromcastle Road	26	D1	Cymric Road	39	A3	Dartmouth Lane	38	E4 [6]	Deerpark Square	54	F3
Cromlech Close	62	F2	Cypress Avenue	56	E2 [2]	Dartmouth Place	38	E4 [4]	Deerpark Terrace	54	F3
Cromlech Court	11	C4	Cypress Court	64	E1	Dartmouth Road	38	E4	Deerpark View	54	F3
Cromlech Fields	64	E1	Cypress Drive	46	D3	Dartmouth Square East	38	E4 [16]	Deerpark Way	54	F3
Cromwell's Quarters	37	B3 [3]	Cypress Garth	46	D4	Dartmouth Square North	38	E4 [14]	Del Val Avenue	27	C2
Cromwellsfort Road	45	C2	Cypress Grove North	46	D3	Dartmouth Square South	38	E4 [15]	Del Val Court	27	C2 [2]
Crosbie House	38	E4 [35]	Cypress Grove Road	46	D3	Dartmouth Square West	38	E4 [17]	Delaford Avenue	55	C1
Cross Avenue (Booterstown)	48	F3	Cypress Grove South	46	D4	Dartmouth Terrace	38	E4 [5]	Delaford Drive	55	C1
Cross Avenue (Dun Laoghaire)	50	D4	Cypress Lawn	46	D4	Dartry Cottages	47	B2 [1]	Delaford Grove	55	C1
Cross Lane	17	C3	Cypress Park	46	D4	Dartry Park	47	A2	Delaford Lawn	55	C1
Crosstrees Court	30	D2 [13]	Cypress Road	48	E3	Dartry Road	47	A2	Delaford Park	55	C1
Crosthwaite Park East	60	D1	Cypress Springs	20	D4 [1]	David Park	25	A4	Delbrook Manor	57	C2 [4]
Crosthwaite Park South	60	D1				David Road	25	A4	Delbrook Park	57	C2
Crosthwaite Park West	60	D1	**D**			*Davis Place	37	C3	Delhurst Avenue	21	B1
Crosthwaite Terrace	50	D4 [15]	*Daisy Market (on Parnell Street)	38	D2	(off Thomas Davis St Sth)			Delhurst Court	21	B1 [3]
*Crostick Alley (off Meath St)	37	C3	Dakota Avenue	12	F4	Davitt Park	60	D4	Delhurst Grove	21	B1 [1]
Crotty Avenue	45	C1	Dal Riada	3	C4	Davitt Road	36	F4	*Delhurst Lane	21	B1
*Crow Street (off Dame St)	38	D2	Dalcassian Downs	24	F4	Davitt Road (Bray)	67	C2	Delhurst Mews	21	B1 [2]
*Crown Alley (Off Temple Bar)	38	D2	Dale Close	58	E1 [1]	Dawson Court	48	F3	Delhurst Terrace	21	B1
Croydon Gardens	25	C4	Dale Drive	58	E1	*Dawson Court	38	D3	Delville Road	25	A2
Croydon Green	25	C4	Dale Road	58	E1	(off Stephen St Lower)			Delvin Road	24	F4 [3]
Croydon Park Avenue	25	C4	Dale Tree Avenue	55	B2	Dawson Lane	38	E3 [18]	Delwood Close	22	E3
Croydon Terrace	25	C3 [4]	Dale Tree Drive	55	C2	Dawson Street	38	E3	Delwood Drive	22	E3
Cruagh Avenue	62	E1	Dale Tree Grove	55	C2	De Burgh Road	37	B2 [14]	Delwood Grove	22	E3
Cruagh Close	62	E1	Dale Tree Park	55	C3	De Courcy Square	25	A4 [2]	Delwood Lawn	22	E3
Cruagh Court	62	E1	Dale Tree Road	55	C3	De Selby Close	54	D2	Delwood Park	22	E3
Cruagh Green	62	E1	Dale View	60	E4	De Selby Court	54	D2	Delwood Road	22	E3
Cruagh Rise	62	E1	Dale View Park	60	E4 [2]	De Selby Crescent	54	D2	Delwood Walk	22	E3
Cruagh Wood	62	E1	Dale View Road	1	C1	De Selby Downs	54	D2	Demesne	26	E3
Crumlin	46	D1	Dalepark Road	55	A2	De Selby Drive	54	D2	Denmark Street Great	38	D1
Crumlin Park(off Crumlin Road)	46	D1	Daletree Close	55	C3	De Selby Green	54	D2	Denville Court	60	D4
Crumlin Road	37	B4	Daletree Crescent	55	C2	De Selby Lane	54	D2	Denzille Lane	38	E3
Cuala Grove	68	D3	Daletree Road	55	C2	De Selby Lawns	54	D2	*Derby Square (off Werburgh St)	38	D3
Cuala Road	24	F4	Dalkey	60	F1	De Selby Park	53	C2	Dermot O'Hurley Avenue	39	A3
Cuala Road	68	D3	Dalkey Avenue	60	F2	De Selby Road	54	D2	Derravaragh Road	46	E2
Cuan na Mara	30	D1 [13]	Dalkey Court	60	F2 [23]	De Velara Place	38	D1 [19]	Derry Drive	46	D1
Cuckoo Lane	38	D2	Dalkey Grove	60	F2 [6]	*De Vesci Court (Flats)	49	C4	Derry Park	46	D1
Cuffe Lane	38	D3	Dalkey Park	60	E2	(off Sloperton)			Derry Road	46	D1
Cuffe Street	38	D3	Dalkey Rock	60	F2	De Vesci Terrace	49	C4	Derrynane Gardens	39	A3
Cul na Greine	54	F2	Dalymount	37	C1	Dean Street	38	D3	Derrynane Parade	38	D1 [33]
Cullen's Cottages	49	A4 [7]	Damastown Avenue	8	F3	Dean Swift Green	25	A2	Deselby	54	D2
Cullen's Wood House	38	E4 [37]	Damastown Close	8	F3	Dean Swift Road	25	A2	Desmond Avenue	50	D4 [3]
*Cullenswood Court	47	B1	Damastown Court	9	A3	Dean Swift Square	37	C3	Desmond Cottages	60	F2 [20]
(off Cullenswood Park)			Damastown Drive	8	E3	Deans Court	59	B1 [10]	Desmond Street	38	D4 [2]
Cullenswood Gardens	47	B1	Damastown Green	8	F3	Deans Grange	59	B2	Devenish Road	46	E1
Cullenswood Park	47	B1	Damastown Road	8	E3	Dean's Grange Road	59	B1	Deverell Place	38	E2 [5]
Cullenswood Road	47	B1 [11]	Damastown Road	9	A4	Deansrath Avenue	34	F4	Devery's Lane	25	A4 [4]
Culmore Park	35	C2 [1]	Damastown Walk	8	E3	Deansrath Crescent	43	C1	Devitt Villas	60	E1 [8]
Culmore Road	35	C2	Damastown Way	8	F3	Deansrath Green	43	C1	Devlin's Place	38	E3 [22]
*Cumberland Place North	37	C1	Dame Court	38	D3 [16]	Deansrath Grove	34	F4	Devon Close	59	B1 [11]
(on North Circular Road)			Dame Lane	38	D3 [7]	Deansrath Lawn	34	F4	Devoy Road	37	A3
Cumberland Road	38	E4	Dame Lane	38	D2 [42]	Deansrath Park	43	C1	Dewberry Park	4	D4
Cumberland Street	49	C4	Dame Street	38	D2	Deansrath Road	43	C1	Dexter Terrace	38	E4 [29]
Cumberland Street North	38	E1	Dane Road	11	C4	Deanstown Avenue	24	D2	Diamond Terrace	67	B2 [15]
Cumberland Street South	38	E3 [1]	Danes Court	27	A4	Deanstown Drive	24	D2	Diamond Valley (Apts.)	67	B2
Cumman Naomh Peregríne CLG	22	D1	Danesfort	39	B1	Deanstown Green	24	D2	Digges Lane	38	D3 [38]
Cunningham Drive	60	F2	Daneswell Road	25	A4	Deanstown Park	24	D2	Digges Street Upper	38	D3
Cunningham Road	60	F2	Dangan	41	A2	Deanstown Road	24	D2	*Dillon Place South	38	D3
Curlew Road	36	F4	Dangan Avenue	46	D2	Decies Road	36	E3	(off John Dillon St)		
Curracloe Drive	27	A1 [4]	Dangan Drive	46	D2	Deepdales	67	B4	Dillon's Row	17	C2
Curragh Hall	9	B3	Dangan Park	46	D2	Deerhaven	8	F4	Dingle Road	24	E4
Curragh Hall Avenue	9	B3	Daniel Street	38	D3	Deerhaven Avenue	8	F4	Dispensary Lane (Lucan)	34	D1 [6]
Curragh Hall Close	9	B3	Danieli Drive	26	E2	Deerhaven Close	8	F4	Dispensary Lane (Willbrook)	46	F4
Curragh Hall Court	9	B3	Danieli Road	26	E2	Deerhaven Crescent	8	F4	Distillery Lane	20	D4
Curragh Hall Crescent	9	B3	Dara Court	32	D3	Deerhaven Green	8	F4	Distillery Road	25	B4
Curragh Hall Drive	9	B3	Dara Crescent	32	D3	Deerhaven Park	8	F4	Diswellstown Cottages	22	E4
Curragh Hall Green	9	B3	Dargan Court	68	D2 [6]	Deerhaven View	8	F4	Dixon Villas	60	E1 [9]
Curragh Hall Grove	9	B3	Dargan Street	67	B2 [10]	Deerhaven Walk	8	F4	Docklands Innovation Park	39	A1
Curragh Hall Hall	9	B3	Dargle Crescent	67	B2 [5]	Deerpark	67	B4	Doctor's Lane	17	C3
Curragh Hall Lane	9	B3				Deerpark Avenue	23	A4	Dodder Avenue	55	B2

STREET NAME	PAGE/GRID REFERENCE
Dodder Bank	47 B2 [10]
Dodder Court	55 B2
Dodder Crescent	55 B2
Dodder Dale	46 F4
Dodder Green	55 B2
Dodder Lawn	55 B2
Dodder Park Drive	46 F3 [3]
Dodder Park Grove	46 F3
Dodder Park Road	46 F3
Dodder Road Lower	47 A3
Dodder Terrace	39 A3 [18]
Dodder Vale	47 A3 [13]
Dodder View Cottages	38 F4 [9]
Dodsboro Cottages	33 B2
Dodsboro Road	33 C2
D'Olier Street	38 E2
Dollymount	27 A4
Dollymount Avenue	27 A4
Dollymount Grove	26 F4
Dollymount Park	27 A4
Dollymount Rise	27 A4
Dolly's Grove	5 C2
Dolmen Court	12 D4
Dolphin Avenue	37 C4
Dolphin Court	37 B4 [7]
Dolphin House	37 B4 [1]
*Dolphin Market (off Dolphin's Barn St)	37 B4
Dolphin Park	37 B4 [5]
Dolphin Road	37 B4
Dolphin's Barn	37 B4
Dolphin's Barn Street	37 B4
Dominick Lane	38 D2 [35]
Dominick Place	38 D1
Dominick Street	50 D4
Dominick Street Lower	38 D2
Dominick Street Upper	38 D1
Domville Drive	46 D4
Domville Green	46 D4
Domville Grove	64 E1 [9]
Domville Road	46 D4
Donaghmede	14 E4
Donaghmede Avenue	27 B1
Donaghmede Drive	27 B1
Donaghmede Park	27 B1
Donaghmede Road	27 B1
Donaghmore	18 F3
Donard Road	36 F4
Donmore Green	46 E2
Donnellan Avenue	37 B3 [7]
Donnybrook	47 C1 [23]
Donnybrook	47 C1
Donnybrook Castle	47 C1
Donnybrook Court	47 C1
Donnybrook Green	48 D2 [3]
Donnybrook Manor	47 C1
Donnybrook Mews	47 C1
Donnybrook Road	47 C1
Donnycarney	26 D3
Donnycarney Church	26 D3
Donnycarney Road	26 D3
Donomore Avenue	54 E2
Donomore Crescent	54 E2
Donomore Green	54 E2
Donomore Park	54 E2
Donore Avenue	37 C3
Donore Road	37 C3
Donore Terrace	37 C3 [55]
Donovan Lane	37 C4 [21]
Doon Avenue	37 B1 [6]
Doon Court	11 C4
Doonamana Road	60 D3
Doonanore Park	60 D3
Doonsalla Drive	60 D3
Doonsalla Park	60 D3
Doris Street	38 F3
Dornden Park	48 E2
Dorney Court	64 E3
Dorset Lane	38 D1
*Dorset Place (off Dorset Street Lower)	38 D1
Dorset Street Lower	38 D1
Dorset Street Upper	38 D1
Double Lane	17 C3
Dowland Road	46 D1
Dowling's Court	38 E2 [15]
Downpatrick Road	37 B4
Downpatrick Road	46 E1
Dowth Avenue	24 F4
Drapier Green	24 F2 [1]
Drapier Road	24 F2
Drayton Close	49 B4 [16]
Drimnagh	36 F4
Drimnagh Road	45 C1
Drimnigh Road	14 E3
Drinaghmore	58 F4
Drinaghmore Avenue	58 F4
Drinaghmore Close	58 F4
Drinaghmore Court	58 F4
Droim na Coille Avenue	34 F2
Droim na Coille Court	34 F2
Droim na Coille Place	34 F2
Dromard Road	36 F4
Dromard Terrace	39 A4 [17]
Dromawling Road	25 C2
Drombawn Avenue	25 C2
Dromcarra Avenue	54 E2
Dromcarra Drive	54 E2
Dromcarra Green	54 D2
Dromcarra Grove	54 E2
Dromeen Avenue	25 C2
Dromheath Avenue	9 B4
Dromheath Drive	9 B4
Dromheath Gardens	9 B4
Dromheath Grove	9 B4
Dromheath Park	9 B4
Dromlee Crescent	25 C2
Dromnanane Park	25 C2 [3]
Dromnanane Road	25 C2 [2]
Dromore Road	37 A4
Druid Court	11 C4
Druid Valley	63 C1
Drumahill	58 D1
Drumalee Avenue	37 B1
Drumalee Court	37 B1 [14]
Drumalee Drive	37 B1
Drumalee Grove	37 B1
Drumalee Park	37 B1
Drumalee Road	37 B1
Drumcairn Avenue	54 D1
Drumcairn Drive	54 D1
Drumcairn Gardens	54 D1
Drumcairn Green	54 E1
Drumcairn Park	54 E1
Drumcliffe Drive	24 E4
Drumcliffe Road	24 E4
Drumcondra	25 B4
Drumcondra Park	38 E1 [18]
Drumcondra Road Lower	25 B4
Drumcondra Road Upper	25 B3
Drumfinn Avenue	35 C2
Drumfinn Park	36 D3
Drumfinn Road	36 D2
Drumkeen Manor	60 D3
Drummartin Close	48 D4
Drummartin Crescent	58 D1 [1]
Drummartin Park	58 D1
Drummartin Road	48 D4
Drummartin Terrace	48 D4
*Drummond Place (off Mount Drummond Ave)	37 C4
Drumnigh Wood	14 E3
Drury Street	38 D3 [55]
Drynam Close	2 E4
Drynam Copse	2 E4
Drynam Court	2 D2
Drynam Crescent	2 E3
Drynam Drive	2 E3
Drynam Glen	2 E3
Drynam Green	2 E3
Drynam Grove	2 E3
Drynam Hall	2 E3
Drynam Lane	2 E2
Drynam Place	2 E4
Drynam Rise	2 E4
Drynam Road	2 D2
Drynam Square	2 E3
Drynam View	2 E3
Drynam Walk	2 E3
Drynam Way	2 E3
Drysdale Close	55 A2
Dublin City Service Sports and Social Club	35 B2
Dublin Road	7 C3
Dublin Road	18 D3
Dublin Road	18 F3
Dublin Road	29 A1
Dublin Road	48 F4
Dublin Road (Bray)	67 B1
Dublin Road (Celbridge)	32 D3
Dublin Road (Kilbarrack)	27 C2
Dublin Road (Malahide)	3 A3
Dublin Road (Shankill)	64 E3
Dublin Road (Swords)	1 C3
Dublin Street (Baldoyle)	15 A4
Dublin Street (Swords)	2 D2
Duck Lane	37 C2
Dufferin Avenue	37 C4
Duke Lane Lower	38 E3 [17]
Duke Lane Upper	38 D3 [32]
Duke Row	38 E1 [57]
Duke Street	38 D3
Dun an Oir	54 F2
Dun Aonghasa	54 F2
Dun Emer Drive	57 C1
Dun Emer Park	57 C1
Dun Emer Road	57 C1
Dun Laoghaire	50 D4
Dunard Avenue	37 A1
Dunard Court	37 B1
Dunard Drive	37 B1
Dunard Park	37 B1
Dunard Road	37 B1 [11]
Dunard Road	37 B1
Dunard Walk	37 B1
Dunawley Avenue	44 D1
Dunawley Drive	44 D1
Dunawley Grove	44 D1
Dunawley Way	44 D1
Dunbo Hill	30 D1 [4]
Dunbo Terrace	30 D1 [1]
Dunboy	59 A4
Dunboyne	7 B2
Dunboyne Road	18 D2
Dunbro Lane	11 C1
Dunbur Terrace	67 C2 [21]
Duncairn Avenue	67 C2
Duncairn Terrace	67 C2
Duncarraig	29 B2
Dundaniel Road	26 D1
Dundela Avenue	60 E1
Dundela Crescent	60 E1
Dundela Haven	60 E1 [24]
Dundela Park	60 E1
Dundrum	57 C1
Dundrum By Pass	57 C1
Dundrum Gate Apts	57 C1 [9]
Dundrum Road	47 C3
Dundrum Wood	57 B1
Dunedin Court	59 C1
Dunedin Drive	59 C1 [8]
Dunedin Terrace	59 C1
Dungar Terrace	50 D4 [12]
Dungriffan Road	30 D2
Dungriffan Villas	30 D2 [8]
Dunleary Hill	49 C4
Dunleary Road	49 C4
Dunluce Road	26 E3
Dunmanus Road	24 E4
Dunmore Grove	44 F2
Dunmore Lawn	44 F3
Dunmore Park	44 F2
Dunne Street	38 E1
Dunree Park	26 F1
Dunsandle Court	23 A3
Dunsandle Grove	23 A3
Dunseverick Road	26 E4
Dunsink Avenue	24 D2
Dunsink Drive	24 D2
Dunsink Gardens	24 D2
Dunsink Green	24 D2
Dunsink Lane	23 A2
Dunsink Park	24 D2
Dunsink Road	24 D2
Dunsoghly	23 C1
Dunsoghly Avenue	23 C1
Dunsoghly Close	23 C1
Dunsoghly Court	23 C1
Dunsoghly Drive	23 C1
Dunsoghly Green	23 C1
Dunsoghly Grove	23 C1
Dunsoghly Park	23 C1
Dunstaffnage Hall Apts	58 F1 [6]
Dunville Avenue	47 B1
Durham Place	60 D1 [18]
Durham Road	39 B4
Durrow Road	46 E1
Dwyer Park	67 C1

E

STREET NAME	PAGE/GRID REFERENCE
Eagle Hill	49 A3 [15]
Eagle Hill Avenue	46 F2 [4]
Eagle Park	26 D1
Eagle Terrace	57 C1 [3]
*Eagle Terrace (Dalkey) (Sorento Rd)	60 F2
Eagle Valley	66 E4
Eaglewood	59 C2 [5]
Eaglewood House	59 C2 [5a]
Eaglewood Mews	59 C2 [5b]
Earl Place	38 D2 [19]
Earl Street North	38 D2
Earl Street South	37 C3
Earls Court	37 B1
Earls Court	46 F2 [15]
Earlscroft	67 C4
Earlsfort	34 F3
Earlsfort Avenue	34 F3
Earlsfort Close	34 F3
Earlsfort Court	34 F2
Earlsfort Drive	34 F3
Earlsfort Gardens	34 F2
Earlsfort Green	34 F3
Earlsfort Grove	34 F3
Earlsfort Lane	34 F3
Earlsfort Lawn	34 F2
Earlsfort Meadows	34 F2
Earlsfort Park	34 F2
Earlsfort Rise	34 F3
Earlsfort Road	34 F2
Earlsfort Terrace	38 E4
Earlsfort Vale	34 F3
Earlsfort View	34 F3
Earlsfort Way	34 F3
East Pier (Dun Laoghaire)	50 E3
East Pier (Howth)	30 D1
East Road	38 F2
East Wall	38 F1
East Wall Road	38 F1
Eastmoreland Lane	38 F4 [4]
Eastmoreland Place	38 F4 [1]
Easton Park	19 C4
Easton Road	32 F1
Eastwood	23 C2 [1]
Eaton Brae	47 A3
Eaton Brae	64 E2
Eaton Court	46 F2 [22]
Eaton Court	68 D3 [1]
Eaton Hall	46 F2 [18]
Eaton Place	49 B4
Eaton Road	46 F2
Eaton Square (Monkstown)	49 B4
Eaton Square (Terenure)	46 F2
Eaton Wood Avenue	64 E3
Eaton Wood Court	64 E3
Eaton Wood Green	64 E3
Eaton Wood Grove	64 E3
Ebenezer Terrace	37 C3 [53]
Eblana Avenue	50 D4
Eblana Villas (Lr Grand Canal St)	38 F3 [2]
*Eblana Villas (off Arbour Hill)	37 B2
Eccles Court	38 D1 [20]
Eccles Place	38 D1
Eccles Street	38 D1
Echlin Street	37 C3
Eden Avenue	57 A1
Eden Court	57 A1
Eden Crescent	57 A1

STREET NAME	PAGE/GRID REFERENCE
Eden Grove	57 A1
Eden Park	60 D1
Eden Park Avenue	58 D1
Eden Park Drive	48 D4
Eden Park Road	58 D1
Eden Quay	38 E2
Eden Road Lower	60 D1
Eden Road Upper	60 D1
*Eden Terrace (Botanic Ave)	25 A4
Eden Terrace (Dun Laoghaire)	60 D1
Eden Villas	60 D1 [5]
Edenbrook Court	56 F1 [5]
Edenbrook Drive	46 E4
Edenbrook Park	46 E4
Edenmore Avenue	26 F1
Edenmore Crescent	27 A2
Edenmore Drive	26 F2
Edenmore Gardens	26 F2
Edenmore Green	26 F2
Edenmore Grove	26 F2
Edenmore Park	26 F2
Edenvale Road	47 B1
Edenwood	48 D4 [1]
Edgewood	25 B4 [10]
Edgewood Lawns	22 E1
Edmondsbury Court	34 E1 [1]
Edmondstown	56 E3
Edmondstown Green	56 E2
Edmondstown Road	56 E3
Edward Road	68 D3
*Edward Terrace	60 F2
(Off Nerano Rd)	
Edwards Court	56 E2
Edwin Court	60 E2 [5]
Effra Road	47 A1
Eglington Road	67 C2 [3]
Eglinton Court	47 C1
Eglinton Park (Donnybrook)	47 C1
Eglinton Road	47 C1
Eglinton Square	47 C1 [13]
Eglinton Terrace (Donnybrook)	47 C1
Eglinton Terrace (Dundrum)	47 C4
*Eglinton Terrace	38 D1
(Royal Canal Bank)	
Eglinton Wood	47 C1 [22]
Elderberry	34 D3
Elderwood Road	35 B2
*Elford Terrace	37 C3
(off Donore Avenue)	
Elgin Heights	67 A4
Elgin Road	38 F4
Elgin Wood	67 A4
Elizabeth Street	25 B4
Elkwood	56 E1
Ellenfield Road	25 C2
Ellensborough	54 F3
Ellensborough Avenue	54 F3
Ellensborough Close	54 F3
Ellensborough Copse	54 F3
Ellensborough Court	54 F3
Ellensborough Crescent	54 F3
Ellensborough Dale	54 F3
Ellensborough Downs	54 F3
Ellensborough Grange	54 F3
Ellensborough Green	54 F3
Ellensborough Grove	54 F3
Ellensborough Lane	54 F3
Ellensborough Meadows	54 F3
Ellensborough Park	54 F3
Ellensborough Rise	54 F3
Ellensborough View	54 F3
Ellensborough Walk	54 F3
Ellesmere	58 F2 [4]
Ellesmere Avenue	37 B1
Ellis Court	37 C2 [44]
Ellis Quay	37 C2
Ellis Street	37 C2 [38]
Ellis Street (off Benburb Street)	37 C2
Elm Close	34 E3
Elm Court	34 E3
Elm Court	54 D2
Elm Dene	34 E3
Elm Drive	34 E3
Elm Drive	54 D2
Elm Green	34 E3
Elm Grove	34 E3
Elm Grove	54 D2
Elm Mount Avenue	25 C2
Elm Mount Close	26 D2
Elm Mount Court	26 D3
Elm Mount Crescent	26 D2
Elm Mount Drive	26 D2
Elm Mount Grove	26 D2
Elm Mount Heights	26 D2
Elm Mount Lawn	26 D2
Elm Mount Park	26 D2
Elm Mount Rise	26 D2
Elm Mount Road	26 D2
Elm Mount View	26 D2
Elm Park	48 D1
Elm Park (Celbridge)	32 D3
Elm Park Terrace	46 F2
Elm Road (Donnycarney)	26 D3
Elm Road (Fox & Geese)	45 A1
Elm Vale	34 E3
Elm Way	34 E3
Elm Way	57 A2 [3]
Elm Wood	34 E3
Elmbrook	34 E2
Elmbrook Crescent	34 E2
Elmbrook Lawn	34 E2
Elmbrook Walk	34 E2
Elmcastle Close	45 A3
Elmcastle Court	45 A3
Elmcastle Drive	45 A3
Elmcastle Green	45 A3
Elmcastle Park	45 A3
Elmcastle Walk	45 A3
Elmdale Crescent	35 C3
Elmdale Drive	35 C3
Elmdale Park	35 C3
Elmfield Avenue	14 D4
Elmfield Close	14 D4 [2]
Elmfield Close	14 D4
Elmfield Close	14 E4
Elmfield Court (Clondalkin)	44 E1
Elmfield Court	14 D4
Elmfield Drive	14 E4
Elmfield Green	14 D4
Elmfield Grove	14 D4
Elmfield Lawn	14 E4
Elmfield Rise	14 D4
Elmfield Vale	14 E4
Elmfield Walk	14 D4
Elmfield Way	14 D4
Elmgrove	49 A4
Elmgrove	60 D4
Elmgrove Terrace	67 C2 [22]
Elmpark Apts	48 E2
Elmpark Avenue	47 B1
Elms	48 F3
Elmwood	21 B1
Elmwood Avenue Lower	47 B1
Elmwood Avenue Upper	47 B1
Elmwood Court	1 C1 [1]
Elmwood Drive	1 C1
Elmwood Park	1 C1
Elmwood Road	1 C1
Elner Court	4 D4
Elton Court	26 F1 [1]
Elton Court	32 F1
Elton Court	60 E1
Elton Court (Dunboyne)	7 C3
Elton Drive	27 A1
Elton Drive (Dunboyne)	7 B2
Elton Drive (Dunboyne)	7 C2
Elton Grove (Dunboyne)	7 C3
Elton Park (Coolock)	27 A1
Elton Park (Dalkey)	60 E1
Elton Walk	27 A1 [1]
Ely Close	55 B3
Ely Crescent	55 B3 [1]
Ely Drive	55 B3
Ely Green	55 B3 [3]
Ely Grove	55 B3 [2]
Ely Place	38 E3
Ely Place Upper	38 E3 [31]
Ely View	55 B3
Embassy Lawn	47 C2
Emerald Cottages	38 F3 [34]
Emerald Place	38 E2 [23]
Emerald Square	37 B3 [20]
Emerald Street	38 F2 [1]
Emerald Terrace	37 C3 [63]
Emmet Court	37 A3
Emmet Road	37 A3
Emmet Square	48 F3
Emmet Street (Harold's Cross)	37 C4 [10]
Emmet Street (Nth Circular Rd)	38 E1
Emmet Street (Sallynoggin)	60 D1 [4]
Emor Street	38 D4
Emorville Avenue	38 D4
Empress Place	38 E1
*Enaville Avenue	38 F1
(off Annesley Place)	
Enaville Road	38 F1 [10]
*Engine Alley (off Meath St)	37 C3
English Row	32 D4
Ennafort Avenue	26 F2
Ennafort Court	26 F3
Ennafort Drive	26 F3
Ennafort Grove	26 F2
Ennafort Park	26 F3
Ennafort Road	26 F2
Ennel Avenue	26 F2
Ennel Court	64 E1 [6]
Ennel Drive	26 F2
Ennel Park	26 F2
Ennis Grove	39 A3 [19]
Enniskerry	66 D3
Enniskerry Road (Phibsborough)	25 A4 [3]
Enniskerry Road (Sandyford)	58 D4
Erne Place	38 F3 [21]
Erne Place Little	38 E3 [4]
Erne Place Lower	38 E2 [2]
Erne Street Lower	38 E2
Erne Street Upper	38 E3
Erne Terrace Front	38 E3 [20]
Erne Terrace Rere	38 E3 [21]
Errigal Gardens	45 C1
Errigal Road	36 F4
Errigal Road	45 C1
Erris Road	24 E4
Esker Drive	34 D2
Esker Lane	34 E1
Esker Lane	34 E2
Esker Lawns	34 D1
Esker Lodge	34 E2
Esker Lodge Avenue	34 E2
Esker Lodge Close	34 E2
Esker Lodge View	34 E2
Esker Meadow	34 E2
Esker Meadow Close	34 E2
Esker Meadow Court	34 E2
Esker Meadow Green	34 E2
Esker Meadow Grove	34 E2
Esker Meadow Lawn	34 E2
Esker Meadow Rise	34 E2
Esker Meadow View	34 E2
Esker Park	34 E2
Esker Pines	34 E1
Esker Road	34 D3
Esker South	34 D3
Esker Villas	47 A1 [11]
Esker Wood Close	34 E2
Esker Wood Court	34 E2
Esker Wood Drive	34 E2
Esker Wood Grove	34 E2
Esker Wood Rise	34 E2
Esker Wood View	34 E2
Esker Wood Walk	34 E2
Esker Woods	34 E2
Esmond Avenue	25 C4
Esmonde Terrace	67 B2 [18]
Esplanade Terrace	68 D2 [3]
Esposito Road	45 C1 [5]
*Essex Gate (off Essex Quay)	38 D2
Essex Quay	38 D2
Essex Street East	38 D2
*Essex Street West	38 D2
(off Fishamble St)	
Estate Avenue	48 E1
Estate Cottages	38 F3 [16]
(Northumberland Rd)	
Estate Cottages (Shelbourne Rd)	38 F4 [13]
Estuary Court	2 D1
Estuary Road	2 F2
Estuary Row	3 B2
Eugene Street	37 C3
Eustace Street	38 D2
Everton Avenue	37 B1 [3]
Evora Crescent	30 D1 [12]
Evora Park	30 D1
Evora Terrace	30 D1 [2]
Ewington Lane	37 B3 [12]
Exchange Hall	54 F1
*Exchange Street Lower	38 D2
(off Wood Quay)	
*Exchange Street Upper	38 D2
(off Lord Edward St)	
Exchequer Street	38 D3

F

STREET NAME	PAGE/GRID REFERENCE
Faber Grove	59 B1 [9]
Fade Street	38 D3 [39]
Fagan's Lane	17 C3 [2]
Fair Haven	3 B2 [1]
Fairbrook Lawn	46 F4
Fairfield Avenue	38 F1
Fairfield Park	47 A2
Fairfield Road	25 A4
Fairgreen	53 B2
Fairgreen Court	67 C2 [50]
Fairgreen Road	67 B2 [11]
Fairgreen Terrace	67 C2 [32]
Fairhaven	3 B2
Fairlawn Park	24 E2
Fairlawn Road	24 E2
Fairlawns	60 E2 [6]
Fairview	25 C4
Fairview Avenue Lower	25 C4
Fairview Avenue Upper	25 C4
Fairview Court	25 C4 [14]
Fairview Green	25 C4 [7]
Fairview Lawn	64 D1
Fairview Passage	25 C4 [10]
Fairview Strand	25 C4
Fairview Terrace	25 C4 [11]
Fairways	46 E4
Fairway's Avenue	24 F2
Fairway's Green	24 F2
Fairways Grove	24 E2
Fairway's Park	24 F2
Fairy Castle	61 C2
Fairyhill	59 A1
Fairyhill	67 B3
Faith Avenue	38 F1
Falcarragh Road	25 B2
Falls Road	64 D2
Farmhill Drive	47 C4
Farmhill Park	47 C4
Farmhill Road	47 C4
Farmleigh Avenue	58 F1
Farmleigh Close	58 F1
Farmleigh Park	58 F1
Farney Park	39 A4
Farnham Crescent	24 E2
Farnham Drive	24 E2
Farrenboley Cottages	47 B3
Farrenboley Park	47 B3
Fassaroe	66 F3
Fassaroe Lane	67 A3
Father Colohan Terrace	67 C2 [1]
Father Mathew Square	37 C2 [26]
Fatima Mansions	37 B3 [23]
(off James's Walk)	
Fatima Terrace	67 C2
Faughart Road	46 E1 [3]
Faughs G.A.A. Club	45 C4
Faulkner's Terrace	37 B3 [37]
Faussagh Avenue	24 E4
Faussagh Road	24 F4
Feltrim	3 A4
Feltrim Hall	2 E3
Feltrim Road	2 F4
Fenian Street	38 E3
Fergus Road	46 F2
Ferguson Road	25 A3
Fern Court	55 B3

STREET NAME	PAGE/GRID REFERENCE
Fernbrook	67 B1 [6]
Ferncarrig Avenue	58 D3
Ferncarrig Court	58 D3
Ferncarrig Rise	58 D3
Ferncourt Avenue	55 B3
Ferncourt Close	55 B3
Ferncourt Crescent	55 B3 [5]
Ferncourt Drive	55 B3 [4]
Ferncourt Green	55 B3
Ferncourt Park	55 B3
Ferncourt View	55 B3
Ferndale	8 F4
Ferndale	21 C1
Ferndale	55 A2
Ferndale Avenue	24 F2
Ferndale Court	67 B1
Ferndale Glen	64 D3
Ferndale Hill	64 D4
Ferndale Road	24 F2
Ferndale Road (Bray)	67 A1
Ferndale Road (Shankill)	64 D3
Fernhill Avenue	45 C3
Fernhill Park	45 C3
Fernhill Road	45 C3
Fernleigh	22 D3
Fernleigh (Estate)	22 D3
Fernleigh Close	22 D3
Fernleigh Court	22 D3
Fernleigh Crescent	22 D4
Fernleigh Dale	22 D3
Fernleigh Dene	22 D4
Fernleigh Drive	22 D3
Fernleigh Grange	22 D3
Fernleigh Green	22 D3
Fernleigh Grove	22 D4
Fernleigh Heath	22 D4
Fernleigh Lawn	22 D3
Fernleigh Park	22 D3
Fernleigh Place	22 D4
Fernleigh Vale	22 D3
Fernleigh View	22 D4
Fernley Court	38 D3
Ferns Road	46 E1
Fernvale Drive	46 D1
Fernwood Avenue	54 E1
Fernwood Close	54 E1
Fernwood Court	54 E1
Fernwood Lawn	54 E1
Fernwood Park	54 E1
Fernwood Way	54 E1
Ferrard Road	46 F2
Ferrycarrig Avenue	13 B4
Ferrycarrig Drive	13 B4
Ferrycarrig Green	13 B4 [3]
Ferrycarrig Park	13 B4
Ferrycarrig Road	13 B4
Ferryman's Crossing	38 F2 [14]
Fertullagh Road	24 F4 [3]
Fettercairn Road	44 E4
Fey Yerra	58 F2 [8]
Fforster	34 E2
Fforster Close	34 E2
Fforster Court	34 E2
Fforster Lawn	34 E2
Fforster Park	34 E2
Fforster Walk	34 E2
Field Avenue	45 C1 [1]
Field's Terrace	47 B1 [5]
Fieldview Cottages	49 A4 [6]
Fiery Lane	62 D4
Findlater Building (Apts.)	30 D1 [16]
Findlater Place	38 D2 [25]
Findlater Street (Dun Laoghaire)	60 E1 [7]
Findlater Street (Nth Circular Rd)	37 B2 [10]
Fingal Place	37 C1 [5]
Fingal Street	37 C3 [11]
Fingallians GAA Club/ Lawless Memorial Park	2 E2
Finglas	24 D1
Finglas East	24 E1
Finglas Park	24 E1
Finglas Place	24 E2
Finglas Road	24 E2
Finglas Road Old	24 F3
Finglas South	24 E2
Finglas West	24 D1
Finglaswood Road	24 D2
Finn Street	37 B2 [12]
Finneber Fort	24 E2
Finneber Fort Square	24 E2
Finnscourt	34 D3
Finnsgreen	34 D3
Finnsgrove	34 D3
Finnslawn	34 D3
Finnspark	34 D3
Finnstown Fairways	34 D3
Finnsvale	34 D3
Finnsview	34 D3
Finnswalk	34 D3
Finnswood	34 D3
Finsbury Green	47 B4
Finsbury Park	47 B4
Firgrove	60 E4 [8]
Firhouse	55 C1
Firhouse Road	55 B2
Firhouse Road West	55 A2
First Avenue	44 F4
First Avenue (Sarsfield Road)	36 F3
First Avenue (Seville Place)	38 F2 [3]
Fishamble Street	38 D2
Fishermans Wharf	39 A2 [1]
Fitzgerald Park	59 C1 [6]
Fitzgerald Street	38 D4 [1]
Fitzgibbon Lane	38 E1 [21]
Fitzgibbon Street	38 E1
Fitzmaurice Road	24 F2
Fitzmaurice Road (City West)	52 F2
Fitzpatrick's Cottages	46 F1 [6]
Fitzroy Avenue	25 B4
Fitzwilliam Court	38 E3 [38]
Fitzwilliam Court	48 E3
Fitzwilliam Lane	38 E3
Fitzwilliam Place	38 E3
Fitzwilliam Place North (Grangegorman)	37 C2 [23]
Fitzwilliam Quay	39 A3
Fitzwilliam Square East	38 E3
Fitzwilliam Square North	38 E3
Fitzwilliam Square South	38 E3
Fitzwilliam Square West	38 E3
Fitzwilliam Street (Ringsend)	39 A3 [2]
Fitzwilliam Street Lower	38 E3
Fitzwilliam Street Upper	38 E3
Fitzwilliam Terrace	68 D2 [21]
Fleet Street	38 D2
Fleming Road	25 A3
Fleming's Place	38 E4
Flemingstown Park	47 B4
Flemming House	38 E4 [39]
Fleurville	49 A4
Floraville Avenue	44 E1
Floraville Drive	44 E2
Floraville Estate	44 E1
Floraville Lawn	44 E1
Florence Road	67 C2
Florence Street	38 D4 [17]
Florence Terrace	67 C2 [39]
*Florence Terrace (Leeson Park Avenue)	38 E4
Florence Villas	67 C2 [40]
*Florence Villas (Sandymount)	39 A4
Flower Grove	60 D2
Foley Street	38 E2
Fontenoy Street	38 D1
Fontenoy Terrace	68 D3
Fonthill Abbey	56 F1 [3]
Fonthill Park	56 F1
Fonthill Road (Clondalkin)	35 A2
Fonthill Road (Rathfarnham)	56 F1
Fonthill Road South	44 E2
Forbes Lane	37 C3
Forbes Street	38 F2
Forest Avenue	1 B3
Forest Avenue	45 A3
Forest Boulevard	1 B3
Forest Close	45 A3
Forest Court	1 B2
Forest Crescent	1 B3
Forest Dale	1 B2
Forest Drive	1 B3
Forest Drive	45 A3
Forest Fields	1 C3
Forest Fields Road	1 C3
Forest Green	1 B3
Forest Green	45 A3
Forest Grove	1 B3
Forest Hills	52 E2
Forest Hills	52 E2
Forest Lawn	45 A2
Forest Park	1 B2
Forest Park	32 F1
Forest Park	45 A3
Forest Road	1 B4
Forest View	1 B3
Forest Walk	1 C3
Forest Way	1 C3
Fort Ostman	37 B4
Fortescue Lane	38 D4
Fortfield Avenue	46 E3
Fortfield Court	46 E3 [2]
Fortfield Drive	46 E3
Fortfield Gardens	47 A2
Fortfield Grove	46 E3
Fortfield Park	46 E3
Fortfield Road	46 E2
Fortfield Road	46 E3
Fortfield Terrace	47 A2
Forth Road	38 F1
Forthill Court	56 F1 [6]
Fortlawn Avenue	22 D1
Fortlawn Drive	22 D1
Fortlawn Park	22 D1
Fortlawns	60 E2
Fortrose Park	46 E4
Fortunestown	53 C1
Fortunestown Close	53 C1
Fortunestown Crescent	53 C1
Fortunestown Lane	53 B1
Fortunestown Road	54 D2
Fortunestown Way	54 D1
Fortview Avenue	39 C1
Foster Place North	38 E1 [41]
Foster Place South (College Grn)	38 D2 [38]
Foster Terrace	38 E1
Fosterbrook	48 E2
Fosters Avenue	48 E3
Fountain Place	37 C2
Fountain Road	37 B2
Fourth Avenue	44 F4
Fourth Avenue (Seville Place)	38 F2 [8]
*Fownes Street Lower (off Temple Bar)	38 E4
Fownes Street Upper	38 D2 [47]
*Fownes Street Upper (off Dame St)	38 D2
Fox and Geese	45 A1
Foxborough Avenue	34 E3
Foxborough Close	34 F3
Foxborough Court	34 F3
Foxborough Crescent	34 F3 [2]
Foxborough Downes	34 E3
Foxborough Drive	34 E3
Foxborough Gardens	34 F3
Foxborough Glen	34 F3
Foxborough Green	34 F3
Foxborough Grove	34 F3
Foxborough Hall	34 F3 [1]
Foxborough Heights	34 F3
Foxborough Hill	34 E3
Foxborough Lane	34 F3
Foxborough Lawn	34 F3
Foxborough Manor	34 F3
Foxborough Meadows	34 E3
Foxborough Park	34 E3
Foxborough Place	34 E3
Foxborough Rise	34 E3
Foxborough Road	34 E3
Foxborough Row	34 F3
Foxborough Walk	34 F3
Foxborough Way	34 E3
Foxdene Avenue	34 F3
Foxdene Drive	34 F3
Foxdene Gardens	34 F3
Foxdene Green	34 F3
Foxdene Grove	34 F3
Foxdene Park	34 F3
Foxes Grove	64 E3
Foxfield	34 D3
Foxfield Avenue	27 B2
Foxfield Crescent	27 B2
Foxfield Drive	27 B2
Foxfield Green	27 B2
Foxfield Grove	27 B2
Foxfield Heights	27 B2
Foxfield Lawn	27 B2
Foxfield Park	27 B2
Foxfield Road	27 B2
Foxfield St John	27 B2
Foxford	34 F2
Foxhill Avenue	27 A1
Foxhill Close	27 A1
Foxhill Court	27 A1
Foxhill Crescent	27 A1
Foxhill Drive	27 A1
Foxhill Green	14 D4
Foxhill Grove	27 A1
Foxhill Lawn	27 A1
Foxhill Park	27 A1
Foxhill Way	27 A1
Foxpark	34 D3
Foxrock	59 A3
Foxrock Avenue	59 A2
Foxrock Close	59 B2
Foxrock Court	59 A2
Foxrock Crescent	59 B2
Foxrock Green	59 A2
Foxrock Grove	59 B2
Foxrock Manor	58 F2
Foxrock Mount	59 A2 [4]
Foxrock Park	59 A2
Foxrock Wood	59 B2
Fox's Lane	27 B2
Foxwood	2 D2
Foxwood	34 D3
Foyle Road	25 C4
Fr Kit Court	46 D1 [3]
Francis Street	37 C3
Frankfort	47 B4 [10]
Frankfort Avenue	47 A2
Frankfort Cottages	38 E1
Frankfort Court	46 F2 [8]
Frankfort Flats	46 F2 [9]
Frankfort Park	47 B4
Frascati Court	49 A3
Frascati Park	49 A3
Frascati Road	49 A3
Frederick Court	38 D1 [46]
Frederick Lane North	38 D1 [14]
Frederick Street North	38 D1
Frederick Street South	38 E3
French Park	9 B2
Frenchman's Lane	38 E2 [20]
Friar's Walk	44 E1 [5]
Friarsland Avenue	47 C3 [3]
Friarsland Crescent	47 C3
Friarsland Road	47 C3
Friary Avenue	37 C2 [6]
Friary Grove	37 C2 [41]
*Friary Grove (off Friary Avenue)	37 C2
Friel Avenue	36 D4
Fumbally Lane	38 D3
Furry Park	26 E3
Furry Park Court	26 E3
Furry Park Road	26 E3
Furze Road	36 E1
Furze Road	58 E2

G

STREET NAME	PAGE/GRID REFERENCE
Gables	27 A1 [6]
Gael Na Trionóide CLG	14 E3
Gaelic Street	38 F1 [6]
Gainsborough Avenue	2 F3
Gainsborough Close	2 F3
Gainsborough Court	2 F3
Gainsborough Crescent	2 F3
Gainsborough Downs	2 F3

STREET NAME	PAGE/GRID REFERENCE	
Gainsborough Green	2	F3
Gainsborough Lawn	2	F3
Gainsborough Park	2	F3
Gallaun Road	11	C4
Galloping Green	58	F1
Galloping Green	59	A1 [9]
Gallows Hill	1	C2
Galmoy Road	24	F4
Galtrim Park	67	C2
Galtrim Road	67	C2
Galtymore Close	36	F4
Galtymore Drive	37	A4
Galtymore Park	36	F4
Galtymore Road	37	A4
Gandon Close	46	F1 [9]
Gandon Mews	34	D1 [10]
Garden Lane	37	C3 [21]
*Garden Terrace (off Clanbrassil St Upper)	37	C4
Garden View	38	D4 [42]
Gardiner Lane	38	E1
Gardiner Place	38	D1
Gardiner Row	38	D1 [40]
Gardiner St Middle	38	E1
Gardiner Street Lower	38	E1
Gardiner Street Upper	38	D1
Garnett Hall	7	A2
Garnett Vale	7	A2
Garrynisk Close	44	F3
Garrynisk Road	44	F3
Garryowen Road	36	E3
Gartan	2	E1
Gartan Avenue	25	A4
Gartan Court	2	E1
Gartan Drive	2	E1
Garter Lane	53	B1
Garville Avenue	47	A2
Garville Avenue Upper	46	F2
Garville Court	47	A2 [10]
Garville Drive	47	A2 [6]
*Garville Drive (off Garville Ave)	47	A2
Garville Lane	47	A2
Garville Place	47	A2 [5]
Garville Road	47	A2
Gas Yard Lane	3	B2
Gateway Avenue	25	A1
Gateway Court	25	A1
Gateway Crescent	25	A1
Gateway Gardens	25	A1
Gateway Mews	25	A1
Gateway Place	25	A1
Gateway View	25	A1
Gaybrook Lawns	3	A3
Gazelle Avenue	9	B2
Gazelle Lane	9	B2
Gazelle Mews	9	B2
Gazelle Terrace	9	B2
Gazelle Walk	9	B2
Geoffrey Keating Road	37	C3 [30]
*George Reynolds Flats (off Oliver Plunkett Ave)	39	A3
George's Avenue (Blackrock)	49	A3
George's Dock	38	E2 [36]
George's Hill	38	D2 [6]
George's Lane	37	C2 [3]
George's Place	38	D1 [43]
George's Place (Blackrock)	49	A3 [6]
George's Place (Dun Laoghaire)	50	D4
George's Quay	38	E2
Georges Road	24	E1 [1]
George's Street Great North	38	D1
George's Street Great South	38	D3
George's Street Lower (Dun Laoghaire)	50	D4
George's Street Upper (Dun Laoghaire)	50	D4
Georgian Hamlet	15	A4
Georgian Village	23	A4
Gerald Street	38	F3 [9]
Geraldine Court	17	C3 [4]
Geraldine Street	38	D1
Geraldstown Woods Apts	12	D4 [1]
Gertrude Terrace	67	B2 [25]
Gilbert Road	37	C4 [12]
Gilford Avenue	39	B4
Gilford Court	39	A4 [10]
Gilford Drive	39	A4
Gilford Park	39	A4
Gilford Place	38	E1 [30]
Gilford Road	39	A4
Gilford Terrace	39	B4 [1]
Giltspur Brook	67	C3
Giltspur Heights	67	B4
Giltspur Lane	67	B4
Giltspur Wood	67	B3
Glandore Park	59	C1
Glandore Road	25	C3
Glasanaon Court	24	E2
Glasanaon Park	24	E2
Glasanaon Road	24	E2
Glasaree Road	24	E2
Glasaree Court	24	E2
Glasilawn Avenue	24	F2
Glasilawn Road	24	F2
Glaslyn	26	D4
Glasmeen Road	24	F2
Glasmore Park	1	C1
Glasnamana Place	24	F2 [2]
Glasnamana Road	24	F2
Glasnevin	24	F3
Glasnevin Avenue	24	F1
Glasnevin Court	24	E3
Glasnevin Downs	24	F3
Glasnevin Drive	25	A1
Glasnevin Hill	25	A3
Glasnevin North	24	F1
Glasnevin Oaks	24	F3 [3]
Glasnevin Park	24	F1
Glasnevin Woods	24	E3
Glasson Court	47	B3
Glasthule Buildings	60	E1 [11]
Glasthule Road	60	E1
Gleann na Rí	64	D1
Gleann na Smol	49	B4
Gleann na Smol	54	F2
Glebe	41	C3
Glebe	52	D3
Glebe View	24	E2 [7]
Gledswood Avenue	47	C3
Gledswood Close	47	C3
Gledswood Drive	47	C3 [5]
Gledswood Park	47	C3
Glen Avenue	59	B3
Glen Close	59	B3
Glen Dale	59	B3
Glen Drive	59	B3
Glen Druid	64	E1 [11]
Glen Easton (Estate)	19	B4
Glen Easton Avenue	19	B4
Glen Easton Court	19	B4
Glen Easton Gardens	19	B4
Glen Easton Grove	19	B4
Glen Easton Manor	19	B4
Glen Easton Park	19	B4
Glen Easton Rise	19	B4
Glen Easton Woods	19	B4
Glen Ellan Avenue	1	C1
Glen Ellan Close	1	C1
Glen Ellan Court	1	C1
Glen Ellan Crescent	1	C1
Glen Ellan Drive	1	C1
Glen Ellan Gardens	1	C1
Glen Ellan Green	1	C1
Glen Ellan Grove	1	C1
Glen Ellan Park	1	C1
Glen Ellan Pines	1	C1
Glen Ellan Walk	1	C1
Glen Garth	59	B3
Glen Grove	59	B3
Glen Lawn Drive	59	B3
Glen na Smol	67	C4
Glen Terrace	60	E1 [10]
Glen Walk	59	B3
Glenaan Road	25	B2
Glenabbey Road	48	E4
Glenacre	62	E4
Glenageary Avenue	60	D2
Glenageary Court	60	D2
Glenageary Hall	60	E2
Glenageary Lodge	60	D2
Glenageary Park	60	D2
Glenageary Road Lower	60	D1
Glenageary Road Upper	60	D1
Glenageary Woods	60	D1
Glenagle Grove	64	E1
Glenalbyn Road	58	F1
Glenalua Heights	60	E3
Glenalua Road	60	E3
Glenalua Terrace	60	E3
Glenamuck Cottages	63	A1
Glenamuck North	62	F1
Glenamuck Road	59	B4
Glenamuck Road	62	F2
Glenamuck Road	63	A2
Glenann	46	F4 [4]
Glenanne	46	E2
Glenard Avenue	37	B1 [5]
Glenard Avenue	67	C2
Glenard Hall	47	C3 [7]
Glenarm Avenue	25	B4
Glenarriff Road	23	C3
Glenart Avenue	48	F4
Glenaulin	36	D2
Glenaulin Drive	36	D2
Glenaulin Park	36	D2
Glenaulin Road	35	C2
Glenavon Park	64	D1
Glenavy Park	46	E2
Glenayle Road	26	F1
Glenayr Road	46	F2
Glenbeigh Park	37	B1
Glenbeigh Road	37	B1
Glenbourne Avenue	58	F4
Glenbourne Close	58	F4
Glenbourne Crescent	58	F4
*Glenbourne Drive	58	F4
Glenbourne Green	58	F4
Glenbourne Grove	58	F4
Glenbourne Park	58	F4
Glenbourne Road	58	F4
Glenbourne View	58	F4
Glenbourne Walk	58	F4
Glenbourne Way	58	F4
Glenbower Park	47	B4 [1]
Glenbrian Hall	26	D4 [8]
Glenbrook	67	B3 [6]
Glenbrook Park	46	F4
Glenbrook Road	23	C3
Glenburgh Terrace	67	B2 [2]
Glencairn	58	E3
Glencairn Avenue	58	E3
Glencairn Chase	58	E3
Glencairn Close	58	E3
Glencairn Copse	58	E3
Glencairn Court	58	E4
Glencairn Crescent	58	E3
Glencairn Dale	58	E3
Glencairn Drive	58	E3
Glencairn Garth	58	E3 [1]
Glencairn Glade	58	E3
Glencairn Glen	58	F4
Glencairn Green	58	E3
Glencairn Grove	58	F4
Glencairn Heath	58	E3 [2]
Glencairn Heath	58	E3
Glencairn Heights	58	E3
Glencairn Oaks	58	E3
Glencairn Park	58	E3
Glencairn Place	58	E3
Glencairn Rise	58	E3
Glencairn Road	58	E3
Glencairn Thicket	58	F3
Glencairn View	58	E3
Glencairn Walk	58	E3
Glencairn Way	58	E3
Glencar Road	37	B1 [2]
Glencarr Court	64	E1 [8]
Glencarr Lawn	64	E1
Glencarraig	29	B1
Glencarrig Court	55	B2
Glencarrig Drive	55	B2
Glencarrig Green	55	B2
Glencloy Road	25	B2
Glencorp Road	25	C2
Glencourt Estate	67	B3
Glencullen	61	C3
Glencullen	62	E4
Glendale	20	D4
Glendale Drive	67	C3
Glendale Meadows	20	E4
Glendale Park	46	D3
Glendalough Road	25	A4 [6]
*Glendenning Lane (off Wicklow Street)	38	D3
Glendhu Park	23	C3
Glendhu Road	23	C3
Glendoher Avenue	56	F1
Glendoher Close	56	E1
Glendoher Drive	56	F1
Glendoher Park	56	E1
Glendoher Road	56	E1
Glendoo Close	45	B3
Glendown Avenue	46	D3
Glendown Close	46	D3
Glendown Court	46	D3
Glendown Crescent	46	D3
Glendown Drive	46	D3
Glendown Green	46	D3
Glendown Grove	46	D3
Glendown Lawn	46	D3
Glendown Park	46	D3
Glendown Road	46	D3
Glendun Road	25	B2
Glenealy Downs	8	F4
Glenealy Road	37	B4
Gleneaston	19	B4
Gleneaston Close	19	B4
Gleneaston Crescent	19	B4
Gleneaston Drive	19	B4
Gleneaston Green	19	B4
Gleneaston Lawns	19	B4
Gleneaston Square	19	B4
Gleneaston View	19	B4
Gleneaston Way	19	B4
Glenfarne Road	26	F1
Glenfield Avenue	35	A2
Glenfield Close	35	A2
Glenfield Drive	35	A2
Glenfield Grove	35	A2
Glenfield Park	35	A2
Glengara Close	60	D1 [15]
Glengara Park	60	D1
Glengariff Parade	38	D1 [64]
Glengarriff Crescent	38	D1 [18]
Glengarriff Parade	38	D1
Glenhill Avenue	24	E2
Glenhill Court	24	E2
Glenhill Drive	24	E2
Glenhill Grove	24	E2
Glenhill Road	24	E2
Glenhill Villas	24	E2 [2]
Glenlucan	67	B2
Glenlyon	55	C2
Glenlyon Crescent	55	C2
Glenlyon Grove	55	C2
Glenlyon Park	55	C2
Glenmalure Park	37	B3 [13]
Glenmalure Square	47	B2
*Glenmalure Villas (Rialto)	37	B3
Glenmaroon Park	35	C2
Glenmaroon Road	35	C2
Glenmore Court	56	F2
Glenmore Park	56	F2
Glenmore Road	37	B1 [1]
Glenmurry Park	45	C3 [2]
Glenomena Grove	48	E2
Glenomena Park	48	E2
Glenpark Close	35	B1
Glenpark Drive	35	B1
Glenpark Road	35	B1
Glenshane Close	54	D1
Glenshane Crescent	54	D1
Glenshane Drive	54	D1
Glenshane Gardens	54	D1
Glenshane Green	54	D1
Glenshane Grove	54	D1
Glenshane Lawns	54	D1
Glenshane Park	54	D1
Glenshesk Road	25	C2

STREET NAME	PAGE/GRID REFERENCE	STREET NAME	PAGE/GRID REFERENCE	STREET NAME	PAGE/GRID REFERENCE	STREET NAME	PAGE/GRID REFERENCE
Glenside Villas	35 C1 [2]	Graham Court	38 D1 [13]	Grangemore Road	14 D4	Greenmount Lane	37 C4
Glenthorn	67 B3	Graham's Row	38 D1 [54]	Grangewood	59 C1	Greenmount Lawns	46 F2
Glenties Drive	24 D2	Graigue Court	11 C4	(Kill O' The Grange)		Greenmount Lodge	62 F2
Glenties Park	24 D2	Granby Lane	38 D1	Granite Hall	60 D1 [7]	Greenmount Road	46 F2
Glentow Road	25 B2	Granby Place	38 D2	Granite Place	38 F4 [10]	Greenmount Square	37 C4 [14]
Glentworth Park	27 A1 [2]	Granby Row	38 D1	Granite Terrace	36 F3 [11]	Greenore Terrace	38 F3 [26]
Glenvale	34 E3	Grand Canal Docks	38 F3	Granitefield	59 C3	Greenpark Road	33 C2
Glenvar Park	48 F3	Grand Canal Place	37 C3 [2]	Granitefield	60 D3	Greenridge Court	22 E1
Glenvara Park	55 C2	Grand Canal Quay	38 F3	Grantham Place	38 D4	Greentrees Drive	45 C2
Glenview	60 D3	Grand Canal Street Lower	38 F3	Grantham Street	38 D4	Greentrees Park	45 C2
Glenview	66 D3	Grand Canal Street Upper	38 F3	Grant's Row	38 E3 [5]	Greentrees Road	45 C2
Glenview Drive	55 B1	Grand Canal View	37 A3	Granville Close	60 D3	Greenview	14 E2
Glenview Lawns	55 B1	Grand Parade	38 E4	Granville Crescent	60 D3 [2]	Greenville Avenue	37 C4 [11]
Glenview Park	55 B1	Grange Abbey Crescent	14 E4	Granville Park	59 A1	*Greenville Parade (Blackpitts)	37 C3
Glenville Avenue	22 E2	Grange Abbey Drive	14 E4	Granville Road (Cabinteely)	59 C3	Greenville Place	37 C4 [35]
Glenville Court	22 E3	Grange Abbey Grove	14 E4	Granville Road (Deans Grange)	59 A2	Greenville Road	49 B4
Glenville Drive	22 E3	Grange Abbey Road	14 E4	Grattan Court	31 C4	Greenville Terrace	37 C4
Glenville Garth	22 E3	Grange Avenue	14 F4	Grattan Court East	38 F3 [28]	Greenwood Avenue	14 D4
Glenville Green	22 E2	Grange Brook	56 F2	Grattan Crescent	36 F3	Greenwood Close	14 D4
Glenville Grove	22 E2	Grange Close	27 C1	Grattan Hall	14 E4	Greenwood Court	14 D4
Glenville Lawn	22 E2	Grange Close	59 C3	Grattan Lodge	14 E4	Greenwood Drive	14 D4
Glenville Road	22 E3	Grange Cottages	58 F1 [3]	Grattan Parade	25 A4	Greenwood Park	14 D4
Glenville Terrace	47 C4 [8]	Grange Cottages	59 B1 [6]	Grattan Place	38 F3 [29]	Greenwood Walk	14 D4
Glenville Way	22 E2	Grange Court	57 A1	Grattan Street	38 E3	Greenwood Way	14 D4
Glenwood	67 B2	Grange Crescent	59 B2	Gray Square	37 C3 [41]	Grenville Lane	38 D1 [15]
Glenwood Road	26 F1	Grange Downs	57 A1	*Gray Street (off Meath St)	37 C3	Grenville Street	38 D1
Glin Avenue	13 B4	Grange Drive	27 C1	Great Western Avenue	37 C1 [18]	Greygates	48 E4 [1]
Glin Crescent	13 B4	Grange Grove	59 B1 [2]	Great Western Square	37 C1 [8]	Greygates	48 E4
Glin Drive	13 B4	Grange Hall	57 B3	Great Western Villas	37 C1 [9]	Grey's Lane	30 D2
Glin Grove	13 B4	Grange Hall (Apts.)	27 A2	Greeg Court	38 D2	Greythorn Park	60 D1
Glin Park	13 B4	Grange Manor	34 D3	Greek Street	38 D2	Griffeen	34 E3
Glin Road	13 B4	Grange Manor Avenue	57 A1	Green Acre Court	56 D1	Griffeen Avenue	34 D3
Gloucester Diamond	38 E1 [52]	Grange Manor Close	57 A1	Green Hallows Quarries	30 D3	Griffeen Glen Avenue	34 E3
*Gloucester Lane (off Sean McDermott Street Lower)	38 E1	Grange Manor Drive	57 A1	Green Isle Court	44 D2 [2]	Griffeen Glen Boulevard	34 E3
		Grange Manor Grove	57 A1	Green Lane	31 A2	Griffeen Glen Chase	34 E3
Gloucester Place	38 E1 [25]	Grange Manor Road	57 A1	Green Lane (Leixlip)	19 C4	Griffeen Glen Court	34 F3
Gloucester Place Lower	38 E1 [53]	Grange Parade	27 C1	Green Oak Drive	52 F2	Griffeen Glen Crescent	34 E3
Gloucester Place Lower	38 E1 [54]	Grange Park (Baldoyle)	14 F4	Green Park (Rathgar)	47 B3	Griffeen Glen Dene	34 E3
Gloucester Place Upper	38 E1 [24]	Grange Park (Cornelscourt)	59 B2	Green Park Road	67 B2	Griffeen Glen Drive	34 E3
Gloucester Street South	38 E2	Grange Park (Willbrook)	56 F1	Green Road (Blackrock)	48 F3	Griffeen Glen Green	34 E3
Glovers Alley	38 D3 [28]	Grange Park Avenue	27 A2	Green Street	38 D2	Griffeen Glen Grove	34 E3
*Glovers Court (off York Street)	38 D3	Grange Park Close	27 B2	Green Street East	38 F2	Griffeen Glen Lawn	34 E3
Goatstown	48 D4	Grange Park Crescent	27 B2	Green Street Little	38 D2 [8]	Griffeen Glen Park	34 E3
Goatstown Avenue	47 C4	Grange Park Drive	27 A2	Greencastle Avenue	26 E1	Griffeen Glen Road	34 D3
Goatstown Road	47 C4	Grange Park Green	27 B2	Greencastle Crescent	26 E1	Griffeen Glen Road	34 E3
*Godfrey Place (off Oxmanstown Road)	37 B1	Grange Park Grove	27 A2	Greencastle Drive	13 B4	Griffeen Glen Vale	34 E3
		Grange Park Rise	27 B1	Greencastle Parade	26 F1	Griffeen GlenWay	34 E3
Gofton Hall	24 E1 [2]	Grange Park Road	27 A2	Greencastle Road	26 E1	Griffeen Way	34 E2
Golden Ball	62 F2	Grange Park View	27 B1	Greendale Avenue	27 C2	Griffin Rath Hall	18 D4
Golden Lane	38 D3	Grange Park Walk	27 A2	Greendale Court	27 B2 [2]	Griffin Rath Manor	18 D4
Goldenbridge Avenue	37 A3	Grange Rise	14 F4	Greendale Road	27 B2	Griffith Avenue	25 B3
Goldenbridge Gardens	37 A3 [4]	Grange Road (Baldoyle)	14 F4	Greenfield Close	17 C4	Griffith Close	24 F2
Goldenbridge Terrace	37 A3 [5]	Grange Road (Marley Park)	57 A2	Greenfield Crescent	48 D2	Griffith Court	25 C4
Goldenbridge Walk	36 F4	Grange Road (Rathfarnham)	46 F4	Greenfield Drive	18 D4	Griffith Downs	25 B3
Goldenbridge Walk	37 A3 [16]	Grange Road (The Priory)	56 F1	Greenfield Manor	48 D2 [4]	Griffith Drive	24 F2
Goldsmith Street	38 D1	Grange View Court	43 B1	Greenfield Park	48 D2	Griffith Hall	25 C3
Goldsmith Terrace	67 C2 [25]	Grange View Close	43 B1	Greenfield Park	55 C2	Griffith Lawns	25 A3
Gordon Avenue	59 A3	Grange View Green	43 B1	*Greenfield Place (off Mount Drummond Ave)	37 C4	Griffith Parade	24 F2
Gordon Place	38 D4 [23]	Grange View Grove	43 B1			Griffith Road	24 F2
Gordon Street	38 F3	Grange View Lawn	43 B1	Greenfield Road (Mount Merrion)	48 E3	Griffith Square	37 C4 [22]
Gorsefield Court	26 F2 [1]	Grange View Park	43 B1			Grosvenor Avenue	68 D3 [3]
Gort na Mona Drive	59 B3	Grange View Road	43 B1	Greenfield Road (Sutton)	29 B1	Grosvenor Court	26 E4
Gortbeg Avenue	24 E3	Grange View Walk	43 B1	Greenfort Avenue	35 A2	Grosvenor Court	46 D3
Gortbeg Drive	24 E3	Grange View Way	43 B1	Greenfort Close	35 A2	Grosvenor Lane	47 A1
Gortbeg Park	24 E3	Grange View Wood	43 B1	Greenfort Crescent	35 A2	Grosvenor Lodge	47 A1
Gortbeg Road	24 E3	Grange Way	27 C1	Greenfort Drive	35 A2	Grosvenor Park	47 A1 [7]
Gortmore Avenue	24 E2	Grange Wood (Ballinteer)	57 A2	Greenfort Gardens	35 A2	Grosvenor Place	47 A1
Gortmore Drive	24 E2	Grangebrook Avenue	56 F2	Greenfort Lawns	35 A2	Grosvenor Road	47 A1
Gortmore Park	24 E3	Grangebrook Close	56 F2	Greenfort Park	35 A2	Grosvenor Square	47 A1
Gortmore Road	24 E3	Grangebrook Park	56 F2	Greenhills	45 B3	Grosvenor Terrace (Dalkey)	60 F2 [17]
Gosworth Park	60 E1	Grangebrook Vale	56 F2	Greenhills Boys A.F.C.	45 C2	Grosvenor Terrace (Dun Laoghaire)	49 C4 [9]
Gowrie Park	60 D1	Grangefield	57 B3	Greenhills Park	45 C2		
Grace O'Malley Drive	30 D2	Grangegorman Lower	37 C2	Greenhills Road	45 A4	*Grosvenor Villas (Dalkey) (Off Sorrento Rd)	60 F2
Grace O'Malley Road	30 D2	Grangegorman Upper	37 C1	Greenhills Sports and Leisure	45 C2		
Grace Park Avenue	25 B4	*Grangegorman Villas (Grangegorman Upper)	37 C1	Greenlands	58 D2	Grosvenor Villas (Rathmines)	47 A1
Grace Park Court	25 C2			Greenlawns	13 B4 [1]	Grotto Avenue	48 F2
Grace Park Gardens	25 B4	Grangemore	14 E4	Greenlea Avenue	46 E2	Grotto Place	48 F2
Grace Park Heights	25 C3	Grangemore Avenue	14 D4	Greenlea Drive	46 E2	Grove Avenue	3 C3
Grace Park Manor	25 B3	Grangemore Court	14 D4	Greenlea Grove	46 E2	Grove Avenue (Finglas)	24 E1
Grace Park Meadows	25 C3	Grangemore Crescent	14 D4	Greenlea Park	46 E3	Grove Avenue (Harold's Cross)	38 D4 [47]
Grace Park Road	25 C3	Grangemore Drive	14 E4	Greenlea Place	46 F2 [12]	Grove Avenue (Mount Merrion)	48 F4
Grace Park Terrace	25 C3	Grangemore Grove	14 E4	Greenlea Road	46 E3		
Gracefield Avenue	26 C2	Grangemore Lawn	14 E4	Greenmount Avenue	37 C4 [9]	Grove Court	1 A2 [1]
Gracefield Road	26 E2	Grangemore Park	14 E4	Greenmount Court	37 C4 [19]	Grove Court	36 F4 [4]
Grafton Street	38 D3	Grangemore Rise	14 D4			Grove House Gardens	48 F4 [5]

STREET NAME	PAGE/GRID REFERENCE
Grove Lane	13 C4
Grove Lawn	48 F4
Grove Lawns (Malahide)	3 C3
Grove Paddock	48 F4
Grove Park	13 C4
Grove Park (Rathmines)	38 D4
Grove Park Avenue	24 F1
Grove Park Crescent	24 F1
Grove Park Drive	24 F1
Grove Park Road	24 F1
Grove Road (Finglas)	24 E1
Grove Road (Malahide)	3 C3
Grove Road (Rathmines)	38 D4
Grove Wood	24 E1
Grovedale	63 B2
Guild Street	38 F2
Guilford Terrace	64 E3 [1]
Gulistan Cottages	47 A1
Gulistan Place	47 A1
Gulistan Terrace	47 A1
Gurteen Avenue	36 D3
Gurteen Park	36 D3
Gurteen Road	36 D2

H

STREET NAME	PAGE/GRID REFERENCE
Hacketsland	64 E1
Haddington Lawns	60 E2
Haddington Park	60 E2
Haddington Place	38 F3 [18]
Haddington Road	38 F3
Haddington Terrace	50 D4 [7]
Haddon Court	39 B1 [1]
Haddon Park	26 D4 [5]
Haddon Road	26 E4
Hadleigh Court	23 A3
Hadleigh Green	23 A3 [2]
Hadleigh Park	23 A3
Hagan's Court	38 E3 [39]
Haigh Terrace	50 D4
Hainault Drive	59 B3
Hainault Grove	59 B3 [2]
Hainault Lawn	59 B3 [3]
Hainault Park	59 A3
Hainault Road	59 A3
Halliday Road	37 C2
Halliday Square	37 B2 [2]
Halston Street	38 D2
Hamilton Court (Dunboyne)	7 B3 [3]
*Hamilton Court (off Strand St Little)	38 D2
Hamilton Hall	7 B3
Hamilton Street	37 C4 [1]
Hammond Lane	37 C2
Hammond Street	37 C3 [56]
Hampstead Avenue	25 A2
Hampstead Court	25 A2
Hampstead Park	25 A3
Hampton Court	36 F3 [16]
Hampton Crescent	48 E3
Hampton Estate	26 F4
Hampton Green	37 B1
Hampton Park	48 E3
Hampton Square	37 B1
Hamwood	6 F3
Hanbury Lane (Lucan)	34 D1 [3]
Hanbury Lane (The Coombe)	37 C3
Hanlon's Lane	61 B1
Hannaville Park	46 F2
Hanover Lane	38 D3 [1]
Hanover Quay	38 F2
Hanover Square	38 D3 [47]
Hanover Street East	38 E2
Hanover Street West	37 C3 [47]
Hansfield	8 E4
Hansted Crescent	34 D4
Hansted Park	34 D4
Hansted Road	34 D4
Harbour Court	38 E2 [18]
Harbour Crescent	60 F1
Harbour Master Place	38 E2 [34]
Harbour Road (Dalkey)	60 F1
Harbour Road (Dun Laoghaire)	50 D4
Harbour Road (Howth)	30 D1
Harbour Terrace	49 C4 [8]
Harbour View	30 D1 [6]
Harcourt Lane	38 D4 [14]
Harcourt Lodge	37 A3 [22]
Harcourt Road	38 D4
Harcourt Street	38 D3
Harcourt Terrace	38 E4
*Harcourt Villas (off Dundrum Rd/Mulvey Pk)	47 C3
Hardebeck Avenue	45 C1
Hardiman Road	25 A3
*Hardwicke Arch (off Hardwicke St)	38 D1
Hardwicke Lane	38 D1 [45]
Hardwicke Place	38 D1 [12]
Hardwicke Street	38 D1
Harelawn Avenue	35 A3
Harelawn Crescent	35 A3
Harelawn Drive	35 A2
Harelawn Green	35 A3
Harelawn Grove	35 A2
Harelawn Park	35 A2
Harlech Crescent	48 D3
Harlech Downs	47 C3
Harlech Grove	48 D3
Harlech Villas	47 C3 [4]
Harman Street	37 C3 [54]
Harmonstown Road	26 F2
Harmony Avenue	47 C1 [5]
Harmony Row	38 E3 [23]
Harold Bridge Court	37 C4 [36]
*Harold Crescent (off Eden Rd Lower)	60 E1
Harold Road	37 C2
Harold Ville Avenue	37 B3
Harold's Cross	46 F1
Harold's Cross Cottages	37 C4 [18]
Harold's Cross Cottages	38 D4 [54]
Harold's Cross Road	46 F1
Harold's Grange Road	57 B3
Harrington Street	38 D4
Harrison Row	46 F2
Harristown	5 A2
Harry Street	38 D3 [17]
Hartstown	21 B1
Hartstown Road	21 C1
Harty Avenue	45 C1
Harty Court	45 C1 [8]
*Harty Court (off Daniel Street)	38 D3
Harty Place	38 D3
Harvard	48 D3
Hastings Street	38 F3 [5]
Hastings Terrace	60 E1 [12]
Hatch Lane	38 E4 [2]
Hatch Place	38 E4 [13]
Hatch Street Lower	38 E4
Hatch Street Upper	38 D4
Hatter's Lane	37 C4 [15]
Havelock Square	38 F3
Havelock Terrace	39 A3 [17]
Haven View	3 B2 [2]
Haverty Road	25 C4
Hawkins Street	38 E2
Hawthorn Avenue	38 F1
Hawthorn Drive	57 B1 [2]
Hawthorn Lawn	22 F3
Hawthorn Lodge	22 F3
Hawthorn Manor	59 A1 [4]
Hawthorn Park	1 C2
Hawthorn Road	44 F1
Hawthorn Road	67 B1
Hawthorn Terrace	38 F1
Hawthorn View	32 D2
Hawthorns Road	58 D2
Hayden's Lane	34 D3
Haydens Park	34 D3
Haydens Park Avenue	34 D3
Haydens Park Close	34 D3
Haydens Park Dale	34 D3
Haydens Park Drive	34 D3
Haydens Park Glade	34 D3
Haydens Park Green	34 D3
Haydens Park Grove	34 D3
Haydens Park Lawn	34 D3
Haydens Park View	34 D3
Haydens Park Walk	34 D3
Haydens Park Way	34 D3
Haymarket	37 C2
Haymarket House	37 C2
Hayworth Drive	21 B1
Hayworth View	21 B1 [5]
Hazel Avenue	58 D1
Hazel Court	14 F2 [7]
Hazel Grove	14 F2
Hazel Grove	54 D2
Hazel Lawn	22 E2
Hazel Lawn	59 C2 [4]
Hazel Park	46 E2 [2]
Hazel Road	26 D3
Hazel Villas	58 D1
Hazelbrook	45 B4
Hazelbrook Apartments	46 E2 [7]
Hazelbrook Court	46 E2
Hazelbrook Drive	46 E2
Hazelbrook Road	46 E2
Hazelbury Green	8 E4
Hazelbury Park	8 E4
Hazelcroft Gardens	24 E2
Hazelcroft Park	24 E2
Hazelcroft Road	24 E2
Hazeldene	47 C1
Hazelgrove Court	54 E2
Hazelhatch	41 B1
Hazelhatch Road	41 C3
Hazelwood (Bray)	67 B2
Hazelwood (Shankill)	64 E2
Hazelwood Avenue	21 C1
Hazelwood Bank	44 D2
Hazelwood Close	44 D2
Hazelwood Court	21 C1
Hazelwood Court	26 D1
Hazelwood Crescent	21 C1
Hazelwood Crescent	44 D2
Hazelwood Drive	26 D2
Hazelwood Green	21 C1
Hazelwood Grove	26 E1
Hazelwood House	38 D4
Hazelwood Lane	44 D2
Hazelwood Park	26 E1
Hazelwood View	44 D2
Headford Grove	47 B4
Healthfield Road	46 F2
*Healy Street (off Rutland Place North)	38 E1
Heaney Avenue	35 C4
Heany Avenue	60 F2 [19]
Heath Square	24 E1 [3]
Heather Close	57 A2
Heather Drive	57 A2
Heather Gardens	4 D4
Heather Grove (Ballinteer)	57 B2
Heather Grove (Palmerston)	35 B4
Heather Lawn	57 A2
Heather Park	57 B2
Heather Road	57 A2
Heather Road	58 E2
Heather View Avenue	54 F2
Heather View Close	54 F2
Heather View Drive	54 F2
Heather View Lawn	54 F2
Heather View Park	54 F2
Heather View Road	54 F2
Heather Walk	4 D4
Heatherwood	67 B4
Heathfield	49 B4 [17]
*Heatley Villas (on Pearse Road)	59 C2
Heidelberg	48 D3
Hempenstal Terrace	39 B4 [5]
Hendrick Place	37 C2 [9]
Hendrick Street	37 C2
Henley Court	47 B4 [8]
Henley Park	47 B4
Henley Villas	47 B4
Henrietta Lane	38 D1
Henrietta Place	38 D2
Henrietta Street	38 D2
Henry Place	38 D2 [16]
Henry Road	36 D4
Henry Street	38 D2
Herbert Avenue	48 E1
Herbert Cottages	38 F4 [4]
Herbert Crescent	22 F2 [1]
Herbert Lane	38 E3 [41]
Herbert Park	38 F4
Herbert Park	67 B3
Herbert Park Lane	38 F4
Herbert Park Mews	47 C1
Herbert Place (Baggot Street Lower)	38 E3
*Herbert Place (off Bath St)	39 A3
Herbert Road	67 B3
Herbert Road (Blanchardstown)	22 F2
Herbert Road (Sandymount)	39 A4
Herbert Street	38 E3
Herbert View	67 B2 [26]
Herberton Drive	37 B4
Herberton Park	37 B3 [15]
Herberton Road	37 B4
Hermitage Avenue (Grange Road)	56 F1
Hermitage Close (Grange Road)	56 F1
Hermitage Court (Grange Road)	57 A1
Hermitage Crescent (Lucan)	34 F1
Hermitage Downs	57 A1
Hermitage Drive (Grange Road)	56 F1
Hermitage Garden (Lucan)	34 F1
Hermitage Green (Lucan)	34 F1
Hermitage Grove (Grange Road)	56 F1
Hermitage Lawn (Grange Road)	56 F1
Hermitage Manor (Lucan)	34 F1
Hermitage Park (Grange Road)	56 F1
Hermitage Park (Lucan)	34 F1
Hermitage Place (Lucan)	34 F1
Hermitage Road (Lucan)	34 F1
Hermitage Valley (Lucan)	34 F1
Hermitage View (Grange Road)	56 F1
Hermitage Way (Lucan)	34 F1
Heronford Lane	63 C2
Heuston Square	37 A3 [11]
*Hewardine Terrace (off Killarney Street)	38 E1
Heytesbury Lane	38 F4
Heytesbury Street	38 D4
Hibernian Avenue	38 F1 [5]
Hibernian Terrace	36 E2 [3]
High Park	25 C2
High Street	38 D3
High Street	55 A1 [2]
Highdownhill	51 C1
Highfield Avenue (Dundrum)	57 A2
Highfield Close	1 C2
Highfield Court	47 A2 [3]
Highfield Crescent	1 C2
Highfield Downs	1 C2
Highfield Drive	57 A2
Highfield Green	1 C2
Highfield Grove	47 A2
Highfield Lawn	1 C2
Highfield Park	33 A1
Highfield Park	47 B3
Highfield Road	47 A2
Highland Avenue	59 B3
Highland Grove	59 B3
Highland Lawn	59 B3
Highland View	59 B3
Highridge Green	58 E1
Highthorn Park	59 C1
Highthorn Woods	59 C1 [10]
Hill Cottages	60 E3 [1]
Hill Court	14 F1
Hill Drive	3 B3
Hill Street	38 D1
Hill View (Ballinteer)	57 B1
Hill View Court	57 B1
Hillbrook Woods	22 D1
Hillcourt	47 A2
Hillcourt Park	60 D2
Hillcourt Road	60 D2
Hillcrest	3 A2 [1]
Hillcrest	34 D2
Hillcrest (Templeogue)	46 D4 [1]
Hillcrest Avenue	33 C2
Hillcrest Close	33 C2
Hillcrest Court	34 D2
Hillcrest Downs	58 D3

STREET NAME	Page	Grid
Hillcrest Drive	33	C2
Hillcrest Green	33	C2
Hillcrest Grove	34	D2
Hillcrest Heights	33	C2
Hillcrest Lawns	33	C2
Hillcrest Manor	46	D4 [2]
Hillcrest Park	24	F2
Hillcrest Park	33	C2
Hillcrest Road (Lucan)	34	D2
Hillcrest Road (Sandyford)	58	D3
Hillcrest View	33	C2 [1]
Hillcrest View	33	C2
Hillcrest Walk	33	C2
Hillcrest Way	33	C2
Hillsbrook Avenue	46	D2
Hillsbrook Crescent	46	D2
Hillsbrook Drive	46	D2
Hillsbrook Grove	46	D2
Hillside	60	E2
Hillside Drive	47	A3
Hillside Park	56	E1
Hillside Terrace	30	D2 [7]
Hilltop Lawn	64	D3
Hilltown	1	B3
Hilltown Close	1	C2
Hilltown Court	1	C2
Hilltown Crescent	1	A2
Hilltown Green	1	C2
Hilltown Grove	1	C2
Hilltown Lawn	1	C2
Hilltown Park	1	C2
Hilltown Road	1	C2
Hilltown Way	1	C2
Hillview	52	E2
Hillview Cottages	59	C2 [1]
Hillview Court	47	B1 [6]
Hillview Drive	59	C2
Hillview Glade	57	B1 [5]
Hillview Grove	57	B1
Hillview Lawns	59	C2
Hilton Gardens	57	C2
*Hoeys Court (off Werburgh Street)	38	D3
Hogan Avenue	38	F3 [27]
Hogan Place	38	E3
Holles Place	38	E3 [34]
Holles Row	38	E3 [7]
Holles Street	38	E3
Holly Avenue	58	D1
Holly Court	64	D1 [4]
Holly Court	64	D1
Holly Park	64	E2
Holly Park Avenue	59	A1
Holly Road (Donnycarney)	26	D3
Holly Road (Fox and Geese)	44	F1
Hollybank Avenue Lower	47	B1
Hollybank Avenue Upper	47	B1
Hollybank Road	25	A4
Hollybrook Court	26	D4 [3]
Hollybrook Court Drive	26	D4 [2]
Hollybrook Grove	26	D4
Hollybrook Park	26	D4
Hollybrook Park	67	C4
Hollybrook Road	26	D4
Hollybrooke	36	E4 [4]
Hollystown	9	B1
Hollystown Demense	9	B1
Hollystown Park	9	B1
Hollyville Lawn	35	C1
Hollywell	11	C4
Hollywood Drive	48	D4
Hollywood Park	48	D4
*Holme's Cottages (Church Avenue Rathmines)	47	A1
Holmston Avenue	60	D1
Holmwood	59	B4
Holycross Avenue	25	B4 [5]
*Holycross Cottages (off Holycross Avenue)	25	B4
Holyrood Park	39	A4
Holywell	58	D1
Holywell Avenue	27	B1
Holywell Crescent	27	B1
Holywell Road	27	B1
Home Farm Park	25	B3
Home Farm Road	25	A3
Home Villas	47	C1
Homelawn Avenue	55	B1
Homelawn Drive	55	B1
Homelawn Gardens	55	B1
Homelawn Road	55	B1
Homelawn Villas	55	A1
Homelee	39	A4 [11]
Homeleigh	22	D4
Homeville	55	C1 [4]
Homeville Court	55	C1 [3]
Honey Park	60	D2 [1]
Hope Avenue	38	F1
*Hope Street (off Gordon Street)	38	F3
Horton Court	46	F2
Hospital Lane	37	A2 [2]
Hotel Yard	38	D2 [29]
Houghton Terrace	37	C2 [28]
*Howard Street (off Gordon Street)	38	F3
Howth	30	D2
Howth Hill Lodge Nursing Home	30	E3
Howth House Apts	30	D1 [10]
Howth Junction Cottages	27	B1 [1]
Howth Lodge (Apts.)	29	C1
Howth Peninsula Apts	30	D1 [14]
Howth Road (Howth)	29	C1
Howth Road (Killester)	26	E3
Howth Road (Marino)	26	D4
Howth Road (Raheny)	26	F3
Howth Road (Raheny)	27	B2
Howth Road (Sutton)	29	B1
Howth Terrace	30	D1 [5]
Howth View Park	27	B1
Huband Road	36	F4
Hudson Road	60	E1
Hughes Road East	45	C1
Hughes Road North	45	C1
Hughes Road South	45	C1
Hume Avenue	35	C4
Hume Street	38	E3
Hunters Avenue	55	C3
Hunters Court	55	C3
Hunters Run	8	E4
Hunters Run The Close	8	E4
Hunters Run The Drive	8	F4
Hunters Run The Glade	8	E4
Hunters Run The Grove	8	E4
Hunters Run The Park	8	E4
Hunters Run The Rise	8	F4
Hunters Run The View	8	F4
Hunters Run The Way	8	F4
Hunters Way	55	C3
Huntstown Avenue	21	C1
Huntstown Close	8	F4
Huntstown Court	8	F4
Huntstown Drive	8	F4
Huntstown Glen	8	F4
Huntstown Green	8	F4
Huntstown Grove	8	F4
Huntstown Lawn	22	D1 [1]
Huntstown Park (Mulhuddart)	8	F4
Huntstown Rise	9	A4
Huntstown Road	21	C1
Huntstown Way	9	A4
Huntstown Wood	8	F4
Hutchinson's Strand	2	E1
Huttonread	51	C4
Huxley Crescent	37	C3 [8]
Hyacinth Street	38	F1 [7]
Hybreasal	37	A3 [1]
Hyde Park (Dalkey)	60	E1
Hyde Park (Templeogue)	46	E3
Hyde Park Avenue	48	F3
Hyde Park Gardens	48	F3
Hyde Road	60	F1
Hynestown	42	D2

I

STREET NAME	Page	Grid
Idrone Avenue	56	D1
Idrone Close	56	D1
Idrone Drive	56	D1
Idrone Mews	49	A3 [11]
Idrone Park	56	D1
Idrone Terrace	49	A3
Imaal Road	37	C1
Inagh Court	64	E1
Inagh Road	36	D3
Inbhir Ide	3	A2
Inbhir Ide Close	3	A2
Inbhir Ide Drive	3	A2
Inchicore	36	F3
Inchicore Road	37	A3
Inchicore Square	36	F3 [13]
Inchicore Terrace North	36	F3 [3]
Inchicore Terrace South	36	F3
Infirmary Road	37	B2
Inglewood Close	21	C2
Inglewood Crescent	21	C2
Inglewood Drive	21	C2
Inglewood Road	21	C2
Ingram Road	37	C4 [2]
Inis Fail	54	F2
Inis Thiar	54	F2
*Inkerman Cottages (off Amiens Street)	38	E2
Innisfallen Parade	38	D1
Innishmaan Road	25	B2
*Innishmore Terrace (St Mary's Road)	46	D1
Innismore	46	D1
*Inns Court (on Winetavern Street)	38	D2
Inver Road	24	E4
Invermore Grove	27	A1 [3]
Inverness Road	25	C4
Iona Crescent	25	A4
Iona Drive	25	A4
Iona Park	25	A4
Iona Road	25	A4
Iona Villas	25	A4
Iris Grove	48	E3
Irishtown	39	A3
Irishtown (Bray)	67	C4
Irishtown Road	39	A3
Irvine Cottages	38	F2 [10]
Irvine Terrace	38	F2
Irwin Court	37	B3 [24]
Irwin Street	37	B3 [1]
Island Street	37	C2
Island View	3	C3
Island View (Kilbarrack)	27	C2
Island View Apts.	30	D1 [9]
Island Villa	38	F3 [3]
Islandbridge	37	A2
Islandbridge Court	37	A2 [1]
Islington Avenue	50	E4
Isolda Road	39	A3
Isolde Gardens	36	E2 [6]
Ivar Street	37	C2
Iveagh Buildings	38	D3 [4]
Iveagh Gardens	37	A4 [1]
Iveagh Gardens	37	A4
Iveleary Road	25	B2
Iveragh Court	38	F4 [17]
Iveragh Road	25	B2
Ivy Court	25	C1
Ivy Terrace	37	C3 [61]

J

STREET NAME	Page	Grid
James Connolly Park	35	A4
James Connolly Square	67	C2 [5]
James Everett Park	67	B2
James Joyce Street	38	E2
James Larkin Road	27	B2
James McCormack Gardens	29	A1 [1]
James's Place East	38	E3
James's Street	37	B3
James's Street East	38	E3
James's Street North	38	F1 [20]
James's Terrace	3	B2
Jamestown	62	F1
Jamestown Avenue	36	F4
Jamestown Cottages	62	E1
Jamestown Court	36	F4
Jamestown Road (Finglas)	24	E1
Jamestown Road (Inchicore)	36	F4
*Jane-Ville (Off Tivoli Road)	50	D4
Jervis Lane Lower	38	D2 [11]
Jervis Lane Upper	38	D2 [10]
Jervis Street	38	D2
Jobstown	54	D2
Jobstown Road	54	D2
John Dillon Street	38	D3
John F Kennedy Avenue	45	A1
John F Kennedy Drive	45	A1
John F Kennedy Park	36	D4
John F Kennedy Road	36	D4
John Field Road	38	D3 [40]
John MacCormack Avenue	45	C1
*John Street North (off Ellis Quay)	37	C2
John Street South	37	C3
John Street West	37	C3
John's Lane East	38	D3 [52]
John's Lane West	37	C3 [50]
Johnsbridge	34	D3
Johnsbridge Avenue	34	D3
Johnsbridge Close	34	D3
Johnsbridge Green	34	D3
Johnsbridge Grove	34	D3
Johnsbridge Meadows	34	D3
Johnsbridge Park	34	D3
Johnsbridge Walk	34	D3
Johnson Place	38	D3 [36]
Johnson's Court	38	D3 [30]
Johnstown	51	C4
Johnstown Avenue	59	C3
Johnstown Court	59	C2
Johnstown Gardens	24	E2 [5]
Johnstown Grove	59	C3
Johnstown House	24	F2 [3]
Johnstown Lane	59	C3
Johnstown Park (Cornelscourt)	59	C3
Johnstown Park (Glasnevin)	24	F2
Johnstown Road	52	E2
Johnstown Road	59	C3
Jones Terrace	68	D2 [18]
Jones's Road	38	E1
Jordanstown	42	F4
Josephine Avenue	38	D1 [25]
*Joy Street (off Gordon Street)	38	F3
Joyce Avenue	59	A3
Joyce Hall	59	B4
Joyce Road	25	A3
Joyce Way	35	C4
Jugback Court	1	C1
Jugback Crescent	1	C1
Jugback Lane	1	C1

K

STREET NAME	Page	Grid
Kavanagh Avenue	36	D4
Keadeen Avenue	45	B2
Kearn's Place	37	A3 [1]
Keatingspark	52	D2
*Keegan's Cottages (off Merrion Rd)	48	E1
Keeloges	42	D3
Keeper Road	37	B4
Kells Road	46	E1
Kelly's Avenue	50	D4
Kelly's Lane	17	C3 [1]
Kelly's Lane	38	D1 [22]
Kelly's Row	38	D1
Kellystown Road	57	B4
Kelston Avenue	59	A2
Kelston Drive	59	A2
Kelston Hall	59	A2 [11]
Kelston Park	59	A2
Kelston View	59	A2
Kelvin Close	4	D4
Kempton	23	C3
Kempton Avenue	23	C3
Kempton Court	23	C3
Kempton Green	23	C3
Kempton Grove	23	C3
Kempton Heath	23	C3
Kempton Lawn	23	C3
Kempton Park	23	C3
Kempton Rise	23	C3
Kempton View	23	C3
Kempton Way	23	C3

STREET NAME	PAGE/GRID REFERENCE
Kenah Court	60 E3
Kengar Mews	46 F1 [14]
Kenilworth Lane	46 F1
Kenilworth Manor	46 F1 [11]
Kenilworth Park	46 F1
Kenilworth Road	47 A1
Kenilworth Square	46 F1
Kenilworth Square East	47 A1
Kenilworth Square North	46 F1
Kenilworth Square South	46 F1
Kenilworth Square West	46 F1
Kenmare Parade	38 D1 [31]
Kennedy Court	39 A3 [31]
Kennedy Park	67 C3 [5]
Kennelsfort Green	35 B2
Kennelsfort Road Lower	35 C1
Kennelsfort Road Upper	35 C2
Kennington Close	45 C4
Kennington Crescent	45 C4
Kennington Lawn	45 C4
Kennington Road	45 C3
*Kent Terrace (on Barnhill Road Dalkey)	60 F2
Kentfield	64 E2
Kerlogue Road	39 A3
Kerrymount Avenue	59 A4
Kerrymount Close	59 B3 [1]
Kerrymount Green	59 B3
Kerrymount Mall	59 B3
Kerrymount Rise	59 B3
Kettles Lane	2 E4
*Kevin Barry (off Church Street Upper)	37 C2
*Kevin Street Cross (on Bride St New)	38 D3
Kevin Street Lower	38 D3
Kevin Street Upper	38 D3
Kew Park	33 C1
Kew Park Avenue	33 B2
Kew Park Crescent	33 B1
Kickham Road	37 A3
Kilakea Close	45 B3
Kilakea Drive	45 B3
Kilakee Road	56 D4
Kilbarrack	27 C1
Kilbarrack Avenue	27 C2
Kilbarrack Gardens	27 C2
Kilbarrack Grove	27 C2
Kilbarrack Parade	27 B1
Kilbarrack Road	27 B1
Kilbarrack Way	27 B1
Kilbarron Avenue	26 D1
Kilbarron Court	26 D1 [1]
Kilbarron Drive	26 D1
Kilbarron Park	26 D1
Kilbarron Road	26 D1
Kilbegnet Close	60 F2 [24]
Kilbogget Grove	59 C4
Kilbogget Villas	59 C4 [1]
*Kilbride Cottages (Killarney Road)	67 B3
*Kilbride Court (Killarney Road)	67 B3
Kilbride Grove	67 B3
Kilbride Lane	67 B3
Kilbride Road	26 E3
Kilbrina	7 B2
Kilcarberry Ave	43 B2
Kilcarberry Close	43 B2
Kilcarberry Court	43 B2
Kilcarberry Lawn	43 B2
Kilcarrig Avenue	44 E4
Kilcarrig Close	54 E1
Kilcarrig Crescent	44 E4
Kilcarrig Green	44 E4
Kilclare Avenue	54 E2
Kilclare Crescent	54 E2
Kilclare Drive	54 E2
Kilclare Gardens	54 E2
Kilcloon	5 A2
Kilcloon Lawns	5 A2
Kilcock Maynooth Leixlip ByPass	32 E1
Kilcock Road	17 C3
Kilcolman Court	60 E2 [4]
Kilcoran Lawns	34 F4 [1]
Kilcronan Avenue	34 E4
Kilcronan Close	34 E4
Kilcronan Crescent	34 E4
Kilcronan Grove	34 E4
Kilcroney Lane	67 A4
Kilcross Avenue	58 D3
Kilcross Close	58 D3
Kilcross Court	57 C3
Kilcross Crescent	57 C3
Kilcross Drive	57 C3
Kilcross Grove	57 C3
Kilcross Lawn	58 D3
Kilcross Park	57 C3
Kilcross Road	58 D3
Kilcross Square	57 C3
Kilcross Way	57 C3
Kildare Bridge	18 D2
Kildare Park	46 D1
Kildare Place	38 E3 [25]
Kildare Road	46 D1
Kildare Street	38 E3
Kildonan Avenue	24 D1
Kildonan Court	24 D1
Kildonan Drive	24 D1
Kildonan Road	24 D1
Kilfenora Drive	27 A1
Kilfenora Road	46 E1
Kilgarran	66 D3
Kilgarron Park	66 D3
Kilgobbin Heights	58 E4
Kilgobbin Lane	58 D4
Kilgobbin Lawn	58 E4
Kilgobbin Road	58 E3
Kilgobbin Wood	58 E4
Kilgraigue	5 B3
Kilgrastor Court	67 B3 [5]
Kilkieran Court	24 E4 [1]
Kilkieran Road	24 E4
Kill Abbey	59 B1
Kill Avenue	59 B1
Kill Lane	59 B2
Kill O' the Grange	59 C1
Killadoon Park	31 C4
Killakee Avenue	55 B2
Killakee Court	55 B2
Killakee Gardens	55 B2
Killakee Green	55 B2
Killakee Grove	55 B2
Killakee Lawns	55 B2
Killakee Park	55 B2
Killakee View	55 B2
Killakee Walk	55 B2
Killakee Way	55 B2
Killala Road	24 E4
Killan Road	38 F2
Killarney Avenue	38 E1 [13]
Killarney Court	67 B3 [4]
Killarney Glen	67 B3
Killarney Heights	67 B3
Killarney Lane	67 B3
Killarney Parade	38 D1 [30]
Killarney Park	67 B3
Killarney Road	67 B3
Killarney Street	38 E1
Killarney Villas	67 C2 [48]
Killary Grove	27 B1
Killeany	5 A4
Killeck	1 A2
Killeck Lane	1 A3
Killeen	2 F3
Killeen Avenue	2 F3
Killeen Court	2 F3
Killeen Crescent	2 F3
Killeen Mews	3 B3
Killeen Park	2 F3
Killeen Road	36 D4
Killeen Road (Fox and Geese)	45 A1
Killeen Road (Rathmines)	47 B1
Killeen Terrace	3 B2
Killegar	65 C1
*Killery Terrace (Upper Dargle Road)	67 B2
Killester	26 E3
Killester Avenue	26 E3
Killester Court	26 E3 [4]
Killester Park	26 E3 [5]
Killester Park	26 E3
Killinarden	54 E3
Killinarden Estate	54 E2
Killinarden Heights	54 E2
Killinarden Road	54 E3
Killiney	60 E3
Killiney Avenue	60 E4 [7]
Killiney Avenue	60 E4
Killiney Court	64 E1 [1]
Killiney Gate	60 E4
Killiney Grove	60 E2
Killiney Heath	60 E4
Killiney Hill Road	60 E3
Killiney Hill Road	64 E1
Killiney Oaks	64 E1 [2]
Killiney Road	60 E2
Killiney Terrace	60 E1 [15]
Killiney Towers	60 E2 [2]
Killiney View	60 E1
*Killiney View (off Albert Road)	60 E1
Killininney Cottages	55 B2
Killininny Court Apts	55 B2 [2]
Killininny / Scholarstown Link Rd	55 B2
Killininny Cottages	55 B2
Kilmactalway	42 F3
Kilmacud Avenue	58 E1
Kilmacud Park	58 E1
Kilmacud Road Upper	58 E1
Kilmahuddrick Avenue	43 B1
Kilmahuddrick Close	43 B1
Kilmahuddrick Court	43 B1
Kilmahuddrick Crescent	43 B1
Kilmahuddrick Drive	43 B1
Kilmahuddrick Green	43 B1
Kilmahuddrick Grove	43 B1
Kilmahuddrick Lawn	43 B1
Kilmahuddrick Place	43 B1
Kilmahuddrick Road	43 B1
Kilmahuddrick Walk	43 B1
Kilmahuddrick Way	43 B1
Kilmainham	37 A3
Kilmainham Lane	37 B3
Kilmalin	65 C3
Kilmantain Place	67 C2 [10]
Kilmartin Avenue	54 D1
Kilmartin Crescent	44 D4
Kilmartin Drive	54 D1
Kilmartin Gardens	54 D1
Kilmartin Green	54 D1
Kilmartin Park	54 D1
Kilmashogue Close	45 B3
Kilmashogue Drive	45 B3
Kilmashogue Grove	45 B3
Kilmashogue Lane	56 F3
Kilmore	26 D1
Kilmore Avenue (Coolock)	26 E1
Kilmore Avenue (Killiney)	60 E4
Kilmore Close	26 E1
Kilmore Court	26 D1 [5]
Kilmore Crescent	26 E1
Kilmore Drive	26 E1
Kilmore Road	26 D1
Kilmorony Close	27 A1
Kilnamanagh	45 A3
Kilnamanagh Estate	45 A3
Kilnamanagh Road	45 C1
Kilohan Grove	45 B3
Kilrock Road	30 E2
Kilronan Court	26 D4 [7]
Kilshane	10 E2
Kilshane Road	10 E3
Kilshane Road	23 C2
Kiltalown	54 D3
Kiltalown Avenue	54 D2
Kiltalown Close	54 D2
Kiltalown Court	54 D2
Kiltalown Crescent	54 D2
Kiltalown Drive	54 D2
Kiltalown Green	54 D2
Kiltalown Grove	54 D2
Kiltalown Heights	54 D2
Kiltalown Park	54 D2
Kiltalown Road	54 D2
Kiltalown View	54 D2
Kiltalown Walk	54 D2
Kiltalown Way	54 D2
Kilteragh Drive	59 A3
Kilteragh Pines	59 A3 [2]
Kilteragh Road	59 A3
Kiltiernan	62 F2
Kiltipper	54 F3
Kiltipper Avenue	55 A2
Kiltipper Close	55 A2
Kiltipper Drive	55 A2
Kiltipper Rise	54 F3
Kiltipper Road	55 A3
Kiltipper View	54 F3
Kiltipper Way	54 F2
Kiltuck Park	64 E4 [1]
Kilvere	46 E4
Kilwogan Manor	31 C2
Kilworth Road	36 F4
Kimmage	46 D2
Kimmage Court	46 E2 [3]
Kimmage Grove	46 E2
Kimmage Road Lower	46 F1
Kimmage Road West	46 D2
Kinahan Street	37 B2 [4]
Kincora Avenue	26 E4
Kincora Court	39 C1
Kincora Drive	26 E4
Kincora Grove	26 E4
Kincora Park	26 E4
Kincora Road	26 E4
King Edward Court	67 C2 [53]
King Edward Lawn	67 C2
King Edward Park	67 B2
King Edward Road	67 B2
King Street North	37 C2
King Street South	38 D3
Kingram Place	38 E4
King's Avenue	38 E1
King's Court	37 C1 [19]
King's Hall	36 E2
Kings Inns	38 D2
King's Inns Street	38 D2
Kingsbury	17 C4
Kingsland Parade	38 D4 [5]
Kingsland Park Avenue	38 D4 [4]
Kingsmill Road	67 C2
Kingston	57 B3
Kingston Avenue	57 B3
Kingston Close	57 B3
Kingston Court	56 F2
Kingston Crescent	57 B3
Kingston Drive	57 C3
Kingston Green	57 B3
Kingston Grove	57 B3
Kingston Hall	57 B3
Kingston Heights	57 C3
Kingston Lawn	57 B3
Kingston Lodge	25 B4 [4]
Kingston Park	57 B3
Kingston Rise	57 B3
Kingston View	57 B3
Kingston Walk	57 B3
Kingswood	43 C3
Kingswood Avenue	44 F3
Kingswood Avenue (City West)	43 C4
Kingswood Castle	45 A2
Kingswood Drive	43 C4
Kingswood Drive	44 F3
Kingswood Heights	44 F3
Kingswood Road	53 C1
Kingswood Road	43 C4
Kingswood View	44 F3
Kinsaley	14 D1
Kinsaley Lane	3 A4
Kinsealy Court	2 E3
Kinsealy Downs	2 E3
Kinsealy Lane	14 D1
Kinsealy Riding Centre	13 C2
Kinvara Avenue	24 D4
Kinvara Drive	23 C4
Kinvara Grove	23 C4
Kinvara Park	24 D4
Kinvara Road	23 C4
Kippure Avenue	45 B3

STREET NAME	PAGE/GRID REFERENCE
Kippure Park	24 D3
Kirkfield	22 D2 [2]
Kirkpatrick Avenue	22 D3
Kirkpatrick Drive	22 D3
Kirkwood	39 A4
Kirwan Street	37 C2
Kirwan Street Cottages	37 C1 [10]
Kitestown Road	30 E3
Knapton Court	49 C4 [21]
Knapton Lawn	49 C4 [22]
Knapton Road	49 C4
Knapton Terrace	49 C4 [27]
*Knapton Villas (Knapton Road)	49 C4
Knights Bridge	26 E4 [4]
Knights Wood	12 F4
Knock Riada	36 D2
Knockaire	56 D1
Knockandinny	52 E4
Knockaulin	20 D4
Knockcullen	56 D1
Knockcullen Drive	56 D1
Knockcullen Lawn	56 D1
Knockcullen Park	56 D1
Knockcullen Rise	56 D1
Knockdara	3 C3
Knockfield Manor	55 C1
Knocklyon	56 D1
Knocklyon Avenue	55 C1
Knocklyon Close	56 D1
Knocklyon Court	56 D1
Knocklyon Drive	56 D1
Knocklyon Gate Apts	55 C2 [9]
Knocklyon Green	56 D1
Knocklyon Grove	56 D1
Knocklyon Heights	55 C1
Knocklyon Mews	55 C1 [2]
Knocklyon Park	55 C1
Knocklyon Road	55 C1
Knocklyon Road	56 D1
Knockmaree Apartments	36 E2
Knockmaroon Hill	36 D1
Knockmaroon Road	36 D1
Knockmeenagh Lane	44 E2
Knockmeenagh Road	44 E2
Knockmitten Close	44 F1 [1]
Knockmitten Lane	45 A1
Knockmitten Lane North	44 F1 [2]
Knockmore Avenue	54 E2
Knockmore Crescent	54 E2
Knockmore Drive	54 E2
Knockmore Gardens	54 E2
Knockmore Green	54 E2
Knockmore Grove	54 E2
Knockmore Park	54 E2
Knocknacree Grove	60 F2
Knocknacree Park	60 F2
Knocknacree Road	60 F2
Knocknagow	49 B4 [23]
Knocknarea Avenue	37 A4
Knocknarea Road	37 A4
Knocknarrow Terrace	37 B3 [34]
Knocknashee	47 C4
Knocknashee	48 D4
Knocksedan Drive	1 A2
Knocksedan Wood	1 A2
Knocksinna	59 A2
Knocksinna Court	59 A2 [2]
Knocksinna Crescent	59 A2
Knocksinna Grove	59 A2 [1]
Knocksinna Park	59 A2
Knowth Court	11 C4
Kyber Road	36 F2
Kyle-Clare Road	39 A3 [13]
Kylemore Avenue	36 D3
Kylemore Drive	36 D3
Kylemore Park North	36 D4
Kylemore Park South	36 D4
Kylemore Park West	36 D4
Kylemore Road	36 D2

L

STREET NAME	PAGE/GRID REFERENCE
La Touche Court	36 F4 [3]
La Touche Court	57 B2
La Touche Drive	36 E4
La Touche Road	36 F4
La Vallee	67 A3
La Vista Avenue (Howth)	29 B2
Labre Park	36 E4
Laburnum Road	47 C2
Laburnum Walk	35 B2
Lad Lane	38 E3
Lad Lane Upper	38 E4
Lady's Lane	37 A3 [13]
Lady's Well Road	9 A4
Lagan Road	24 E3
Lake Drive	43 C4
Lake Drive	53 C1
Lakelands Avenue	58 D1
Lakelands Close	58 D1
Lakelands Crescent	58 E1
Lakelands Drive	58 E1
Lakelands Grove	58 D1
Lakelands Lawn	58 D1
Lakelands Park	46 E3
*Lakelands Place	58 D1
Lakelands Road	58 E1
Lakeshore Drive	2 D3
Lakeview Drive	2 D3
Lally Road	36 E3
Lamb Alley	37 C3
Lambay Close	64 E1
Lambay Court	3 C3
Lambay Drive	64 E1
Lambay Road	25 A3
Lambourne Avenue	21 C2
Lambourne Court	21 C2
Lambourne Drive	21 C2
Lambourne Park	21 C2
Lambourne Road	21 C2
Lambourne Village	26 E4 [3]
Lambourne Wood	59 C4
Lamb's Brook	58 D3 [1]
*Lamb's Court (off James Street)	37 B3
Landen Road	36 E3
Landore	47 A3 [9]
Landscape Avenue	47 A3
Landscape Crescent	47 A4
Landscape Gardens	47 B4
Landscape Park	47 A4
Landscape Road	47 A3
Landsdowne Valley (Apts)	45 C1
Landsdowne Valley Park	36 F4 [5]
Lanesborough Avenue	11 B4
Lanesborough Court	11 B4
Lanesborough Drive	11 B4
Lanesborough Gardens	11 B4
Lanesborough Grove	11 B4
Lanesborough Mews	11 B4
Lanesborough Road	11 B4
Lanesborough Square	11 B4
Lanesborough Terrace	11 B4
Lanesborough View	11 B4
Lanesville	59 B1
Langrishe Place	38 E1 [23]
Lanndale Lawn	54 E1
Lansdowne Crescent	38 F3 [43]
Lansdowne Gardens	38 F4 [7]
Lansdowne Hall	39 A3 [25]
Lansdowne Lane	38 F3 [20]
Lansdowne Park (Ballsbridge)	38 F3
Lansdowne Park (Templeogue)	56 D1
Lansdowne Road	38 F4
Lansdowne Square	39 A4 [24]
Lansdowne Terrace	38 F3 [37]
Lansdowne Village	39 A3
Lansdowne Villas	38 F3 [44]
Laracor Gardens	27 A1 [5]
Laragh	60 E4
Laragh (Flats)	25 C2 [4]
Laragh Close	27 A1
Laragh Grove	27 A1
Laraghbryan East	17 B2
Laraghbryan West	17 A2
Laraghon	34 D1
Larch Drive	56 E2 [3]
Larch Grove (Clonsilla)	21 C2
Larch Grove (Donnybrook)	47 B1
Larchfield	47 C4
Larchfield (Dunboyne)	7 C3
Larchfield Park	47 C4
Larchfield Road	47 C4
Larkfield	34 F2
Larkfield Avenue	34 F2
Larkfield Avenue	46 F1
Larkfield Close	34 F2
Larkfield Court	34 F2
Larkfield Gardens	46 F1
Larkfield Green	34 F2
Larkfield Grove	34 F2
Larkfield Grove	46 F1
Larkfield Mews	32 D3
Larkfield Park	46 F1
Larkfield Place	34 F2
Larkfield Rise	34 F2
Larkfield View	34 F2
Larkfield Way	34 F2
Larkhill Road	25 B2
Latchford	21 B1
Latchford Close	21 B1
Latchford Court	21 B1
Latchford Green	21 B1
Latchford Park	21 B1
Latchford Row	21 B1
Latchford Square	21 B1
Latchford Terrace	21 B1
Lauderdale Estate	67 C3
Lauderdale Terrace	67 C3 [16]
*Lauderdale Terrace (on New Row South)	38 D3
Lauder's Lane	29 A1
Laundry Lane	46 F1
Laurel Avenue	57 B1
Laurel Avenue	64 E1
Laurel Court	22 E3
Laurel Drive	57 B1
Laurel Hill	60 D1 [6]
Laurel Lodge Road	22 F3
Laurel Place	44 E1
Laurel Road	57 B1
Laurelton	1 C1
Laurelton	46 F3
Laurence Brook	36 E2
Laurence Court	46 F1
Laurence Place East	38 F2 [5]
Laurleen	58 F1
Lavarna Grove	46 E2
Lavarna Road	46 E2
Laverna Avenue	22 E3
Laverna Dale	22 E3
Laverna Grove	22 E3
Laverna Way	22 E3
Lavery Avenue	35 C4
Lavista Avenue (Killester)	26 E3
Lawnswood Park	58 F1
Lawrence Grove	26 D4
Lawrence's Avenue	18 D4
Lawson Spinney	3 A3
Lawson Terrace	60 E1 [14]
Le Bas Terrace	46 F1 [2]
Le Brett Terrace	46 F3 [7]
Le Brocquy Avenue	36 D4
Le Fanu Drive	36 D3 [1]
Le Fanu Road	36 D3
Le Vere Terrace	37 C4 [38]
*Le Vere Terrace (off Harold's Cross Road)	46 F1
Lea Crescent	39 B4
Lea Road	39 B4
Leahy's Terrace	39 A3
Lealand Avenue	43 C1
Lealand Close	43 C1
Lealand Crescent	43 C1
Lealand Drive	43 C1
Lealand Gardens	43 C1
Lealand Grove	43 C1
Lealand Road	43 C1
Lealand Walk	43 C1
Leaunstown	59 C4
Ledwidge Crescent	67 B1
Lee Road	24 E3
Leeson Close	38 E4 [1]
Leeson Lane	38 E3
Leeson Park	38 E4
Leeson Park Avenue	38 E4
Larchfield Park	47 C4
Larchfield Road	47 C4
Larkfield	34 F2
Leeson Place	38 E4 [3]
Leeson Street Lower	38 E3
Leeson Street Upper	38 E4
Leeson Village	38 E4 [30]
Leeson Walk	38 E4 [19]
Lehaunstown Road	63 C1
Leicester Avenue	47 A1
Leicester Celtic F.C.	57 A1
Leighlin Road	46 E1
Lein Gardens	26 F2
Lein Park	26 F2
Lein Road	26 F2
Leinster Avenue	38 F1
Leinster Court	18 D3 [2]
Leinster Lane	38 E3 [13]
Leinster Lawn	47 C3
Leinster Lodge Apartments	18 D3 [1]
Leinster Market	38 E2 [11]
Leinster Park	18 D3
Leinster Place	46 F1
Leinster Road	47 A1
Leinster Road West	46 F1
Leinster Square	47 A1 [2]
Leinster Street	17 C3
Leinster Street East	38 F1 [21]
Leinster Street North	24 F4
Leinster Street South	38 E3
Leinster Terrace	44 D1 [2]
Leitrim Place	38 F3 [33]
Leix Road	37 C1
Leixlip	33 B1
Leixlip Park	32 F1
Leixlip Road	33 B1
Lemon Street	38 D3 [31]
Lennox Place	38 D4
Lennox Street	38 D4
Lennox Terrace	38 D4 [31]
Lentisk Lawn	27 A1
Leo Avenue	38 D1 [24]
Leo Street	38 D1
Leonard's Court	37 C4
Leopardstown	58 F3
Leopardstown Abbey	58 F4
Leopardstown Avenue	58 F2
Leopardstown Court	58 F2 [1]
Leopardstown Drive	58 F2
Leopardstown Gardens	58 F2
Leopardstown Grove	58 F2
Leopardstown Heights	58 E3
Leopardstown Lawn	58 F2 [2]
Leopardstown Oaks	58 F2
Leopardstown Park	58 F2
Leopardstown Rise	58 E3
Leopardstown Road	58 F2
Leopardstown Valley	58 F4
Leslie Avenue	60 F1
Leslie's Buildings	37 C1 [7]
Leukos Road	39 A3 [11]
Liberty House	38 E1 [64]
Liberty Lane	38 D3 [20]
Library Road	50 D4
Library Road	64 E2
Library View Villas	38 D1 [61]
Liffey Close	34 F2
Liffey Court	34 F2
Liffey Crescent	34 F2
Liffey Dale	34 F2
Liffey Downs	34 F2
Liffey Drive	34 F2
Liffey Fitness Centre	35 B2
Liffey Gardens	34 F2
Liffey Glen	34 F2
Liffey Hall	34 F2 [1]
Liffey Junction	24 E3
Liffey Lawn	34 F2
Liffey Park	34 F2
Liffey Place	34 F2
Liffey Road	34 F2
Liffey Row	34 F2
Liffey Street Lower	38 D2
Liffey Street South	36 F3
Liffey Street Upper	38 D2
Liffey Street West	37 C2 [19]
Liffey Terrace	36 E2 [7]
Liffey Vale	34 F2

STREET NAME	PAGE/GRID REFERENCE
Liffey Valley Ave	34 F2
Liffey Valley Park	34 F2
Liffey View	34 F2
Liffey View Apts	33 A1 [2]
Liffey Villas	34 F2
Liffey Walk	34 F2
Liffey Way	34 F2
Lilys Way	21 A1
Lime Street	38 E2
Limekiln Avenue	45 C3
Limekiln Close	45 C3
Limekiln Drive	45 C3
Limekiln Green	45 B3
Limekiln Grove	45 C2
Limekiln Lane (Harold's Cross)	37 C4 [16]
Limekiln Lane (Kimmage)	45 C2
Limekiln Park	45 C3
Limekiln Road	45 C3
Limelawn Park	22 D2
Limes Road	58 D2
Limetree Avenue	3 C4
Limewood Avenue	26 F1
Limewood Park	26 F1
Limewood Road	27 A1
Lincoln Lane	37 C2 [43]
*Lincoln Lane (off Arran Quay)	37 C2
Lincoln Place	38 E3
Linden Grove	48 F4
Linden Square	48 F4
Linden Lea Park	58 F1
Lindenvale	49 A4 [4]
Lindisfarne Avenue	43 C1
Lindisfarne Drive	43 C1
Lindisfarne Green	43 C1
Lindisfarne Grove	43 C1
Lindisfarne Lawns	43 C1
Lindisfarne Park	34 F4
Lindisfarne Vale	43 C1
Lindisfarne Walk	43 C1
Lindsay Road	25 A4
Linenhall Parade	38 D2 [4]
*Linenhall Street (off King Street North)	38 D2
Linenhall Terrace	38 D2 [1]
Link Road	60 E1
Linnetfield	8 E4
Linnetfield Avenue	8 E4
Linnetfield Close	8 E4
Linnetfield Drive	8 E4
Linnetfield Green	8 E4
Linnetfield Rise	8 E4
Linnetfield Square	8 E4
Linnetfield View	8 E4
Linnetsfields Court	21 A1
Linnetsfields Estate	21 A1
Linnetsfields Green	21 A1
Linnetsfields Park	21 A1
Linnetsfields Walk	21 A1
Lioscian	1 B1
Lios na Sidhe	54 F2
Lisalea	49 A3 [22]
Lisburn Street	38 D2 [2]
Liscannor Road	24 E4
Liscanor	60 F1 [9]
Liscarne Court	35 A3
Liscarne Gardens	35 A3
Lisle Road	46 D1
Lismeen Grove	26 E1 [1]
Lismore	18 E4
Lismore Road	46 E1
Lissadel Avenue	37 A4
Lissadel Court	37 A4
Lissadel Crescent	2 F2
Lissadel Drive	37 A4
Lissadel Green	37 A4 [2]
Lissadel Grove	2 F2
Lissadel Park	2 F2
Lissadel Road	37 A4
Lissadel Wood	2 F2
Lissen Hall	2 D1
Lissenfield	38 D4 [53]
Lissenhall Avenue	2 D1
Lissenhall Court	2 D1
Lissenhall Drive	2 D1
Lissenhall Park	2 D1
Little Britain Street	38 D2
Little Fitzwilliam Place	38 E3 [29]
Little Meadow	59 C3 [1]
Littlepace	8 E4
Littlepace Close	8 E4
Littlepace Court	8 E4
Littlepace Crescent	8 E4
Littlepace Drive	8 E4
Littlepace Gallops	8 E4
Littlepace Meadow	8 E4
Littlepace Park	8 E4
Littlepace View	8 E4
Littlepace Walk	8 E4
Littlepace Way	8 E4
Littlepace Woods	8 E4
Littlewood	58 D4
Litton Lane	38 D2 [18]
*Litton Lane (off Bachelors Walk)	38 D2
Llewellyn Close	57 A1
Llewellyn Court	57 A1
Llewellyn Grove	57 A1
Llewellyn Lawn	57 A1
Llewellyn Park	57 A1
Llewellyn Way	57 A1
Lock Road	34 D3
Lockkeeper's Walk	24 D3
Loftus Lane	38 D2
Loftus Square	46 F4 [14]
Lohunda Crescent	21 C2
Lohunda Dale	22 D2
Lohunda Downs	22 D2
Lohunda Drive	22 D2
Lohunda Grove	22 D2
Lohunda Park	21 C2
Lohunda Road	22 D2
Lombard Court	38 E2 [33]
Lombard Street East	38 E2
Lombard Street West	38 D4
Lomond Avenue	25 C4
Londonbridge Drive	39 A3 [20]
Londonbridge Road	39 A3
Long Lane	38 D3
Long Lane (New Street)	38 D1 [49]
Long Lane Close (off Long Lane)	38 D3
Long Mile Road	45 B1
Longdale Terrace	25 A1
Longdale Way	25 A1
Longford Lane	38 D3 [45]
Longford Place	49 C4
Longford Street Great	38 D3 [8]
Longford Street Little	38 D3 [9]
Longford Terrace	49 C4
Longlands	2 D2
Longmeadow	59 C3
Longmeadow Grove	59 C3
Long's Place	37 C3 [5]
Longwood Avenue	38 D4
Longwood Park	46 F4
Lorcan Avenue	25 C1
Lorcan Crescent	25 C1
Lorcan Drive	25 B1
Lorcan Green	25 C1
Lorcan Grove	25 C1
Lorcan O'Toole Court	46 D2 [2]
Lorcan O'Toole Park	46 D2
Lorcan Park	25 C1
Lorcan Road	25 B1
Lorcan Villas	25 C1
Lord Edward Street	38 D3
Lordello Road	64 D3
Lords Walk	37 A1
Loreto Avenue	47 A4
Loreto Avenue (Dalkey)	60 F1
Loreto Court	47 A4
Loreto Crescent	47 A4
Loreto Grange	67 C3
Loreto Park	47 A4
Loreto Road	37 C3
Loreto Row	47 A4
Loreto Terrace	46 F4
Loretto Terrace	67 C2 [34]
Loretto Terrace	67 C2 [35]
Loretto Villas	67 C2 [54]
*Lorne Terrace (off Almeida Avenue)	37 B3
Lotts	38 D2
Lough Conn Avenue	36 D2
Lough Conn Drive	36 D2
Lough Conn Road	36 D2
Lough Conn Terrace	36 D2
Lough Derg Road	27 A2
Loughlinstown	64 D1
Loughlinstown Drive	64 D1
Loughlinstown Park	64 D1
Loughlinstown Wood	64 D1
Lough-na-Mona	19 C3
Loughtown Lower	41 C1
Loughtown Lower	42 D1
Loughtown Upper	42 E1
Louis Lane	47 A1 [23]
*Louis Lane (off Leinster Road)	47 A1
Louisa Vally	19 C4
Lourdes House	38 E1 [61]
Lourdes Road	37 B3
Louvain	48 D3
Louvain Glade	48 D3
Love Lane East	38 F3 [15]
Lower Dargle Road	67 B2
Lower Glen Road	36 D1
Lower Kilmacud Road (Goatstown)	48 D4
Lower Kilmacud Road (Stillorgan)	58 D1
Lower Lucan Road	21 C4
Lower Road (Shankill)	64 E3
Lower Road (Strawberry Beds)	35 B1
Luby Road	37 A3
Lucan	34 D2
Lucan Bypass	34 D2
Lucan Heights	34 E1
Lucan-Newlands Road	34 F3
Lucan Road (Chapelizod)	36 D2
Lucan Road (Lucan)	34 D1
Lucan Road (near Qaurryvale)	35 A1
Lucan Road (Palmerston)	35 C1
Ludford Drive	57 B1
Ludford Park	57 B1
Ludford Road	57 B2
Lugg	52 F4
Lugmore	54 D3
Lugmore Lane	53 C3
Lugnaquilla Avenue	45 B3
Luke Street	38 E2 [25]
Lurgan Street	38 D2 [3]
Lutterell Hall	7 A2
Luttrell Park	22 D3
Luttrell Park Close	22 D3
Luttrell Park Court	22 D3
Luttrell Park Crescent	22 E3
Luttrell Park Drive	22 E3
Luttrell Park Green	22 E3
Luttrell Park Grove	22 D3
Luttrell Park Hall	22 D3
Luttrell Park Heath	22 E3
Luttrell Park Lawn	22 D3
Luttrell Park View	22 D3
Luttrellstown Avenue	22 E4
Luttrellstown Chase	22 D4
Luttrellstown Close	22 E4
Luttrellstown Court	22 D4
Luttrellstown Dale	22 D4
Luttrellstown Drive	22 D4
Luttrellstown Glade	22 D4
Luttrellstown Green	22 D4
Luttrellstown Grove	22 D4
Luttrellstown Heath	22 D4
Luttrellstown Heights	22 D4
Luttrellstown Lawn	22 D4
Luttrellstown Oaks	22 D4
Luttrellstown Park	22 D4
Luttrellstown Place	22 D4
Luttrellstown Rise	22 D3
Luttrellstown Thicket	22 D4
Luttrellstown View	22 E4
Luttrellstown Walk	22 D4
Luttrellstown Way	22 D4
Luttrellstown Wood	22 E4
Lyllymore Terrace	37 C4 [6]
Lymewood Mews	12 E4
Lynches Lane	34 E4
Lynch's Lane	36 E3 [2]
Lynch's Place	38 D1 [2]
Lyndon Gate	24 D4 [4]
Lynton Court	39 A4 [12]
Lynwood	57 C1
Lyons	41 A4
Lyons Road	41 A3
Lyons Road	41 C4
Lyreen Court	17 C3
Lyreen Manor	17 C3
Lyreen Park	18 D2

M

STREET NAME	PAGE/GRID REFERENCE
Mabbot Lane	38 E2 [17]
Mabel Street	25 B4
Macken Street	38 F3
Macken Villa	38 F3 [31]
Mackies Place	38 E3 [33]
Mackintosh Park	59 C2
Macroom Avenue	13 B4
Macroom Road	13 B4
Madden Road	37 C3 [31]
*Madden's Court (off Thomas Street)	37 C3
Madden's Lane	60 E4
Madison Road	37 B3 [10]
*Magdalen Terrace (off Oliver Plunket Ave)	39 A3
Magennis Place	38 E2 [3]
Magennis Square	38 E2 [29]
Magenta Crescent	25 B1
Magenta Hall	25 B1
Magenta Place	60 D1 [8]
Magna Drive	53 C2
*Maher's Terrace (Main Street Dundrum)	47 C4
Maidens Row	36 E2 [2]
Main Street	7 B2
Main Street	17 C3
Main Street	42 D4
Main Street	52 F2
Main Street	67 C2
Main Street (Baldoyle)	15 A4
Main Street (Blackrock)	49 A3
Main Street (Blanchardstown)	22 F2
Main Street (Celbridge)	32 D3
Main Street (Clondalkin)	44 E1
Main Street (Dundrum)	47 C4
Main Street (Finglas)	24 E2
Main Street (Howth)	30 D2
Main Street (Leixlip)	33 A1
Main Street (Lucan)	34 D1
Main Street (Raheny)	27 A2
Main Street (Rathfarnham)	46 F4
Main Street (Swords)	2 D2
Main Street (Tallaght)	55 A1
Main Street (Tallaght)	55 A1
Maitland Street	67 B2
Malachi Place	38 F1 [18]
Malachi Road	37 C2 [45]
*Malachi Road (off Halliday Road)	37 C2
Malahide	3 C2
Malahide Golf Club	14 D1
Malahide Road	2 E2
Malahide Road (Artane)	26 E2
Malahide Road (Balgriffin)	14 D3
Malahide Road (Coolock)	26 F1
Malahide Road (Marino)	26 D4
Malborough Court	60 E2 [8]
Mallin Avenue	37 B3 [17]
Malone Gardens	38 F3 [12]
Malpas Court	38 D3 [50]
*Malpas Place (off Malpas Street)	38 D3
*Malpas Street	38 D3
Malpas Terrace	38 D3 [46]
Mander's Terrace	38 E4 [10]
Mangerton Road	36 F4
Mannix Road	25 A4
Manor Avenue	46 E3
Manor Close	57 A2
Manor Court	17 C3
Manor Crescent	21 B1

STREET NAME	PAGE/GRID REFERENCE
Manor Drive	14 D4
Manor Green	57 A2
Manor Grove	46 D2
Manor Heath	57 A1
Manor Mews (off Norseman Place)	37 C2 [50]
Manor Mills	17 C3
Manor Park (Ballinteer)	57 A2
Manor Park (Palmerston)	35 C2
Manor Place	21 A1
Manor Place	37 C2
Manor Rise	57 A2
Manor Road	35 C2
Manor Square	21 A1
Manor Street	37 C2
Manor Villas	46 F1 [4]
Manorfields	21 B1
Mantua Park	2 D1 [2]
Maolbuille Road	25 A2
Mapas Avenue	60 E2
Mapas Road	60 E2
Maple Avenue	22 E3
Maple Avenue (off Blackthorn Drive)	58 D2
Maple Close	22 E3
Maple Drive	7 B2
Maple Drive	22 E3
Maple Drive	46 F2 [6]
Maple Glen	22 E3
Maple Green	22 E3
Maple Grove	22 E3
Maple Grove	52 F2
Maple Grove	67 B2
Maple Lawn	22 E3
Maple Manor	59 C3
Maple Road	47 C2
Maples Road	58 D2
Maplewood Avenue	54 E1
Maplewood Close	54 E1
Maplewood Court	54 E1
Maplewood Drive	54 E1
Maplewood Green	54 E1
Maplewood Lawn	54 E1
Maplewood Park	54 E1
Maplewood Road	54 E1
Maplewood Way	54 E1
Maretimo Gardens East	49 A3
Maretimo Gardens West	49 A3 [4]
Maretimo Place	49 A3 [17]
Maretimo Road	49 A3 [2]
Maretimo Terrace	49 A3 [16]
Maretimo Villas	49 A3 [18]
Margaret Place	38 F3 [11]
Marguerite Road	25 A4
Marian Crescent	46 E4
Marian Drive	46 E4
Marian Grove	46 E4
Marian Park (Baldoyle)	27 C1
Marian Park (Blackrock)	59 A1
Marian Park (Templeogue)	46 E4
Marian Road	46 E4
Mariavilla	17 C2
Marie Villas	67 C2 [55]
Marigold Court	13 C4
Marigold Crescent	13 C4
Marigold Grove	13 C4
Marigold Park	13 C4
Marina House Apts	49 C4 [32]
Marina Village	3 B2
Marine Avenue	60 E1
Marine Court	50 D4
Marine Court	60 E1
Marine Cove	28 D1 [4]
Marine Drive	39 A4
Marine Parade	50 E4
Marine Road	50 D4
Marine Terrace	50 D4 [9]
Marine Terrace	68 D2 [17]
Marine View	48 F3
Marine Villas	30 D1 [7]
Mariners Court	27 C2 [1]
Mariners Cove	30 E2
Mariner's Port	38 F2 [16]
Marino	25 C4
Marino Avenue	25 C4
Marino Avenue East	60 E4
Marino Avenue West	60 E4
Marino Court	25 C4 [13]
Marino Crescent	26 D4
Marino Green	25 C4
Marino Mart	25 C4 [9]
Marino Park	25 C4
Marino Park Avenue	25 C4
Marion Villas	37 C3 [59]
Mark Street	38 E2 [26]
Market Square	67 C2 [49]
Market Street South	37 C3 [4]
Mark's Alley West	37 C3 [22]
Mark's Lane	38 E2 [4]
Marlay View	57 B2
Marlborough Court	38 E2 [35]
Marlborough Lane	47 B1
Marlborough Mews	37 B1
Marlborough Park	60 D1 [9]
Marlborough Place	38 E2 [7]
Marlborough Road (Donnybrook)	47 C1
Marlborough Road (Glenageary)	60 E1
Marlborough Road (Nth Circular Rd)	37 B1
Marlborough Street	38 D2
Marlborough Terrace	68 D2 [16]
Marley Avenue	57 A1
Marley Close	57 A1
Marley Court North	57 A1
Marley Court South	57 A1
Marley Drive	57 A1
Marley Grove	57 A1
Marley Lawn	57 A1
Marley Rise	57 A1
Marley Villas	57 A1 [1]
Marley Walk	57 A1
Marlfield	59 C3
Marlfield Close	54 F3
Marlfield Court	54 F3
Marlfield Crescent	54 F3
Marlfield Gardens	59 C3
Marlfield Green	54 F3
Marlfield Grove	54 F3
Marlfield Lawn	54 F3
Marlfield Place	54 F3
*Marmion Court (on Blackhall Street)	37 C2
Marne Villas	37 C1 [13]
Marrowbone Lane	37 C3 [66]
Marrowbone Lane	37 C3
*Marrowbone Lane Close (off Marrowbone Lane)	37 C3
Marshal Court Apts	37 C3 [1]
Marshal Lane	37 C3 [1]
Marsham Court	58 E1
Mart Lane	59 B3
Martello Avenue	50 D4 [14]
Martello Court	4 D4
Martello Mews	48 E1
Martello Terrace	29 B3 [2]
Martello Terrace	67 C2 [2]
Martello Terrace (Booterstown)	48 F3 [1]
Martello Terrace (Dun Laoghaire)	50 E4 [2]
Martello View	39 B4 [3]
Martello Wood	39 B4 [6]
Martin Grove	24 D4
Martin Savage Park	23 C3
Martin Street	38 D4 [34]
Martin White Chalets	39 A4 [9]
Martin's Row	36 E2
*Martin's Terrace (off Hanover Street East)	38 E2
Mary Street	38 D2
Mary Street Little	38 D2 [32]
Maryfield Avenue	26 E2 [1]
Maryfield Crescent	26 E2
Maryfield Drive	26 D2
Maryland	64 E2 [5]
Mary's Abbey	38 D2
Mary's Lane	38 D2
Maryville Road	26 F3
Mask Avenue	26 E2
Mask Crescent	26 E2
Mask Drive	26 E2
Mask Green	26 E2
Mask Road	26 E2
Mather Road North	48 E3
Mather Road South	48 D3
Matt Talbot Court	38 E1 [28]
Maunsell Place	38 D1 [52]
Maxwell Court	47 A1 [18]
Maxwell Lane	47 A2
Maxwell Road	47 A1
Maxwell Street	37 C3 [10]
May Lane	37 C2
May Park	26 D3
*May Street (off Fitzroy Ave)	25 B4
Mayberry Park	45 A4
Mayberry Road	45 A4
Mayfair	3 C2
Mayfield	47 A2
Mayfield Park	35 B4
Mayfield Road (Kilmainham)	37 B3 [11]
Mayfield Road (Terenure)	46 F2
Mayfield Terrace	67 C3 [17]
Mayfield Terrace (Ballinteer)	57 C2
Maynooth	17 C2
Maynooth	18 D2
Maynooth Park	18 D4
Maynooth Road	7 A3
Maynooth Road (Celbridge)	31 C1
Mayola Court	47 B3
Mayor Street Lower	38 E2
Mayor Street Upper	38 F2
Mayville Terrace	60 F1 [11]
Maywood Avenue	27 B2
Maywood Close	27 B2
Maywood Crescent	27 B3
Maywood Drive	27 B2
Maywood Grove	27 B2
Maywood Lawn	27 B3
Maywood Park	27 B2
Maywood Road	27 B2
McAuley Avenue	26 F2
McAuley Drive	26 F2
McAuley Park	26 F2
McAuley Road	26 F2
McCabe Villas	48 E3
McCarthy Terrace	37 B3 [25]
McCreadies Lane	3 A3
McDowell Avenue	37 B3 [8]
McGrane Court	57 C1 [5]
McKee Avenue	24 E1
McKee Park	37 B1
McKee Road	24 E1
McKelvey Avenue	11 A4
McKelvey Road	11 A4
McMahon Street	38 D4 [27]
McMorrough Road	46 F2 [14]
Meade's Terrace	38 E3 [6]
Meadow Avenue	57 B1 [1]
Meadow Close (Dundrum)	57 A1
Meadow Close (Newtown Park Ave)	59 A1
Meadow Copse	21 C1
Meadow Court	60 D4 [2]
Meadow Dale	21 C1 [1]
Meadow Downs	21 C1
Meadow Drive	21 C1
Meadow Green	21 C1
Meadow Grove	57 B1
Meadow Mount	57 A1
Meadow Park	57 A1
Meadow Park Avenue	47 A4
Meadow Vale	59 B2
Meadow View	7 B2
Meadow View	57 A1
Meadow Villas	57 A1 [2]
Meadow Way	21 C1
Meadowbank	46 F3
Meadowbrook	17 C4
Meadowbrook Ave	17 C4
Meadowbrook Avenue	28 D1
Meadowbrook Close	17 C4
Meadowbrook Court	17 C4
Meadowbrook Crescent	17 C4
Meadowbrook Drive	17 C4
Meadowbrook Grange	6 E4
Meadowbrook Green	17 C4
Meadowbrook Lawn	28 D1
Meadowbrook Lawns	17 C4
Meadowbrook Park	28 D1
Meadowbrook Road	17 C4
Meadowfield	58 E4
Meadowlands	59 C1
Meadowview Grove	33 C2
Meakstown Cottages	11 B3
Meath Market	37 C3 [16]
Meath Place	37 C3
Meath Place	67 C2
Meath Road	68 D2
Meath Square	37 C3 [42]
Meath Street	37 C3
*Meath Terrace (on Meath Place)	37 C3
*Meathville Terrace (on Long Lane)	38 D3
Meetinghouse Lane	38 D2 [33]
Méile an Rí Crescent	34 F3
Méile an Rí Drive	34 F3
Méile an Rí Green	34 F3
Méile an Rí Park	34 F3
Méile an Rí Road	34 F3
Méile an Rí View	34 F3
Mellifont Avenue	50 D4
Mellowes Avenue	24 D1
Mellowes Court	24 D2 [3]
Mellowes Crescent	24 D2 [4]
Mellowes Park	24 D1
Mellowes Road	24 D1
Melrose Avenue (Clondalkin)	43 C1
Melrose Avenue (Fairview)	25 C4
Melrose Crescent	43 C1
Melrose Green	34 F4
Melrose Green	43 C1
Melrose Grove	43 C1
Melrose Lawn	34 F4
Melrose Park	2 E3
Melrose Park	43 C1
Melrose Road	34 F4
Melville Close	11 B4
Melville Court	11 B4
Melville Crescent	11 B4
Melville Drive	11 B4
Melville Green	11 B4
Melville Grove	11 B4
Melville Park	11 B4
Melville Terrace	11 B4
Melville View	11 B4
Melville Way	11 B4
Melvin Road	46 F2
Memorial Road	37 A3 [7]
Memorial Road	38 E2
Mercer Street Lower	38 D3
Mercer Street Upper	38 D3
Merchamp	26 F4
*Merchants Arch (off Temple Bar)	38 D2
Merchant's Quay	37 C2
Merchant's Road	39 A1
Merchant's Square	38 F2 [15]
Meretimo Villas	68 D3 [2]
Merlyn Drive	48 D1
Merlyn Park	48 D1
Merlyn Road	48 D1
Merrion	48 E1
Merrion Close	38 E3 [26]
Merrion Court	48 E1 [1]
Merrion Crescent	48 E2 [3]
Merrion Gates	48 E1 [1]
Merrion Grove	48 E3
Merrion Park	48 E3
Merrion Place	38 E3 [8]
Merrion Road	39 A4
Merrion Row	38 E3
Merrion Square East	38 E3
Merrion Square North	38 E3
Merrion Square South	38 E3
Merrion Square West	38 E3
Merrion Strand	48 E1
Merrion Street Lower	38 E3 [27]
Merrion Street Upper	38 E3
Merrion View Avenue	48 D1 [1]
Merrion Village	48 E1

STREET NAME	PAGE/GRID REFERENCE	STREET NAME	PAGE/GRID REFERENCE	STREET NAME	PAGE/GRID REFERENCE	STREET NAME	PAGE/GRID REFERENCE	STREET NAME	PAGE/GRID REFERENCE
Merton Avenue	37 C4 [25]	Millwood Court	27 A1	Montpelier Drive	37 B2	Mount Argus Way	46 F1		
Merton Drive	47 B1	Millwood Park	27 A1	Montpelier Gardens	37 B2 [5]	Mount Auburn	60 E3 [2]		
Merton Park	37 C4 [27]	Millwood Villas	27 A1	Montpelier Gardens	37 B2	Mount Bellew Crescent	34 F2		
Merton Road	47 B2	Milton Terrace	67 C2 [13]	Montpelier Hill	37 B2	Mount Bellew Green	34 F2		
Merville Avenue (Fairview)	25 C4	Milward Terrace	68 D2 [13]	Montpelier Manor	49 B4 [2]	Mount Bellew Rise	34 F2		
Merville Avenue (Stillorgan)	58 F1	Mine Hill Lane	63 B3	Montpelier Parade	49 B4	Mount Bellew Way	34 E2		
Merville Road	58 F1	*Minstrel Court	58 F2	Montpelier Park	37 B2	Mount Brown	37 B3		
Mespil Estate	38 E4	(Charles Sheil's Houses)		Montpelier Place	49 B4 [1]	Mount Carmel Avenue	47 C4		
Mespil Road	38 E4	Misery Hill	38 F2	Montrose Avenue	26 D2	Mount Carmel Park	55 C1		
Michael Collins Park	44 D1	Moat Lane	1 A2	Montrose Close	26 D2	Mount Carmel Road	47 C4		
Middle Third	26 E3	Moatfield Avenue	26 F1	Montrose Court	26 D2	Mount Dillon Court	26 E2		
Milesian Avenue	2 E2	Moatfield Park	26 F1	Montrose Crescent	26 D1	Mount Drinan Avenue	2 E3		
Milesian Court	2 E2	Moatfield Road	26 F1	Montrose Drive	26 D1	Mount Drinan Crescent	2 E3		
Milesian Grove	2 E2	Moatview Avenue	13 B4	Montrose Grove	26 D2	Mount Drinan Grove	2 E3		
Milesian Lawn	2 E2	Moatview Court	13 B4	Montrose Park	26 D2	Mount Drinan Lawn	2 E3		
Milestown	6 F4	Moatview Drive	13 B4	Moore Lane	38 D2 [15]	Mount Drinan Park	2 E3		
Milestown	19 C1	Moatview Gardens	13 B4	Moore Street	38 D2	Mount Drinan Walk	2 E3		
Milford	3 A2	Mobhi Court	25 A3 [16]	Moorefield	60 E4	Mount Drummond Avenue	37 C4		
Military Road	37 B3	Mobhi Road	25 A3	Moore's Cottages	59 A1 [3]	Mount Drummond Court	37 C4 [30]		
Military Road (Killiney)	60 E4	Moeran Road	45 C1	Mooretown	1 B1	Mount Drummond Square	38 D4		
Military Road (Phoenix Park)	36 F2	*Moira Road	37 B1	Mooretown Avenue	1 C1	Mount Eagle Court	58 E3		
Military Road (Rathmines)	38 D4	(off Oxmanstown Road)		Mooretown Grove	1 C1	Mount Eagle Drive	58 E3		
Military Road (Woodtown)	56 D3	Moland Place	38 E2 [21]	Mooretown Park	1 C1	Mount Eagle Green	58 E3		
Mill Bank	34 D1 [15]	Molesworth Close	1 A2	Mooreview (Apts.)	13 C4	Mount Eagle Grove	58 E3		
Mill Brook (Apts.)	35 C1	Molesworth Place	38 E3 [24]	Moorfield	35 A4	Mount Eagle Lawn	58 E3		
Mill Court Avenue	43 C1	Molesworth Street	38 E3	Moorfield Avenue	35 A4	Mount Eagle Park	58 E3		
Mill Court Drive	43 C1	Molyneux Yard	37 C3 [19]	Moorfield Close	35 A4 [2]	Mount Eagle Rise	58 D3		
Mill Field	66 E3	Monalea Grove	55 C1	Moorfield Drive	35 A4	Mount Eagle View	58 E3		
Mill House	62 F3	Monalea Park	55 C1	Moorfield Green	35 A4	Mount Eagle Way	58 E3		
Mill Lane	33 A1	Monalea Wood	55 C1	Moorfield Grove	35 A4	Mount Eden Road	47 C1		
Mill Lane (Ashtown)	23 B3 [1]	Monaloe Avenue	59 C3	Moorfield Lawns	35 A4	Mount Eustace	9 A2		
Mill Lane (Loughlinstown)	64 E2	Monaloe Court	59 B3 [6]	Moorfield Parade	35 A4	Mount Eustace Avenue	9 B2		
Mill Lane (Newmarket)	37 C3 [26]	Monaloe Crescent	59 B3 [4]	Moorfield Walk	35 A4	Mount Eustace Close	9 A2		
*Mill Lane	67 C2	Monaloe Drive	59 C3	Moracrete Cottages	37 B4 [4]	Mount Eustace Drive	9 A2		
(off Castle Street Bray)		Monaloe Park	59 C3	Moran's Cottages	47 B1 [12]	Mount Eustace Green	9 B2		
Mill Lane (Palmerston)	35 C1	Monaloe Park Road	59 C3	Moreen Avenue	58 D2 [8]	Mount Eustace Grove	9 A2		
Mill Park	44 D1	Monaloe Way	59 C3	Moreen Avenue	58 D2	Mount Eustace Park	9 A2		
Mill Road (Blanchardstown)	22 F2	Monasterboice Road	46 E1	Moreen Close	58 D2	Mount Eustace Rise	9 B2		
Mill Road (Saggart)	53 A2	Monastery	66 E3	Moreen Lawn	58 D2 [2]	Mount Eustace Walk	9 B2		
Mill Street	37 C3	Monastery Crescent	44 E1	Moreen Park	58 D2	Mount Gandon	34 D1 [9]		
Mill Street (Dun Laoghaire)	50 D4 [19]	Monastery Drive	44 E1	Moreen Road	58 D2	Mount Harold Terrace	46 F1 [1]		
Millbank	14 F2	Monastery Gate	44 F1	Moreen Walk	58 D2	Mount Merrion	48 E4		
Millbourne Avenue	25 A4	Monastery Gate Avenue	44 F1	Morehampton Lane	38 F4	Mount Merrion Avenue	48 F3		
Millbrook Avenue	27 A1	Monastery Gate Close	44 F1	Morehampton Mews	38 F4 [12]	Mount Norris Villas	68 D2 [19]		
Millbrook Court	37 B3 [35]	Monastery Gate Copse	44 F1	Morehampton Road	38 F4	Mount Olive Grove	27 B1		
Millbrook Drive	27 A1	Monastery Gate Green	44 F1	Morehampton Square	38 F4 [11]	Mount Olive Park	27 B1		
Millbrook Grove	27 A1	Monastery Gate Lawn	44 F1	Morehampton Terrace	47 B1	Mount Olive Road	27 B1		
Millbrook Lawns	55 A1	Monastery Gate Villas	44 F1	Morgan Place	37 C2 [14]	Mount Prospect Avenue	26 F4		
Millbrook Road	27 A1	Monastery Grove	66 E2	Morgans Place	23 A3	Mount Prospect Drive	26 F4		
Millbrook Terrace	37 A3 [24]	Monastery Heath	44 E1	Moritz House	55 B2	Mount Prospect Grove	26 F4		
Millbrook Village	47 C1 [17]	Monastery Heath Avenue	44 E1	Morning Star Avenue	37 C2 [24]	Mount Prospect Lawn	26 F4		
Millennium Park	22 D2	Monastery Heath Court	44 E1	Morning Star Road	37 B3 [19]	Mount Prospect Park	26 F4		
Blanchardstown		Monastery Heath Green	44 E1	Mornington Avenue	50 E4 [1]	Mount Salus Road	60 F2		
Millers Wood	67 B3	Monastery Heath Square	44 E1	Mornington Grove	26 E2	Mount Sandford	47 C1 [14]		
Millfarm	7 C2	Monastery Heights	44 E1 [2]	Mornington Park	26 E2	Mount St Agnes	47 B2		
Millfield	14 F2	Monastery Park	44 E1	Mornington Road	47 B1	Mount Street Crescent	38 F3 [32]		
Millgate Drive	45 C3	Monastery Rise	44 E1	Morrogh Terrace	25 C3 [2]	Mount Street Lower	38 E3		
Millmount Avenue	25 A4	Monastery Road	44 E1	Moss Street	38 E2	Mount Street Upper	38 E3		
Millmount Grove	47 B3	Monastery Walk	44 E1	Mount Albany	59 A1	Mount Symon Avenue	21 C2		
Millmount Place	25 B4	Monck Place	37 C1	Mount Albion Road	57 B1 [3]	Mount Symon Close	21 C2		
Millmount Terrace	25 B4	Monks Hill	66 E2	Mount Albion Road	57 B1	Mount Symon Crescent	21 C2		
(Drumcondra)		Monks Meadow	4 D4	Mount Alton	55 C1	Mount Symon Dale	21 B2		
Millmount Villas	25 A4 [1]	Monksfield	44 F1	Mount Alton Court	56 D1	Mount Symon Drive	21 C2		
Millrose Estate	36 E4 [2]	Monksfield Court	44 F1	Mount Andrew	34 F2	Mount Symon Estate	21 B2		
Millstead	22 F2	Monksfield Downs	44 F1	Mount Andrew Avenue	34 F2	Mount Symon Green	21 B2		
Millstream	14 F2	Monksfield Grove	44 F1	Mount Andrew Close	34 F2	Mount Symon Lawn	21 C2		
Millstream Road	33 C2	Monksfield Heights	44 F1	Mount Andrew Court	34 F1	Mount Symon Park	21 C2		
Milltown	42 F2	Monksfield Lawn	44 F1	Mount Andrew Dale	34 F2	Mount Symon Rise	21 B2		
Milltown	47 C2	Monksfield Meadows	44 F1	Mount Andrew Grove	34 F1	Mount Tallant Avenue	46 F2		
Milltown Bridge Road	47 C2	Monksfield Walk	44 F1	Mount Andrew Rise	34 F1	Mount Temple Road	37 C2		
*Milltown Collonade	47 B2	Monkstown	49 B4	Mount Annville Road	48 D4	Mount Venus Road	56 D4		
(on Milltown Road)		Monkstown Avenue	59 B1	Mount Annville Wood	48 D4	Mount View Road	22 D2		
Milltown Drive	47 A3	Monkstown Crescent	49 C4	Mount Anthony Estate	47 A1 [22]	Mount Wood	59 C1		
Milltown Grove	47 B2 [6]	Monkstown Farm	59 C1	Mount Anville Lawn	48 D4	Mountain Park	55 A1		
Milltown Grove	47 A3	Monkstown Gate	49 C4 [29]	Mount Anville Park	48 D4	Mountain View	54 D2		
Milltown Hill	47 B2 [7]	Monkstown Grove	59 C1	Mount Argus Avenue	46 F1	Mountain View Apartments	67 C3 [11]		
Milltown Park	47 B2	Monkstown Road	49 B4	Mount Argus Close	46 F1	Mountain View Avenue	46 F1		
Milltown Path	47 B2	Monkstown Square	59 B1 [12]	Mount Argus Court	46 F1	Mountain View Cottages	22 D4		
Milltown Road	47 B1	Monkstown Valley	49 B4	Mount Argus Crescent	46 F1	(Castleknock)			
Milltown Terrace (Dundrum)	47 B3 [4]	Montague Court	38 D3 [25]	Mount Argus Green	46 F1	Mountain View Cottages	47 B1 [13]		
Millview	44 E1 [7]	Montague Lane	38 D3 [13]	Mount Argus Grove	46 F1	(Ranelagh)			
Millview Close	3 A3	Montague Place	38 D3 [26]	Mount Argus Park	46 F1	*Mountain View Court	38 E1		
Millview Court	3 A2	Montague Street	38 D3	Mount Argus Road	46 F1	(off Summerhill Place)			
Millview Lawns	3 A3	Monte Vella	60 F2 [9]	Mount Argus Terrace	46 F1	Mountain View Drive	57 A1		
Millview Road	3 A3	Montebello Terrace	68 D2 [2]	Mount Argus View	46 F1	Mountain View Park	47 A4		

STREET NAME	PAGE/GRID REFERENCE		STREET NAME	PAGE/GRID REFERENCE		STREET NAME	PAGE/GRID REFERENCE		STREET NAME	PAGE/GRID REFERENCE	
Mountain View Road	47	B1	Muirfield Drive	36	F4 [1]	New Park Road	59	A1	Newtown Road	13	C4
Mountain View Road	60	E4 [5]	Mulally's Lane	52	F2	New Rathmore Terrace	67	B2 [23]	Newtown Road	17	B4
Mountain Villa	60	E4 [3]	Mulberry Crescent	22	F4	New Ravenswell Row	67	B2 [20]	Newtown Road	17	C3
Mountainview Drive	67	C4	Mulberry Drive	22	E4	New River Road	23	A2	Newtown Road	32	D4
Mountbrook	48	E3 [2]	Mulberry Park	22	E4	New Road	2	D2 [5]	Newtown Upper	52	D4
Mountdown Avenue	45	C3	Muldowney Court	3	C3	New Road (Clondalkin)	44	E2	Newtown Villas	47	A3 [4]
Mountdown Drive	45	C3	Mulgrave Street	50	D4	New Road (Howth)	30	E3	Newtown Villas	49	A3 [1]
Mountdown Park	45	C3	Mulgrave Terrace	50	D4	New Road (Inchicore)	36	F3	Newtownpark House	59	A1 [11]
Mountdown Road	45	C3	Mulhuddart	9	A4	New Row	36	E2 [12]	Newtownsmith	50	E4
Mountgorry Wood (Apts.)	2	E2	Mulhuddart Wood	9	A4	New Row South	37	C3	Niall Street	37	B2 [11]
Mountjoy Parade	38	E1 [36]	Mullauns	42	D1	New Row Square	37	C3 [32]	Nicholas Avenue	37	C2 [7]
Mountjoy Place	38	E1 [22]	Mullinastill Road	64	D2	New Street	3	B2	Nicholas Street	38	D3
Mountjoy Square	38	E1	Mullingar Terrace	36	E2 [10]	New Street	38	D3	Ninth Lock Road	44	D1
Mountjoy Square Apts	38	E1 [65]	Mulroy Road	24	E4	New Street	38	D3	Noel Purcell Park	38	D3 [55]
Mountjoy Square East	38	E1	Mulvey Park	47	C3	*New Street Garden's	38	D3	Nore Road	24	E3
Mountjoy Square North	38	E1	Munster Street	24	F4	(off New Street)			Norfolk Road	24	F4
Mountjoy Square South	38	E1	Munster Terrace	60	E1 [16]	*New Street North	37	C2	*Norseman Court	37	C2
Mountjoy Square West	38	D1	Murphy's Lane	63	B4	(off Church Street)			(off Norseman Place)		
Mountjoy Street	38	D1	Murphy's Lane	66	E1	New Vale	64	E3	Norseman Place	37	C2
Mountjoy Street Middle	38	D1 [9]	Murphystown Road	58	E3	New Vale Cottages	64	D3	North Avenue	48	E4
Mountpleasant Avenue Lower	38	D4	Murray's Cottages	36	F3 [4]	New Vale Crescent	64	E3	North Bull Island	27	B4
Mountpleasant Avenue Upper	38	D4	Murtagh Road	37	C2 [30]	New Wapping Street	38	F2	North Circular Road	37	C1
Mountpleasant Parade	38	D4 [39]	Muskerry Road	36	E3	Newbridge Avenue	39	A3	(Phibsborough)		
Mountpleasant Place	38	E4 [22]	Mutton Lane	56	E4	Newbridge Drive	39	A3	North Circular Road	37	B1
Mountpleasant Square	38	D4	Myra Cottages	37	A3 [21]	Newbrook Avenue	27	B1	(Phoenix Park)		
Mountpleasant Terrace	38	D4 [40]	Myrtle Avenue	60	D1 [3]	Newbrook Road	27	B1	North Clarence St Flats	38	E1 [66]
*Mountpleasant Terrace Upper	38	E4	Myrtle Grove	58	F1	Newbury Avenue	13	A4	North Great George's St	38	D1
(off Mountpleasant Place)			Myrtle Grove	67	B1 [3]	Newbury Drive	13	A4	North Quay Extension	39	A2
Mountpleasant Villas	67	B2 [13]	Myrtle Park	60	D1	Newbury Grove	13	A4	North Road	11	A4
*Mountpleasant Villas	38	E4	Myrtle Street	38	D1 [23]	Newbury Lawns	13	B4	North Road (Phoenix Park)	37	A1
(off Mountpleasant Place)						Newbury Park	13	A4	North Strand Road	38	F1
Mountsandel	59	B4	**N**			Newbury Terrace	13	A4 [1]	North Street	2	D1
Mountshannon Road	37	B3				Newcastle	41	C4	North Wall	38	F2
Mounttown Cottages	49	C4 [26]	N.U.I. Maynooth	17	C2	Newcastle Demesne	41	B4	North Wall Quay	38	F2
Mounttown Lower	59	C1	Naas Road	45	A1	Newcastle Farm	41	B4	Northbrook Avenue (Ranelagh)	38	E4
Mounttown Park	59	C1 [3]	Naas Road	52	F1	Newcastle Road	34	D2	Northbrook Avenue Lower	38	F1
Mounttown Road Upper	49	C4	Naas Road	52	F2	Newcastle Road	52	E1	Northbrook Avenue Upper	38	F1
Mourne Road	37	A4	Naas Road (Saggart)	53	B1	Newcomen Avenue	38	E1	Northbrook Lane	38	E4 [20]
Moy Elta Road	38	F1	Nagle Court	18	D2	Newcomen Court	38	E1 [29]	Northbrook Road	38	E4
Moy Glas Avenue	34	E3	Nangor Crescent	44	D1 [5]	Newcourt	2	D1	Northbrook Terrace	38	F1 [1]
Moy Glas Chase	34	E3	Nangor Place	43	C1 [2]	Newcourt	68	D4	*Northbrook Villas	38	E4
Moy Glas Close	34	E3	Nangor Road	43	A2	Newcourt Avenue	68	D3	(on Northbrook Road Ranelagh)		
Moy Glas Court	34	E3	Nangor Road	45	A1	Newcourt Road	68	D3	Northcote Avenue	49	C4
Moy Glas Dale	34	E3	Nangor Road (Clondalkin)	44	D1	Newcourt Villas	67	C3 [8]	Northcote Place	49	C4 [23]
Moy Glas Dene	34	E3	Nangor Road (Fox & Geese)	44	F1	Newgrange Road (Cabra)	24	F4	Northcote Terrace	49	C4 [20]
Moy Glas Drive	34	E3	Nanikin Avenue	27	A3	Newgrove Avenue	39	B4	Northern Close	13	B3
Moy Glas Glen	34	E3	Nash Street	36	F3	Newhall Court	54	D2	Northland Drive	24	F3 [2]
Moy Glas Grove	34	E3	Nashville Park	30	E2	Newlands Avenue	44	E2	Northland Grove	24	F3 [1]
Moy Glas Lawn	34	E3	Nashville Road	30	D2	Newlands Drive	44	E2	Northumberland Avenue	50	D4
Moy Glas Park	34	E3	Nassau Street	38	E3	Newlands Manor	44	D3	Northumberland Park	50	D4 [11]
Moy Glas Road	34	E3	Naul Road	1	C4	Newlands Manor Court	44	D3	Northumberland Place	38	F3 [42]
Moy Glas Vale	34	E3	Navan Road	8	F4	Newlands Manor Drive	44	D3	Northumberland Place	50	D4
Moy Glas View	34	E3	Navan Road (Blanchardstown)	22	E1	Newlands Manor Fairway	44	D3	Northumberland Road	38	F3
Moy Glas Way	34	E3	Navan Road (Cabra)	24	D4	Newlands Manor Green	44	D3	Northumberland Square	38	E2 [8]
Moy Glas Wood	34	E3	Navan Road (Clonee)	8	E3	Newlands Manor Park	44	D2	Northway Estate	11	A4
Moyclare Avenue	28	D1	Navan Road (Dunboyne)	7	B2	Newlands Park	44	E2	Northwood	12	E4
Moyclare Close	28	D1	Neagh Road	46	E2	Newlands Road	34	F3	Norton's Avenue	37	C1 [9]
Moyclare Drive	28	D1	Neillstown Avenue	35	A3	Newlands Road	44	E2	Norwood	64	E1
Moyclare Gardens	28	D1 [6]	Neillstown Crescent	35	A3	Newman Place	18	D3	Norwood Park	47	C1 [7]
Moyclare Park	28	D1	Neillstown Drive	35	A3	Newmarket	37	C3	Nottingham Street	38	F1
Moyclare Road	28	D1	Neillstown Gardens	35	A3	Newmarket Street	37	C3 [25]	Novara Avenue	67	C2
Moycullen Road	35	C3	Neillstown Park	35	A3	Newport Street	37	C3	Novara Mews	67	C2 [57]
Moygaddy	18	D1	Neilstown Cottages	35	A4 [3]	Newtown	7	A3	Novara Park	67	C2 [5]
Moyglare	17	A1	Neilstown Road	35	A3	Newtown	56	E3	Novara Terrace	67	C2 [27]
Moyglare Abbey	17	B2	Neilstown Village Court	35	A3 [1]	Newtown	62	E3	Nugent Road	47	A4
Moyglare Abbey	17	C2	Nelson Street	38	D1	Newtown	66	E4	Nunciature Road	23	C4
Moyglare Meadows	17	C2	Nephin Road	24	D4	Newtown Avenue	26	F1	Nurney Lawn	14	D4
Moyglare Road	17	C2	Neptune Terrace	60	E1 [17]	Newtown Avenue	49	A3	Nutgrove Avenue	47	B4 [1]
Moyglare Village	17	C2	Nerano Road	60	F2	Newtown Cottages	11	A1	Nutgrove Avenue	47	A4
Moyle Crescent	44	E1	Nerney's Court	38	D1 [44]	Newtown Cottages	26	F1	Nutgrove Court	47	A4 [2]
Moyle Road	24	E3	Nethercross Court	2	E2	Newtown Court	13	C4	Nutgrove Crescent	57	A1
Moyne Court	47	B1 [22]	Nethercross Court	24	D2 [8]	Newtown Court	17	B4	Nutgrove Park (Clonskeagh)	47	C2
Moyne Park	14	F3	Neville Road	47	A2	Newtown Court	17	B4	Nutgrove Way	57	A1
Moyne Road	47	B1	Nevinstown Lane	1	C3	Newtown Court	47	A3 [5]	Nutley Avenue	48	D1
Moyne Road (Balgriffin)	14	E3	New Bawn Drive	55	A2	Newtown Drive	26	F1	Nutley Lane	48	D2
Moynihan Court	55	B1 [6]	New Bawn Park	55	A2	Newtown Glendale	20	D4	Nutley Park	48	D2
Moyville	56	E2	New Brighton Terrace	67	C2 [47]	Newtown Grove	17	C3	Nutley Road	48	D1
Moyville Lawns	56	E1	New Grange Park	68	D2 [22]	Newtown House	47	A3 [12]	Nutley Square	48	D2 [1]
Muckross Avenue	46	D2	New Grange Road	59	A1	Newtown Lower	51	C4			
Muckross Crescent	46	D2	(Deans Grange)			Newtown Lower	52	D4	**O**		
Muckross Drive	46	D2 [1]	New Grove Estate	14	E4	Newtown Park	20	D4			
Muckross Green	46	D2	New Hall Court	54	D1	Newtown Park	26	F1	O Neill's Park	18	D3
Muckross Grove	46	D2	New Ireland Road	37	B3	Newtown Park (Blackrock)	59	A1	Oak Apple Green	47	A2
Muckross Parade	38	D1 [32]	New Nangor Road	43	C1	Newtown Park (Tallaght)	55	B1	Oak Avenue	12	F4
Muckross Park	46	D2	New Park Lodge	59	A2 [3]	Newtown Park Avenue	49	A4	Oak Court	12	F4
						Newtown Park Court	59	A1 [8]	Oak Crescent	12	F4

STREET NAME	PAGE/GRID REFERENCE
Oak Dene	60 E3
Oak Downs	44 D2
Oak Drive	12 F4
Oak Glen Park	67 C4
Oak Glen View	67 C4
Oak Green	12 F4
Oak Grove	12 F4
Oak Lawn	12 F4
Oak Lawn (Castleknock)	22 F3
Oak Lodge	23 A4
Oak Rise	12 F4
Oak Rise	44 D2
Oak Road (Donnycarney)	26 D3
Oak Road (Fox & Geese)	44 F1
Oak View	12 E4
Oak Way	44 D2
Oakcourt Avenue	35 C2
Oakcourt Close	35 C2
Oakcourt Drive	35 C2
Oakcourt Grove	35 C2
Oakcourt Lawn	35 C2
Oakcourt Park	35 C2
Oakdale Close	55 B3
Oakdale Crescent	55 B3
Oakdale Drive	55 B3
Oakdale Drive	59 C2
Oakdale Grove	55 B3
Oakdale Road	55 B3
Oakdale View	55 B3
Oakdown Road	47 A4
Oakfield Place	38 D4 [50]
Oaklands Avenue	2 D2
Oaklands Crescent	47 A2
Oaklands Drive (Rathgar)	47 A2
Oaklands Drive (Sandymount)	39 A4
Oaklands Park	2 D2
Oaklands Park	39 A4
Oaklands Terrace	46 F2
Oaklawn	19 C4
Oaklawn Close	19 C4
Oaklawn West	19 C4
Oakleigh	31 C4
Oakley Court (Flats)	47 B1 [10]
Oakley Grove	49 A4
Oakley Park (Blackrock)	49 A4
Oakley Park (Clontarf)	26 F4
Oakley Park (Ranelagh)	47 B1 [23]
Oakley Road	47 B1
Oakpark Avenue	25 C1
Oakpark Close	25 C1
Oakpark Drive	25 C1
Oakpark Grove	25 C1
Oakton Court	60 E4 [1]
Oakton Drive	60 D4
Oakton Green	60 D4 [3]
Oakton Park	60 D4
Oaktree Avenue	22 E3
Oaktree Drive	22 E3
Oaktree Green	22 E3
Oaktree Grove	22 E3
Oaktree Lawn	22 E3
Oaktree Road	58 F1
Oakview Avenue	21 C1
Oakview Close	21 C1
Oakview Court	21 C1
Oakview Drive	21 C1
Oakview Grove	21 C1 [2]
Oakview Lawn	21 C1
Oakview Park	21 C1
Oakview Rise	21 C1
Oakview Walk	21 C1
Oakview Way	21 C1
Oakwood	49 C4 [7]
Oakwood Avenue	1 C2
Oakwood Avenue	24 E1
Oakwood Close	24 E1
Oakwood Grove Estate	35 A4
Oakwood Park	24 E1
Oakwood Road	24 E1
Oatfield Avenue	35 B3
Oatfield Close	35 B3
*Oatfield Crescent (off Oatfield Drive)	35 B2
Oatfield Drive	35 B3
Oatfield Grove	35 B3

STREET NAME	PAGE/GRID REFERENCE
Oatfield Lawn	35 B3
Oatfield Park	35 B3
Obelisk Court	3 A3 [1]
Obelisk Lane	18 E4
Obelisk Rise	59 A1
Oblate Drive	36 F3 [14]
O'Brien Road	45 C1
O'Brien's Place North	25 A3 [13]
O'Brien's Terrace	25 A4 [15]
Observatory Lane	47 A1 [14]
O'Byrne Road	67 C3
O'Byrne Villas	67 C3 [9]
O'Carolan Road	37 C3 [29]
O'Connell Avenue	38 D1 [6]
O'Connell Gardens	39 A3
O'Connell Street	38 D2
*O'Curry Avenue (off O'Curry Road)	37 C3
O'Curry Road	37 C3
O'Daly Road	25 A3
Odd Lamp Road	36 F1
O'Devaney Gardens	37 B2
O'Donnell Gardens	60 D1 [1]
O'Donoghue Street	36 F3
O'Donovan Road	37 C4
O'Dwyer Road	45 C1 [4]
Offaly Road	24 F4
Offington Avenue	29 B2
Offington Court	29 B2
Offington Drive	29 B2
Offington Lawn	29 B2
Offington Manor Apts	29 B1 [4]
Offington Park	29 B1
O'Hanlon's Lane	3 B2
O'Hara Avenue	38 D4
O'Hogan Road	36 E3 [1]
O'Hogan Road	36 E3
Olaf Road	37 C2 [33]
Old Bawn Avenue	55 A2
Old Bawn Close	55 A2
Old Bawn Court	55 A1 [5]
Old Bawn Drive	55 A2
Old Bawn Park	55 A2
Old Bawn Road	55 A2
Old Bawn Terrace	55 A2
Old Bawn Way	55 A2
Old Belgard Road	44 F4
Old Blessington Road	55 A1
Old Brazil Way	1 A2
Old Bridge Road	46 D4
Old Brighton Terrace	67 C2 [46]
Old Cabra Road	37 B1
Old Camac Bridge	37 A3
Old Carrickbrack Road	30 D4
Old Conna Wood	67 B1
Old Connaught	67 A1
Old Connaught Avenue	67 B1
Old Connaught Grove	67 B2
Old Connaught View	67 B2
Old Corduff Road	22 E1
Old Cornmill Road	33 C2
Old County Glen	37 B4
Old County Road	37 A4
Old Dunleary	49 C4
Old Fairgreen	7 B2
Old Fort Road	1 A2
Old Greenfield	17 C3
Old Greenfield	17 C4
Old Hill	20 D4
Old Kilmainham	37 B3
Old Kilmainham Village	37 B3 [2]
Old Mill Court	37 C3 [52]
Old Mountpleasant	38 E4 [9]
Old Naas Road	36 E4
Old Naas Road Cottages	36 E4 [1]
Old Quarry	60 F2
Old Quay	29 B2
Old Quay Mews	29 B2
Old Quay Terrace	29 B2
Old Rathmichael	64 D3
Old Rathmore Terrace	67 B2 [22]
Old Ravenswell Row	67 B2 [19]
Old Rectory	34 D1 [11]
Old Rectory Park	47 C4
Old Road (Portmarnock)	14 E2

STREET NAME	PAGE/GRID REFERENCE
Old Street	3 B2
Old Yellow Walls Road	2 F2
Oldbawn	55 A2
Oldbridge	34 E3
Oldbridge Close	34 E3
Oldbridge Court	34 E3
Oldbridge Glen	34 E3
Oldbridge Green	34 E3
Oldbridge Grove	34 E3
Oldbridge Park	34 E3
Oldbridge View	34 E3
Oldbridge Walk	34 E3
Oldbridge Way	34 E3
Oldcarton	18 F1
Oldcastle Avenue	29 B2
Oldcastle Drive	43 B1
Oldcastlepark	43 B1
Oldcastlepark Close	43 B1
Oldcastlepark Green	43 B1
Oldcastlepark Grove	43 B1
Oldcastlepark Lawn	43 B1
Oldcastlepark View	43 B1
Oldchurch Avenue	43 C1
Oldchurch Close	43 C1
Oldchurch Court	43 C1
Oldchurch Crescent	43 C1
Oldchurch Drive	43 C1
Oldchurch Grove	43 C1
Oldchurch Lawns	43 C1
Oldchurch Park	43 C1
Oldchurch Way	43 C1
Oldcourt	67 B3
Oldcourt Avenue	55 B2
Oldcourt Avenue	67 B3
Oldcourt Close	55 B2
Oldcourt Cottages	55 B3
Oldcourt Drive	67 B3
Oldcourt Grove	67 B4
Oldcourt Lawn	55 B2 [1]
Oldcourt Lodge	55 B2
Oldcourt Manor	55 B3
Oldcourt Park	67 B3
Oldcourt Road	55 B3
Oldcourt Terrace	67 C3 [15]
Oldcourt View	55 B2
Oldfarm	22 E3
Oldfarm Lane	22 E3
Oldtower Crescent	35 A2
Oldtown Avenue	25 A1
Oldtown Cottages	31 C3
Oldtown Mill	31 C3
Oldtown Mill Glade	31 C3
Oldtown Mill Road	31 C3
Oldtown Park	25 A1 [3]
Oldtown Road	25 A1
O'Leary Road	37 A3
Olivemount Grove	47 C3 [2]
Olivemount Road	47 C3
Olivemount Terrace	47 C3 [6]
Oliver Bond Street	37 C2
Oliver Plunkett Avenue (Dun Laoghaire)	59 C1
Oliver Plunkett Avenue (Ringsend)	39 A3
Oliver Plunkett Road	59 C1
Oliver Plunkett Square	59 C1 [1]
Oliver Plunkett Terrace	59 C1 [5]
Oliver Plunkett Villas	59 B1 [3]
Olney Crescent	46 F2
Olney Grove	46 F2 [17]
Omni Park	25 B1
O'Moore Road	36 E3
O'Neachtain Road	25 A3 [14]
O'Neill's Buildings	38 D3 [14]
Ongar Chase Estate	21 A1
Ongar Lodge Apts	21 B1 [4]
Ongar Park Estate	21 B1
Ongar Road	21 B2
Ongar Village	21 A1
Ontario Terrace	38 D4 [11]
Onward Close	3 C4
Onward Walk	3 C4
Ophaly Court	47 C4 [1]
*O'Quinn Avenue (off Mount Brown)	37 B3

STREET NAME	PAGE/GRID REFERENCE
O'Quinns Avenue	37 B3 [40]
O'Rahilly House Flats	39 A3 [28]
O'Rahilly Parade	38 D2 [26]
Oranmore Road	35 C3
Oratory Mews Court	50 D4 [24]
Orby Avenue	58 E3
Orby Close	58 F3
Orby Court	58 F3
Orby Lawn	58 F3
Orby Park	58 F3
Orby View	58 E3
Orby Village	58 E3
Orby Way	58 E3
Orchard Avenue	21 C2
Orchard Avenue	53 B1
Orchard Avenue (City West)	53 B1
Orchard Close	22 D2
Orchard Cottages	59 A1 [1]
Orchard Court	22 E2
Orchard Green	22 D2
Orchard Grove	22 E2
Orchard Grove	42 D4
Orchard Lane	38 E4 [24]
Orchard Lane (Blackrock)	59 A1
Orchard Lane (Clondalkin)	44 E1
Orchard Lawns	35 C3
Orchard Road (Ballybough)	25 B4
Orchard Road (Raheny)	27 B2
Orchard Road South	47 B2
Orchard Square	47 B3
Orchard Terrace	67 C3 [19]
*Orchard Terrace (Grangegorman Upper)	37 C1
*Orchard View (Grangegorman Upper)	37 C1
Orchardstown Avenue	46 E4
Orchardstown Drive	46 E4
Orchardstown Park	46 E4
Orchardstown Villas	46 E4
Orchardstown Villas	56 E1
Orchardton	56 E1 [1]
Ordnance Survey Road	36 E1
O'Reilly Avenue	37 B3 [9]
Oriel Street Lower	38 F1
Oriel Street Upper	38 E2
Orlagh Avenue	56 D2
Orlagh Close	56 D2
Orlagh Court	56 D2
Orlagh Crescent	56 D2
Orlagh Downs	56 D2
Orlagh Grange	56 D2
Orlagh Green	56 D2
Orlagh Grove	56 D2
Orlagh Lawn	56 D2
Orlagh Lodge	56 D2
Orlagh Meadows	56 D2
Orlagh Park	56 D2
Orlagh Pines	56 D2
Orlagh Rise	56 D2
Orlagh View	56 D2
Orlagh Way	56 D2
Orlagh Wood	56 D2
Ormeau Drive	60 F1 [2]
Ormeau Street	38 F3 [7]
Ormond Avenue	1 B1
Ormond Close	1 B1
Ormond Crescent	1 B1
Ormond Drive	1 B1
Ormond Grove	1 B1
Ormond Lawn	1 B1
*Ormond Market (off Ormond Quay Upper)	38 D2
*Ormond Place (off Ormond Quay Upper)	38 D2
Ormond Quay Lower	38 D2
Ormond Quay Upper	38 D2
Ormond Road	25 B4
Ormond Road South (Rathmines)	47 B1
Ormond Square	38 D2 [37]
Ormond Street	37 C3
*Ormond Terrace (off Sorrento Road)	60 F2
Ormond View	1 B1
Ormond Way	1 B1

STREET NAME	PAGE/GRID REFERENCE	STREET NAME	PAGE/GRID REFERENCE	STREET NAME	PAGE/GRID REFERENCE	STREET NAME	PAGE/GRID REFERENCE
O'Rourke Park (Sallynoggin)	59 C2	Palmers Copse	35 B2	Parker Hill	47 A1 [12]	Pavillion Gate	59 A4
Orpen	58 F1	Palmers Court	35 B2	Parkgate Street	37 B2	Pea Field	48 F3
Orpen Close	48 F4	Palmers Crescent	35 B2	Parkhill Avenue	44 F3	Peamount	42 D2
Orpen Dale	48 F4 [2]	Palmers Drive	35 B2	Parkhill Close	45 A3	Peamount Road	42 D3
Orpen Green	48 F4 [6]	Palmers Glade	35 B2	Parkhill Court	44 F3	Peamount Road	42 E2
Orpen Green	58 F1	Palmers Grove	35 B2	Parkhill Drive	44 F3	Pear Tree Field	58 F1 [5]
Orpen Hill	58 F1	Palmers Lawn	35 B2	Parkhill Green	44 F3	Pearse Avenue	60 D2
Orpen Rise	58 F1	Palmers Park	35 B2	Parkhill Heights	45 A3 [1]	Pearse Brothers Park	56 F1
Orwell Bank	47 A3 [7]	Palmers Road	35 B2	Parkhill Lawn	44 F3	Pearse Close	60 D2 [3]
Orwell Court	47 A3 [3]	Palmers Walk	35 B2	Parkhill Rise	44 F3	Pearse Drive	60 D2
Orwell Gardens	47 A3	Palmerston	35 C1	Parkhill Road	44 F3	Pearse Gardens	59 C2
Orwell Mews	47 A2 [8]	Palmerston Close	47 B1 [21]	Parkhill Way	45 A3	Pearse Green	60 D2
Orwell Park	45 C3	*Palmerston Close	47 B1	Parkhill West	44 F4	Pearse Grove	38 F3 [38]
Orwell Park	45 C4	(rere of Palmerston Road)		Parklands	18 D3	Pearse House	38 E2 [1]
Orwell Park	47 A3	Palmerston Court	47 A1	Parklands	22 F3	Pearse Park	60 D2
Orwell Park Avenue	46 D3	Palmerston Gardens	47 B2	Parklands Avenue	55 B2	Pearse Road	60 D2
Orwell Park Close	46 D3	Palmerston Grove	47 C2 [5]	Parklands Close	18 D3	Pearse Road	67 B2 [12]
Orwell Park Crescent	46 D3	Palmerston Lane	47 B2	Parklands Court	18 D3	Pearse Square (Bray)	67 B2
Orwell Park Dale	45 C4	Palmerston Park	35 B2	Parklands Court	55 B2	Pearse Street	38 E2
Orwell Park Drive	46 D3	Palmerston Park	47 B2	Parklands Crescent	18 D3	Pearse Street (Sallynoggin)	60 D2
Orwell Park Glade	45 C3	Palmerston Place	38 D1 [8]	Parklands Drive	55 B2	Pearse Villas	60 D2
Orwell Park Glen	46 D3	Palmerston Road	47 B1	Parklands Grove	18 D3	Pebble Hill	18 D2
Orwell Park Green	46 D3	Palmerston Villas	47 A2	Parklands Lawns	18 D3	Pebble Hill	18 D2
Orwell Park Grove	45 C3	Palmerstown Avenue	35 C2	Parklands Rise	18 D3	Pebble Hill Lodge	18 D2
Orwell Park Heights	45 C4	Palmerstown Close	35 B2	Parklands Road	55 B2	Peck's Lane	23 A3
Orwell Park Lawns	45 C3	Palmerstown Court	35 C2	Parklands Square	18 D3	Pelletstown Avenue	23 C3
Orwell Park Rise	45 C4	Palmerstown Drive	35 C2	Parklands View	55 B2	Pemberton	67 A3
Orwell Park View	45 C4	Palmerstown Green	35 B2	Parklands Way	18 D3	Pembroke Cottages	48 F3 [2]
Orwell Park Way	46 D3	Palmerstown Heights	35 B2	Parkmore	23 A3	(Booterstown)	
Orwell Road	47 A2	Palmerstown Lawn	35 B2	Parkmore Drive	46 E2	Pembroke Cottages	47 C1 [2]
Orwell Walk	47 A3	Palmerstown Manor	35 B2	Parknasilla Avenue	64 D2	(Donnybrook)	
Orwell Woods	47 A2	Palmerstown Woods	35 B4	Parknasilla Close	64 D2	Pembroke Cottages (Dundrum)	47 C4 [5]
*Osborne Terrace	38 E4	Paradise Place	38 D1	Parknasilla Lane	64 D2	Pembroke Cottages (Ringsend)	39 A2
(Northbrook Road)		Park Avenue	1 B2	Parknasilla Rise	64 D2	Pembroke Gardens	38 F4
Oscar Square	37 C3 [23]	Park Avenue	22 F3	Parknasillog	65 C2	Pembroke Lane	38 E3
Oscar Traynor Road	26 E1	Park Avenue (Deans Grange)	59 A1	Parkvale	28 D1	(Lr Baggot Street)	
O'Shea's Cottages	59 C3 [4]	Park Avenue (Sandymount)	39 B4	Parkvale	57 C1	Pembroke Lane	38 F4
Osprey Avenue	45 C3	Park Avenue (Willbrook)	56 F1	Parkview	1 B2	(Pembroke Road)	
Osprey Drive	45 C3	Park Avenue West	37 B2 [13]	Parkview	45 A3 [2]	Pembroke Park	38 F4
Osprey Lawn	45 C3	Park Boulevard	9 B2	Parkview Avenue	46 F1	Pembroke Place (Ballsbridge)	38 F4 [15]
Osprey Park	45 C3	Park Close (Sallynoggin)	60 D2	(Harold's Cross)		Pembroke Place	38 E4 [32]
Osprey Road	45 C3	Park Court (Sandymount)	39 A4 [16]	Parkview Court	37 A1 [1]	(Pembroke St Upr)	
Ossory Road	38 F1	Park Court Apts	23 A3 [4]	Parkview Court	46 F1 [8]	Pembroke Road	38 F4
Ostman Place	37 C2 [1]	Park Crescent	37 A1	*Parkview Court	37 A1	Pembroke Row	38 E3
O'Sullivan Avenue	38 E1 [1]	Park Crescent (Kimmage)	46 D2	(on Blackhorse Avenue)		Pembroke Street	39 A3
Oswald Road	39 A3	Park Crescent House	24 D4 [6]	Parkview Place	39 A3 [14]	Pembroke Street Lower	38 E3
Otranto Place	60 E1	Park Drive (Cabinteely)	59 B3	Parkview Terrace	67 B2 [16]	Pembroke Street Upper	38 E3
Otterbrook	46 F4 [16]	Park Drive (Ranelagh)	47 B1	Parkwood Avenue	55 A2	Pembroke Terrace	47 C4 [4]
Oulart	1 C3	Park Drive Avenue	22 F3	Parkwood Grove	55 A2	Penrose Street	38 F3 [6]
Oulton Road	26 E4	Park Drive Close	22 F3	Parkwood Lawn	55 A2	Percy French Road	45 C1 [3]
*Our Lady's Close	37 C3	Park Drive Court	22 F3	Parkwood Road	55 A2	Percy Lane	38 F3
(off Our Lady's Road)		Park Drive Crescent	22 F3	Parliament Street	38 D2	Percy Place	38 F3
Our Lady's Road	37 C3	Park Drive Green	22 F3	Parlickstown Court	9 A4	Perrystown Manor Estate	45 C2
Outlands	1 C1	Park Drive Grove	22 F3	Parlickstown Gardens	9 A3	Community Centre	
Ovoca Road	38 D4	Park Drive Lawn	22 F3	Parlickstown Green	9 A4	Peter Place	38 D4 [19]
Owendoher Lodge	56 E1	Park Lane	50 D4 [21]	Parnell Avenue	37 C4	Peter Row	38 D3
Owendore Avenue	46 F4	Park Lane (Chapelizod)	36 E2 [1]	Parnell Cottages	3 B3	Peter Street	38 D3
Owendore Crescent	46 F4	Park Lane (Sandymount)	39 A4	Parnell Court	37 C4 [13]	Peter's Court	38 D1 [38]
Owen's Avenue	37 B3 [39]	Park Lawn	27 A4	Parnell Park G.A.A.	26 D3	Peterson's Court	38 E2 [16]
Owenstown Park	48 D3	Park Lodge	22 F3	Parnell Place	38 D1 [16]	Petrie Road	37 C4
Oxford Road	38 E4	Park Manor	22 E3	Parnell Road	37 C4	Pheasant Run	8 F4
*Oxford Terrace	38 F1	Park Place	37 A2 [4]	Parnell Road	67 C2	Pheasant Run The Drive	8 F4
(on Hawthorn Terrace)		Park Road (Dun Laoghaire)	50 D4	Parnell Square East	38 D1	Pheasant Run The Green	8 F4
*Oxford Terrace	38 F1	Park Road (off Navan Road)	23 C3	Parnell Square North	38 D1	Pheasant Run The Grove	8 F4
(off Church Road)		Park Road (Sallynoggin)	60 D2	Parnell Square West	38 D1	Pheasant Run The Park	8 F4
Oxmantown Lane	37 C2 [21]	Park Spring's	24 D4 [5]	Parnell Street	38 D2	Phelan Avenue	24 D3
Oxmantown Road	37 B1	Park Street	36 F3 [1]	Parnell Street (Sallynoggin)	60 D1	Phibsboro	37 C1 [22]
		*Park Street	37 C3	Parochial Avenue	15 A4 [2]	Phibsborough	37 C1
P		(off Hanover St West)		Parslickstown Avenue	9 A4	Phibsborough	38 D1
		Park Terrace (Coombe)	37 C3 [6]	Parslickstown Close	9 A4	Phibsborough Avenue	37 C1 [6]
Pace Avenue	8 E4	*Park Terrace	67 B2	Parslickstown Drive	9 A4	Phibsborough Place	38 D1 [1]
Pace Crescent	8 E4	(on Lower Dargle Road)		Parson Court	17 C3	Phibsborough Road	38 D1
Pace Road	8 E4	Park View	26 F4 [1]	Parson Lodge	17 C3	Philipsburgh Avenue	25 C4
Pace View	8 E4	Park View	47 A3 [10]	Parson Street	17 C3	Philipsburgh Terrace	25 C4
Pacelli Avenue	27 C1	Park View (Cabra)	37 B1	Parsons Hall	17 B3	*Philomena Terrace	39 A3
Pairc Gleann Trasna	55 A3	Park View (Castleknock)	23 B4	Partridge Terrace	36 F3 [5]	(off Oliver Plunket Ave)	
Pairc Mhuire	53 A2	Park View (Clonsilla)	22 D2	Path (Robswall)	4 D3	Phoenix Avenue	23 A3
Pairc Ó Ruaire Sports Ground	30 D2	Park View Court	46 F1	Patrician Park	59 C1 [2]	Phoenix Court	23 A3
Pakenham	49 C4 [28]	Park View (Portmarnock)	15 A1	Patrician Villas	48 F4	Phoenix Court	37 B1 [15]
Pakenham Road	49 C4	Park View Lawns	44 D2	Patrick Doyle Road	47 B2	Phoenix Court	37 B2 [17]
*Palace Street (off Dame Street)	38 D2	Park Villas	23 A3	Patrick Street	38 D3	Phoenix Drive	23 A3
Palatine Square	37 B2	Park Villas	48 F4 [3]	Patrick Street (Dun Laoghaire)	50 D4	Phoenix Gardens	23 A3
Palmer Park	56 E2	Park West Avenue	35 C4	Patrick's Row	49 A3 [14]	Phoenix Manor	37 B1 [19]
Palmer Park	56 F2	Park West Road	35 C4	Patrickswell Place	24 D2	Phoenix Manor	37 B1
Palmers Avenue	35 B2	Park West Road	36 D4	Paul Street	37 C2 [36]	Phoenix Place	23 A3
Palmers Close	35 B2						

STREET NAME	PAGE/GRID REFERENCE	STREET NAME	PAGE/GRID REFERENCE	STREET NAME	PAGE/GRID REFERENCE	STREET NAME	PAGE/GRID REFERENCE
Phoenix Street	36 F3 [2]	Polo Road	37 A1	Priorswood Road	13 C4	Raglan Lane	38 F4
Phoenix Street West	37 C2 [15]	Poolbeg Quay	39 A3	Priory Avenue	48 F4	Raglan Road	38 F4
Phoenix Terrace	48 F3	Poolbeg Street	38 E2	Priory Chase	31 C4	Raheen Avenue	54 E1
Phoenix View	37 B3 [43]	Poole Street	37 C3 [38]	Priory Close	31 C4	Raheen Close	54 E1
Phrompstown	66 E1	Poplar Row	38 F1	Priory Court	57 A2 [1]	Raheen Court	54 E1
Pickford's Terrace	38 F2 [13]	Poppintree	11 C4	Priory Court (Celbridge)	31 C4	Raheen Crescent	54 E1
Pig Lane	38 E1	Port Tunnel	39 A1	Priory Crescent	31 C4	Raheen Drive (Ballyfermot)	36 D3
*Pig Lane (off Summer Place)	38 E1	Port View House	39 A2	Priory Drive	48 F4	Raheen Drive (Tallaght)	54 E1
Pigeon House Road	39 B3	Porters Avenue	22 D2	Priory Drive (Celbridge)	31 C4	Raheen Green	54 E1
Pigeon House Road (Ringsend)	39 A3	Porters Gate	21 C2	Priory East	24 D4	Raheen Park (Ballyfermot)	36 D3
*Pile's Terrace (Sandwith St Upper)	38 E3	Porters Gate Avenue	21 C2	Priory Green	31 C4	Raheen Park (Bray)	68 D3
Pilot View	60 F1 [14]	Porters Gate Close	21 B2	Priory Grove	48 F4	Raheen Park (Tallaght)	54 E1
Pim Street	37 C3	Porters Gate Court	21 B2	Priory Grove (Celbridge)	31 C4	Raheen Road	54 E1
Pimlico	37 C3	Porters Gate Crescent	21 B2	Priory Hall	46 D2	Raheny	27 A2
Pimlico Cottages	37 C3 [12]	Porters Gate Drive	21 B2	Priory Hall	48 E4	Raheny Park	27 A3
Pine Avenue	59 A2	Porters Gate Green	21 B2	Priory Lodge	31 C4	Raheny Road	27 A1
Pine Copse Road	57 B1	Porters Gate Grove	21 B2	Priory North	24 D3	Rail Park	18 D4
Pine Court	15 A1	Porters Gate Heights	21 C2	Priory Road	46 F1	Railpark	18 E3
Pine Court	59 A1	Porters Gate Rise	21 C2	Priory Square	31 C4	Railway Avenue	3 B2
Pine Grove	56 D1 [2]	Porters Gate View	21 B2	Priory View	31 C3	Railway Avenue (Baldoyle)	28 D1
Pine Grove Park	1 C1	Porters Gate Way	21 B2	Priory Walk	31 C4	Railway Avenue (Inchicore)	36 F3
Pine Grove Road	1 C1	Porters Road	22 D2	Priory Walk	46 D2	Railway Cottages	39 A4 [8]
Pine Haven	48 F3	Portersfield (Apts.)	22 D2	Priory Way	31 C3	Railway Court	3 B2 [3]
Pine Hurst	24 E4	Portersgate Green	21 B2	Priory Way	46 D2	Railway Road	60 F2 [2]
Pine Lawn (Deans Grange)	59 A1	Portersgate Lawn	21 B2	Priory West	24 D4	Railway Street	38 E1
Pine Lawn (Tallaght)	55 A2	Porterstown	5 A3	Proby Garden	49 A4	*Railway Terrace (off Macken St)	38 F3
Pine Road	39 A3	Porterstown Road	22 D2	Proby Hall	60 E2	Rainsford Avenue	37 C3 [3]
Pine Valley Avenue	57 B2	Portland Close	38 E1 [50]	Proby Park	60 E2	Rainsford Lane	60 E4 [6]
Pine Valley Drive	57 B3	*Portland Court (off Portland Place)	38 D1	Proby Square	49 A4	Rainsford Street	37 C3
Pine Valley Grove	57 B3	Portland Lock	38 E1	Proby's Lane	38 D2 [28]	Ralahine	60 D4
Pine Valley Park	57 B3	Portland Place	38 D1	Promenade Road	39 A1	Raleigh Square	46 D1
Pine Valley Way	57 B3	Portland Row	38 E1	Prospect Avenue	25 A4	Ralph Square	33 A1 [1]
Pinebrook Avenue	26 D2	Portland Square	38 E1 [70]	Prospect Avenue	56 E2	Ramillies Road	36 E3
Pinebrook Close	21 C1	Portland Street North	38 E1	Prospect Court	56 E3	Ramleh Close	47 C2
Pinebrook Crescent	26 D2	Portland Street West	37 C3	Prospect Drive	56 E2	Ramleh Park	47 C2
Pinebrook Downs	21 C1	Portmahon Drive	37 B3	Prospect Glen	56 E2	Ramparts	63 C1
Pinebrook Drive	26 E2	Portmarnock	15 A1	Prospect Grove	56 E2	Ramor Park	22 E2
Pinebrook Glen	21 C1	Portmarnock Adventure Club	14 F2	Prospect Heath	56 E2	Ranelagh	38 E4
Pinebrook Grove	26 E2	Portmarnock Avenue	15 A1	Prospect Heights	56 E2	Ranelagh Avenue	38 E4
Pinebrook Heights	21 C1	Portmarnock Crescent	15 A1	Prospect Lane	47 C2 [1]	Ranelagh Road	38 E4
Pinebrook Lawn	21 C1	Portmarnock Drive	4 D4	Prospect Lawn	59 B3	Raphoe Road	46 D1
Pinebrook Rise	26 D2	Portmarnock Driving Range	14 E2	Prospect Manor	56 E2	Rathbeal Court	1 C1 [2]
Pinebrook Road	26 D2	Portmarnock Golf Links and Hotel	15 A1	Prospect Meadows	56 E2	Rathbeale Court	1 C1
Pinebrook Vale	21 C1	Portmarnock Grove	4 D4	Prospect Road	25 A4	Rathbeale Crescent	1 C1
Pinebrook View	21 C1	Portmarnock Park	4 D4	Prospect Square	25 A4 [5]	Rathbeale Rise	1 C2
Pinebrook Way	21 C1	Portmarnock Rise	15 A1	Prospect Terrace (Kilmainham)	37 A3 [14]	Rathbeale Road	1 C1
Pinecroft	62 F1	Portmarnock Walk	4 D4	Prospect Terrace (Sandymount)	39 B3 [1]	Rathborne Avenue	23 C3
Pinetree Crescent	44 F4 [1]	Portobello Harbour	38 D4 [6]	Prospect View	56 E2	Rathborne Close	23 C3
Pinetree Grove	44 F3 [1]	Portobello Harbour Apts	38 D4 [58]	Prospect Way	25 A4	Rathborne Drive	23 C3
Pineview Avenue	55 A2	Portobello Place	38 D4 [36]	Protestant Row	38 D3 [12]	Rathborne Place	23 C3
Pineview Drive	55 A2	Portobello Road	38 D4	Proud's Lane	38 D3 [24]	Rathborne Way	23 C3
Pineview Grove	55 A2	Portside Court	38 F1 [22]	Provost Row	37 C2 [46]	Rathclaren	67 B3 [2]
Pineview Lawn	55 A2	Pottery Road	59 C2	Prussia Street	37 C1	Rathcoole Park	52 F2
Pineview Park	55 A2	Pound Hill	17 C1	Pucks Castle Lane	63 C3	Rathcreedan	52 D1
Pineview Rise	55 A2	Pound Lane	17 C3	*Purcell Lane (off Main Street Bray)	67 C2	Rathdown Avenue	46 F3
Pineview Road	55 A2	Pound Park	17 C3	Purley Park	3 C4	Rathdown Court (off Templeogue Road)	46 F2 [10]
Pinewood	60 D4	Pound Street	33 A1	Purser Gardens	47 A1 [10]	Rathdown Crescent	46 F3
Pinewood Avenue	24 F1	Power's Court	38 F3	Putland Road	67 C3	Rathdown Drive	46 E3
Pinewood Close	67 C4	*Power's Square (off John Dillon Street)	38 D3	Putland Villas	67 C3 [14]	Rathdown Grove	58 D2 [9]
Pinewood Court	8 F4	Prebend Street	37 C2	Pyro Villas	37 C3 [60]	Rathdown Park	46 F3
Pinewood Crescent	24 F1	Premier Square	24 E2			Rathdown Road	37 C1
Pinewood Drive	24 F1	Preston Street	38 E1 [14]	**Q**		Rathdown Square	37 C1 [20]
Pinewood Green	24 F1	*Price's Lane (Aston Quay)	38 D2	Quarry Cottages	26 E3 [3]	Rathdown Terrace (Sandyford)	58 D2 [5]
Pinewood Grove	25 A1 [1]	Price's Place (Ranelagh)	38 D4	Quarry Drive	45 C2	Rathdown Villas	46 F3
Pinewood Park	56 E1	Priestfield Cottages	37 C4 [4]	Quarry Road	24 E4	Rathdrum Road	37 B4
Pinewood Villas	24 F1	Priestfield Drive	37 C4 [28]	Quarry Road	64 D4	Rathfarnham	46 F3
Pinewoods	44 D2	Primrose Avenue	38 D1	Quartiere Bloom	38 D2	Rathfarnham Park	46 F3
Pipe Hill	1 C2	Primrose Grove	13 C4	Queen's Park	49 B4	Rathfarnham Road	46 F3
Pleasants Lane	38 D3 [15]	Primrose Hill	32 D3	Queen's Road	50 D4	Rathfarnham Wood	46 F4
Pleasants Place	38 D3 [21]	Primrose Hill	49 C4 [25]	Queen's Street	37 C2	Rathgar	47 A2
Pleasants Street	38 D3	Primrose Lane	34 D1	Quinn's Lane	38 E3	Rathgar Avenue	46 F2
Pluckstown	51 A2	*Primrose Street (off Wellington Street Upper)	38 D1	Quinn's Road	64 E3	Rathgar Park	46 F2 [16]
Plums Road	58 D1	Prince Arthur Terrace	47 A1 [3]	Quinsborough	51 A4	Rathgar Park	47 A2 [7]
Plunkett Avenue (Finglas)	24 D1	Prince Edward Terrace Lower	49 A4 [2]	Quinsborough Road	67 C2	Rathgar Place	47 A1
Plunkett Avenue (Foxrock)	59 A3	Prince Edward Terrace Upper	49 A4 [3]			Rathgar Road	47 A1
Plunkett Crescent	11 A4	Prince of Wales Terrace	39 A4 [7]	**R**		Rathgar Villas	46 F2 [11]
Plunkett Drive	24 D1	Prince of Wales Terrace	67 C2 [26]	Radcliffe	29 A1 [3]	Rathingle Road	1 B3
Plunkett Green	24 D1	Prince's Street North	38 D2 [20]	Radlett Grove	4 D4	Rathland Drive	46 E2 [4]
Plunkett Grove	24 D1	Prince's Street South	38 E2 [12]	*Rafter's Avenue (off Rafter's Road)	37 A4	Rathland Road	46 E2
Plunkett Hall	7 A2	Princeton	48 D3	Rafter's Lane	37 A4	Rathlawns	52 E2
Plunkett Hall Crescent	7 A2	Prior Hall	37 B3 [36]	Rafter's Road	37 A4	Rathlin Road	25 A3
Plunkett Road	24 D1			Raglan Hall Apts	38 F4 [20]	Rathlyon	55 C2
Poddle Close	46 E1					Rathlyon Estate	55 C2
Poddle Green	46 E1 [6]					Rathlyon Park	55 C2
Poddle Park	46 E2						

STREET NAME	PAGE/GRID REFERENCE
Rathmichael	63 C3
Rathmichael Dales	64 D3
Rathmichael Haven	64 D3
Rathmichael Hill	63 C2
Rathmichael Lane	63 C2
Rathmichael Manor	64 D2
Rathmichael Park	64 E2
Rathmichael Road	63 C2
Rathmichael Woods	64 E2
Rathmines	47 A1
Rathmines Avenue	47 A1
Rathmines Avenue Court	47 A1 [25]
Rathmines Close	47 A1
Rathmines Park	47 A1 [1]
Rathmines Road Lower	47 A1
Rathmines Road Upper	47 A1
Rathmintan Close	54 D2
Rathmintan Court	54 D2
Rathmintan Crescent	54 D2
Rathmintan Drive	54 D2
Rathmore	14 F2
Rathmore Avenue	58 D1
Rathmore Park	27 A2
Rathmore Villas	46 F2
Rathsallagh Avenue	64 E2
Rathsallagh Drive	64 E2
Rathsallagh Grove	64 E2
Rathsallagh Park	64 E2
Rathvale Avenue	26 F1
Rathvale Drive	26 F1
Rathvale Grove	26 F1
Rathvale Park	26 F1
Rathvilly Drive	24 D2
Rathvilly Park	24 D2
Ratoath Avenue	24 D2
Ratoath Drive	23 C1
Ratoath Estate	24 D3
Ratoath Road	24 E4
Ratoath Road (Hollystown)	9 B1
Ratra Park	23 C4
Ratra Road	23 C4
Ravens Court	24 D2 [5]
Ravens Rock Road	58 E2
Ravensdale Drive (off Ravensdale Park)	46 E2
Ravensdale Park	46 E2
Ravensdale Road	38 F1
Ravenswell Road	67 C2
Ravenswood Avenue	21 B1
Ravenswood Crescent	21 B1
Ravenswood Drive	21 B1
Ravenswood Estate	21 B1
Ravenswood Green	21 B1
Ravenswood Lawn	21 B1
Ravenswood Rise	21 B1
Ravenswood Road	21 B1
Ravenswood View	21 B1
Raverty Villas	67 B1 [1]
Raymond Street	37 C4
Rectory Slopes	67 B3
Rectory Way	67 A3
Red Brick Terrace	59 A1 [2]
Red Cow Cottages	35 C1 [1]
Red Cow Lane	37 C2
Redberry	34 D3
Redesdale Crescent	48 D4
Redesdale Road	48 D4
Redfern Avenue	3 C4
Redgap	52 E3
Redmond's Court	27 B1 [3]
Redmond's Hill	38 D3 [11]
Redwood Avenue	45 A4
Redwood Close	45 A4
Redwood Court (Churchtown)	47 A3
Redwood Court (Tallaght)	44 F4
Redwood Drive	44 F4
Redwood Grove	48 F3
Redwood Heights	45 A4
Redwood Lawn	44 F4
Redwood Park	45 A4
Redwood Rise	45 A4
Redwood View	45 A4
Redwood Walk	44 F4
Reginald Square	37 C3 [43]
Reginald Street	37 C3
Rehoboth Avenue	37 C4 [3]
Rehoboth Place	37 B4
Reilly's Avenue	37 B4 [6]
Reuben Avenue	37 B3
Reuben Street	37 B3
*Rhodaville (off Mountpleasant Ave)	38 D4
Rialto Buildings	37 B3 [14]
Rialto Cottages	37 B3
Rialto Drive	37 B4 [3]
*Rialto Park(off Rialto Street)	37 B3
Rialto Street	37 B3
Ribh Avenue	26 F2
Ribh Road	26 F2
Richelieu Park	48 E1
Richmond	59 A1
Richmond Avenue (Fairview)	25 B4
Richmond Avenue (Monkstown)	49 C4
Richmond Avenue South	47 B2
Richmond Cottages (Summerhill)	38 E1 [9]
Richmond Cottages North	38 E1 [37]
Richmond Court	47 B2
Richmond Crescent	38 E1 [8]
Richmond Estate	25 C4
Richmond Green	49 C4 [12]
Richmond Grove	49 C4
Richmond Hill (Monkstown)	49 C4
Richmond Hill (Rathmines)	38 D4
Richmond Lane	38 E1 [20]
Richmond Manor	38 D2
Richmond Mews	38 D4 [43]
Richmond Parade	38 E1 [10]
Richmond Park	49 B4
Richmond Park	67 A4
Richmond Place (Rathmines)	38 D4 [10]
Richmond Place South (Sth Richmond St)	38 D4 [44]
Richmond Road	25 B4
Richmond Row	38 D4 [7]
Richmond Street North	38 E1
Richmond Street South	38 D4
Richmond Terrace	68 D2 [12]
Richmond Villas	38 D4 [22]
Richview	47 C2
Richview Park	47 B2
Richview Villas	47 C2 [11]
Riddlesford	67 C4
Ridge Hill	64 E1
Ridgewood Avenue	1 B3
Ridgewood Close	1 B3
Ridgewood Close	1 B3
Ridgewood Court	1 B3
Ridgewood Green	1 B3
Ridgewood Grove	1 B3
Ridgewood Park	1 B3
Ridgewood Place	1 B3
Ridgewood Square	1 B3
Rinawade Avenue	32 E1
Rinawade Close	32 E1
Rinawade Crescent	32 E1
Rinawade Downs	32 E1
Rinawade Glade	32 E1
Rinawade Grove	32 E1
Rinawade Lawns	32 E1
Rinawade Park	32 F1
Rinawade Rise	32 E1
Rinawade View	32 E1
Ring Street	36 F3 [12]
Ring Terrace	36 F3
Ringsend	39 A3
Ringsend Park	39 A2
Ringsend Road	38 F3
Rinn na Mara	27 A4 [3]
Ripley Court	67 B3
Ripley Hills	67 B3
River Close	64 E1 [23]
River Court	7 B3 [2]
River Court	7 B3 [2]
River Drive	24 D3
River Forest	20 D3
River Forest View	19 C3
River Forest View	20 D3
River Gardens	25 A3 [15]
River Lane (Bray)	67 B2
River Lane (Loughlinstown)	64 E2 [1]
River Lawns	31 C4
River Road	22 F2
River Road	23 C3
River Road Cottages	23 A2
River Valley Avenue	1 C2
River Valley Close	1 B2
River Valley Court	1 B2
River Valley Drive	1 C2
River Valley Grove	1 C3
River Valley Heights	1 C2
River Valley Lawn	1 C2
River Valley Park	1 C2
River Valley Rise	1 C3
River Valley Road	1 C2
River Valley View	1 B2
River Valley Way	1 B2
River View	31 C4
Riverbank	47 A3 [6]
Riverbank Hall	24 F3
Riverdale	20 D4
Riverpark View	9 A4 [3]
Riversdale	35 C1
Riversdale (Herbert Hill)	57 C1
Riversdale Avenue	46 F3
Riversdale Avenue (Clondalkin)	44 E1
Riversdale Avenue (Palmerston)	35 C1
Riversdale Court	35 C1
Riversdale Crescent	44 E1
Riversdale Drive	44 E1
Riversdale Green	35 B4
Riversdale Grove	35 B1
Riversdale Grove	46 E2 [1]
Riversdale Park	35 C1
Riversdale Park	44 E1
Riversdale Road	44 E1
Riverside	44 E1 [6]
Riverside Avenue	13 A4
Riverside Cottages	46 E4
Riverside Crescent	13 A4
Riverside Drive (Coolock)	13 B4
Riverside Drive (Palmerston)	35 C1
Riverside Drive (Rathfarnham)	47 A3
Riverside Grove	13 A4
Riverside Park	13 A4
Riverside Road	13 A4
Riverston Abbey	24 D4
Rivervale	23 C3
Rivervale Apts	67 B2 [27]
Riverview	35 C1
Riverview	55 A2
Riverview Apartments	32 D4
Riverview Court	36 E2 [11]
Riverwood Chase	22 D3
Riverwood Close	22 D3
Riverwood Copse	22 D3
Riverwood Court	22 D3
Riverwood Crescent	22 D3
Riverwood Dale	22 D3
Riverwood Dene	22 D3
Riverwood Drive	22 D3
Riverwood Gardens	22 D3
Riverwood Glebe	22 D3
Riverwood Glen	22 D3
Riverwood Green	22 D3
Riverwood Grove	22 D3
Riverwood Hall	22 D3
Riverwood Heath	22 D3
Riverwood Lawn	22 D3
Riverwood Park	22 D3
Riverwood Place	22 D3
Riverwood Road	22 D3
Riverwood Terrace	22 D3
Riverwood Vale	22 D3
Riverwood View	22 D3
Riverwood Way	22 D3
Robert Emmett Close	37 C2 [48]
Robert Place	25 B4 [7]
Robert Street (James's Street)	37 C3
Robert Street (Jones's Road)	25 B4 [6]
Robin Villas	35 C1
Robinhood Park	45 B1
Robinhood Road	45 A1
Robswall	3 C3
Roby Place	50 D4 [17]
Rochestown Avenue	59 C2
Rochestown House (Apts)	59 C2 [6]
Rochestown Park	60 D2
Rochfort Avenue	34 F2
Rochfort Close	34 F2
Rochfort Crescent	34 F3
Rochfort Downs	34 F2
Rochfort Green	34 F2
Rochfort Park	34 E1
Rochfort Way	34 F3
Rock Field Drive (Clondalkin)	44 D2
Rock Hall	49 A3
*Rock Lane (Baggot St Lower)	38 E3
Rock Lodge	60 E3
Rock Road	49 A3
Rockbrook	56 E4
Rockfield	18 D4
Rockfield	34 D3
Rockfield (Dundrum)	57 C1
Rockfield Avenue	18 D4
Rockfield Avenue	46 D2
Rockfield Close	22 D3
Rockfield Drive (Coolmine)	22 D3
Rockfield Drive (Kimmage)	46 D2
Rockfield Gardens	18 D3
Rockfield Green	18 D3
Rockfield Lodge	18 D4
Rockfield Manor	18 D4
Rockfield Park	18 D4
Rockfield Park	22 D2
Rockfield Rise	18 D3
Rockfield Square	18 D3
Rockfield Walk	18 D3
Rockford Manor	59 B1
Rockford Park	59 B1
Rockford Terrace	49 B4 [14]
Rockfort Avenue	60 F2
Rockingham Avenue	19 C4
Rockingham Green	19 C4
Rockingham Grove	19 C4
Rockingham Park	19 C4
Rockingham Terrace	2 D2
Rocklands	60 F1 [6]
Rockstown	30 E2
Rockview	57 C3
Rockville	62 F2
Rockville Crescent	49 B4
Rockville Drive	49 B4
Rockville Drive	63 A1
Rockville Estate	49 A4 [9]
Rockville Park	49 B4
Rockville Road	49 A4
Rockwell Cove Apts	49 A3 [9]
Rockwood	34 D3
Rocwood	58 F2
Roe Lane	37 C2
Roebuck Avenue	48 E3
Roebuck Castle	48 D3
Roebuck Crescent	47 C3 [10]
Roebuck Downs	47 C3
Roebuck Drive	46 D2
Roebuck Hill	48 D3
Roebuck Lawn	47 C3 [9]
Roebuck Road	48 D3
Roger Casement Park	67 B2
Roger's Lane	38 E3 [15]
Roland Court	47 A1 [20]
Rollins Court	60 D1 [12]
Rollins Villas	59 C1 [15]
Rollins Villas	60 D1
Ronanstown	35 A4
Roncalli Road	27 C1
Roosevelt Cottages	24 D4 [1]
Rooske Road	7 B3
Rope Walk Place	39 A3
Ropewalk Pace	39 A3 [30]
Rory O'Connor Park	59 B1
Rosary Gardens East	50 D4 [2]
Rosary Gardens West	49 C4 [1]
Rosary Road	37 B3
Rosary Terrace (Ringsend)	39 A3
*Rosary Terrace (off Library Road)	50 D4
Rosbeg Court	27 C2
Rosberry	34 E3

STREET NAME	PAGE/GRID REFERENCE	
Rosberry Avenue	34	E3
Rosberry Court	34	E3
Rosberry Lane	34	E3
Rosberry Park	34	E3
Rosberry Place	34	E3
Rose Park	59	C1
Roseacre	58	E3
Rosebank	55	A2
Rosebank Court	35	B4 [1]
Rosebank Hall	35	B4 [3]
Rosebank Place	35	B4 [4]
Rosebank View	35	B4 [2]
Rosedale	8	E4
Rosedale Estate	21	B1
*Rosedale Terrace (Lower Clanbrassil St)	37	C4
Roseglen Avenue	27	B2
Roseglen Road	27	B2
Rosehaven	22	D3 [1]
Rosehill	59	A1 [5]
Roselawn	34	E1
Roselawn Avenue	22	E2
Roselawn Close	22	F2
Roselawn Court	22	F2
Roselawn Crescent	22	E2
Roselawn Drive	67	C3
Roselawn Drive (Castleknock)	22	E2
Roselawn Glade	22	E2
Roselawn Grove	22	E2
Roselawn Park	67	C3 [2]
Roselawn Road	22	E2
Roselawn Road	22	F2
Roselawn View	22	E2
Roselawn Walk	22	E2
Roselawn Way	22	F2
Rosemount	26	D3
Rosemount (Churchtown)	47	C4
Rosemount Avenue	26	E2
Rosemount Court	47	C4
Rosemount Court	48	E3
Rosemount Court (Inchicore Rd)	37	A3 [19]
Rosemount Crescent (Roebuck Road)	47	C3
Rosemount Glade	47	C4
Rosemount Hall	47	C4
Rosemount Park	47	C4
Rosemount Park Drive	10	D4
Rosemount Park Road	10	D4
Rosemount Road	37	C1 [4]
Rosemount Terrace (Arbour Hill)	37	C2 [29]
Rosemount Terrace (Booterstown)	48	F3
Rosemount Terrace (Dundrum)	47	B4 [11]
Rosevale Court	26	F3
Rosevale Mansions	26	F3
Roseville Court	67	B1 [7]
Roseville Terrace	47	C4 [4]
Rosewood Grove	34	F3
Rosmeen Gardens	50	D4
Rosmeen Park	60	D1
Ros Mór View	56	D2
Ross Road	38	D3
Ross Street	37	B1
Ross View	35	C1
Rossaveal Court	36	D2 [1]
Rossfield Avenue	54	D1
Rossfield Crescent	54	D1
Rossfield Drive	54	D1
Rossfield Gardens	54	D1
Rossfield Grove	54	D1
Rossfield Park	54	D1
Rossfield Way	54	D1
Rosslyn	67	C2 [37]
Rosslyn Court	67	C2
Rosslyn Grove	67	C2 [4]
Rossmore Avenue	45	C4
Rossmore Avenue (Ballyfermot)	36	D3
Rossmore Avenue (Templeogue)	45	C4
Rossmore Close	46	D4
Rossmore Crescent	46	D4
Rossmore Drive (Ballyfermot)	36	D2
Rossmore Drive (Templeogue)	45	C4
Rossmore Grove	45	C4
Rossmore Grove	46	D4

STREET NAME	PAGE/GRID REFERENCE	
Rossmore Lawns	46	D4
Rossmore Park	46	D4
Rossmore Road (Ballyfermot)	36	D2
Rossmore Road (Templeogue)	46	D4
Rostrevor Road	47	A3
Rostrevor Terrace (Lr Grand Canal St)	38	F3 [25]
Rostrevor Terrace (Orwell Road)	47	A2
Rothe Abbey	37	A3
Rowan Avenue	58	D2
Rowan Close	32	D3
Rowan Grove	67	B2
Rowan Hall	47	C1 [15]
Rowan Park	49	B4
Rowanbyrn	49	B4
Rowanbyrn	59	B1
Rowans Road	58	D2
Rowlagh Avenue	35	A3
Rowlagh Crescent	35	A3
Rowlagh Gardens	35	A3
Rowlagh Green	35	A3
Rowlagh Park	35	A3
Rowserstown Lane	37	A3 [20]
Royal Canal Avenue	23	C3
Royal Canal Bank	25	A4
Royal Canal Bank	38	D1
Royal Canal Terrace	37	C1 [12]
Royal Canal Way	25	A4
Royal Canal Way	38	E1
Royal Hibernian Way	38	E3 [10]
Royal Marine Terrace	67	C2 [12]
Royal Oak	12	F4
Royal Terrace East	60	D1
Royal Terrace Lane	60	D1 [10]
Royal Terrace North	60	D1 [2]
Royal Terrace West	60	D1
Royse Road	25	A4
Royston	46	D2
Royston Village	46	D2
Ruby Hall	59	C2
Rugby Road	47	B1
Rugby Villas	47	B1 [6]
*Rus in Urbe Terrace (on Glenageary Road Lr)	60	D1
Rushbrook	22	E2
Rushbrook Avenue	45	C3
Rushbrook Court	45	C4
Rushbrook Crescent	45	C3
Rushbrook Drive	45	C3
Rushbrook Grove	45	C3
Rushbrook Park	45	C3
Rushbrook Road	45	C3
Rushbrook View	45	C3
Rushbrook Way	45	C3
Rusheeney	21	B1
Rusheeney Avenue	21	B1
Rusheeney Close	21	B1
Rusheeney Court	21	B1
Rusheeney Crescent	8	F4
Rusheeney Green	21	B1
Rusheeney Grove	21	B1
Rusheeney Manor	21	B1
Rusheeney Park	21	B1
Rusheeney View	21	B1
Rusheeney Way	21	B1
Rus-in-Urbe Terrace	60	D1 [19]
Russell Avenue	38	E1
Russell Avenue	54	D1
Russell Avenue East	38	F1 [14]
Russell Close	54	D2
Russell Court	54	D2
Russell Crescent	54	D2
Russell Downs	54	D1
Russell Drive	54	D2
Russell Green	54	D2
Russell Grove	54	D2
Russell Lane	54	D1
Russell Lawns	54	D2
Russell Meadows	54	D1
Russell Place	54	D1
Russell Rise	54	D1
Russell Street	38	E1
Russell View	54	D2
Russell Walk	54	D1

STREET NAME	PAGE/GRID REFERENCE	
Rutland Avenue	37	B4
Rutland Avenue	46	E1
Rutland Cottages	38	E1 [55]
Rutland Court	38	E1
Rutland Grove	46	F1
Rutland Place North	38	E1 [48]
Rutland Place West	38	D1
Rutland Street Lower	38	E1
Rutledge Terrace	37	C4 [26]
Ryan's Cottages (Harold's Cross)	46	F1 [7]
Ryder's Row	38	D2 [9]
Rye River Avenue	20	D4
Rye River Close	20	D4
Rye River Court	20	D4
Rye River Crescent	20	D4
Rye River Gardens	20	D4
Rye River Grove	20	D4
Rye River Mall	20	D4
Rye River Park	20	D4
Ryecroft	67	C3
Ryemont Abbey	20	D4
Ryevale Lawns	20	D4
Rynville Manor	67	B3

S

STREET NAME	PAGE/GRID REFERENCE	
Sackville Avenue	38	E1
Sackville Gardens	38	E1 [2]
Sackville Place	38	D2 [24]
Saddlers Avenue	9	A4
Saddlers Close	9	A4
Saddlers Court	38	D4 [55]
Saddlers Crescent	9	A4
Saddlers Drive	9	A4
Saddlers Glade	9	A4
Saddlers Grove	9	A4
Saddlers Lawn	9	A4
Sadleir Hall	7	A2
Saggart	53	B2
Saggart Abbey	53	C2
Saintsbury Avenue	60	E4
Salamanca	48	D4
Salem Court	47	A1 [17]
Salestown	6	D4
Sally Park	55	C1
Sally Park Close	55	C1
Sallyglen Road	50	D2
Sallymount Avenue	47	B1
Sallymount Gardens	47	B1 [1]
Sallymount Terrace	47	B1 [14]
Sallynoggin	60	D2
Sallynoggin Park	59	C2
Sallynoggin Road	59	C2
Salmon Pool Apts	37	A2 [5]
Salthill	49	C4
*Salthill Place (off Crofton Road)	50	D4
Saltzburg	48	D4
Sampson's Lane	38	D2 [14]
Sandford Avenue (Donnybrook)	47	C1
Sandford Avenue (Donore Avenue)	37	C4
Sandford Close	47	B1
Sandford Gardens	37	C4 [33]
Sandford Gardens (Donnybrook)	47	C1 [10]
*Sandford Gardens (off Donore Avenue)	37	C4
Sandford Park	37	C4 [32]
*Sandford Park (off O'Donovan Road)	37	C4
Sandford Road	47	B1
Sandford Terrace	47	B1
Sandford Wood	1	C1
Sandford Wood	1	C2
Sandon Cove	26	E4
Sandwith Street Lower	38	E2
Sandwith Street Upper	38	E3
Sandycove Avenue East	60	E1
Sandycove Avenue North	50	E4
Sandycove Avenue West	60	E1
Sandycove Lane East	60	E1
Sandycove Point	50	E4
Sandycove Road	60	E1
Sandyford	58	D2
Sandyford Downs	58	D3
Sandyford Hall	58	E3

STREET NAME	PAGE/GRID REFERENCE	
Sandyford Hall Avenue	58	E3
Sandyford Hall Close	58	E4
Sandyford Hall Court	58	E3
Sandyford Hall Crescent	58	E3
Sandyford Hall Drive	58	E4
Sandyford Hall Green	58	E3
Sandyford Hall Grove	58	E4
Sandyford Hall Lawn	58	E3
Sandyford Hall Place	58	E3
Sandyford Hall Rise	58	E3
Sandyford Hall View	58	E3
Sandyford Hall Walk	58	E3
Sandyford Park	58	D2
Sandyford Road	57	C1
Sandyford View	57	C3
Sandyford Village	58	D3
Sandyhill Avenue	24	F1
Sandyhill Gardens	24	F1
Sandymount	39	A4
Sandymount Avenue	39	A4
Sandymount Castle	39	A4 [5]
Sandymount Castle Drive	39	A4 [3]
Sandymount Castle Park	39	B4 [2]
Sandymount Castle Road	39	A4 [2]
Sandymount Court	39	A3 [26]
Sandymount Green	39	A4 [1]
Sandymount Road	39	A3
Sans Souci Park	48	F3
Sans Souci Wood	67	C3
Santa Sabina Manor	29	B2
Santry Avenue	12	E4
Santry Close	12	F4
Santry Court	12	F4
Santry Villas	12	E4
Sarah Curran Avenue	56	F1
Sarah Curran Road	56	F1 [1]
Sarah Place	37	A2 [3]
Sarney	6	E2
Sarsfield Court	34	D1 [1]
Sarsfield Park	34	D1
Sarsfield Quay	37	C2 [8]
Sarsfield Road	36	F3
Sarsfield Street (Phibsborough)	38	D1 [5]
Sarsfield Street (Sallynoggin)	60	D1
Sarsfield Terrace	34	D1 [1]
Sarto Lawn	27	C1
Sarto Park	27	C1
Sarto Rise	27	C1
Sarto Road	27	C2
Saul Road	46	E1
Saval Grove	60	E2
Saval Park Crescent	60	E2
Saval Park Gardens	60	E2
Saval Park Road	60	E2
Scarriff Apts	22	F1
Scholarstown Park	56	D2
Scholarstown Road	56	D2
School Avenue	26	E2
School Street	37	C3
Schoolhouse Lane	25	B1
Schoolhouse Lane	38	E3 [12]
*Schoolhouse Lane West (off High Street)	38	D3
Schools Road	67	B4
Scott Park	67	C3
Scribblestown Road	23	B3
Sea Road	3	A2
Seabank Court	60	E1 [21]
Seabrook Manor (Apts.)	14	E2
Seabury	48	E1
Seabury Avenue	2	F2
Seabury Close	2	F2
Seabury Court	2	F2
Seabury Crescent	2	F2
Seabury Dale	2	F2
Seabury Downs	2	F2
Seabury Drive	3	A2
Seabury Gardens	2	F2
Seabury Glen	2	F2
Seabury Green	2	F2
Seabury Grove	2	F2
Seabury Heights	2	F2
Seabury Lane	2	F2
Seabury Lawns	2	F2
Seabury Meadows	2	F2

STREET NAME	PAGE/GRID REFERENCE	STREET NAME	PAGE/GRID REFERENCE	STREET NAME	PAGE/GRID REFERENCE	STREET NAME	PAGE/GRID REFERENCE
Seabury Orchard	2 F2	Seaview Wood	64 E2	Shaw's Lane	38 F3 [13]	Silverdale	34 D3
Seabury Parade	2 F2	Second Avenue	44 F4	Shea's Court	37 C1 [23]	Silverpine	67 B3
Seabury Park	2 F2	Second Avenue (Seville Place)	38 F2 [6]	Sheelan Drive	64 E1	Silverwood	34 D3
Seabury Place	2 F2	Sefton	59 C2	Sheelin Avenue	64 E1	Silverwood Drive	46 E4
Seabury Road	2 F2	Sefton Green	59 C2	Sheelin Drive	64 E1 [15]	Silverwood Road	46 E4
Seabury Vale	2 F2	Sefton Hall	59 A2	Sheelin Grove	64 E1 [7]	Simmon's Court	48 D1 [3]
Seabury View	2 F2	Selskar Terrace	38 E4 [21]	Sheelin Hill	64 E1 [13]	*Simmon's Place	38 E1
Seabury Walk	2 F2	Serpentine Avenue	39 A4	Sheelin Walk	64 E1 [14]	(off Thompson's Cottages)	
Seabury Wood	2 F2	Serpentine Park	39 A4	Sheephill Avenue	9 C4	Simons Ridge	57 C3
Seacliff Avenue	27 C1	Serpentine Road	39 A4	Sheephill Green	9 C4	Simmonscourt Avenue	48 D1 [2]
Seacliff Drive	27 C1	Serpentine Terrace	39 A4	Sheephill Park	9 C4	Simmonscourt Castle	48 D1
Seacliff Road	27 C1	Seskin View Avenue	55 A2	Sheepmoor Avenue	22 D1	Simmonscourt Road	39 A4
Seacourt	26 F4	Seskin View Drive	55 A2	Sheepmoor Close	22 D1	Simmonscourt Terrace	47 C1 [18]
Seacrest	67 C3	Seskin View Park	55 A2	Sheepmoor Crescent	22 D1	Simmonstown	41 A1
Seafield	28 D1 [2]	Seskin View Road	55 A2	Sheepmoor Gardens	22 D1	Simmonstown Manor	32 D4
Seafield (Shankill)	64 F2	Setanta Place	38 E3 [11]	Sheepmoor Green	22 D1	Simmonstown Park	32 D4
Seafield Avenue (Clontarf)	26 F4	Seven Houses	60 D1 [13]	Sheepmoor Grove	22 D1	Simpsons Lane	39 A3 [32]
Seafield Avenue (Monkstown)	49 B4	Seven Oaks	25 B3	Sheepmoor Lawn	22 D1	Sion Hill Avenue	46 F1
Seafield Close	48 E2	Seville Place	38 E1	Sheepmoor Way	22 D1	Sion Hill Court	25 C3 [5]
Seafield Court	64 E1	Seville Terrace	38 E1 [59]	Shelbourne Avenue	38 F4 [5]	Sion Hill Road	25 C3
Seafield Court (Malahide)	3 B2	Seymour Road	67 C2	Shelbourne Lane	38 F4 [3]	Sion Road	60 D2
Seafield Crescent	48 E2	Shaldon Grange	62 F2	Shelbourne Park Mews	38 F3 [50]	Sir Ivor Mall	58 F2 [7]
Seafield Downs	26 F4	Shamrock Cottages	38 E1 [31]	Shelbourne Road	38 F3	Sir John Rogerson's Quay	38 F2
(off Kincora Road Clontarf)		Shamrock Place	38 E1 [15]	Shelbourne Village	38 F3 [51]	Sisters of Charity Stella Maris	30 D4
Seafield Drive	48 E2	Shamrock Street	38 D1 [69]	Shelerin Road	21 C2	*Sitric Place (off Sitric Road)	37 C2
Seafield Grove	27 A4 [1]	Shamrock Terrace	38 E1 [16]	Shellys Banks Road	39 B3	Sitric Road	37 C2
Seafield Park	48 E2 [1]	Shamrock Villas	46 F1	Shelmalier Road	38 F1	Skeagh	41 A3
Seafield Road (Ballybrack)	64 E1	Shanagarry	47 B2 [9]	Shelmartin Avenue	25 C4	Skelly's Lane	26 D2
Seafield Road (Booterstown)	48 E2	Shanard Avenue	25 A1	Shelmartin Terrace	25 C4 [2]	Skreen Road	37 A1
Seafield Road (Killiney)	60 E4	Shanard Road	25 A1	Shelton Drive	46 D2	Slade Row	37 C2 [35]
Seafield Road East	26 F4	Shanboley Road	25 C1	Shelton Gardens	46 D2	Slademore Avenue	26 F1
Seafield Road West	26 E4	Shancastle Avenue	35 A2	Shelton Grove	46 D2	Slademore Close	26 F1
Seafield Terrace	60 F2 [15]	Shancastle Close	35 A2	Shelton Park	46 D2	Slademore Court	13 C4
Seafort Avenue	39 A4	Shancastle Crescent	35 A2	Sheriff Street Lower	38 E2	Slademore Court	26 F1
Seafort Cottages	39 A4 [18]	Shancastle Drive	35 A2	Sheriff Street Upper	38 F2	Slademore Drive	26 F1
Seafort Gardens	39 A3 [10]	Shancastle Lawns	35 A2	Sherkin Gardens	25 B3	Slane Road	37 B4
Seafort Parade	48 F3	Shancastle Park	35 A2	Sherrard Avenue	38 D1 [28]	Slaney Close	24 E3
Seafort Terrace	39 A4 [19]	Shandon Crescent	24 F4	*Sherrard Court	38 D1	Slaney Road	24 E3
Seafort Villas	39 A4 [20]	Shandon Drive	24 F4	(off Portland Place)		Slate Cabin Lane	57 C3
Seagrange Avenue	14 F4	Shandon Gardens	24 F4	Sherrard Street Lower	38 D1	Slemish Road	37 A1
Seagrange Drive	27 C1	Shandon Green	24 F4 [8]	Sherrard Street Upper	38 D1	Slí an Chanáil	19 C4
Seagrange Road	27 C1	Shandon Mill	24 F4 [9]	Sherrards Court	38 D1 [65]	Slieve Bloom Park	45 C1
Seagrave	14 F2	Shandon Park (Monkstown)	49 B4	Shielmartin Drive	29 B3	Slieve Rua Drive	58 D1
Seamount	48 E3	Shandon Park (Phibsborough)	24 F4	Shielmartin Park	29 B3 [1]	Slievebloom Park	45 C1
Seamount Drive	3 C3	Shandon Road	24 F4	Shielmartin Road	29 B3	Slievebloom Road	45 C1
Seamount Grove	3 C3	Shangan Avenue	25 B1	Ship Street Great	38 D3	Slievemore Road	37 A4
Seamount Heights	3 C3	Shangan Crescent	25 A1	Ship Street Little	38 D3	Slievenamon Road	37 A4
Seamount Park	3 C3	Shangan Gardens	25 B1	Shrewsbury	39 A4	Sloan Terrace	68 D2 [8]
Seamount Road	3 C3	Shangan Green	25 B1	Shrewsbury Hall	64 E3	*Sloan Terrace (on Meath Road)	67 C2
Seamount View	2 E2	Shangan Park	25 B1	Shrewsbury House	59 C4	Sloperton	49 C4
Seamus Ennis Road	24 E1	Shangan Road	25 A1	Shrewsbury Lawn	59 C4	Smithfield	37 C2
Sean MacDermott Street Lower	38 E1	Shanganagh Cliffs	64 E2	Shrewsbury Lodge	59 C3	Smithfield Terrace	37 C2 [37]
Sean MacDermott Street Upper	38 D2	Shanganagh Grove	64 E3	Shrewsbury Park	48 D1	Smith's Cottages (Donnybrook)	47 B1 [18]
Sean Moore Road	39 A3	Shanganagh Road	25 A4	Shrewsbury Road	48 D1	Smith's Lane	46 F1 [13]
Sean O'Casey Avenue	38 E1 [47]	Shanganagh Road	64 E1	Shrewsbury Road	64 E3	Smith's Villas	49 C4 [3]
Sean Tracey House	38 E1 [12]	Shanganagh Terrace	60 E4	Shrewsbury Woods	59 C4	Smyth Gardens	49 C4 [34]
Sean Walsh Memorial Park	54 F1	Shanganagh Vale	60 D4	Sibthorpe Lane	38 E4 [28]	Snowdrop Walk	13 C4
Seapark	3 C3	Shanganagh Wood	64 E2 [8]	Sidbury Court	68 D2 [5]	Snugborough Road	22 F1
Seapark (Dollymount)	26 F4	Shanglas Road	25 C1	Sidmont Gardens	67 C2	Snugborough Road (Extention)	22 D2
Seapark Drive	26 F4	Shanid Road	46 F1	Sidmonton Avenue	67 C2	Solus Tower Estate	67 C1
Seapark Hill	3 C3	Shankill	64 E3	Sidmonton Court	68 D3 [5]	Somerset Street	38 F3 [8]
Seapark Road	26 F4	Shankill View	67 C2 [38]	Sidmonton Gardens	67 C2 [36]	Somerton Mews Est	59 C2
Seapoint Avenue	49 B3	Shanliss Avenue	25 B1	Sidmonton Gardens	67 C2	Somerville Avenue	45 C1
Seapoint Avenue (Baldoyle)	15 A4 [1]	Shanliss Drive	25 B1	Sidmonton Park	68 D2	Somerville Drive	46 D1
Seapoint Court	15 A4 [7]	Shanliss Gardens	25 A1 [2]	Sidmonton Place	67 C2 [6]	Somerville Park	45 C1 [7]
Seapoint Court	67 C1	Shanliss Grove	25 B1	Sidmonton Road	67 C2	Somerville Park	45 C1
Seapoint Road	67 C2	Shanliss Park	25 B1	Sidmonton Square	67 C2 [1]	Sommerton Lane	22 E4
Seapoint Terrace	39 A3 [4]	Shanliss Road	25 A1	Sigurd Road	37 C2 [31]	Sommerville	47 C4
Seapoint Terrace	67 C2 [24]	Shanliss Walk	25 B1	Silchester Court	60 D1	Sonesta	3 A2
Seapoint Terrace (Blackrock)	49 B3 [4]	Shanliss Way	25 B1	Silchester Crescent	60 D1	Sophie Baret Residence	48 D4 [4]
Seapoint Villas	67 C2 [20]	Shannon Terrace	37 B3 [4]	Silchester Park	60 D1	Sorbonne	48 D4
Seatown Road	2 D1	Shanowen Avenue	25 A1	Silchester Road	60 D1	Sorrel Dale	22 D2
Seatown Terrace	2 D2	Shanowen Crescent	25 B1	Silchester Wood	60 D1 [16]	Sorrel Drive	21 C2
Seatown Villas	2 D1	Shanowen Drive	25 B1	Silken Vale	17 C3	Sorrel Heath	21 C2
Seatown Walk	2 D2	Shanowen Grove	25 A1	Silken Vale	17 C3	Sorrel Park	21 C2
Seatown West	2 D1	Shanowen Park	25 A1	Silleachain Lane	20 D4	Sorrento Close	60 F2 [25]
Seaview Avenue East	38 F1	Shanowen Road	25 B1	Silloge Avenue	25 A1	Sorrento Court	60 F2 [29]
Seaview Avenue North	26 D4	Shanrath Road	25 B1	Silloge Gardens	25 A1	Sorrento Drive	60 F2 [12]
Seaview Cottages	63 C4	Shantalla Avenue	25 C1	Silloge Road	25 A1	Sorrento Heights	60 F2 [30]
Seaview Lawn	64 E2	Shantalla Drive	25 C2	Silver Birches	7 B2	Sorrento Lawn	60 F2
Seaview Park	64 E2	Shantalla Park	25 C2	Silver Birches	47 C4	Sorrento Mews	60 F2 [28]
Seaview Terrace (Donnybrook)	48 D1	Shantalla Road	25 C2	Silver Birches Close	7 B2	*Sorrento Park (on Sorrento Rd)	60 F2
Seaview Terrace (Dun Laoghaire)	49 C4 [15]	Shanvarna Road	25 B1	Silver Birches Crescent	7 B2	Sorrento Road	60 F2
		Sharavogue	60 E2	Silver Pines	58 F2 [3]	Sorrento Terrace	60 F2
Seaview Terrace (Howth)	30 D2 [2]	Shaw Street	38 E2 [10]	Silverberry	34 D3	South Avenue	48 F4

STREET NAME	PAGE/GRID REFERENCE	STREET NAME	PAGE/GRID REFERENCE	STREET NAME	PAGE/GRID REFERENCE	STREET NAME	PAGE/GRID REFERENCE
South Bank Road	39 B3	*St Agatha Court (off William St N)	38 E1	St Brigids Green	26 E2	St Finbarr's Close	45 B3
South Circular Road (Dolphin's Barn)	37 B3	St Agnes Park	46 D1	St Brigids Grove	26 E2	St Finbarr's Road	24 E4
South Circular Road (Islandbridge)	37 A2	St Agnes Road	46 D1	St Brigid's Avenue	14 F2 [4]	St Finians Grove	34 D2
South Circular Road (Kilmainham)	37 B3	St Agnes Terrace (Rathfarnham)	46 F3 [2]	St Brigid's Church Road	58 F1	St Finnians Avenue	34 D2
South Circular Road (Portobello)	37 C4	St Aidan's Drive	48 D4	St Brigid's Cottages (Blanchardstown)	22 F2	St Finnians Close	34 D2
*South City Market (on South Great Georges St)	38 D3	St Aidan's Park	25 C4 [6]	St Brigid's Cottages (Clondalkin)	44 F2	St Finnians Crescent	34 D2
South Dock Place	38 F3 [35]	St Aidan's Park Avenue	25 C4	St Brigid's Cottages (North Strand)	38 F1 [24]	St Fintan Road (Cabra)	24 F4
South Dock Road	38 F3 [24]	St Aidan's Park Road	25 C4	St Brigid's Court	26 E3 [2]	St Fintan Terrace (Cabra)	24 F4
South Dock Street	38 F3	St Aidan's Terrace	67 C2 [23]	St Brigid's Crescent	26 E2	St Fintan's Crescent	29 B3
South Esplanade	68 D2	St Aiden's Halting Site	54 D1	St Brigid's Drive (Clondalkin)	44 E2	St Fintan's Grove	29 B3
South Great George's St	38 D3	St Alban's Park	48 E1	St Brigid's Drive (Killester)	26 E3 [1]	St Fintan's High School	29 A1
South Hill	29 C3	St Alban's Road	37 C4	St Brigid's Lawn	26 E2	St Fintan's Park (Dean's Grange)	59 B1
South Hill	47 B2	St Alphonsus Avenue	25 A4 [11]	St Brigid's Park (Clondalkin)	44 E2 [1]	St Fintan's Park (Sutton)	29 B2
South Hill Avenue	48 F3	St Alphonsus Rd	25 A4	St Brigid's Park (Cornelscourt)	59 B3	St Fintan's Road (Sutton)	29 B3
South Hill Park	48 F3	St Andrew Street	38 D3	St Brigid's Pk (Blanchardstown)	22 F2	St Fintan's Terrace	35 C1 [5]
South Lotts Road	38 F3	St Andrews	34 F2	St Brigid's Road (Artane)	26 E2	St Fintan's Villas	59 B1
South Park	1 C1	St Andrews Drive	34 F2	St Brigid's Road (Clondalkin)	44 E2	St Francis Square	38 D3 [48]
South Park	59 B2	St Andrews Fairway	34 F2	St Brigid's Road Lower	25 A4	St Gabriel's	59 C3
South Park Drive	59 B2	St Andrews Green	34 F2	St Brigid's Road Upper	25 A4	St Gabriel's Court	27 A4 [2]
South Western Area Health Board	18 D2	St Andrew's Grove	3 B3	St Brigid's Terrace	67 C2 [33]	St Gabriel's Road	26 F4
South Winds	60 F1 [4]	*St Andrew's Lane (off Exchequer Street)	38 D3	St Broc's Cottages	47 C1 [1]	St Gall Gardens North	47 B3 [2]
South Wood Park	48 F3	St Andrews Park	1 C1	St Canice's Park	24 F2	St Gall Gardens South	47 B3 [3]
Southdene	49 B4 [18]	St Andrews Wood	34 F2	St Canice's Road	25 A2	St Gatien Road	56 F1 [2]
Southern Cross Avenue	37 A3	St Anne's	38 E4	St Catherine's Avenue	37 C4	St George's Avenue (Clonliffe Road)	25 B4
Southern Cross Route	57 B3	St Annes	46 E2	St Catherines Grove	43 C1 [3]	St George's Avenue (Killiney)	60 E3
Southview Terrace	37 B3 [38]	St Annes Court	27 A3 [2]	St Catherine's Lane West	37 C3 [14]	St George's Villas (Inchicore)	36 F3 [18]
Spa Road	36 F3	St Anne's Avenue	27 A3	St Catherine's Park	60 E1	St Gerard's Road	45 C2
Spa Road (Phoenix Park)	37 A1	St Anne's Drive	27 A3	St Catherine's Road	60 E1	St Helena's Court	24 E2 [3]
Spafield Terrace	39 A4 [13]	St Anne's Park	64 E3	St Catherine's Terrace	29 A1 [2]	St Helena's Drive	24 E2
Spawell Cottages	45 C4 [1]	St Anne's Road North	25 A4	St Catherine's View	20 E4	St Helena's Road	24 E2
Spawell Hotel Leisure and Sports Centre	45 C4	St Anne's Road South	37 C4 [5]	St Clair's Lawn	67 B3	St Helen's	60 E1 [22]
Spencer Dock	38 F2 [12]	St Anne's Square (Blackrock)	49 A3 [7]	St Clair's Terrace	67 B3 [3]	St Helen's Road	48 E2
Spencer Dock (Guild Street)	38 F2	St Anne's Square (Portmarnock)	14 F2	St Clare's Avenue	37 C4 [20]	St Helen's Villas	48 F2 [1]
*Spencer Place (off Spencer Street N)	38 F1	St Anne's Terrace	52 E2	St Clare's Terrace (on Mount Drummond Avenue)	38 D4	St Helen's Wood	48 E3
Spencer Row	38 E2 [22]	St Anne's Terrace (Cabra)	24 F4	*St Clement's Road	25 A4	St Helier's Copse	48 F4 [1]
Spencer Street North	38 F1	*St Anne's Terrace (off Northbrook Lane)	38 E4	St Colmcilles Court	2 D2 [3]	St Ignatius Avenue	38 D1 [17]
Spencer Street South	38 D4 [48]	St Anne's Terrace (Raheny)	27 A3	St Columbanus Avenue	47 B3	St Ignatius Road	25 A4
*Spencer Terrace (off Cork Street)	37 B3	St Ann's Square	14 F2 [6]	St Columbanus Place	47 B3 [1]	St Ita's Road	25 A3 [6]
Spencer Villas	60 E1	St Ann's Square Lower	14 F2 [5]	St Columbanus Road	47 B3	St Ives	3 B2
Sperrin Road	37 A4	St Anthony's Avenue	44 E2	St Columbas Heights	1 C2	St James Avenue (Clonliffe Road)	38 E1
Spiddal Park	35 C3	St Anthony's Crescent	45 C2	St Columbas Rise	1 C2	*St James Place (Sandymount Road)	39 A3
Spiddal Road	35 C3	*St Anthony's Place (off Temple Street North)	38 D1	St Columba's Road	45 B2	St James Terrace (Sandymount)	39 A3 [23]
Spire View	24 D4	St Anthony's Road	37 B3	St Columba's Road Lower	25 A4	St James's Avenue (James's Street)	37 B3 [21]
Spire View Lane	47 A1	St Aongus Court	45 B4	St Columba's Road Upper	25 A4	St James's Place (Inchicore)	36 F3 [17]
Spitalfields	37 C3 [46]	St Aongus Crescent	45 B4	St Columcille's Crescent	2 D2 [1]	St James's Road	45 B2
Spittal Hill	2 D1	St Aongus Green	45 B4	St Columcille's Drive	2 D2	St James's Terrace (Dolphin's Barn)	37 B4 [2]
Spring Garden Lane	38 E2 [14]	St Aongus Grove	45 B4	St Columcille's Terrace	67 C2 [18]	St James's Walk	37 B3
Spring Garden Street	38 E1	St Aongus Lawn	45 B4	St Columcills Park	2 D2	St Jarlath Road	24 F4
Springbank Cottages	53 A2	St Aongus Park	45 B4	St Conleth's Road	45 C2	St John of God's	26 D1
Springdale Road	26 F2	St Aongus Road	45 B4	St Cronan's Avenue	1 B2	St John Street	37 C3 [58]
Springfield (Cabra)	37 A1	St Assam's Avenue	27 A2	St Cronan's Close	1 B2	St Johns Court (Donnycarney)	26 D3
Springfield (Tallaght)	54 F1	St Assam's Drive	27 A2	St Cronan's Cottages	1 C2	St John's	48 E1
Springfield Avenue	46 E4	St Assam's Park	27 A2	St Cronan's Court	1 B1	St John's Avenue	37 C3 [39]
Springfield Close	31 C4	St Assam's Road East	27 B2	St Cronan's Grove	1 C1	St John's Avenue	44 D2
Springfield Crescent	46 E4	St Assam's Road West	27 A2	St Cronan's Lawn	1 B1	St John's Close	44 D2
Springfield Drive	46 E4	St Attracta Road	24 F4	St Cronan's Road	67 C2 [8]	St John's Cottages	37 B3 [28]
Springfield Park (Deans Grange)	59 A2	St Aubyn's Court	64 E1 [5]	St Cronan's View	1 B2	St John's Court	44 D2
Springfield Park (Templeogue)	46 E4	*St Audoen's Terrace (off High Street)	38 D3	St Cronan's Way	1 C2	St John's Court (Beaumont)	26 D1
Springfield Road	46 E3	St Augustine Street	37 C2	St David's	26 D2	St John's Crescent	44 D2
Springhill Avenue	59 A1	St Augustine's Park	59 A1 [7]	St David's Court	26 E4 [5]	St John's Drive	44 D2
Springhill Cottages	59 B1 [5]	St Augustine's Park (Estate)	59 A1	St David's Park	26 D2	St John's Green	44 D2
Springhill Park (Dalkey)	60 E1	St Barnabas Gardens	38 F1 [12]	St David's Terrace (Blackhorse Avenue)	37 B1 [7]	*St John's Lane (off Strand Road)	48 E1
Springhill Park (Deans Grange)	59 B1	St Begnet's Villas	60 E1	St David's Terrace (Glasnevin)	25 A3 [3]	St John's Lawn	44 D2
Springlawn	22 E2	St Benedicts Gardens	38 D1 [35]	St Davids Wood	26 D2	St John's Park (Dun Laoghaire)	49 C4
Springlawn Close	22 E2	St Brendan's Avenue	26 E2	St Declan's Road	25 C4	St John's Park East	44 D2
Springlawn Court	22 E2	St Brendan's Cottages	39 A3 [6]	St Declan's Terrace	25 C4 [5]	St Johns Park West	44 D1
Springlawn Drive	22 E2	St Brendan's Crescent	45 B2	St Domhnach's Well	28 D1 [3]	St John's Road	44 D2
Springlawn Heights	22 E2	St Brendan's Drive	26 E2	St Dominic's Avenue	55 A1	St John's Road East	48 E1
Springlawn Road	22 E2	St Brendan's Park	26 F2	St Dominic's Court	55 A1 [4]	St John's Road West	37 B2
Springmount Apartments	24 D2	St Brendan's Road	25 A4 [12]	St Dominic's Road	55 A1	St John's Road West	44 D2
Springvale	56 E2	St Brendan's Terrace (Coolock)	26 E1	St Dominic's Terrace	55 A1	St John's Terrace (Mount Brown)	37 B3 [33]
Spruce Avenue	58 D2	St Brendan's Terrace (Dun Laoghaire)	49 C4 [19]	St Donagh's Crescent	27 B1	St John's Wood	26 E4 [2]
St Aengus CBSI Scout Den	45 B4	St Brendan's Terrace (Rockbrook)	56 E4	St Donagh's Park	27 B1	St John's Wood	44 D2
*St Agnes Terrace (on St Agnes Rd)	46 D1	St Bricin's Park	37 B2	St Donagh's Road	27 B1	St John's Wood West	44 D2
		St Bridget's Avenue (North Strand)	38 F1	St Edmundsbury Hospital	34 E1	St Joseph Street	38 D1 [27]
		St Bridget's Drive (Greenhills)	45 B2	St Eithne Road	24 F4	St Joseph's	23 C2
		St Bridget's Flats	47 C2 [8]	St Elizabeth's Court	37 C1 [14]	St Joseph's Avenue (Ballybough)	25 B4 [2]
				St Enda's Drive	56 F1		
				St Enda's Park	56 F1		
				St Enda's Road	46 F2		
				St Finbarrs Court	24 E4 [2]		

STREET NAME	PAGE/GRID REFERENCE
St Joseph's Avenue (Drumcondra)	25 A4
St Joseph's Cottages	23 C4 [3]
St Joseph's Court	37 C1 [16]
St Joseph's Grove	47 C4 [9]
St Joseph's Mansions	38 E1 [60]
St Joseph's Parade	38 D1
St Joseph's Place	37 C1 [15]
St Joseph's Place	38 D1 [59]
St Joseph's Road (Aughrim Street)	37 C1
St Joseph's Road (Walkinstown)	45 C2
St Joseph's Square	39 C1 [2]
*St Joseph's Street (off Leo Street)	38 D1
St Joseph's Terrace	38 E1 [35]
St Joseph's Terrace (Fairview)	25 C4 [4]
*St Joseph's Terrace (off Dolphin's Barn)	37 B4
*St Joseph's Terrace (off Pembroke Street)	39 A3
*St Joseph's Terrace (on Tivoli Road)	50 D4
St Joseph's Villas (Summerhill)	38 E1 [38]
St Judes Apts	31 C3 [3]
St Judes G.A.A. Club	45 C4
*St Kevin's Avenue (off Blackpitts)	37 C3
St Kevin's Cottages	38 D4 [29]
St Kevin's Court	47 A2
St Kevin's Gardens	47 A2
St Kevin's Parade	38 D4 [52]
St Kevin's Park (Rathgar)	47 A2
St Kevin's Park (Stillorgan)	58 D1
St Kevin's Road	38 D4 [3]
St Kevin's Square	67 C2
St Kevin's Terrace	67 C2 [14]
*St Kevin's Terrace (New Bride St)	38 D3
St Kevin's Villas	60 D1
St Killian's Avenue	45 B2
St Killians Crescent	67 B4
St Killian's Park	44 E1 [1]
St Laurence Grove	36 E2 [4]
St Laurence Park	48 F4
St Laurence Place	38 D1 [66]
*St Laurence Place (Fontenoy Street)	38 D1
*St Laurence Place (Lr Sheriff Street)	38 F2
St Laurence Road	36 E2
St Laurence Terrace (Chapelizod)	36 E2 [9]
St Laurence's Terrace	67 C2 [17]
St Lawrence Building (Apts.)	30 D1 [14]
St Lawrence O'Toole Avenue	14 F2 [1]
St Lawrence Quay	30 D1 [8]
St Lawrence Road (Clontarf)	26 D4
St Lawrence Road (Howth)	30 D1
St Lawrence's Court	26 D4
St Lawrences Glen	36 E3 [5]
St Lawrence's Terrace (Howth)	30 D2 [1]
St Loman's Road	34 F2
St. Luke's Avenue	37 C3
St Luke's Court	26 D1 [3]
St Luke's Crescent	47 B2 [3]
St Luke's Gate	37 C3
St Maelruans Park	55 A1
St Maelruans Park (Estate)	55 A1
St Maignenn's Terrace	37 B3 [6]
St Malachy's Drive	45 C2
St Malachy's Road	25 A3 [7]
St Margarets Close	60 E1 [30]
St Margaret's	11 B1
St Margaret's	48 F3
St Margaret's (Booterstown)	48 F3
St Margaret's Avenue	3 B3
St Margaret's Avenue (Kilbarrack)	27 C2
*St Margaret's Avenue (off Pimlico)	37 C3
St Margaret's Avenue North	38 E1 [34]
St Margaret's Court	11 A4 [1]
St Margaret's Halting Site	11 C4
St Margaret's Park	3 B3
St Margaret's Road	3 B3
St Margaret's Road (Ballymun)	12 D4
St Margaret's Road (Finglas)	11 A4
St Margaret's Terrace	37 C3 [7]
St Mark's Avenue	35 A2
St Mark's Crescent	35 A3
St Mark's Drive	35 A3
St Mark's Gardens	35 A3
St Mark's Green	35 A3
St Mark's Grove	35 A3
St Marnock's Avenue	14 F2
St Martin's Drive	46 E2
St Martin's Park	46 E1
St Mary's Ave North (Mountjoy Street)	38 D1 [7]
St Mary's Avenue (Rathfarnham)	46 F4
St Mary's Avenue West	36 F3
St Mary's Crescent	45 C1
St Mary's Drive	45 C1
St Mary's Lane	38 F3 [17]
St Mary's Mansions	38 E1 [62]
St Mary's Park	20 D4
St Mary's Park	23 C2
St Mary's Park	45 C1
St Mary's Place (Howth)	30 D2 [4]
St Mary's Place North	38 D1 [48]
St Mary's Road (Crumlin)	46 D1
St Mary's Road (Howth)	30 D2 [3]
St Mary's Road North (East Wall)	38 F1
St Mary's Road South (Ballsbridge)	38 F4
St Mary's Street	49 C4 [5]
St Marys Terrace	68 D2 [20]
St Mary's Terrace	7 B2 [1]
St Mary's Terrace	67 C4 [6]
St Mary's Terrace (Arbour Hill)	37 C2 [34]
*St Mary's Terrace (Bath Street)	39 A3
*St Mary's Terrace (Chapelizod)	36 E2 [5]
St Mary's Terrace (Mountjoy Street)	38 D1 [10]
St Mary's Terrace (Rathfarnham)	46 F4 [5]
St Mathias Wood	60 D4
St Mel's Avenue	45 B3
*St Michael's Close (off High Street)	38 D3
St Michael's Estate	37 A3 [8]
*St Michael's Hill (off High Street)	38 D3
St Michael's House	47 C4
St Michael's Place	38 D1 [51]
St Michael's Road	25 A3 [8]
St Michael's Terrace (Blackpitts)	37 C3 [57]
St Michael's Terrace (Dun Laoghaire)	49 C4 [18]
*St Michan's Place (off Chancery Street)	38 D2
St Michan's Street	38 D2 [44]
St Mobhi Avenue	25 A3
St Mobhi Boithirin	25 A3
St Mobhi Drive	25 A3
St Mobhi Grove	25 A3 [10]
St Mobhi Road	25 A3
St Mochtas Avenue	22 D3
St Mochtas Chase	22 D2
St Mochtas Drive	22 D3
St Mochtas Green	22 D3
St Mochtas Grove	22 D3
St Mochtas Lawn	22 D2
St Mochtas Road	22 D3
St Mochtas Vale	22 D3
St Mura's Terrace	38 F1 [17]
St Nathy's House	47 B4 [5]
St Nathy's Villas	47 B4 [17]
St Nessans Apts	30 E2 [3]
St Nessan's Close	30 D2 [9]
St Nessans Court	30 D2 [12]
St Nessan's Terrace	30 D2 [5]
St Nicholas Place	38 D3 [2]
St Oliver's Park	35 B3
St Pappin's Green	24 F2
St Pappin's Road	25 A2
St Patricks Avenue	14 F2
St Patrick's Avenue (Clondalkin)	44 D1 [1]
St Patrick's Avenue (Dalkey)	60 F2 [1]
St Patrick's Avenue (Fairview)	38 F1 [16]
St Patrick's Close	38 D3
St Patrick's Close	59 C1 [9]
St Patrick's College Maynooth	17 C3
St Patrick's Cottages	46 F4
St Patrick's Crescent	52 E2
St Patrick's Crescent	59 C1
St Patrick's Parade	25 A4
St Patrick's Park (Clondalkin)	44 D1
St Patrick's Park	58 E3
St Patrick's Park	7 B2
St Patrick's Park	32 D3
St Patrick's Park	62 E1
St Patrick's Park (Blanchardstown)	22 E2
*St Patrick's Place (off Royal Canal Bank)	25 A4
St Patrick's Road (Clondalkin)	35 A4
St Patrick's Road (Dalkey)	60 F2 [8]
St Patrick's Road (Drumcondra)	25 A4
St Patrick's Road (Walkinstown)	45 C2
St Patrick's Square	60 F2 [4]
St Patrick's Square	67 C1 [1]
St Patrick's Terrace (Inchicore)	36 F3 [9]
St Patrick's Terrace (Kill O' the Grange)	59 C1 [7]
*St Patrick's Terrace (Nth Brunswick St)	37 C2
*St Patrick's Terrace (off Fitzroy Avenue)	25 B4
St Patrick's Terrace (Russell Street)	38 E1
St Patrick's Villas	39 A3 [3]
St Paul's Terrace	60 E1 [5]
St Peregrines G.A.A.	22 D1
St Peter's Avenue	37 C1
St Peter's Close	38 D1 [62]
*St Peter's Close (off Royal Canal Bank)	38 D1
St Peter's Crescent	45 C2
St Peter's Drive	45 C2
St Peter's Park	7 B2
St Peter's Road (Bray)	67 B1
St Peter's Road (Phibsborough)	37 C1
St Peter's Road (Walkinstown)	45 C2
St Peter's Square	38 D1 [37]
St Peter's Terrace	67 B1 [2]
St Peter's Terrace (Dun Laoghaire)	60 E1 [6]
St Peter's Terrace (Howth)	30 D2
St Peter's Terrace Walkinstown (off Peters Road)	45 C2 [1]
St Philomenas	9 C4
St Philomena's Court	9 C4
St Philomena's Park	9 C4
St Philomena's Road	24 F4 [1]
St Raphaels Avenue	31 C4
St Ronan's Avenue	35 A3
St Ronan's Close	35 A3
St Ronan's Crescent	35 A3
St Ronan's Drive	35 A3
St Ronan's Gardens	35 A3
St Ronan's Green	35 A3
St Ronan's Grove	35 A3
St Ronan's Park	35 A3
St Ronan's Way	35 A3
St Stephen's Green East	38 E3
St Stephen's Green North	38 E3
St Stephen's Green South	38 D3
St Stephen's Green West	38 D3
St Sylvester Villas	3 B3
St Teresa's Gardens	37 C3
St Teresa's Place	25 A4 [9]
St Teresa's Road (Crumlin)	46 D2
St Teresa's Road (Glasnevin)	25 A4 [8]
St Thomas Mead	48 E3
St Thomas Road (Ardee Street)	37 C3
St Thomas's Road (Mount Merrion)	48 E3
St Ultan's Flats	38 D4 [21]
St Vincent Street North	38 D1 [4]
St Vincent Street South	38 D4
St Vincent Street West	37 A3
St Vincent's Cottages	23 C4 [2]
St Vincent's Court	25 C3 [7]
St Vincent's Park	49 A4
St Werburghs	2 E2
St Wolston's Abbey	32 D4
Stable Lane (Harcourt Street)	38 D3 [19]
Stable Lane (Leeson St Lr)	38 E3 [37]
Stable Lane (Smithfield)	37 C2 [16]
Staffordstown	5 C2
Staffordstown Little	5 C1
Stamer Street	38 D4
Stanford Green	45 C1
Stanhope Street	37 C2 [2]
Stanley Street	37 C2 [39]
*Stanley Street (off Brunswick Street North)	37 C2
Stannaway Avenue	46 D1
Stannaway Court	46 D2 [3]
Stannaway Drive	46 E1
Stannaway Road	46 E1
Stapolin Lawns	14 F4
Station Road	7 B3
Station Road	19 C4
Station Road	64 E2 [6]
Station Road (Glenageary)	60 E1
Station Road (Killiney)	60 E4
*Station Road (off Clover Hill Road)	35 A4
Station Road (Portmarnock)	14 E2
Station Road (Raheny)	27 A2
Station Road (Sutton)	29 A1
Station View Apts	22 D3 [4]
Stationcourt	22 D3
Stationcourt Hall	22 D3
Stationcourt Park	22 D3
Stationcourt View	22 D3
Stationcourt Way	22 D3
Steelstown	51 C3
Steeven's Lane	37 B2
Stella Avenue	25 A3
Stella Gardens	39 A3
Stepaside	58 E4
Stepaside Lane	62 E1
Stepaside Park	58 E4
Stepaside Park	62 E1
Stephen Street Lower	38 D3
Stephen Street Upper	38 D3
Stephen's Lane	38 E3
Stephen's Place	38 E3 [36]
Stephen's Road	37 A3
Sterling Square Apts.	8 D3
Stillorgan	58 E1
Stillorgan Court	58 E1 [2]
Stillorgan Grove	48 F4
Stillorgan Heath	58 E1 [3]
Stillorgan Heath	58 E1
Stillorgan Park	48 F4
Stillorgan Park Avenue	58 F1
Stillorgan Road (Donnybrook)	48 D1
Stillorgan Road (Foxrock)	59 A2
Stillorgan Road (Mount Merrion)	48 E3
Stillorgan Road (Stillorgan)	48 E4
Stillorgan Wood	58 E1
Stirling Park	47 A3 [2]
*Stirrup Lane (off Church Street)	37 C2
Stockhole Lane	12 F1
Stocking Lane	56 D3
Stockton Court	23 A3
Stockton Drive	23 A3
Stockton Green	23 A3
Stockton Grove	23 A3
Stockton Lawn	23 A3
Stockton Park	23 A3
Stokes Place	38 D3 [27]
Stone Mews	47 A1 [8]
Stone Park Orchard	46 F4 [17]
Stonebridge	21 B2
Stonebridge Avenue	21 B2
Stonebridge Close	64 E3 [2]
Stonebridge Drive	21 B2
Stonebridge Lane	64 D2 [1]
Stonebridge Road	21 B2
Stonebridge Road	64 D2
Stonemasons Way	57 A2

STREET NAME	PAGE/GRID REFERENCE	STREET NAME	PAGE/GRID REFERENCE	STREET NAME	PAGE/GRID REFERENCE	STREET NAME	PAGE/GRID REFERENCE
Stonepark Abbey	46 F4	Summerhill Road	7 A2	Swords Manor Drive	1 B1	Tamarisk Court	45 A3
Stoneview Place	50 D4 [13]	Summerhill Road	50 D4	Swords Manor Grove	1 B2	Tamarisk Dale	45 A3
Stoney Park	52 F2	Summerseat Court	8 D4	Swords Manor View	1 B1	Tamarisk Drive	45 A3
Stoney Road (Dundrum)	47 C4	Summerville	39 B1	Swords Manor Way	1 B1	Tamarisk Grove	45 A3
Stoney Road (East Wall)	38 F1 [2]	Summerville Park	47 A1	Swords Road	25 B1	Tamarisk Heights	45 A3
Stoneybatter	37 C2	*Summerville Terrace	60 F2	Swords Road (Collinstown)	12 F2	Tamarisk Lawn	45 A3
Stoneylea Terrace	67 C3 [10]	(on Dalkey Ave)		Swords Road (Malahide)	3 A3	Tamarisk Park	45 A3
Store Street	38 E2	Sunbury Gardens	47 A2	Swords Street	37 B2 [8]	Tamarisk View	45 A3
Stormanstown Road	25 A2	Suncroft Avenue	14 F2 [3]	Sybil Hill Avenue	26 F3	Tamarisk Walk	45 A3
Stradbrook Close	59 B1	Suncroft Drive	54 D2	Sybil Hill Road	26 F3	Tamarisk Way	45 A3
Stradbrook Gardens	49 B4 [8]	Suncroft Park	54 D2	Sycamore Avenue (Cabinteely)	59 B3	Tandys Lane	33 C3
Stradbrook Grove	49 B4	Sundale Avenue	54 D2	Sycamore Avenue (Castleknock)	22 E3	Taney Avenue	47 C4
Stradbrook Hall	49 B4 [20]	Sundale Close	54 D2	Sycamore Avenue (Mt Merrion)	48 E4	Taney Court	47 C4
Stradbrook Hill	59 B1 [4]	Sundale Crescent	54 D1	Sycamore Avenue (Tallaght)	45 A3	Taney Crescent	47 C4
Stradbrook Lawn	49 B4	Sundale Green	54 D1	Sycamore Close	44 F3	Taney Drive	47 C4
Stradbrook Park	49 B4	Sundale Grove	54 D2	Sycamore Close	59 B3	Taney Grove	47 C4
Stradbrook Road	49 B4	Sundale Heights	54 D1	Sycamore Court	59 C2 [3]	Taney Lawn	47 C4
Straffan Way	17 C4	Sundale Lawn	54 D1	Sycamore Crescent	48 E4 [4]	Taney Manor	47 C4
Straleek	41 B1	Sundale Meadows	54 D1	Sycamore Crescent (Cabinteely)	59 B3	Taney Park	47 C4
Stralem Court	21 B1	Sundale Parade	54 D1	Sycamore Drive (Cabinteely)	59 B4	Taney Rise	47 C4
Stralem Mews	21 B1	Sundale Park	54 D2	Sycamore Drive (Castleknock)	22 E3	Taney Road	47 C4
Stralem Terrace	21 B1	Sundale Road	54 D2	Sycamore Drive (Dundrum)	57 B1 [4]	*Tangier Lane	38 D3
Strand Lane	48 E1 [3]	Sundale Villas	54 D1	Sycamore Drive (Tallaght)	45 A3	(off Grafton Street)	
Strand Road (Baldoyle)	15 A4	Sundale Walk	54 D1	Sycamore Green (Cabinteely)	59 B3	Tara Hill Crescent	46 F4
Strand Road (Bray)	67 C2	Sundrive Park	46 E1	Sycamore Grove	59 A2 [7]	Tara Hill Grove	46 F4 [2]
Strand Road (Merrion)	48 E1	Sundrive Road	46 E1	Sycamore Grove	59 B3	Tara Hill Road	46 F4
Strand Road (Portmarnock)	4 D4	Sunnybank Court	47 C4	Sycamore Lawn (Cabinteely)	59 B3	Tara Lawn	27 A1
Strand Road (Portmarnock)	14 F2	Sunnyside	62 F3	Sycamore Lawn (Castleknock)	22 E3	Tara Street	38 E2
Strand Road (Portmarnock)	15 A1	Sunville Green	46 D1 [1]	Sycamore Park (Castleknock)	22 E3	Tassagard Greens	53 B2
Strand Road (Sandymount)	39 B4	Susan Terrace	37 C3	Sycamore Park (Finglas)	24 E1	Tay Lane	52 E2
Strand Road (Sutton)	29 B2	Susanville Road	25 B4	Sycamore Park (Tallaght)	45 A3	Taylor's Hall	57 A3
Strand Street	3 B2	Sussex Road	38 E4	Sycamore Road (Dundrum)	57 B1	Taylor's Lane (Ballyboden)	56 E1
Strand Street	39 A3	Sussex Street	50 D4 [16]	Sycamore Road (Finglas)	24 E1	Taylor's Lane (Pimlico)	37 C3 [13]
Strand Street Great	38 D2	Sussex Terrace	38 E4 [11]	Sycamore Road (Fox & Geese)	45 A1	Temple Bar	38 D2
Strand Street Little	38 D2 [36]	Sutton	29 A1	Sycamore Road	48 E4	Temple Buildings	38 D1 [60]
Strand Terrace	47 B2 [2]	Sutton Castle (Apts.)	29 B3	(Mount Merrion)		Temple Cottages	38 D1
Strandmill Avenue	14 F2	Sutton Castle Hotel	29 B3	Sycamore Street	38 D2 [21]	Temple Court	37 B2 [16]
Strandmill Park	15 A2	Sutton Court	28 D1 [1]	Sycamore View	22 E3	Temple Court (Off Hogan Place)	38 F3 [46]
Strandmill Road	15 A2	Sutton Dinghy Club	29 B3	Sycamore Walk	59 B4	Temple Court Apartments	12 E4
Strandville Avenue	38 F1 [4]	Sutton Downs	28 D1	Sydenham	50 D4 [23]	Temple Crescent	49 B4
(North Strand)		Sutton Grove	28 D1	Sydenham Mews	68 D3	Temple Gardens	12 E4
Strandville Avenue East	26 D4	Sutton Lane	63 A3	*Sydenham Place	47 C4	Temple Gardens	47 B2
(Clontarf)		Sutton Lawns	28 D1	(on Kilmacud Rd Upr)		Temple Hill	49 B4
Strandville House	26 D4 [4]	Sutton Park	28 D1	Sydenham Road (Ballsbridge)	39 A4 [4]	Temple Hill	46 E2
Strandville Place	38 F1 [19]	Sutton Park School	29 B3	Sydenham Road (Dundrum)	47 C4	(on Terenure Road West)	
Strangford Drive	42 D4	Sutton Road	67 B2 [9]	Sydenham Villas	57 C1	Temple Lane North	38 D1 [41]
Strangford Gardens	38 F1	Sutton Villas	67 B2 [17]	Sydenham Villas	68 D3 [6]	Temple Lane South	38 D2 [46]
Strangford Road	38 F1	Swallowbrook	8 F4	Sydney Avenue	49 A3	Temple Lawns	32 D3
Strasburg Terrace	39 A3 [21]	Swallowbrook Crescent	8 F4	Sydney Parade Avenue	48 E1	Temple Manor	7 B2
Stratford	47 A2 [9]	Swallowbrook Park	8 F4	Sydney Terrace	49 A3	Temple Manor	31 C4
Strathmore Road	60 E4	Swallowbrook View	8 F4	Sykes Lane	46 F2	Temple Manor	45 C3
Streamville Court	64 E1 [10]	Swan Alley	37 C3 [51]	Sylvan Avenue	45 A3	Temple Manor Avenue	45 C3
Streamville Road	27 A1	Swan Grove	38 E4 [23]	Sylvan Close	44 F3	Temple Manor Close	45 C3
Strong's Court	38 D1 [67]	Swan Place	38 E4 [31]	Sylvan Drive	44 F3	Temple Manor Court	45 C3
*Strong's Court	38 D2	*Swan Yard (off Harry Street)	38 D3	Sylvester Villas	3 B3	Temple Manor Drive	45 C3
(off Findlater Place)		Swanbrook	67 C4	Synge Lane	38 D4 [25]	Temple Manor Grove	45 C3
Suffolk Street	38 D2	Swan's Nest Apts	27 B1 [6]	Synge Place	38 D4 [24]	Temple Manor Way	45 C3
Sugarloaf Crescent	67 C3	Swan's Nest Avenue	27 B1	Synge Street	38 D4	Temple Park	47 B2
Sugarloaf Terrace	67 C3 [21]	Swan's Nest Court	27 B1 [2]	Synge Way	35 C4	Temple Park Avenue	49 B3
Suir Road	37 A3	Swan's Nest Road	27 B1	Synnott Place	38 D1	Temple Place	38 E4 [26]
Sullivan Street	37 B2 [3]	Swanville Place	47 A1 [4]	Synnott Row	38 D1 [26]	Temple Road (Blackrock)	49 A3
*Summer Arch	38 E1	Swanward Court	37 C4 [39]	Synnott Terrace	49 C4 [16]	Temple Road (Rathgar)	47 B2
(off Summer St N)		Sweeney's Terrace	37 C3 [36]			Temple Square	47 B2 [5]
Summer Place	38 E1 [46]	Sweetbriar Lane	58 D1	**T**		Temple Street North	38 D1
*Summer Row	38 E1	Sweetman's Avenue	49 A3 [21]			Temple Street West	37 B2 [7]
(off Summer Street North)		Sweetman's Avenue	49 A3	Taaffe's Place	38 F1 [15]	Temple Terrace	60 F2 [16]
Summer Street North	38 E1	Sweetmount Avenue	47 B4 [15]	Talbot	2 F3	*Temple Villas (Arbour Hill)	37 C2
Summer Street South	37 C3	Sweetmount Drive	57 B1	Talbot Avenue	2 F3	*Temple Villas	47 B1
Summerfield	39 A3	Sweetmount House	47 B4 [18]	Talbot Court	3 A2	(on Palmerston Road)	
Summerfield	55 A2 [1]	Sweetmount Park	47 B4	Talbot Court	22 F2	Templemore Avenue	47 A2
Summerfield Avenue	22 E2	Swift Hall	59 B4	Talbot Downs	22 F2	Templeogue	46 D4
Summerfield Close	22 E2	Sweetmount Park	57 B1	Talbot Lane	38 E2 [6]	Templeogue Lodge	46 D4
Summerfield Close	60 F2 [10]	Swiftbrook	54 D1	Talbot Lane	60 E3 [7]	Templeogue Road	46 E3
Summerfield Green	22 E2	Swiftbrook Avenue	54 D1	Talbot Lodge	48 F4	Templeogue United F.C.	45 C4
Summerfield Grove	22 E2	Swiftbrook Close	54 D1	Talbot Park	2 F3	Templeogue Wood	46 D4
Summerfield Lawns	22 E2	Swiftbrook Drive	54 D1	Talbot Place	38 E2	Templeroan	56 D1
Summerfield Meadows	22 E2	Swiftbrook Park	54 D1	Talbot Road	2 F3	Templeroan Avenue	56 D1
Summerfield Park	22 E2	Swift's Alley	37 C3	Talbot Road	60 E3 [3]	Templeroan Close	56 E1
Summerfield Rise	22 E2	Swift's Grove	13 A3	Talbot Street	38 E2	Templeroan Court	56 D1
Summerhill	38 E1	*Swift's Row (off Ormond Quay)	38 D2	Tallaght	55 A1	Templeroan Crescent	56 D1
Summerhill Court	50 E4 [3]	Swilly Road	24 E4	Tallaght Bypass	54 F1	Templeroan Downs	56 E1
Summerhill Parade	50 D4 [6]	Swords	2 D1	Tallaght Road	45 C4	Templeroan Drive	56 D1
(Dun Laoghaire)		Swords Manor Avenue	1 B2	Tallaght Road	55 B1	Templeroan Green	56 D2
Summerhill Parade (Summerhill)	38 E1	Swords Manor Court	1 B1	Tamarisk Avenue	45 A3	Templeroan Grove	56 D1
Summerhill Place	38 E1 [26]	Swords Manor Crescent	1 B1	Tamarisk Close	45 A3	Templeroan Lodge	56 D2

STREET NAME	PAGE/GRID REFERENCE
Templeroan Meadows	56 E1
Templeroan Mews	56 D1
Templeroan Park	56 D1
Templeroan View	56 D1
Templeroan Way	56 D1
Templeview Avenue	14 D4
Templeview Close	14 D4
Templeview Copse	14 D4
Templeview Court	14 D4
Templeview Crescent	14 D4
Templeview Downs	14 D4
Templeview Drive	14 D4
Templeview Green	14 D4
Templeview Grove	14 D4
Templeview Lawn	14 D4
Templeview Park	14 D4
Templeview Place	14 D4
Templeview Rise	14 D4
Templeview Row	14 D4
Templeview Square	14 D4
Templeview Vale	14 D4 [1]
Templeview Walk	14 D4
Templeview Way	14 D4
Templeville Avenue	46 D3
Templeville Drive	46 D3
Templeville Park	46 E3 [1]
Templeville Road	46 D3
Terenure	46 F2
Terenure Enterprise Centre	46 F2
Terenure Park	46 F2
Terenure Place	46 F2 [3]
Terenure Road East	46 F2
Terenure Road North	46 F2
Terenure Road West	46 E2
Terminal Road North	39 C2
Terminal Road South	39 C2
Termon Court	11 C4 [1]
*Terrace Place (off Bella St)	38 E1
Tetrarch Grove	7 C1
Texas Lane	3 A2
The Alders	49 B4 [6]
The Ancorage	49 C4 [33]
The Appian Way	38 E4
The Arches	17 C3
The Avenue	7 A2
The Avenue (St Wolstan's Abbey)	32 D4
The Avenue (Ballinteer)	57 C2
The Avenue (Ballyboden)	56 E2
The Avenue (Celbridge)	32 D3
The Avenue (Grange Manor)	34 D3
The Avenue (Kinsaley)	2 E3
The Avenue (Lutterell Hall)	7 B2
The Avenue (Louisa Valley)	19 C4
The Avenue (Manorfields)	21 B1
The Avenue (Mulhuddart)	9 A4
The Avenue (Plunkett Hall)	7 A2
The Avenue (Swords)	2 D1
The Avenue (Tallaght)	44 F3
The Avenue (Templeogue)	46 D3
The Bawn	3 B3
The Bawn Grove	3 B3
The Beeches	27 A1
The Beeches	49 B4 [21]
The Beeches	56 F1 [8]
The Beeches (Abberley)	64 E1 [22]
The Belfry	27 B1
The Belfry	37 A3 [17]
The Birches	59 A3
The Black Avenue	33 B1
The Bramblings	26 E3
The Briars	35 C1
The Bridge	64 E3
The Burgage	60 F2
The Castlelands	46 F4 [11]
The Cedars	49 B4 [5]
The Cedars (Abberley)	64 E1 [21]
The Chase (Charles Sheil's Houses)	58 F2
The Cherries	57 A2 [2]
The Cloisters	25 B3 [5]
The Cloisters	46 F2
The Close	7 A2
The Close	25 C1
The Close	31 C3
The Close (Ballinteer)	57 C2
The Close (Ballyboden)	56 E2
The Close (Grange Manor)	34 D3
The Close (Kinsaley)	2 E3
The Close (Manorfields)	21 B1
The Close (Mount Merrion)	48 E3
The Close (Old Town Mill)	31 C3 [2]
The Close (Tallaght)	44 F3
The Close (Tallaght)	55 A2 [2]
The Close (Temple Manor)	31 C4
The Close (Templeogue)	46 D3
The Coombe	37 C3
The Coppice	35 C1
The Coppice	35 C2
The Coppins	32 D3
The Coppins (Foxrock)	59 A3
The Copse	25 B3
The Court	7 A2
The Court	25 C2
The Court	27 B3 [2]
The Court	31 C3
The Court (Ballinteer)	57 B2
The Court (Clontarf)	26 D4
The Court (Donnybrook)	47 C2
The Court (Larch Hill)	12 F4
The Court (Mulhuddart)	9 A4
The Court (Plunkett Hall)	7 A2
The Court (Sutton)	29 A1
The Court (Swords)	2 D1
The Court (Tallaght)	44 F3
The Court (Tallaght)	44 F4
The Court (Temple Manor)	31 C4
The Court (Templeogue)	46 D3
The Courtyard	22 D3
The Courtyard	46 F4
The Courtyard	67 B2
The Coutryard	59 A2 [10]
The Courtyards	31 C4
The Cove	3 A2
The Covert	35 C1 [1]
The Crescent (Robswall)	4 D3
The Crescent (St Wolstan's Abbey)	32 D4
The Crescent	7 A2
The Crescent	33 C2
The Crescent	2 D2 [4]
The Crescent (Abbeyfarm)	31 C4
The Crescent (Ballinteer)	57 B2 [1]
The Crescent (Ballyboden)	56 E2
The Crescent (off Beaumont Rd)	25 C2 [8]
The Crescent (Castleknock)	22 F3 [1]
The Crescent (Donnybrook)	47 C1 [4]
The Crescent (Grange Manor)	34 D3
The Crescent (Kinsaley)	2 E3
The Crescent (Larch Hill)	12 F4
The Crescent (Oldtown Mill)	31 C3
The Crescent (Sutton)	29 A1
The Crescent (Swords)	2 D1
The Crescent (Tallaght)	44 E4
The Crescent (Tallaght)	44 F3
The Crescent (Tallaght)	55 A1
The Crescent (Temple Manor)	31 C4
The Crescent (Whitehall)	25 B3
The Croft	32 D2
The Dale	31 C3
The Dale	44 F3
The Dale	44 F4
The Dale	67 B2
The Dale (Lutterell Hall)	7 B2
The Dale (Manorfields)	21 B1
The Deanery	31 C3 [1]
The Dell	57 A2
The Dingle	35 B2
The Downs	32 D4
The Drive	7 A2
The Drive	7 B2
The Drive	67 C1
The Drive (Abbeyfarm)	31 C4
The Drive (Ballinteer)	57 B2
The Drive (Ballyboden)	56 E1
The Drive (Grange Manor)	34 D3
The Drive (Kinsaley)	2 E3
The Drive (Manorfields)	21 B1
The Drive (Mulhuddart)	9 A4
The Drive (Oldtown Mill)	31 C3
The Drive (Swords)	2 D1
The Drive (Tallaght)	55 A1
The Drive (Temple Manor)	31 C4
The Dunes	15 A1
The Elms	7 B2
The Elms	48 E2
The Elms	64 E1 [4]
The Elms (Celbridge)	32 D2
The Fairways	14 E2
The Fairways	67 C1
The Fairways Apts.	8 D3
The Falls	46 F3 [5]
The Farm (Apts)	45 C4
The Fosters	48 E3
The Gables	43 B1
The Gables (Dundrum)	57 B1
The Gables	59 A3 [5]
The Gallops	58 E3
The Garth	44 E4
The Garth	44 F3
The Gate Lodge	30 E3
The Glade	32 D4
The Glade	44 F4
The Glade (Ballinteer)	57 B2
The Glade (Oldtown Mill)	31 C3
The Glade (Palmerston)	35 B2
The Glebe	34 D2
The Glebe	34 E2
The Glen	60 D1 [14]
The Glen (Ballinteer)	57 B2
The Glen (Ballyboden)	56 E1
The Glen (Louisa Valley)	19 C4
The Glen (Raheny)	27 B3
The Granary	37 C3
The Grange	3 B4
The Grange	59 B1
The Green	17 B2
The Green	25 C1
The Green (Ballinteer)	57 B2
The Green (Ballyboden)	56 E1
The Green (Bray)	67 C1
The Green (Kinsaley)	2 E3
The Green (Larch Hill)	12 F4
The Green (Lutterell Hall)	7 B2
The Green (Malahide)	3 B2
The Green (Manorfields)	21 B1
The Green (Mulhuddart)	9 A4
The Green (Oldtown Mill)	31 C3
The Green (Swords)	2 D1
The Green (Tallaght)	44 F3
The Green (Templeogue)	46 D3
The Green Road	60 F2
The Greenlands	46 F4
The Grove	7 A2
The Grove	27 B3 [1]
The Grove (Abbeyfarm)	31 C4
The Grove (Ballinteer)	57 B2
The Grove (Bray)	67 C1
The Grove (Celbridge)	32 D4
The Grove (Grange Manor)	34 D3
The Grove (Kinsaley)	2 E3
The Grove (Louisa Valley)	19 C4
The Grove (Lutterell Hall)	7 B2
The Grove (Plunkett Hall)	7 A2
The Grove (Swords)	2 D1 [3]
The Grove (Tallaght)	44 E4
The Grove (Tallaght)	44 F3
The Grove (Tallaght)	55 A1
The Grove (Whitehall)	25 B3
The Gunny Hill	55 C3
The Haggard (Howth)	30 D2 [6]
The Haven	3 B2
The Haven	25 A3 [17]
The Hawthorns (Abberley)	64 E1 [20]
The Heath (Tallaght)	44 F4
The Heath (Templeogue)	46 D3
The Hedgerows	59 A3
The Heights (Ballinteer)	57 B2
The Heights (Kinsaley)	2 E3
The Hill	3 B3
The Hill (Ballinteer)	57 C2
The Hill (Monkstown)	49 C4
The Hill (Mulhuddart)	9 A4
The Hill (Stillorgan)	58 F1
The Hole in the Wall Rd	14 E4
The Hollows	34 D2 [1]
The Killigeen	52 D4
The Lakelands	46 F4 [8]
The Larches (Abberley)	64 E1 [16]
The Laurels	36 E4 [3]
The Laurels	46 F4 [13]
The Laurels (Dundrum)	47 B4
The Laurels (Terenure)	46 F2
The Lawn	17 B2
The Lawn	67 C1
The Lawn (Ballinteer)	57 B2
The Lawn (Ballyboden)	56 E2
The Lawn (Finglas)	24 E4
The Lawn (Kinsaley)	2 E3
The Lawn (Oldtown Mill)	31 C3
The Lawn (Plunkett Hall)	7 A2
The Lawn (Tallaght)	44 E4
The Lawns (Abbeyfarm)	31 C4
The Lawns (Temple Manor)	31 C4
The Links	14 F2
The Little Grove	32 D4
The Lodge	60 D1
The Mall	3 B2
The Mall	33 A1
The Mall (Baldoyle)	15 A4 [4]
The Mall (Lucan)	34 D1
The Maltings	67 C2
The Manor	46 D4
The Maples	47 C3
The Maples	49 B4 [4]
The Mayne	8 E2
The Meadow	57 B2
The Meadows	26 F3
The Meadows (Oldtown Mill)	31 C3
The Meadows (Newtownpark Ave)	59 A1
The Meadows East	44 F4
The Meadows West	44 E4
The Mews	47 A1 [19]
The Mews (Clontarf)	26 E4
The Mews (Killester)	26 E3
The Mill Pond Apts	44 D1 [4]
The Moorings	3 C3
The Moorings	36 E2
The New Road	23 B1
The Nurseries	1 C3
The Nurseries	9 A4
The Nurseries	60 E4 [4]
The Nurseries	67 B3
The Nurseries (Swords)	1 C3
The Oaks (Forest Road)	1 B3
The Oaks	9 C1
The Oaks	27 A4
The Oaks	32 D3
The Oaks	44 E4
The Oaks	47 B4
The Oaks	64 D1 [1]
The Oaks (Abberley)	64 E1 [17]
The Oaks (Ballinteer)	57 B2
The Old Forge	34 D3
The Old Golf Links	3 C3
The Old Hill	34 D1
The Orchard	34 D1 [14]
The Orchard	22 D3 [3]
The Orchard	31 C3
The Orchard	59 A1
The Orchard (Apts.)	35 B3
The Orchard (Killester)	26 E3
The Orchard (Kimmage)	46 E2
The Orchard (Palmerston)	35 B1
The Oval	35 C2
The Paddock	17 B2
The Paddock	23 C4
The Paddock	31 C2
The Paddocks	7 B2
The Paddocks	60 F1 [3]
The Paddock's (Clontarf)	26 E4 [6]
The Paddocks (Kilmainham)	37 A3
The Palms	48 D3
The Park	7 A2
The Park (Abbeyfarm)	31 C4
The Park (Beaumont)	25 C1
The Park (Dunboyne)	7 A2
The Park (Grange Manor)	34 D3
The Park (Kinsaley)	2 E3

STREET NAME	PAGE	GRID
The Park (Larch Hill)	12	F4
The Park (Louisa Valley)	19	C4
The Park (Oldtown Mill)	31	C3
The Park (Tallaght)	44	F3
The Park (Tallaght)	55	A2
The Park (Templeogue)	46	D3
The Park (Vanessa Lawns)	31	C3
The Park Lands	46	F4 [7]
The Pines	23	A3
The Pines	26	E3
The Pines	58	D1 [3]
The Pines	67	B3
The Pines	57	B2
The Poplars	49	B4 [7]
The Priory	3	B2 [4]
The Priory	24	D4
The Priory	56	F1
The Rise	3	B3
The Rise	42	D4
The Rise (Ballinteer)	57	B2
The Rise (Ballyboden)	56	E2
The Rise (Dalkey)	60	E2
The Rise (Glasnevin)	25	A2
The Rise (Kinsaley)	2	E3
The Rise (Manorfields)	21	B1
The Rise (Mount Merrion)	48	E4
The Rise (Tallaght)	44	E4
The Rise (Tallaght)	44	F3
The Road (Manorfields)	21	B1
The Rookery	56	D2
The Rose	9	B2
The Rowans (Abberley)	64	E1 [18]
The Sand Holes	22	F4 [1]
The Scalp	63	A4
The Slopes	49	C4
The Spruce	9	B2
The Square (Irishtown)	39	A3 [5]
The Square (Larch Hill)	12	F4
The Square (Lucan)	34	D1 [5]
The Square (Tallaght)	54	F1
The Stables	48	E3 [1]
The Stables Office Park	15	A1
The Steeple	17	B2
The Stiles Road	26	E4
The Summit (Howth)	30	E3
The Sweepstakes	39	A4 [22]
The Sycamores	64	E1 [3]
The Thatch Road	25	C2
The Thicket	59	A3
The Turrets	39	A4
The Vale	35	C1
The View	32	D4
The View (Ballinteer)	57	B2
The View (Larch Hill)	12	F4
The View (Manorfields)	21	B1
The View (Oldtown Mill)	31	C3
The View (Tallaght)	44	F3
The View (Tallaght)	55	B1
The Villa (Kinsaley)	2	E3
The Village	25	B3 [2]
The Village	27	B3
The Village	60	F2
The Village (Clonsilla)	21	C3
The Village Centre	34	D1 [12]
The Village Court	34	D1 [13]
The Village Gate	60	F2
The Walk (Ballinteer)	57	B2
The Walk (Kinsaley)	2	E3
The Walk (Louisa Valley)	19	C4
The Walk (Manorfields)	21	B1
The Walk (Oldtown Mill)	31	C3
The Walk (Tallaght)	55	A1
The Walk (Templeogue)	46	D3
The Walled Gardens	32	D2
The Warren	2	F2
The Weir	36	E2
The Willow	9	B2
The Willows	32	D3
The Willows	47	A3 [1]
The Willows (Abberley)	64	E1 [19]
The Willows (Glasnevin)	24	F3
The Willows (Monkstown)	49	B4 [3]
The Wood	55	A2
The Woodlands	32	D3
The Woodlands	46	F4 [9]
Third Avenue	44	F4
Third Avenue (Seville Place)	38	F2 [7]
Thirlestane Terrace	37	C3 [67]
Thomas Court	37	C3
Thomas Davis Street (South)	37	C3 [49]
Thomas Davis Street (West)	36	F3
Thomas Lane	38	D2 [17]
Thomas Moore Road	45	C1
Thomas Street	37	C3
Thomas Street West	37	C3 [65]
Thomastown Crescent	60	D2 [2]
Thomastown Road	60	D3
Thomond	64	E2 [9]
Thomond Road	36	E3
Thompson's Cottages	38	E1 [49]
Thor Place	37	B2 [1]
Thormanby Grove	30	D2 [10]
Thormanby Lawns	30	D2
Thormanby Lodge	30	E2
Thormanby Road	30	E2
Thormanby Woods	30	E2
Thornberry Apts.	8	F4
Thorncastle Court Apts.	39	A2
Thorncastle Street	39	A2
Thorncliff	47	B2 [8]
Thorncliffe Park	47	B3
Thorndale Avenue	26	D2
Thorndale Court	25	C2 [3]
Thorndale Crescent	26	D2
Thorndale Drive	26	D3
Thorndale Grove	26	D3
Thorndale Lawns	26	D2
Thorndale Park	26	D2
Thornhill Gardens	31	C2
Thornhill Heights	31	C2
Thornhill Lane	27	A4
Thornhill Meadows	31	C2
Thornhill Road	48	E4
Thornhill Road	67	A2
Thornhill View	67	B1 [5]
Thornville Avenue	27	B1
Thornville Drive	27	B2
Thornville Park	27	C1
Thornville Road	27	B1
Thornville Terrace	27	B2 [1]
Three Rock Close	45	B3
Three Rock Grove	57	B3
Three Rock Road	58	E2
Thundercut Alley	37	C2 [20]
Tibradden Close	45	B2 [1]
Tibradden Drive	45	B2
Tibradden Grove	45	B3
Tibradden Lane	56	F4
Tibradden Road	56	F3
Tiknock	61	B1
Ticknock Dale	57	C3
Ticknock Grove	57	C3
Ticknock Hill	57	C3
Ticknock Road	57	B4
Timard	17	A1
Timber Mills (Apts.)	26	E2
Tinkers Hill	21	A4
Tinklers Path	36	E1
Tinnehinch	66	E4
Tivoli Avenue	46	F1
Tivoli Close	59	C1
Tivoli Road	50	D4
Tivoli Terrace East	50	D4
Tivoli Terrace North	49	C4
Tivoli Terrace South	49	C4
Tobernea Terrace	49	B3 [2]
Tolka Cottages	24	F3
Tolka Estate Road	24	F3
Tolka Quay	39	A2
Tolka Quay Road	39	A2
Tolka Road	25	B4
Tolka Vale	24	E3
Tolka Valley Road	24	D3
Tolka Valley View	24	D3
Tom Clarke House	25	B4 [1]
Tom Kelly Road	38	D4 [16]
Tonduff Close	45	B3
Tonguefield Road	46	E1 [1]
Tonlegee Avenue	26	F1
Tonlegee Drive	26	F1
Tonlegee Road	27	A1
Tootenhill	52	D2
Torca Road	60	F2
Torca View	60	F2 [33]
Torcaill	3	C4
Torlogh Gardens	25	C4 [8]
Torlogh Parade	25	C3 [1]
Torquay Road	58	F2
Torquay Wood	58	F2
Totenhill	52	E2
Tourmakeady Road	25	B2 [1]
Tourville Lodge	46	F3 [6]
Tower Avenue	46	F2
Tower Road	44	D1
Tower Road (Castleknock)	22	F4
*Tower Terrace (off Kilmainham Lane)	37	B3
Tower View Cottages	24	F4 [2]
Townsend Street	38	E2
Townyard Lane	3	B2
Traders Wharf	49	C3
Trafalgar Lane	49	B4
Trafalgar Terrace	49	B3
Trafalgar Terrace	67	C2 [31]
Tramway Court	29	A1
Tranquility Grove	26	D1
Traynor Place	37	B3 [41]
*Traynor Place (off Mount Brown)	37	B3
Treepark Avenue	45	A3
Treepark Close	45	A3
Treepark Drive	45	A3
Treepark Road	45	A3
Trees Avenue	48	E4
Trees Road Lower	48	E4
Trees Road Upper	48	E4
Treesdale	48	F4
Tresilian	59	A3
Trim Road	26	D1
Trimelston Apts.	47	C3
Trimleston Avenue	48	E2
Trimleston Drive	48	E2
Trimleston Gardens	48	E2
Trimleston Park	48	E2
Trimleston Road	48	E2
Trinity Gaels G.A.A.	14	E3
Trinity Sports and Leisure Club	14	E4
Trinity Street	38	D2
Trinity Terrace	38	E1 [44]
Tritonville Avenue	39	A3 [8]
Tritonville Close	39	A3 [22]
Tritonville Court	39	A4
Tritonville Crescent	39	A3 [9]
Tritonville Road	39	A3
Trosyrafon Terrace	68	D2 [1]
Tubber Lane Road	33	B2
Tubbermore Avenue	60	F2
Tubbermore Road	60	F2
Tuckett's Lane	30	D2
Tudor Court	2	F2
Tudor Lawns	58	F2
Tudor Road	47	B1
Tullyhall	34	D4
Tullyhall Avenue	34	D4
Tullyhall Close	34	D4
Tullyhall Court	34	D4
Tullyhall Crescent	34	D4
Tullyhall Drive	34	E4
Tullyhall Green	34	D4
Tullyhall Park	34	D4
Tullyhall Rise	34	E4
Tullyhall Way	34	D4
Tullyvale	63	C1
Tulip Court	13	C4
Turnapin Cottages	12	F3
Turnapin Green	12	F3
Turnapin Grove	12	F3
Turnapin Lane	12	F3
Turnberry	28	D1
Turnpike Road	45	A2
Turret Road	35	C2
Turrets Flats	47	A1 [9]
Turvey Avenue	37	A3 [1]
Tuscany Downs	27	A2
Tuscany Park	28	D1
Twin Cottages	49	A4 [5]
Tymon Close	55	A2
Tymon Crescent	54	F2
Tymon Grove	55	A2
Tymon Heights	55	B2
Tymon Lane	45	B4
Tymon Lawn	55	A2
Tymon Lodge (Apts)	45	B4
Tymon North	45	B4
Tymon North Avenue	45	B4
Tymon North Court	45	B4 [1]
Tymon North Gardens	45	B4
Tymon North Green	45	B4
Tymon North Grove	45	B4
Tymon North Lawn	45	B4
Tymon North Park	45	B4
Tymon North Place	45	B4 [2]
Tymon North Road	45	B4
Tymonville Avenue	45	B4
Tymonville Court	45	A4
Tymonville Crescent	45	A4
Tymonville Drive	45	A3
Tymonville Grove	45	B4
Tymonville Lawn	45	B4
Tymonville Park	45	B4
Tymonville Road	45	A4
Tynan Hall	44	F3
Tynan Hall Avenue	44	F3
Tynan Hall Grove	44	F3
Tynan Hall Park	44	F3
Tyrconnell Park	36	F3
Tyrconnell Road	36	F3
Tyrconnell Street	36	F3 [6]
Tyrconnell Villas	36	F3 [7]
Tyrone Place	37	A3 [12]
Tyrrell Place	38	E1 [45]
*Tyrrel's Lane (off Fitzwilliam St Ringsend)	39	A3
Tyrrelstown Way	9	B2

U

STREET NAME	PAGE	GRID
UCD Village Belgrove	48	D3
Ullardmor	60	F2 [27]
Ulster Street	24	F4
Ulster Terrace (North Strand)	38	E1 [58]
Ulster Terrace (Stillorgan Grove)	58	F1 [4]
Ulverton Close	60	F1 [5]
Ulverton Court	60	F1 [13]
Ulverton Road	60	F1
Upper Cliff Road	30	E2 [2]
Upper Dargle Road	67	A2
Upper Glen Road	36	E1
Uppercross	34	F1
Uppercross Road	37	B3
Urney Grove	60	E2 [7]
Usher Lane	1	A2
Usher Street	37	C2
Usher's Island	37	C2
Ushers Lane	1	A2
Usher's Quay	37	C2

V

STREET NAME	PAGE	GRID
*Vale Terrace (on lower Dargle Road)	67	B2
Vale view	67	B2 [21]
Vale View Avenue	59	B3
Vale View Close	59	B3
Vale View Grove	59	B3
Vale View Lawn	59	B3
Valentia Parade	38	D1 [34]
Valentia Road	25	B3
Valeview Crescent	24	D2 [6]
Valeview Drive	24	D2
Valeview Gardens	24	D2 [2]
Valley Avenue	64	D1
Valley Drive	63	C1
Valley Park Avenue	24	D2 [1]
Valley Park Drive	23	C2
Valley Park Road	23	C2
Valley View	1	B2
Vanessa Close	31	C3
Vanessa Lawns	31	C3
Vauxhall Avenue	37	B3 [30]

STREET NAME	PAGE/GRID REFERENCE
Vavasour Square	38 F3
Vehicle Pound Dublin City Council	39 A1
Venetian Hall	26 E3
Ventry Drive	24 D4
Ventry Park	24 E4
Ventry Road	24 E4
Verbena Avenue	27 C1
Verbena Avenue	59 A3
Verbena Grove	27 C1
Verbena Lawn	27 C1
Verbena Park	27 C1
Verdemont	22 D2
Vergemount	47 C1 [12]
Vergemount Hall	47 C1 [9]
Vergemount Park	47 C1 [6]
Verney	62 F3
Vernon Avenue	26 F4
Vernon Court	26 F4
Vernon Court	39 C1 [3]
Vernon Drive	26 F3
Vernon Gardens	26 F4
Vernon Grove (Clontarf)	26 F4
Vernon Grove (Rathgar)	47 A2
Vernon Heath	26 F4
Vernon Park	26 F4
Vernon Rise	26 F3
Vernon Street	38 D3
Vernon Wood	39 C1 [4]
*Veronica Terrace (off Oliver Plunket Ave)	39 A3
Verschoyle Avenue	53 C2
Verschoyle Close	53 C2
Verschoyle Court	38 F3
Verschoyle Crescent	53 C2
Verschoyle Drive	53 C2
Verschoyle Glen	53 C2
Verschoyle Green	53 C2
Verschoyle Heights	53 C2
Verschoyle Park	53 C2
Verschoyle Place (off Lr Mount St)	38 E3
Verschoyle Rise	53 C2
Verschoyle Vale	53 C2
Vesey Mews	49 C4
Vesey Park (Lucan)	34 D2
Vesey Place	49 C4
Vesey Terrace (Lucan)	34 D1 [2]
*Vevay Arcade (on Vevay Road)	67 C3
Vevay Crescent	67 C2 [58]
Vevay Road	67 C3
Vevay Villas	67 C3 [18]
Vicar Street	37 C3 [20]
Vico Road	60 F3
*Vico Terrace (Vico Road)	60 F3
Victoria Avenue	47 C1
Victoria Avenue	68 D2
*Victoria Cottages (off Irishtown Rd)	39 A3
Victoria Lane	25 B4 [9]
*Victoria Lane (South Zion Road)	47 A2
Victoria Quay	37 C2
Victoria Road (Clontarf)	26 E4
Victoria Road (Dalkey)	60 F2
Victoria Road (Killiney)	60 E3
Victoria Road (Terenure)	47 A2
Victoria Street	38 D4
Victoria Terrace (Dalkey)	60 F2 [11]
Victoria Terrace (Dun Laoghaire)	50 D4 [8]
Victoria Terrace (Dundrum)	47 C4
Victoria Village	46 F2 [7]
Victoria Villas (Clontarf)	26 D4
Victoria Villas (Rathgar)	46 F2 [5]
Viking Place	37 C2 [47]
Viking Road	37 C2 [32]
*Villa Bank (Royal Canal Bank)	38 D1
Villa Blanchard	22 F2
Villa Building (Apts.)	30 D1 [15]
Villa Nova	48 F4
Villa Park Avenue	24 D4
Villa Park Drive	24 D4
Villa Park Gardens	24 D4
Villa Park Road	24 D4
*Village Gate Arcade (on Main Street Bray)	67 C2
Village Green (Rathfarnham)	46 F3 [4]
Village Green (Tallagh)	55 A1
Village Heights	9 A4
Village Square (Tallagh)	55 A1
Village Weir	34 D1 [7]
Villarea Park	60 E1
Villiers Road	47 A2
Violet Hill Drive	24 F3
Violet Hill Park	24 F3
Violet Hill Road	24 F3
Virginia Drive	24 D2
Virginia Heights	54 F1
Virginia Park	24 D2
Viscount Avenue	12 F4

W

STREET NAME	PAGE/GRID REFERENCE
Wadelai Green	25 A2
Wadelai Road	25 A2
Wade's Avenue	27 A3
Wainsfort Avenue	46 D3
Wainsfort Crescent	46 D3
Wainsfort Drive	46 D2
Wainsfort Gardens	46 D3
Wainsfort Grove	46 E3
Wainsfort Manor	46 D3
Wainsfort Park	46 E3
Wainsfort Road	46 D3
Waldemar Terrace	47 B4 [12]
Walk (Robswall)	4 D3
Walker's Cottages	38 D4 [37]
Walker's Court	38 D4 [38]
Walkinstown	45 B1
Walkinstown Avenue	45 B1
Walkinstown Close	45 B1
Walkinstown Crescent	45 B1
Walkinstown Cross	45 C2
Walkinstown Drive	45 B1
Walkinstown Green	45 B1
Walkinstown Mall S.C.	45 C1
Walkinstown Parade	45 B1
Walkinstown Park	45 B1
Walkinstown Road	45 C1
Wallace Road	45 C1 [2]
Walnut Avenue (Clondalkin)	44 F3
Walnut Avenue (Whitehall)	25 B3
Walnut Close	44 F3
Walnut Court	25 B2
Walnut Drive	44 F3
Walnut Lawn	25 B3
Walnut Park	25 B3
Walnut Rise	25 B3
Walnut View	56 E2 [5]
Walsh Road	25 A3
Waltersland Road	58 F1
Waltham Terrace	48 F3
Walworth Road	38 D4 [33]
Warburton Terrace	68 D2 [7]
Ward's Hill	37 C3
Warner's Lane	38 E4 [18]
Warren Avenue	22 E3
Warren Close	22 E3
Warren Court	28 D1 [5]
Warren Crescent	22 E4
Warren Green	22 E3
Warren Green	28 D1
Warren Park	22 E3
Warren Street	38 D4 [35]
Warrenhouse Road	28 D1
Warrenmount	37 C3 [27]
Warrenmount Place	37 C3 [28]
Warrenpoint	26 E4 [1]
Warrenstown	9 B4
Warrenstown Close	9 B4
Warrenstown Court	9 B4
Warrenstown Drive	9 B4
Warrenstown Garth	9 B4
Warrenstown Green	9 B4
Warrenstown Grove	9 B4
Warrenstown Lawn	9 B4
Warrenstown Park	9 B4
Warrenstown Place	9 B4
Warrenstown Rise	9 B4
Warrenstown Row	9 B4
Warrenstown Vale	9 B4
Warrenstown View	9 B4
Warrenstown Walk	9 B4
Warrenstown Way	9 B4
Warrington Lane	38 F3 [45]
Warrington Place	38 F3
Warwick Terrace	38 E4 [27]
Wasdale Grove	46 F2
Wasdale Park	46 F3
Washington Lane	46 E4
Washington Park	46 E4
Washington Street	37 C4
Waterfall Avenue	25 B4
Waterfall Road	26 F3
Watergate Estate	55 A1
Waterloo Avenue	38 F1
Waterloo Lane	38 E4
Waterloo Road	38 E4
Watermeadow Drive	54 F2
Watermeadow Park	55 A2
Watermill Avenue	27 A3
Watermill Close	55 A2
Watermill Drive	27 A3
Watermill Grove	55 A2
Watermill Lawn	27 A3 [1]
Watermill Lawn	55 A2
Watermill Park	27 A3
Watermill Road	27 A3
Watermint Court	24 D3 [3]
Waterside Apartments	38 F3 [49]
Waterside Avenue	2 E2
Waterside Court	2 E2
Waterside Crescent	2 E2
Waterside Crescent	3 C4
Waterside King's Hall	2 E2
Waterside Park	2 E2
Waterside Rise	2 E2
Waterside Road	2 E2
Waterside Walk	2 E2
Waterside Way	2 E2
Waterstown Avenue	35 C1
Waterville Apts	22 F1
Watery Lane	1 C1
Watery Lane	44 E1
Watkins Buildings	37 C3 [64]
Watling Street	37 C2
Watson Avenue	60 D4
Watson Drive	60 D4
Watson Park	60 D4
Watson Road	60 D3
Watson's Estate	60 D3
Waverley Avenue	25 C4
Waverley Terrace (Bray)	67 C2 [28]
Waverley Terrace (off Harolds Cross Road)	46 F1 [12]
Waynestown	5 C1
Wayside Cottages	62 F2
Weatherwell Ind.Est.	35 A4
Weaver Lane	38 D1 [39]
Weaver's Close	37 C3 [33]
Weaver's Row	21 C2
Weaver's Square	37 C3 [37]
Weaver's Street	37 C3
Webster's Cottages	49 A4 [8]
Wedgewood Estate	58 D2
Weirview	34 D1
Weirview Drive	58 F1
Weldon's Lane	15 A4
Well Road	2 D2 [2]
Wellesley Place	38 E1 [32]
Wellfield	14 D4
Wellington Cottages	45 C3 [3]
Wellington Court	67 C2 [56]
Wellington Court (on Whitehall Road West)	46 D2 [5]
*Wellington Gardens (off Oakley Road)	47 B1
Wellington House	38 F4 [18]
Wellington Lane (Tallaght Road)	45 C3
Wellington Lane (Wellington Road)	38 F4
Wellington Park	46 D3
Wellington Place (Leeson Street)	38 F4
Wellington Place North	38 D1 [50]
Wellington Quay	38 D3
Wellington Road	38 F4
Wellington Road (Phoenix Park)	37 A2
Wellington Road (Templeogue)	46 D3 [1]
Wellington Street (Dun Laoghaire)	50 D4 [1]
Wellington Street Lower	38 D1
Wellington Street Upper	38 D1
Wellmount Avenue	24 D2
Wellmount Court	24 D2
Wellmount Crescent	24 D2
Wellmount Drive	24 D2
Wellmount Green	24 D2
Wellmount Parade	24 D2
Wellmount Park	24 D2
Wellmount Road	24 D2
Wellpark Avenue	25 B3
Wellview Avenue	9 A3
Wellview Crescent	9 A3
Wellview Green	9 A3
Wellview Grove	9 A3
Wellview Park	9 A3
Wendell Avenue	4 D4
Werburgh Street	38 D3
Wesbury	58 E1
Wesley Heights	57 C2
Wesley House	38 E4 [38]
Wesley Lawns	57 C2
Wesley Place	37 C4 [7]
Wesley Road	47 A2
West Park Drive	24 F2
West Pier (Dun Laoghaire)	49 C3
West Pier (Howth)	30 D1
West Road	38 F1
West Terrace	36 F3
Westbourne Avenue	43 C1
Westbourne Castle	43 C1
Westbourne Close	43 C1
Westbourne Court	43 C1
Westbourne Drive	43 C1
Westbourne Grove	43 C1
Westbourne Lodge	56 D1
Westbourne Manor	43 C1
Westbourne Rise	43 C1
Westbourne Road	46 F3
Westbourne Terrace	67 C2 [52]
Westbourne View	43 C1
Westbrook	46 D2
Westbrook Lawns	53 C2
Westbrook Park	33 C2
Westbrook Road (Windy Arbour)	47 B3
Westbury	34 D3
Westbury Avenue	34 D3
Westbury Close	34 D3
Westbury Drive	34 D3
Westbury Park	34 D3
Westend Village	22 E2
Western Parkway Motorway	22 E4
Western Road	37 C4 [29]
Western Way	38 D1
Westerton Rise	57 C1 [1]
Westfield Avenue	33 B1
Westfield Park	68 D3
Westfield Road	46 F1
Westfield Terrace	49 A3 [10]
Westhampton Place	46 F2 [2]
Westhaven	8 F4
Westland Row	38 E3
Westmanstown	42 D3
Westminster Court	59 A3 [6]
Westminster Lawns	58 F2
Westminster Park	59 A2
Westminster Road	59 A3
Westmoreland Park	47 B1 [1]
Westmoreland Street	38 D2
Weston Avenue	47 B4
Weston Close	33 B1
Weston Close	47 B4
Weston Court	33 B2
Weston Crescent	33 B1
Weston Drive	33 B1
Weston Green	33 B1
Weston Grove	47 B4
Weston Heights	33 B2

STREET NAME	PAGE/GRID REFERENCE	STREET NAME	PAGE/GRID REFERENCE	STREET NAME	PAGE/GRID REFERENCE	STREET NAME	PAGE/GRID REFERENCE
Weston Lawn	33 B1	Whitehall Road (Kimmage)	46 D2	Willington Grove	45 C3	Windmillhill	52 D3
Weston Meadow	33 B2	Whitehall Road West	46 D2	Willington Lawn	45 C3 [1]	Windrush	64 E2 [7]
Weston Park	33 B1	Whitehall Square	45 C2	Willington Park	45 C3	Windsor Avenue	25 C4
Weston Park	47 B4	White's Lane North	38 D1 [3]	Willow Avenue	44 D2	Windsor Court (Dun Laoghaire)	59 B1 [1]
Weston Road	47 B4	White's Road	23 A4	Willow Avenue	64 D1	Windsor Drive	59 B1
Weston Terrace	47 B4 [9]	White's Villas	60 F1 [10]	Willow Bank	49 C4	Windsor Mews	3 B2 [5]
Weston Way	33 B2	Whitestown	22 D1	Willow Bank Drive	56 E1	*Windsor Park	59 B1
Westpark	52 F2	Whitestown Avenue	22 D1	Willow Bank Park	56 E1	Windsor Place	38 E3 [32]
Westpark (Coolock)	26 F2	Whitestown Crescent	22 D1	Willow Court	44 D2	Windsor Road	47 B1
Westpark (Tallaght)	55 A1	Whitestown Drive	22 D1	Willow Court	64 D1	Windsor Terrace	3 B3
Westpark Fitness Centre	45 A4	Whitestown Drive	54 E2	Willow Drive	44 D2	Windsor Terrace	38 D4
Westview Terrace	67 C2 [29]	Whitestown Gardens	22 D1	Willow Gate	57 B1	Windsor Terrace	50 D4
Westway Close	9 C4	Whitestown Green	22 D1	Willow Grove	44 D2	(Dun Laoghaire)	
Westway Grove	9 C4	Whitestown Grove	22 D1	Willow Grove	59 C1 [13]	Windsor Villas	25 C4 [3]
Westway Lawns	22 F1	Whitestown Park	22 D1	Willow Grove	59 B3	Windy Arbour	47 C3
Westway Park	9 C4	Whitestown Road	54 F2	Willow Mews	48 E1	Winetavern Street	38 D2
Westway Rise	9 C4	Whitestown Way	54 F2	Willow Park	59 A2 [6]	Wingfield	62 E1
Westway View	9 C4	Whitestown Walk	22 D1	Willow Park (Dunboyne)	7 B2	Winton Avenue	47 A2
Westwood Avenue	23 C2	Whitethorn	35 B3	Willow Park (Dunboyne)	7 C2	Winton Grove	46 F2 [19]
Westwood Road	23 C2	Whitethorn Avenue	26 D2	Willow Park Avenue	24 F1	Winton Road	38 E4
Wexford Street	38 D3	Whitethorn Close	26 D2	Willow Park Close	24 F1	Wogans Field	33 A1
Wheatfield	67 C3	Whitethorn Crescent	26 D2	Willow Park Crescent	24 F1	Wolfe Tone Avenue	50 D4 [4]
Wheatfield Grove	4 D4	Whitethorn Crescent	35 B3	Willow Park Drive	25 A1	Wolfe Tone F.C.	67 C3
Wheatfield Road	4 D4	Whitethorn Drive	35 B3	Willow Park Grove	24 F1	Wolfe Tone Quay	37 B2
Wheatfield Road	35 C2	Whitethorn Gardens	35 B3	Willow Park Lawn	24 F1	Wolfe Tone Square East	67 C3
Wheatfields Avenue	35 B3	Whitethorn Grove	26 D2	Willow Park Road	24 F1	Wolfe Tone Square Middle	67 C3
Wheatfields Close	35 B3	Whitethorn Park	26 D2	Willow Place	48 F3	Wolfe Tone Square North	67 C3
Wheatfields Court	35 B3	Whitethorn Park	35 B3	Willow Road (Dundrum)	57 B1	Wolfe Tone Square South	67 C3
Wheatfields Crescent	35 B3	Whitethorn Rise	26 D2	Willow Road (Fox & Geese)	45 A1	Wolfe Tone Square West	67 C3
Wheatfields Drive	35 B3	Whitethorn Road (Artane)	26 D2	Willow Terrace	48 F2	Wolfe Tone Street	38 D2 [12]
Wheatfields Grove	35 B3	Whitethorn Road (Milltown)	47 C2	Willow Vale	60 D4	Wolseley Street	37 C4 [24]
Wheatfields Park	35 B3	Whitethorn Walk	59 C2 [2]	Willow Wood Close	21 C2	Wolstan Haven Avenue	31 C3
Wheaton Court	36 F3 [20]	Whitethorn Walk	59 A2 [8]	Willow Wood Downs	21 C2 [1]	Wolstan Haven Road	31 C3
Whelan House Flats	39 A3 [29]	Whitethorn Way	35 B2	Willow Wood Green	21 C2	Wolverton Glen	60 E2
Whelan's Terrace	49 A3 [19]	Whitton Road	46 F2	Willow Wood Grove	21 C2	Wood Avens	35 A3
Whitchurch Drive	56 F2	Whitworth Avenue	38 E1 [40]	Willow Wood Lawn	21 C2	Wood Dale Close	55 B2
Whitchurch Road	56 F2	(off Whitworth Place)		Willow Wood Park	21 C2	Wood Dale Crescent	55 B2
White Gables	64 D2	*Whitworth Parade	25 A4	Willow Wood Rise	21 C2	Wood Dale Drive	55 B2
White Hall (Ballymount Road)	44 F3	(off Saint Patrick's Road)		Willow Wood View	21 C2	Wood Dale Green	55 B2
White Oak	47 C3	Whitworth Place	25 A4 [16]	Willow Wood Walk	21 C1	Wood Dale Green	55 C2
White Oaks	67 B4	Whitworth Road	25 A4	Willowbank (Herbert Hill)	57 C1	Wood Dale Grove	55 C2
Whiteacre Close	25 B1	*Whitworth Terrace	38 E1	Willowbrook Grove	31 C3	Wood Dale Oak	55 C2 [1]
Whiteacre Court	25 B1	(off Russell Ave)		Willowbrook Lawns	31 C3	Wood Dale View	55 C2
Whiteacre Crescent	25 B1	Whyteleaf Grove	14 D4	Willowbrook Lodge	31 C3	Wood Lane	37 C2 [40]
Whitebank Road	39 B3	*Wicklow Lane	38 D3	Willowbrook Park	31 C3	Wood Quay	38 D2
Whitebarn Road	47 A4	(off Wicklow Street)		Willowfield	39 B4	Wood Street	38 D3
Whitebeam Avenue	47 C2	Wicklow Street	38 D3	Willowfield Avenue	47 C4	Woodbank Avenue	23 C2
Whitebeam Road	47 C2	Wigan Road	25 A4	Willowfield Park	47 C4	Woodbank Drive	23 C2
Whitebeams Road	58 D2	Wilderwood Grove	45 C4	Willowmount	48 F3 [3]	Woodberry	22 E3
Whitebrook Park	54 E1	Wilfield	39 A4 [15]	Willows Court	21 C2	Woodberry	34 D3
Whitechapel Avenue	22 D2	Wilfield Park	39 A4	Willows Drive	21 C2	Woodbine Avenue	48 E2
Whitechapel Court	22 D2	Wilfield Road	39 A4	Willows Green	21 C2	Woodbine Close	27 A1
Whitechapel Crescent	22 D2	Wilford Court	67 B1	Willows Road	21 C2	Woodbine Drive	27 A1
Whitechapel Green	22 D2	Wilfrid Road	46 F1	Willsbrook Avenue	34 E2	Woodbine House	48 E2 [4]
Whitechapel Grove	22 D2	Wilfrid Terrace	46 F1 [5]	Willsbrook Crescent	34 F1	Woodbine Park (Booterstown)	48 E2
Whitechapel Lawn	22 D2	Willbrook	46 F4	Willsbrook Drive	34 E1	Woodbine Park (Raheny)	27 A1
Whitechapel Park	22 D2	Willbrook (Estate)	56 F1	Willsbrook Gardens	34 E1	Woodbine Road (Booterstown)	48 E2
Whitechapel Road	22 D2	Willbrook Downs	56 F1	Willsbrook Green	34 E2	Woodbine Road (Raheny)	27 A1
Whitechurch Abbey	56 F1 [4]	Willbrook Grove	46 F4 [1]	Willsbrook Grove	34 E1	Woodbine Terrace (Dundrum)	47 C4 [2]
Whitechurch Avenue	56 F2	Willbrook House	38 E4 [36]	Willsbrook Park	34 E2	Woodbrook Court	22 D3
Whitechurch Close	56 F2	Willbrook Lawn	46 F4	Willsbrook Place	34 F2	Woodbrook Crescent	22 D3
Whitechurch Court	56 F2	Willbrook Park	46 F4	Willsbrook Road	34 E2	Woodbrook Downs	64 E4
Whitechurch Crescent	56 F2	Willbrook Road	46 F4	Willsbrook View	34 E2	Woodbrook Glen	67 C1
Whitechurch Green	56 F2	Willbrook Street	46 F4	Willsbrook Way	34 E1	Woodbrook Hall	22 D3
Whitechurch Grove	56 F2	William Street North	38 E1	Wilmont Avenue	60 E1 [1]	Woodbrook Lawn	67 C3
Whitechurch Hill	56 F2	William Street South	38 D3	Wilson Crescent	48 D4	Woodbrook Park	22 D3
Whitechurch Lawn	56 F2	Williams Avenue	21 A1	Wilson Road	48 E4	Woodbrook Park	46 D4
Whitechurch Park	56 F2	Williams Drive	21 A1	Wilson Terrace	37 C3 [44]	Woodbrook Square	22 D3
Whitechurch Pines	56 F1	Williams Green	21 A1	Wilson's Place	38 E3 [35]	Woodcliff Heights	30 E2
Whitechurch Place	56 F2	William's Lane	38 D2 [27]	Wilton Place	38 E4	Woodfarm Avenue	35 C2
Whitechurch Stream	56 F1 [7]	William's Park	47 A1	Wilton Terrace	38 E4	Woodfarm Drive	35 C2
Whitechurch View	56 F2	*William's Place Lower	38 D1	Windele Road	25 A3 [12]	Woodfield	56 D2
Whitechurch Walk	56 F2	(off Portland Place)		Windermere	21 B2	Woodfield Cottages	36 F3 [8]
Whitechurch Way	56 F2	*William's Place South	38 D3 [6]	Windgate Rise	30 D3	Woodfield Place	36 F3 [15]
Whitecliff	56 F1	William's Place Upper	38 D1 [29]	Windgate Road	30 D3	Woodford	58 E2
*Whitefriar Gardens	38 D3	Williams Rise	21 A1	Windmill Avenue	1 C1	Woodford Avenue	44 F1
(off Whitefriar St)		Williams Row	21 A1	Windmill Avenue	46 D1	Woodford Close	44 F1
Whitefriar Place	38 D3 [42]	Williams Way	21 A1	Windmill Crescent	1 A2	Woodford Court	44 F1
Whitefriar Street	38 D3 [41]	Willie Bermingham Place	37 B3 [31]	Windmill Crescent	46 D1 [2]	Woodford Court	46 F1 [10]
Whitehall	25 B2	Willie Nolan Road	15 A4	Windmill Lands	1 C2	Woodford Crescent	44 E1
Whitehall Close	46 D3	Willington Avenue	45 C3	Windmill Lane	38 E2	Woodford Downs	44 F1
Whitehall Gardens	46 D2	Willington Court	45 C3	Windmill Park	46 D1	Woodford Drive	44 F1
Whitehall Mews	59 A2	Willington Crescent	45 C3	Windmill Rise	1 C1	Woodford Garth	44 E1
Whitehall Park	46 D3	Willington Drive	45 C3	Windmill Road	46 D1	Woodford Green	44 F1
Whitehall Road (Churchtown)	47 A4	Willington Green	45 C3	Windmillhill	51 C3		

STREET NAME	PAGE/GRID REFERENCE		STREET NAME	PAGE/GRID REFERENCE		STREET NAME	PAGE/GRID REFERENCE		STREET NAME	PAGE/GRID REFERENCE	
Woodford Grove	44	F1	Woodlawn Grove	47	B4 [7]	Woodstown Parade	55	C2	Wyattville Road	64	D1
Woodford Heights	44	F1	Woodlawn Park	12	F4	Woodstown Park	55	C2 [3]	Wycham Grove	57	C2
Woodford Hill	44	F1	Woodlawn Park	47	B4	Woodstown Place	55	C2 [7]	Wycham Place	57	C1
Woodford Lawn	44	F1	Woodlawn Park	55	C2	Woodstown Rise	55	C2	Wyckham Park Road	57	B1
Woodford Meadow	44	F1	Woodlawn Park	59	C1 [4]	Woodstown Road	55	C2	Wyckham Way	57	C1
Woodford Parade	44	E1	(Dun Laoghaire)			Woodstown Vale	55	C2 [8]	Wyckham Way Extension	57	C1
Woodford Park	44	F1	Woodlawn Park Avenue	55	B1	Woodstown Vale	55	C2	Wynberg Park	49	B4
Woodford Park Road	44	E1	Woodlawn Park Drive	55	C1	Woodthorpe	58	E1 [5]	Wyndham Park	67	C2
Woodford Rise	44	F1	(Firhouse)			Woodtown	56	D3	Wynnefield Park	47	A1 [21]
Woodford Road	44	E1	Woodlawn Park Grove	55	C2	Woodvale Avenue	21	C1	Wynnefield Road	47	A1
Woodford Terrace	44	F1	Woodlawn Rise	12	F4	Woodvale Crescent	21	C1	Wynnsward Drive	47	C2
Woodford View	44	F1	Woodlawn Terrace	47	B4 [2]	Woodvale Drive	21	C1	Wynnsward Park	47	C2
Woodford Villas	44	E1	Woodlawn View	12	F4	Woodvale Garth	21	C1	Wyvern Estate	60	E3
Woodford Walk	44	F1	Woodlawn Walk	12	F4	Woodvale Green	21	C1			
Woodford Way	44	F1	Woodlawn Way	12	F4	Woodvale Grove	21	C1	**XYZ**		
Woodhaven	47	C2 [10]	Woodleigh	47	A2 [2]	Woodvale Park	21	C1			
Woodhazel Close	25	A1	Woodley Park	58	D1	Woodvale Way	21	C1	Xavier Avenue	38	F1 [3]
Woodhazel Terrace	25	A1	Woodley Road	60	D3	Woodview	33	C2	Yale	48	D3
Woodlands	14	F1 [1]	Woodpark (Ballinteer)	57	B2	Woodview (Celbridge)	32	D2	Yankee Terrace	49	A4
Woodlands	14	F1	Woodpark (Blanchardstown)	22	F2	Woodview (Dunboyne)	7	B3	Yarnhall Street	38	D2 [45]
Woodlands	17	C3	Woodside	19	C4	Woodview Close	27	A1	Yeates Hall	59	B4
Woodlands	22	D1 [3]	Woodside	26	F4	Woodview Cottages	46	F3 [1]	Yeates Way	35	C4
Woodlands	47	A2 [1]	Woodside	30	D2	Woodview Court	58	F1 [1]	Yellow Meadows Ave	44	F1
Woodlands Avenue	59	C3	Woodside	47	A3	Woodview Drive	67	C3 [4]	Yellow Meadows Drive	44	E1
(Cornelscourt)			Woodside Drive	47	A3	Woodview Grove	22	E2	Yellow Meadows Estate	44	F1
Woodlands Avenue (Stillorgan)	48	E4	Woodside Grove	47	A3	Woodview Heights	33	C2	Yellow Meadows Grove	44	E1
Woodlands Court	15	A1	Woodside Road	57	C3	Woodview Heights (Dunboyne)	7	B3	Yellow Meadows Lawn	44	E1
Woodlands Drive	59	C3	Woodstock Gardens	47	B1 [24]	Woodview Park	23	A3	Yellow Meadows Park	44	E1
(Johnstown Road)			Woodstock Park	56	D1	Woodview Park	27	A1	Yellow Meadows Road	44	E1
Woodlands Drive (Stillorgan)	48	E4	Woodstown	55	C2	Woodville Avenue	34	E1	Yellow Meadows Vale	44	E1
Woodlands Park	59	C3	Woodstown Abbey	56	D2 [1]	Woodville Close	34	E1	Yellow Road	25	C2
(Johnstown Road)			Woodstown Avenue	55	C2	Woodville Court	26	E1	Yellow Walls	3	A2
Woodlands Pk (Mount Merrion)	48	F4	Woodstown Close	55	C2 [4]	Woodville Green	34	E1	Yellow Walls Road	3	A2
Woodlands Road	59	C3	Woodstown Court	55	C2 [2]	Woodville Grove	34	E1	Yewlands Terrace	46	F2
Woodlawn	12	F4	Woodstown Crescent	55	C2	Woodville House	26	D1 [4]	York Avenue	47	A1
Woodlawn Avenue	12	F4	Woodstown Dale	55	C2 [5]	Woodville Lawn	34	E1	York Road (Dun Laoghaire)	49	C4
Woodlawn Close	12	F4	Woodstown Drive	55	C2	Woodville Road	25	A4 [7]	York Road (Rathmines)	47	A1
Woodlawn Court	12	F4	Woodstown Gardens	55	C2	Woodville Walk	34	E1	York Road (Ringsend)	39	A2
Woodlawn Crescent	12	F4	Woodstown Heath	55	C2	Woostock Court	47	B1 [2]	York Street	38	D3
Woodlawn Crescent	47	B4	Woodstown Height	55	C2 [6]	*Wormwood Gate	37	C2	York Terrace	49	C4 [4]
Woodlawn Drive	12	F4	Woodstown Hill	55	C2	(off Bridge Street Lower)			Zion Road	47	A2
Woodlawn Green	12	F4	(Shown as Knocklyon Hill)			Wyattville Close	64	D1	Zoo Road	37	A2
Woodlawn Grove	12	F4	Woodstown Lawn	55	C2	Wyattville Hill	64	D1	*Zuma Terrace	37	C4
			Woodstown Meadow	55	C2	Wyattville Park	64	D1	(Mount Drummond Ave)		

LIST OF STREETS NOT NAMED ON MAP BUT SHOWN AS SMALL NUMBERS

PAGE/ GRID REF		STREET NAME
1	A2	1 Grove Court
1	C1	1 Elmwood Court
		2 Rathbeal Court
2	D1	2 Mantua Park
		3 The Grove (Swords)
2	D2	1 St Columcille's Crescent
		2 Well Road
		3 St Colmcilles Court
		4 The Crescent
		5 New Road
3	A2	1 Hillcrest
3	B2	1 Fair Haven
		2 Haven View
		3 Railway Court
		4 The Priory
		5 Windsor Mews
3	C2	1 Obelisk Court
4	D4	1 Alder Court
7	B2	1 St Mary's Terrace
		2 Avondale Square
7	B3	2 River Court
		3 Hamilton Court (Dunboyne)
8	D3	1 Cloncourt Apts
9	A4	1 Ashmount
		2 Ashfield Park
		3 Riverpark View
11	A4	1 St Margaret's Court
11	C4	1 Termon Court
13	A4	1 Newbury Terrace
13	B4	1 Greenlawns
		2 Clonshaugh Rise
		3 Ferrycarrig Green
		4 Clonshaugh Court
14	D4	1 Templeview Vale
		2 Elmfield Close
		3 Clonmellon Grove
		4 Beechbrook Grove
14	F1	1 Woodlands
14	F2	1 St Lawrence O'Toole Avenue
		2 Church Avenue
		3 Suncroft Avenue
		4 St Brigid's Avenue
		5 St Ann's Square Lower
		6 St Ann's Square
		7 Hazel Court
15	A4	1 Seapoint Avenue (Baldoyle)
		2 Parochial Avenue
		3 Back Lane (Baldoyle)
		4 The Mall (Baldoyle)
		5 Breffni Gardens
		6 Brookstone Lane
		7 Seapoint Court
		8 College Street
		9 Admiral Court
17	C3	1 Kelly's Lane
		2 Fagan's Lane
		3 Coate's Lane
		4 Geraldine Lane
		5 Court House Square
		6 Leinster Cottages
		7 Charter House
18	D3	1 Leinster Lodge Apts
		2 Leinster Court
20	D4	1 Cypress Springs
21	B1	1 Delhurst Grove
		2 Delhurst Mews
		3 Delhurst Court
		4 Ongar Lodge Apts
		5 Hayworth View

PAGE/ GRID REF		STREET NAME
21	C1	1 Meadow Dale
		2 Oakview Grove
21	C2	1 Willow Wood Downs
		2 Cedar Grove
22	D1	1 Huntstown Lawn
		2 Briarwood Park
		3 Woodlands
		4 Briarwood Road
		5 Ashcroft Grove
22	D2	1 Coolmine Mews
		2 Kirkfield
22	D3	1 Rosehaven
		3 The Orchard
		4 Station View Apts
22	F2	1 Herbert Crescent
22	F3	1 The Crescent (Castleknock)
		2 Castleknock Court
22	F4	1 The Sand Holes
23	A3	1 Beech Park Crescent
		2 Hadleigh Green
		3 Beechpark Close
		4 Park Court Apts
		5 Castleknock Manor
23	B3	1 Mill Lane (Ashtown)
23	B4	1 Castleknock Gate
23	C2	1 Eastwood
23	C3	1 Compass Court
23	C4	1 Baggot Terrace
		2 St Vincent's Cottages
		3 St Joseph's Cottages
		4 Ashgrove Lodge
24	D1	1 Cardiffsbridge Grove
24	D2	1 Valley Park Avenue
		2 Valeview Gardens
		3 Mellowes Court
		4 Mellowes Crescent
		5 Ravens Court
		6 Valeview Crescent
		7 Church View (Finglas)
		8 Nethercross Court
24	D3	1 Clearwater Court
		2 Cassian Court
		3 Watermint Court
24	D4	1 Roosevelt Cottages
		2 Convent View Cottages
		3 Convent View Crescent
		4 Lyndon Gate
		5 Park Spring's
		6 Park Crescent House
24	E1	1 Georges Road
		2 Gofton Hall
		3 Heath Square
24	E2	1 Ballygall Place
		2 Glenhill Villas
		3 St Helena's Court
		4 Johnstown Gardens
		5 Collins Row
		6 Collins Row
		7 Glebe View
24	E4	1 Kilkieran Court
		2 St Finbarrs Court
24	F2	1 Drapier Green
		2 Glasnamana Place
		3 Johnstown House
24	F3	1 Northland Grove
		2 Northland Drive
		3 Glasnevin Oaks
		4 Bellevue Cottages
		5 Cremore Villas
24	F4	1 St Philomena's Road
		2 Tower View Cottages
		3 Delvin Road

PAGE/ GRID REF		STREET NAME
		4 Bengal Terrace
		5 Fertullagh Road
		6 Connaught Parade
		7 Clareville Court
		8 Shandon Green
		9 Shandon Mill
25	A1	1 Pinewood Grove
		2 Shanliss Gardens
		3 Oldtown Park
25	A3	1 Claremont Avenue
		2 Church Avenue (Glasnevin)
		3 St David's Terrace (Glasnevin)
		4 Barron Place
		5 Comyn Place
		6 St Ita's Road
		7 St Malachy's Road
		8 St Michael's Road
		9 Addison Place
		10 St Mobhi Grove
		11 Clonmore Court
		12 Windele Road
		13 O'Brien's Place North
		14 O'Neachtain Road
		15 River Gardens
		16 Mobhi Court
		17 The Haven
25	A4	1 Millmount Villas
		2 De Courcy Square
		3 Enniskerry Road (Phibsborough)
		4 Devery's Lane
		5 Prospect Square
		6 Glendalough Road
		7 Woodville Road
		8 St Teresa's Road (Glasnevin)
		9 St Teresa's Place
		10 Botanic Villas
		11 St Alphonsus Avenue
		12 St Brendan's Road
		14 Botanic Park
		15 O'Brien's Terrace
		16 Whitworth Place
25	B1	1 Ailesbury
25	B2	1 Tourmakeady Road
25	B3	1 Clonturk Avenue
		2 The Village
		3 Clare Park Villas
		4 Beaucourt
		5 The Cloisters
		6 Clonturk Court
		7 All Hallows Square
25	B4	1 Tom Clarke House
		2 St Joseph's Avenue (Ballybough)
		3 Clonturk Gardens
		4 Kingston Lodge
		5 Holycross Avenue
		6 Robert Street (Jones's Road)
		7 Robert Place
		8 College Manor
		9 Victoria Lane
		10 Edgewood
		11 College Mews
25	C2	1 Chestnut Court
		2 Dromnanane Road
		3 Dromnanane Park
		4 Thorndale Court
		5 Laragh (Flats)
		6 Collindale
		7 Beaumount Hall
		8 The Crescent (off Beaumont Rd)

PAGE/ GRID REF		STREET NAME
25	C3	1 Torlogh Parade
		2 Morrogh Terrace
		3 Calderwood Grove
		4 Croydon Terrace
		5 Sion Hill Court
		6 Collins Court
		7 St Vincent's Court
25	C4	1 Annadale Avenue
		2 Shelmartin Terrace
		3 Windsor Villas
		4 St Joseph's Terrace (Fairview)
		5 St Declan's Terrace
		6 St Aidan's Park
		7 Fairview Green
		8 Torlogh Gardens
		9 Marino Mart
		10 Fairview Passage
		11 Fairview Terrace
		12 Caragh Court
		13 Marino Court
		14 Fairview Court
		15 Bushfield Square
26	D1	1 Kilbarron Court
		2 Cromcastle Close
		3 St Lukes Court
		4 Woodville House
		5 Kilmore Court
		6 Cromcastle Court
26	D3	1 Cherrymount Crescent
		2 Cherrymount Grove
26	D4	1 Brighton Avenue (Clontarf)
		2 Hollybrook Court Drive
		3 Hollybrook Court
		4 Strandville House
		5 Haddon Park
		6 Crescent House
		7 Kilronan Court
		8 Glenbrian Hall
26	E1	1 Lismeen Grove
		2 Brookville Crescent
		3 Coolock Village Close
26	E2	1 Maryfield Avenue
		2 Artane Cottages Lower
		3 Artane Cottages Upper
26	E3	1 St Brigid's Drive (Killester)
		2 St Brigid's Court
		3 Quarry Cottages
		4 Killester Court
		5 Killester Park
26	E4	1 Warrenpoint
		2 St John's Wood
		3 Lambourne Village
		4 Knights Bridge
		5 St David's Court
		6 The Paddock's (Clontarf)
26	F1	1 Elton Court
		2 Ayrefield Park
26	F2	1 Gorsefield Court
26	F4	1 Park View
27	A1	1 Elton Walk
		2 Glentworth Park
		3 Invermore Grove
		4 Curracloe Drive
		5 Laracor Gardens
		6 Gables
27	A3	1 Watermill Lawn
		2 St Annes Court
27	A4	1 Seafield Grove
		2 St Gabriel's Court
		3 Rinn na Mara
27	B1	1 Howth Junction Cottages
		2 Swan's Nest Court

PAGE/GRID REF	STREET NAME
	3 Redmond's Court
	4 Briarsfield Walk
	5 Briarfield Villas
	6 St Berach's Place
27 B2	1 Thornville Terrace
	2 Greendale Court
27 B3	1 The Grove
	2 The Court
27 C1	1 Bayside Crescent
27 C2	1 Mariners Court
	2 Del Val Court
28 D1	1 Sutton Court
	2 Seafield
	3 St Domhnach's Well
	4 Marine Cove
	5 Warren Court
	6 Moyclare Gardens
29 A1	1 James McCormack Gardens
	2 St Catherine's Terrace
	3 Radcliffe
29 B1	1 Corrbridge Terrace (off Claremont Road)
	2 Avalon Apts.
	3 Corr Castle Apts
	4 Offington Manor Apts
29 B3	1 Shielmartin Park
	2 Martello Terrace
30 D1	1 Dunbo Terrace
	2 Evora Terrace
	4 Dunbo Hill
	5 Howth Terrace
	6 Harbour View
	7 Marine Villas
	8 St Lawrence Quay
	9 Island View Apts.
	10 Howth House Apts
	11 Abbey Terrace
	12 Evora Crescent
	13 Cuan na Mara
	14 Howth Peninsula Apts
	15 Villa Building (apts.)
	16 Findlater Building (apts.)
30 D2	1 St Lawrence's Terrace (Howth)
	2 Seaview Terrace (Howth)
	3 St Mary's Road (Howth)
	4 St Mary's Place (Howth)
	5 St Nessan's Terrace
	6 The Haggard (Howth)
	7 Hillside Terrace
	8 Dungriffan Villas
	9 St Nessan's Close
	10 Thormanby Grove
	12 St Nessans Court
	13 Crosstrees Court
30 E2	1 Cannon Rock View
	2 Upper Cliff Road
	3 St Nessans Apts
31 C2	1 Crodaun Court
31 C3	1 The Deanery
	2 The Close (Old Town Mill)
	3 St Judes Apts
31 C4	1 Springfield Close
32 D4	1 Balfe Gardens
33 A1	1 Ralph Square
	2 Liffey View Apts
33 C2	1 Hillcrest View
34 D1	1 Sarsfield Terrace
	2 Vesey Terrace (Lucan)
	3 Hanbury Lane (Lucan)
	4 Sarsfield Court
	5 The Square (Lucan)
	6 Dispensary Lane (Lucan)
	7 Village Weir
	8 Brookvale
	9 Mount Gandon

PAGE/GRID REF	STREET NAME
	10 Gandon Mews
	11 Old Rectory
	12 The Village Centre
	13 The Village Court
	14 The Orchard
	15 Mill Bank
34 D2	1 The Hollows
34 E1	1 Edmondsbury Court
34 F2	1 Liffey Hall
34 F3	1 Foxborough Hall
	2 Foxborough Crescent
34 F4	1 Kilcoran Lawns
35 A3	1 Neilstown Village Court
	2 Liscarne Dale
35 A4	1 Ballymanagin Lane
	2 Moorfield Close
	3 Neilstown Cottages
35 B3	1 Collinstown Crescent
35 B4	1 Rosebank Court
	2 Rosebank View
	3 Rosebank Hall
	4 Rosebank Place
35 C1	1 The Covert
	2 Glenside Villas
	3 Clarkeville Terrace
	4 Red Cow Cottages
	5 St Fintan's Terrace
35 C2	1 Culmore Park
35 C4	1 Cherry Orchard Way
36 D2	1 Rossaveal Court
36 D3	1 Le Fanu Drive
36 E2	1 Park Lane (Chapelizod)
	2 Maidens Row
	3 Hibernian Terrace
	4 St Laurence Grove
	5 St Mary's Terrace (Chapelizod)
	6 Isolde Gardens
	7 Liffey Terrace
	8 Clayton Terrace
	9 St Laurence Terrace (Chapelizod)
	10 Mullingar Terrace
	11 Riverview Court
	12 New Row
	13 Chapelizod Moorings
36 E3	1 O'Hogan Road
	2 Lynch's Lane
	5 St Lawrences Glen
36 E4	1 Old Naas Road Cottages
	2 Millrose Estate
	3 The Laurels
	4 Hollybrooke
36 F3	1 Park Street
	2 Phoenix Street
	3 Inchicore Terrace North
	4 Murray's Cottages
	5 Partridge Terrace
	6 Tyrconnell Street
	7 Tyrconnell Villas
	8 Woodfield Cottages
	9 St Patrick's Terrace (Inchicore)
	10 Abercorn Terrace
	11 Granite Terrace
	12 Ring Street
	13 Inchicore Square
	14 Oblate Drive
	15 Woodfield Place
	16 Hampton Court
	17 St James's Place (Inchicore)
	18 St George's Villas (Inchicore)
	19 Abercorn Square
	20 Wheaton Court

PAGE/GRID REF	STREET NAME
36 F4	1 Muirfield Drive
	2 Bernard Curtis House
	3 La Touche Court
	4 Grove Court
	5 Landsdowne Valley Park
37 A1	1 Parkview Court
37 A2	1 Islandbridge Court
	2 Hospital Lane
	3 Sarah Place
	4 Park Place
	5 Salmon Pool Apts
37 A3	1 Hybreasal
	2 Turvey Avenue
	3 Connolly Gardens
	4 Goldenbridge Gardens
	5 Goldenbridge Terrace
	6 Camac Close
	7 Kearn's Place
	8 St Michael's Estate
	9 Memorial Road
	10 Camac Court
	11 Heuston Square
	12 Tyrone Place
	13 Lady's Lane
	14 Prospect Terrace (Kilmainham)
	15 Carrickfoyle Terrace
	16 Goldenbridge Walk
	17 The Belfry
	18 Beaconsfield Court
	19 Rosemount Court (Inchicore Rd)
	20 Rowserstown Lane
	21 Myra Cottages
	22 Harcourt Lodge
	23 Ashmount Court
	24 Millbrook Terrace
37 A4	1 Iveagh Gardens
	2 Lissadel Green
37 B1	1 Glenmore Road
	2 Glencar Road
	3 Everton Avenue
	4 Ardmore Avenue
	5 Glenard Avenue
	6 Doon Avenue
	7 St David's Terrace (Blackhorse Avenue)
	8 Aughrim Place
	9 Carnew Street
	10 Ashford Street
	11 Dunard Road
	12 Aughrim Villas
	13 Arklow Street
	14 Drumalee Court
	15 Phoenix Court
	16 Ashford Place
	17 Ashford Cottages
	18 Auburn Walk
	19 Phoenix Manor
37 B2	1 Thor Place
	2 Halliday Square
	3 Sullivan Street
	4 Kinahan Street
	5 Montpelier Gardens
	6 Arbour Terrace
	7 Temple Street West
	8 Swords Street
	9 Black Street
	10 Findlater Street (Nth Circular Rd)
	11 Niall Street
	12 Finn Street
	13 Park Avenue West
	14 De Burgh Road
	15 Brodin Row
	16 Temple Court
	17 Phoenix Court
37 B3	1 Irwin Street
	2 Old Kilmainham Village
	3 Cromwell's Quarters

PAGE/GRID REF	STREET NAME
	4 Shannon Terrace
	5 Cameron Square
	6 St Maignenn's Terrace
	7 Donnellan Avenue
	8 McDowell Avenue
	9 O'Reilly Avenue
	10 Madison Road
	11 Mayfield Road (Kilmainham)
	12 Ewington Lane
	13 Glenmalure Park
	14 Rialto Buildings
	15 Herberton Park
	16 Clarke Terrace
	17 Mallin Avenue
	18 Ave Maria Road
	19 Morning Star Road
	20 Emerald Square
	21 St James's Avenue (James's Street)
	22 Church Avenue South (Dolphin's Barn)
	23 Fatima Mansions (off James's Walk)
	24 Irwin Court
	25 McCarthy Terrace
	26 Almeida Avenue
	27 Almeida Terrace
	28 St John's Cottages
	29 Carrick Terrace
	30 Vauxhall Avenue
	31 Willie Bermingham Place
	32 Brandon Terrace
	33 St John's Terrace (Mount Brown)
	34 Knocknarow Terrace
	35 Millbrook Court
	36 Prior Hall
	37 Faulkner's Terrace
	38 Southview Terrace
	39 Owen's Avenue
	40 O'Quinns Avenue
	41 Traynor Place
	42 Burke Place
	43 Phoenix View
37 B4	1 Dolphin House
	2 St James's Terrace (Dolphin's Barn)
	3 Rialto Drive
	4 Moracrete Cottages
	5 Dolphin Park
	6 Reilly's Avenue
	7 Dolphin Court
37 C1	1 Aughrim Lane
	2 Annamoe Parade
	3 Cherrymount Park
	4 Rosemount Road
	5 Fingal Place
	6 Phibsborough Avenue
	7 Leslie's Buildings
	8 Great Western Square
	9 Great Western Villas
	10 Kirwan Street Cottages
	11 Norton's Avenue
	12 Royal Canal Terrace
	13 Marne Villas
	14 St Elizabeth's Court
	15 St Joseph's Place
	16 St Joseph's Court
	17 Castle Terrace (Phibsborough Ave)
	18 Great Western Avenue
	19 King's Court
	20 Rathdown Square
	21 Aughrim Court
	22 Phibsboro
	23 Shea's Court
	24 Phibsborough
37 C2	1 Ostman Place
	2 Stanhope Street
	3 George's Lane

PAGE/GRID REF	STREET NAME
	4 Blackhall Parade
	5 Brown Street North
	6 Friary Avenue
	7 Nicholas Avenue
	8 Sarsfield Quay
	9 Hendrick Place
	10 Arran Quay Terrace
	11 Church Street New
	12 Marshalsea Lane
	13 Blackhall Street
	14 Morgan Place
	15 Phoenix Street West
	16 Stable Lane (Smithfield)
	17 Arran Street West
	18 Burgess Lane
	19 Liffey Street West
	20 Thundercut Alley
	21 Oxmantown Lane
	22 Catherine Lane
	23 Fitzwilliam Place North (Grangegorman)
	24 Morning Star Avenue
	25 Church Avenue West (Church Street)
	26 Father Mathew Square
	27 Ard Right Place
	28 Houghton Terrace
	29 Rosemount Terrace (Arbour Hill)
	30 Murtagh Road
	31 Sigurd Road
	32 Viking Road
	33 Olaf Road
	34 St Mary's Terrace (Arbour Hill)
	35 Slade Row
	36 Paul Street
	37 Smithfield Terrace
	38 Ellis Street
	39 Stanley Street
	40 Wood Lane
	41 Friary Grove
	42 Coke Lane
	43 Lincoln Lane
	44 Ellis Court
	45 Malachi Road
	46 Provost Row
	47 Viking Place
	48 Robert Emmet Close
	49 Marshal Lane
	50 Manor Mews (on Norseman Place)
37 C3	1 Marshal Court Apts
	2 Grand Canal Place
	3 Rainsford Avenue
	4 Market Street South
	5 Long's Place
	6 Park Terrace (Coombe)
	7 St Margaret's Terrace
	8 Huxley Crescent
	9 Darley's Terrace
	10 Maxwell Street
	11 Fingal Street
	12 Pimlico Cottages
	13 Taylor's Lane (Pimlico)
	14 St Catherine's Lane West
	15 Allingham Street
	16 Meath Market
	17 Brabazon Street
	18 Brabazon Row
	19 Molyneux Yard
	20 Vicar Street
	21 Garden Lane
	22 Mark's Alley West
	23 Oscar Square
	24 Cow Parlour
	25 Newmarket Street
	26 Mill Lane (Newmarket)
	27 Warrenmount
	28 Warrenmount Place
	29 O'Carolan Road
	30 Geoffrey Keating Road
	31 Madden Road
	32 New Row Square
	33 Weaver's Close
	34 Ardee Row
	35 Brabazon Place
	36 Sweeney's Terrace
	37 Weaver's Square
	38 Poole Street
	39 St John's Avenue
	40 Brabazon Square
	41 Gray Square
	42 Meath Square
	43 Reginald Square
	44 Wilson Terrace
	45 Catherine Street (Swift's Alley)
	46 Spitalfields
	47 Hanover Street West
	48 Brickfield Lane
	49 Thomas Davis Street (South)
	50 John's Lane West
	51 Swan Alley
	52 Old Mill Court
	53 Ebenezer Terrace
	54 Harman Street
	55 Donore Terrace
	56 Hammond Street
	57 St Michael's Terrace (Blackpitts)
	58 St John Street
	59 Marion Villas
	60 Pyro Villas
	61 Ivy Terrace
	62 Coombe Court
	63 Emerald Terrace
	64 Watkins Buildings
	65 Thomas Street West
	66 Marrowbone Lane Close
	67 Thirlestane Terrace
37 C4	1 Hamilton Street
	2 Ingram Road
	3 Rehoboth Avenue
	4 Priestfield Cottages
	5 St Anne's Road South
	6 Lyllymore Terrace
	7 Wesley Place
	8 Arbutus Avenue
	9 Greenmount Avenue
	10 Emmet Street (Harold's Cross)
	11 Greenville Avenue
	12 Gilbert Road
	13 Parnell Court
	14 Greenmount Square
	15 Hatter's Lane
	16 Limekiln Lane (Harold's Cross)
	17 Clanbrassil Close
	18 Harold's Cross Cottages
	19 Greenmount Court
	20 St Clare's Avenue
	21 Donovan Lane
	22 Griffith Square
	23 Briansboro Terrace
	24 Wolseley Street
	25 Merton Avenue
	26 Rutledge Terrace
	27 Merton Park
	28 Priestfield Drive
	29 Western Road
	30 Mount Drummond Court
	31 Boyne Court
	32 Sandford Park
	33 Sandford Gardens
	34 Leonard's Court
	35 Greenville Place
	36 Harold Bridge Court
	37 Armstrong Street
	38 Le Vere Terrace
	39 Swanward Court
	40 Darley Street
	41 Argus House
38 D1	1 Phibsborough Place
	2 Lynch's Place
	3 White's Lane North
	4 St Vincent Street North
	5 Sarsfield Street (Phibsborough)
	6 O'Connell Avenue
	7 St Mary's Ave North (Mountjoy Street)
	8 Palmerston Place
	9 Mountjoy Street Middle
	10 St Mary's Terrace (Mountjoy Street)
	11 Belvidere Court
	12 Hardwicke Place
	13 Graham Court
	14 Frederick Lane North
	15 Grenville Lane
	16 Parnell Place
	17 St Ignatius Avenue
	18 Glengarriff Crescent
	19 De Velara Place
	20 Eccles Court
	21 Cavendish Row
	22 Kelly's Lane
	23 Myrtle Street
	24 Leo Avenue
	25 Josephine Avenue
	26 Synnott Row
	27 St Joseph Street
	28 Sherrard Avenue
	29 William's Place Upper
	30 Killarney Parade
	31 Kenmare Parade
	32 Muckross Parade
	33 Derrynane Parade
	34 Valentia Parade
	35 St Benedicts Gardens
	36 Arranmore Avenue
	37 St Peter's Square
	38 Peter's Court
	39 Weaver Lane
	40 Gardiner Row
	41 Temple Lane North
	42 Bath Lane
	43 George's Place
	44 Nerney's Court
	45 Hardwicke Lane
	46 Frederick Court
	47 Britain Place
	48 St Mary's Place North
	49 Long Lane (New Street)
	50 Wellington Place North
	51 St Michael's Place
	52 Maunsell Place
	53 Blessington Lane
	54 Graham's Row
	55 Berkeley Avenue
	56 Blessington Court
	57 Berkeley Place
	58 Bethesda Place
	59 St Joseph's Place
	60 Temple Buildings
	61 Library View Villas
	62 St Peter's Close
	64 Glengariff Parade
	65 Sherrards Court
	66 St Laurence Place
	67 Strong's Court
	68 Broadstone Avenue
	69 Shamrock Street
38 D2	1 Linenhall Terrace
	2 Lisburn Street
	3 Lurgan Street
	4 Linenhall Parade
	5 Anne Street North
	6 George's Hill
	7 Anglesea Row
	8 Green Street Little
	9 Ryder's Row
	10 Jervis Lane Upper
	11 Jervis Lane Lower
	12 Wolfe Tone Street
	13 Chapel Lane (Parnell Street)
	14 Sampson's Lane
	15 Moore Lane
	16 Henry Place
	17 Thomas Lane
	18 Litton Lane
	19 Earl Place
	20 Prince's Street North
	21 Sycamore Street
	22 Cope Street
	23 Ball's Lane
	24 Sackville Place
	25 Findlater Place
	26 O'Rahilly Parade
	27 William's Lane
	28 Proby's Lane
	29 Hotel Yard
	30 Bachelors Way
	31 Byrne's Lane (Jervis St)
	32 Mary Street Little
	33 Meetinghouse Lane
	34 Campbell's Court
	35 Dominick Lane
	36 Strand Street Little
	37 Ormond Square
	38 Foster Place South (College Grn)
	39 Aston Place
	40 Crampton Quay
	41 Church Lane (College Green)
	42 Dame Lane
	43 Abbey Cottages
	44 St Michan's Street
	45 Yarnhall Street
	46 Temple Lane South
	47 Fownes Street Upper
	48 Cows Lane
	49 Copper Alley
38 D3	1 Hanover Lane
	2 St Nicholas Place
	3 Castle Street (Cork Hill)
	4 Iveagh Buildings
	5 Cathedral Lane
	6 William's Place South
	7 Dame Lane
	8 Longford Street Great
	9 Longford Street Little
	10 Aungier Place
	11 Redmond's Hill
	12 Protestant Row
	13 Montague Lane
	14 O'Neill's Buildings
	15 Pleasants Lane
	16 Dame Court
	17 Harry Street
	18 Clonmel Street
	19 Stable Lane (Harcourt Street)
	20 Liberty Lane
	21 Pleasants Place
	22 Camden Villas
	23 Aungier Lane
	24 Proud's Lane
	25 Montague Court
	26 Montague Place
	27 Stokes Place
	28 Glovers Alley
	29 Balfe Street
	30 Johnson's Court
	31 Lemon Street
	32 Duke Lane Upper
	33 Anne's Lane
	34 Coppinger Row
	35 Chatham Row
	36 Johnson Place
	37 Bow Lane East
	38 Digges Lane
	39 Fade Street

PAGE/ GRID REF STREET NAME

40 John Field Road
41 Whitefriar Street
42 Whitefriar Place
43 Cathedral View Court
44 Cathedral View Walk
45 Longford Lane
46 Malpas Terrace
47 Hanover Square
48 St Francis Square
49 Coolevin Road
50 Malpas Court
51 Christchurch Square
52 John's Lane East
53 Church Lane South
54 Camden Buildings
55 Bride Close
56 Noel Purcell Park

38 D4 1 Fitzgerald Street
2 Desmond Street
3 St Kevin's Road
4 Kingsland Park Avenue
5 Kingsland Parade
6 Portobello Harbour
7 Richmond Row
8 Blackberry Lane
9 Bessborough Parade
10 Richmond Place
   (Rathmines)
11 Ontario Terrace
12 Atlumney Villas
13 Cheltenham Place
14 Harcourt Lane
15 Albert Place West
16 Tom Kelly Road
17 Florence Street
18 Albert Terrace
19 Peter Place
20 Charlemont Gardens
21 St Ultan's Flats
22 Richmond Villas
23 Gordon Place
24 Synge Place
25 Synge Lane
26 Avenue Road
27 McMahon Street
28 Camden Market
29 St Kevin's Cottages
30 Camden Court
31 Lennox Terrace
32 Charlotte Way
33 Walworth Road
34 Martin Street
35 Warren Street
36 Portobello Place
37 Walker's Cottages
38 Walker's Court
39 Mountpleasant Parade
40 Mountpleasant Terrace
41 Bannaville
42 Garden View
43 Richmond Mews
44 Richmond Place South
   (Sth Richmond St)
45 Alexandra Terrace
   (Portobello)
46 Bloomfield Park
47 Grove Avenue
   (Harold's Cross)
48 Spencer Street South
49 Bloomfield Cottages
50 Oakfield Place
51 Arbutus Place
52 St Kevin's Parade
53 Lissenfield
54 Harold's Cross Cottages
55 Saddlers Court
56 O'Hara Avenue
57 Adelaide Court
58 Portobello Harbour Apts

38 E1 1 O'Sullivan Avenue
2 Sackville Gardens
3 Ardilaun Road

PAGE/ GRID REF STREET NAME

4 Ballybough Lane
5 Charlemont Parade
6 Clonmore Terrace
7 Clinch's Court
8 Richmond Crescent
9 Richmond Cottages
   (Summerhill)
10 Richmond Parade
11 Bailey's Row
12 Sean Tracey House
13 Killarney Avenue
14 Preston Street
15 Shamrock Place
16 Shamrock Terrace
17 Aldborough Parade
18 Drumcondra Park
19 Belvidere Avenue
20 Richmond Lane
21 Fitzgibbon Lane
22 Mountjoy Place
23 Langrishe Place
24 Gloucester Place Upper
25 Gloucester Place
26 Summerhill Place
27 Bella Street
28 Matt Talbot Court
29 Newcomen Court
30 Gilford Place
31 Shamrock Cottages
32 Wellesley Place
33 Brendan Behan Court
34 St Margaret's Avenue
   North
35 St Joseph's Terrace
36 Mountjoy Parade
37 Richmond Cottages North
38 St Joseph's Villas
   (Summerhill)
39 Clonmore Villas
40 Whitworth Avenue
   (off Whitworth Place)
41 Foster Place North
42 Ballybough Avenue
43 Ballybough Court
44 Trinity Terrace
45 Tyrrell Place
46 Summer Place
47 Sean O'Casey Avenue
48 Rutland Place North
49 Thompson's Cottages
50 Portland Close
51 Beaver Close
52 Gloucester Diamond
53 Gloucester Place Lower
54 Gloucester Place Lower
55 Rutland Cottages
56 Buckingham Village
57 Duke Row
58 Ulster Terrace
   (North Strand)
59 Seville Terrace
60 St Joseph's Mansions
61 Lourdes House
62 St Mary's Mansions
63 Avondale House
64 Liberty House
65 Mountjoy Square Apts
66 North Clarence St Flats
67 Clarence St Great North
68 Croke Villas
69 Campbell's Row
   (off Portland Street N)
70 Portland Square
71 Campbell's Lane
   (off Belvidere Ave)

38 E2 1 Pearse House
2 Erne Place Lower
3 Magenis Place
4 Mark's Lane
5 Deverell Place
6 Talbot Lane
7 Marlborough Place

PAGE/ GRID REF STREET NAME

8 Northumberland Square
9 Beresford Lane
10 Shaw Street
11 Leinster Market
12 Prince's Street South
13 Card's Lane (Pearse St)
14 Spring Garden Lane
15 Dowling's Court
16 Peterson's Court
17 Mabbot Lane
18 Harbour Court
19 Abbey Street Old
20 Frenchman's Lane
21 Moland Street
22 Spencer Row
23 Emerald Place
24 Corn Exchange Place
25 Luke Street
26 Mark Street
27 Custom House Harbour
28 Bracken's Lane
29 Magennis Square
30 Brunswick Villas
   (Pearse Street)
31 Crinan Strand
32 Champions Avenue
33 Lombard Court
34 Harbour Master Place
35 Marlborough Court
36 George's Dock

38 E3 1 Cumberland Street South
2 Boyne Lane
3 Bass Place
4 Erne Place Little
5 Grant's Row
6 Meade's Terrace
7 Holles Row
8 Merrion Place
9 Baggot Court
10 Royal Hibernian Way
11 Setanta Place
12 Schoolhouse Lane
13 Leinster Lane
14 Clare Lane
15 Roger's Lane
16 Leeson Lane
17 Duke Lane Lower
18 Dawson Lane
19 College Lane
20 Erne Terrace Front
21 Erne Terrace Rere
22 Devlin's Place
23 Harmony Row
24 Molesworth Place
25 Kildare Place
26 Merrion Close
27 Merrion Street Lower
28 Baggotrath Place
29 Little Fitzwilliam Place
30 Bell's Lane
31 Ely Place Upper
32 Windsor Place
33 Mackies Place
34 Holles Place
35 Wilson's Place
36 Stephen's Place
37 Stable Lane (Leeson St Lr)
38 Fitzwilliam Court
39 Hagan's Court
40 Convent Close
41 Herbert Lane

38 E4 1 Leeson Close
2 Hatch Lane
3 Leeson Place
4 Dartmouth Place
5 Dartmouth Terrace
6 Dartmouth Lane
7 Cambridge Terrace
   (Ranelagh)
8 Chelmsford Avenue
9 Old Mountpleasant

PAGE/ GRID REF STREET NAME

10 Mander's Terrace
11 Sussex Terrace
12 Convent Place
13 Hatch Place
14 Dartmouth Square North
15 Dartmouth Square South
16 Dartmouth Square East
17 Dartmouth Square West
18 Warner's Lane
19 Leeson Walk
20 Northbrook Lane
21 Selskar Terrace
22 Mountpleasant Place
23 Swan Grove
24 Orchard Lane
25 Berystede
26 Temple Place
27 Warwick Terrace
28 Sibthorpe Lane
29 Dexter Terrace
30 Leeson Village
31 Swan Place
32 Pembroke Place
   (Pembroke St Upr)
33 Burlington Gardens
34 Burleigh Court
35 Crosbie House
36 Willbrook House
37 Cullen's Wood House
38 Wesley House
39 Flemming House

38 F1 1 Northbrook Terrace
2 Stoney Road (East Wall)
3 Xavier Avenue
4 Strandville Avenue
   (North Strand)
5 Hibernian Avenue
6 Gaelic Street
7 Hyacinth Street
8 Courtney Place
9 Annesley Avenue
10 Enaville Road
11 Crescent Gardens
12 St Barnabas Gardens
13 Boolavogue Road
14 Russell Avenue East
15 Taaffe's Place
16 St Patrick's Avenue
   (Fairview)
17 St Mura's Terrace
18 Malachi Place
19 Strandville Place
20 James's Street North
21 Leinster Street East
22 Portside Court
23 Austin's Cottages
24 St Brigid's Cottages
   (North Strand)
25 Caledon Court

38 F2 1 Emerald Street
2 Bellman's Walk
3 First Avenue
   (Seville Place)
4 Blythe Avenue
5 Laurence Place East
6 Second Avenue
   (Seville Place)
7 Third Avenue
   (Seville Place)
8 Fourth Avenue
   (Seville Place)
9 Carbury Terrace
10 Irvine Cottages
11 Alexander Terrace
   (North Wall)
12 Spencer Dock
13 Pickford's Terrace
14 Ferryman's Crossing
15 Merchant's Square
16 Mariner's Port

PAGE/GRID REF	STREET NAME
38 F3	1 Clarence Place Great
	2 Eblana Villas (Lr Grand Canal St)
	3 Island Villa
	4 Carlingford Parade
	5 Hastings Street
	6 Penrose Street
	7 Ormeau Street
	8 Somerset Street
	9 Gerald Street
	10 Bath Avenue Place
	11 Margaret Place
	12 Malone Gardens
	13 Shaw's Lane
	14 Albert Place East
	15 Love Lane East
	16 Estate Cottages (Northumberland Rd)
	17 St Mary's Lane
	18 Haddington Place
	19 Cranmer Lane
	20 Lansdowne Lane
	21 Erne Place
	22 Brunswick Place
	23 Conway Court
	24 South Dock Road
	25 Rostrevor Terrace (Lr Grand Canal St)
	26 Greenore Terrace
	27 Hogan Avenue
	28 Grattan Court East
	29 Grattan Place
	30 Albert Court
	31 Macken Villa
	32 Mount Street Crescent
	33 Leitrim Place
	34 Emerald Cottages
	35 South Dock Place
	36 Berkeley Terrace
	37 Lansdowne Terrace
	38 Pearse Grove
	39 Camden Lock
	40 Clanwilliam Terrace
	41 Clanwilliam Square
	42 Northumberland Place
	43 Lansdowne Crescent
	44 Lansdowne Villas
	45 Warrington Lane
	46 Temple Court (Off Hogan Place)
	47 Cannon Mews East
	48 Beggars Bush Court
	49 Waterside Apartments
	50 Shelbourne Park Mews
	51 Shelbourne Village
38 F4	1 Eastmoreland Place
	2 Eastmoreland Lane
	3 Shelbourne Lane
	4 Herbert Cottages
	5 Shelbourne Avenue
	6 Carlton Villas
	7 Lansdowne Gardens
	8 Beatty's Avenue
	9 Dodder View Cottages
	10 Granite Place
	11 Morehampton Square
	12 Morehampton Mews
	13 Estate Cottages (Shelbourne Rd)
	14 Ballsbridge Terrace
	15 Pembroke Place (Ballsbridge)
	16 Crampton Avenue
	17 Iveragh Court
	18 Wellington House
	19 Clyde Court
	20 Raglan Hall Apts
39 A2	1 Fishermans Wharf
	2 Alexandra Quay
39 A3	1 Cambridge Street
	2 Fitzwilliam Street (Ringsend)
	3 St Patrick's Villas
	4 Seapoint Terrace
	5 The Square (Irishtown)
	6 St Brendan's Cottages
	7 Cambridge Avenue
	8 Tritonville Avenue
	9 Tritonville Crescent
	10 Seafort Gardens
	11 Leukos Road
	12 Clonlara Road
	13 Kyle-Clare Road
	14 Parkview Place
	15 Canon Mooney Gardens
	16 Caroline Row
	17 Havelock Terrace
	18 Dodder Terrace
	19 Ennis Grove
	20 Londonbridge Drive
	21 Strasburg Terrace
	22 Tritonville Close
	23 St James Terrace (Sandymount)
	24 Cambridge Court
	25 Lansdowne Hall
	26 Sandymount Court
	27 Cambridge Park
	28 O'Rahilly House Flats
	29 Whelan House Flats
	30 Ropewalk Pace
	31 Kennedy Court
	32 Simpsons Lane
39 A4	1 Sandymount Green
	2 Sandymount Castle Road
	3 Sandymount Castle Drive
	4 Sydenham Road (Ballsbridge)
	5 Sandymount Castle
	6 Churchill Terrace
	7 Prince of Wales Terrace
	8 Railway Cottages
	9 Martin White Chalets
	10 Gilford Court
	11 Homelee
	12 Lynton Court
	13 Spafield Terrace
	14 Adair
	15 Wilfield
	16 Park Court (Sandymount)
	17 Dromard Terrace
	18 Seafort Cottages
	19 Seafort Terrace
	20 Seafort Villas
	21 Claremont Court
	22 The Sweepstakes
	23 Ballsbridge Park
	24 Lansdowne Square
	25 Ballsbridge Gardens
	26 Ballsbridge Avenue
39 B1	1 Alverno
	2 Haddon Court
39 B3	1 Prospect Terrace (Sandymount)
39 B4	1 Gilford Terrace
	2 Sandymount Castle Park
	3 Martello View
	4 Bethany House
	5 Hempenstal Terrace
	6 Martello Wood
39 C1	1 Churchgate Avenue
	2 St Joseph's Square
	3 Vernon Court
	4 Vernon Wood
43 C1	1 Bawnogue Cottages
	2 Nangor Place
	3 St Catherines Grove
44 D1	1 St Patrick's Avenue (Clondalkin)
	2 Leinster Terrace
	3 Beech Row
	4 The Mill Pond Apts
	5 Nangor Crescent
	6 Cherrywood Villas
44 D2	1 Church View (Clondalkin)
	2 Green Isle Court
44 E1	1 St Killian's Park
	2 Monastery Heights
	3 Bettysford
	4 Castle Crescent
	5 Friar's Walk
	6 Riverside
	7 Millview
44 E2	1 St Brigid's Park (Clondalkin)
44 F1	1 Knockmitten Close
	2 Knockmitten Lane North
44 F3	1 Pinetree Grove
	2 Belgard Close
44 F4	1 Pinetree Crescent
45 A3	1 Parkhill Heights
	2 Parkview
45 B2	1 Tibradden Close
45 B3	1 Three Rock Close
45 B4	1 Tymon North Court
	2 Tymon North Place
45 C1	1 Field Avenue
	2 Wallace Road
	3 Percy French Road
	4 O'Dwyer Road
	5 Esposito Road
	6 Landsdowne Valley
	7 Somerville Park
	8 Harty Court
45 C2	1 St Peter's Terrace Walkinstown (off Peters Road)
45 C3	1 Willington Lawn
	2 Glenmurry Park
	3 Wellington Cottages
45 C4	1 Spawell Cottages
46 D1	1 Sunville Green
	2 Windmill Crescent
	3 Fr Kit Court
46 D2	1 Muckross Drive
	2 Lorcan O'Toole Court
	3 Stannaway Court
	4 Beechfield Mews
	5 Wellington Court (on Whitehall Road West)
46 D3	1 Wellington Road (Templeogue)
46 D4	1 Hillcrest (Templeogue)
	2 Hillcrest Manor
46 E1	1 Tonguefield Road
	2 Cloyne Road
	3 Faughart Road
	4 Clonmacnoise Grove
	5 Bedford Court
	6 Poddle Green
46 E2	1 Riversdale Grove
	2 Hazel Park
	3 Kimmage Court
	4 Rathland Drive
	5 Brookfield Green
	6 Brookfield Court
	7 Hazlebrook Apartments
46 E3	1 Templeville Park
	2 Fortfield Court
46 E4	1 Butterfield Meadow
	2 Brookmount Court
46 F1	1 Mount Harold Terrace
	2 Le Bas Terrace
	3 Mountain View Avenue
	4 Manor Villas
	5 Wilfrid Terrace
	6 Fitzpatrick's Cottages
	7 Ryan's Cottages (Harold's Cross)
	8 Parkview Court
	9 Gandon Close
	10 Woodford Court
	11 Kenilworth Manor
	12 Waverley Terrace (off Harolds Cross Road)
	13 Smith's Lane
	14 Kengar Mews
46 F2	1 Ashdale Park
	2 Westhampton Place
	3 Terenure Place
	4 Eagle Hill Avenue
	5 Victoria Villas (Rathgar)
	6 Maple Drive
	7 Victoria Village
	8 Frankfort Court
	9 Frankfort Flats
	10 Rathdown Court (off Templeogue Road)
	11 Rathgar Villas
	12 Greenlea Place
	13 Brighton Green
	14 McMorrough Road
	15 Earls Court
	16 Rathgar Park
	17 Olney Grove
	18 Eaton Hall
	19 Winton Grove
	20 Beechlawn Manor
	21 Beechlawn Mews
	22 Eaton Court
	23 Carlisle Court
46 F3	1 Woodview Cottages
	2 St Agnes Terrace (Rathfarnham)
	3 Dodder Park Drive
	4 Village Green (Rathfarnham)
	5 The Falls
	6 Tourville Lodge
	7 Le Brett Terrace
46 F4	1 Willbrook Grove
	2 Tara Hill Grove
	3 Beaufort Villas
	4 Glenann
	5 St Mary's Terrace (Rathfarnham)
	7 The Park Lands
	8 The Lakelands
	9 The Woodlands
	10 Beaufort Court
	11 The Castlelands
	13 The Laurels
	14 Loftus Square
	15 Blackburn Square
	16 Otterbrook
	17 Stone Park Orchard
47 A1	1 Rathmines Park
	2 Leinster Square
	3 Prince Arthur Terrace
	4 Swanville Place
	5 Castlewood Terrace
	6 Castlewood Place
	7 Grosvenor Park
	8 Stone Mews
	9 Turrets Flats
	10 Purser Gardens
	11 Esker Villas
	12 Parker Hill
	13 Alma Terrace
	14 Observatory Lane
	15 Belgrave Place (Rathmines)
	16 Cambridge Villas
	17 Salem Court
	18 Maxwell Court
	19 The Mews

PAGE/GRID REF	STREET NAME
	20 Roland Court
	21 Wynnefield Park
	22 Mount Anthony Estate
	23 Louis Lane
	24 Castlewood Close
	25 Rathmines Avenue Court
	26 Cosy Lodge
47 A2	1 Woodlands
	2 Woodleigh
	3 Highfield Court
	4 Cowper Mews
	5 Garville Place
	6 Garville Drive
	7 Rathgar Park
	8 Orwell Mews
	9 Stratford
	10 Garville Court
47 A3	1 The Willows
	2 Stirling Park
	3 Orwell Court
	4 Newtown Villas
	5 Newtown Court
	6 Riverbank
	7 Orwell Bank
	8 Crannagh Way
	9 Landore
	10 Park View
	11 Ard Na Greine
	12 Newtown House
	13 Dodder Vale
47 A4	1 Castle Court
	2 Nutgrove Court
47 B1	1 Sallymount Gardens
	2 Woostock Court
	3 Collier's Avenue
	4 Westmoreland Park
	5 Field's Terrace
	6 Rugby Villas
	7 Beechwood Park (Rathmines)
	8 Bushfield Avenue
	9 Charleston Court Flats
	10 Oakley Court (Flats)
	11 Cullenswood Road
	12 Moran's Cottages
	13 Mountain View Cottages (Ranelagh)
	14 Sallymount Terrace
	15 Chelmsford Lane
	16 Belgrave Villas (Rathmines)
	17 Bushfield Place
	18 Smith's Cottages (Donnybrook)
	19 Beechdale Mews
	20 Palmerston Close
	21 Palmerston Close
	22 Moyne Court
	23 Oakley Park (Ranelagh)
	24 Woodstock Gardens
	25 Marlborough Lane
47 B2	1 Dartry Cottages
	2 Strand Terrace
	3 St Luke's Crescent
	4 Balnagowan
	5 Temple Square
	6 Milltown Grove
	7 Milltown Hill
	8 Thorncliff
	9 Shanagarry
	10 Dodder Bank
47 B3	1 St Columbanus Place
	2 St Gall Gardens North
	3 St Gall Gardens South
	4 Milltown Terrace (Dundrum)
47 B4	1 Glenbower Park
	2 Woodlawn Terrace
	3 Beaumont Close
	4 Briarly Court
	5 St Nathy's House

PAGE/GRID REF	STREET NAME
	6 Ardtona Avenue
	7 Woodlawn Grove
	8 Henley Court
	9 Weston Terrace
	10 Frankfort
	11 Rosemount Terrace (Dundrum)
	12 Waldemar Terrace
	13 Airfield Drive
	14 Nutgrove Avenue
	15 Sweetmount Avenue
	16 Annadale
	17 St Nathy's Villas
	18 Sweetmount House
47 C1	1 St Broc's Cottages
	2 Pembroke Cottages (Donnybrook)
	3 Belmont Park
	4 The Crescent (Donnybrook)
	5 Harmony Avenue
	6 Vergemount Park
	7 Norwood Park
	8 Brookvale Road (Donnybrook)
	9 Vergemount Hall
	10 Sandford Gardens (Donnybrook)
	11 Auburn Road (Donnybrook)
	12 Vergemount
	13 Eglinton Square
	14 Mount Sandford
	15 Rowan Hall
	16 Cedar Hall
	17 Millbrook Village
	18 Simmonscourt Terrace
	19 Brookfield
	22 Eglinton Wood
	23 Donnybrook
	24 Donnybrook Castle
47 C2	1 Prospect Lane
	2 Beech Hill Villas
	3 Beech Hill Crescent
	4 Beech Hill Terrace
	5 Palmerston Grove
	6 Clonskeagh Drive
	7 Clonskeagh Square
	8 St Bridget's Flats
	9 Crannagh
	10 Woodhaven
	11 Richview Villas
	12 Byrnes Terrace
47 C3	1 Annaville Grove
	2 Olivemount Grove
	3 Friarsland Avenue
	4 Harlech Villas
	5 Gledswood Drive
	6 Olivemount Terrace
	7 Glenard Hall
	8 Belfield Close
	9 Roebuck Lawn
	10 Roebuck Crescent
47 C4	1 Ophaly Court
	2 Woodbine Terrace (Dundrum)
	3 Alexandra Villas
	4 Roseville Terrace
	5 Pembroke Cottages (Dundrum)
	6 Pembroke Terrace
	7 Claremont Terrace
	8 Glenville Terrace
	9 St Joseph's Grove
48 D1	1 Merrion View Avenue
	2 Simmonscourt Avenue
	3 Simmon's Court
	4 Ailesbury Close
48 D2	1 Nutley Square
	3 Donnybrook Green
	4 Greenfield Manor

PAGE/GRID REF	STREET NAME
48 D4	1 Edenwood
	2 Sophie Baret Residence
48 E1	1 Merrion Court
	2 Merrion Gates
	3 Strand Lane
48 E2	1 Seafield Park
	2 Bellevue Court
	3 Merrion Crescent
	4 Woodbine House
48 E3	1 The Stables
	2 Mountbrook
48 E4	1 Greygates
	2 Beaufield Mews
	3 Ashurst
	4 Sycamore Crescent
48 F2	1 St Helen's Villas
48 F3	1 Martello Terrace (Booterstown)
	2 Pembroke Cottages (Booterstown)
	3 Willowmount
	4 Cherbury Mews
48 F4	1 St Helier's Copse
	2 Orpen Dale
	3 Park Villas
	4 Cedar Square
	5 Grove House Gardens
	6 Orpen Green
49 A3	1 Newtown Villas
	2 Maretimo Road
	3 Ben Inagh Park
	4 Maretimo Gardens West
	5 Craigmore Gardens
	6 George's Place (Blackrock)
	7 St Anne's Square (Blackrock)
	8 Bath Place
	9 Rockwell Cove Apts
	10 Westfield Terrace
	11 Idrone Mews
	12 Brusna Cottages
	13 Collins Court
	14 Patrick's Row
	15 Eagle Hill
	16 Maretimo Terrace
	17 Maretimo Place
	18 Maretimo Villas
	19 Whelan's Terrace
	20 Carbury Place
	21 Sweetman's Avenue
	22 Lisalea
49 A4	1 Avondale Park (Dun Laoghaire)
	2 Prince Edward Terrace Lower
	3 Prince Edward Terrace Upper
	4 Lindenvale
	5 Twin Cottages
	6 Fieldview Cottages
	7 Cullen's Cottages
	8 Webster's Cottages
	9 Rockville Estate
	10 Avoca Hall
	11 Brookfield Grove
	12 Brookfield Court
49 B3	1 Ardenza Terrace
	2 Tobernea Terrace
	3 Ardenza Park
	4 Seapoint Terrace (Blackrock)
49 B4	1 Montpelier Place
	2 Montpelier Manor
	3 The Willows (Monkstown)
	4 The Maples
	5 The Cedars
	6 The Alders
	7 The Poplars
	8 Stradbrook Gardens

PAGE/GRID REF	STREET NAME
	9 Brighton Terrace
	10 Belgrave Place (Monkstown)
	11 Belgrave Terrace (Monkstown)
	12 Brooklawn Avenue
	13 Brooklawn Wood
	14 Rockford Terrace
	15 Beaupark Downs
	16 Drayton Close
	17 Heathfield
	18 Southdene
	19 Arundel
	20 Stradbrook Hall
	21 The Beeches
	22 Brighton Lane
	23 Knocknagow
49 C4	1 Rosary Gardens West
	2 Barrett Street
	3 Smith's Villas
	4 York Terrace
	5 St Mary's Street
	6 Crofton Terrace
	7 Oakwood
	8 Harbour Terrace
	9 Grosvenor Terrace (Dun Laoghaire)
	10 Clifton Lane
	11 Clifton Avenue
	12 Richmond Green
	13 Clifton Terrace
	14 Alma Place
	15 Seaview Terrace (Dun Laoghaire)
	16 Synnott Terrace
	17 Bentley Villas
	18 St Michael's Terrace (Dun Laoghaire)
	19 St Brendan's Terrace (Dun Laoghaire)
	20 Northcote Terrace
	21 Knapton Court
	22 Knapton Lawn
	23 Northcote Place
	24 Cambridge Terrace (Dun Laoghaire)
	25 Primrose Hill
	26 Mounttown Cottages
	27 Knapton Terrace
	28 Pakenham
	29 Monkstown Gate
	30 Alma Park
	31 Clearwater Cove
	32 Marina House Apts
	33 The Ancorage
	34 Smyth Gardens
50 D4	1 Wellington Street (Dun Laoghaire)
	2 Rosary Gardens East
	3 Desmond Avenue
	4 Wolfe Tone Avenue
	5 Charlemont Avenue
	6 Summerhill Parade (Dun Laoghaire)
	7 Haddington Terrace
	8 Victoria Terrace (Dun Laoghaire)
	9 Marine Terrace
	10 Northumberland Place
	11 Northumberland Park
	12 Dungar Terrace
	13 Stoneview Place
	14 Martello Avenue
	15 Crosthwaite Terrace
	16 Sussex Street
	17 Mansions Court
	18 Charlemont Terrace
	19 Mill Street (Dun Laoghaire)
	20 Anglesea Lane
	21 Park Lane
	22 Clarinda Manor

PAGE/ GRID REF	STREET NAME
	23 Sydenham
	24 Oratory Mews Court
	25 Crofton Terrace
	26 Connaught Place
	27 Albert Terrace
	28 Crofton Mansions
50 E4	1 Mornington Avenue
	2 Martello Terrace (Dun Laoghaire)
	3 Summerhill Court
54 D1	1 Brookfield Court
55 A1	1 Allenton Road
	2 High Street
	3 Avonbeg Court
	4 St Dominic's Court
	5 Old Bawn Court
	6 College View
	7 Lippercross Court
55 A2	1 Summerfield
	2 The Close (Tallaght)
	3 Allenton Crescent
55 B1	1 Bolbrook Drive
	3 Bolbrook Avenue
	4 Bolbrook Close
	5 Avonmore Avenue
	6 Moynihan Court
55 B2	1 Oldcourt Lawn
	2 Killininny Court Apts
	3 Tara Crescent
55 B3	1 Ely Crescent
	2 Ely Grove
	3 Ely Green
	4 Ferncourt Drive
	5 Ferncourt Crescent
	6 Beechdale Close
55 C1	1 Brookmount Lawns
	2 Knocklyon Mews
	3 Homeville Court
	4 Homeville
	5 Balrothery Cottages
55 C2	1 Wood Dale Oak
	2 Woodstown Court
	3 Woodstown Park
	4 Woodstown Close
	5 Woodstown Dale
	6 Woodstown Height
	7 Woodstown Place
	8 Woodstown Vale
	9 Knocklyon Gate Apts
56 D1	1 Coolamber Court
	2 Pine Grove
	3 Ballyroan Court
56 D2	1 Woodstown Abbey
56 E1	1 Orchardton
56 E2	1 Beechview
	2 Cypress Avenue
	3 Larch Drive
	4 Beech Walk
	5 Walnut View
56 F1	1 Sarah Curran Road
	2 St Gatien Road
	3 Fonthill Abbey
	4 Whitechurch Abbey
	5 Edenbrook Court
	6 Forthill Court
	7 Whitechurch Stream
	8 The Beeches
57 A1	1 Marley Villas
	2 Meadow Villas
	3 Barton Court
57 A2	1 Priory Court
	2 The Cherries
	3 Elm Way
57 B1	1 Meadow Avenue
	2 Hawthorn Drive
	3 Mount Albion Road

PAGE/ GRID REF	STREET NAME
	4 Sycamore Drive (Dundrum)
	5 Hillview Glade
	6 Hillview Court
57 B2	1 The Crescent (Ballinteer)
	2 Ballinteer Court
	3 Ballinteer Park
57 C1	1 Westerton Rise
	2 Ashgrove Terrace
	3 Eagle Terrace
	4 Castle Court (Dundrum)
	5 McGrane Court
	6 Ballyolaf Manor
	7 Castleview
	8 Ashgrove Court
	9 Dundrum Gate Apts
57 C2	1 Clonlea Wood
	2 College Park Court
	3 College Park Drive
	4 Delbrook Manor
58 D1	1 Drummartin Crescent
	2 Carrick Lawn
	3 The Pines
58 D2	1 Balally Terrace
	2 Moreen Lawn
	3 Blackthorn Grove
	4 Blackthorn Court
	5 Rathdown Terrace (Sandyford)
	6 Blackthorn Green
	7 Blackthorn Close
	8 Moreen Avenue
	9 Rathdown Grove
58 D3	1 Lamb's Brook
58 E1	1 Dale Close
	2 Stillorgan Court
	3 Stillorgan Heath
	4 Convent Court
	5 Woodthorpe
58 E3	1 Glencairn Garth
	2 Glencairn Heath
58 F1	1 Woodview Court
	2 Ard Lorcain Villas
	3 Grange Cottages
	4 Ulster Terrace (Stillorgan Grove)
	5 Pear Tree Field
	6 Dunstaffnage Hall Apts
58 F2	1 Leopardstown Court
	2 Leopardstown Lawn
	3 Silver Pines
	4 Ellesmere
	5 Ballymoss Parade
	6 Arkle Square
	7 Sir Ivor Mall
F2	8 Fey Yerra
58 F4	1 Ballyogan Road
59 A1	1 Orchard Cottages
	2 Red Brick Terrace
	3 Moore's Cottages
	4 Hawthorn Manor
	5 Rosehill
	6 Ardagh Close
	7 St Augustine's Park
	8 Newtown Park Court
	8 Newtownpark House
	9 Galloping Green
	10 Avila Apts
	11 Newtownpark House
59 A2	1 Knocksinna Grove
	2 Knocksinna Court
	3 New Park Lodge
	4 Foxrock Mount
	5 Chestnut Park
	6 Willow Park
	7 Sycamore Grove
	8 Whitethorn Walk
	9 Birch Dale

PAGE/ GRID REF	STREET NAME
	10 The Coutryard
	11 Kelston Hall
59 A3	1 Brighton Cottages
	2 Kilteragh Pines
	3 Avalon
	4 Brighton Lodge
	5 The Gables
	6 Westminster Court
59 B1	1 Windsor Court (Dun Laoghaire)
	2 Grange Grove
	3 Oliver Plunkett Villas
	4 Stradbrook Hill
	5 Springhill Cottages
	6 Grange Cottages
	7 Abbey Court (Monkstown)
	8 Abbey Road
	9 Faber Grove
	10 Deans Court
	11 Devon Close
	12 Monkstown Square
59 B3	1 Kerrymount Close
	2 Hainault Grove
	3 Hainault Lawn
	4 Monaloe Crescent
	5 Clonkeen Lawn
	6 Monaloe Court
59 C1	1 Oliver Plunkett Square
	2 Patrician Park
	3 Mounttown Park
	4 Woodlawn Park (Dun Laoghaire)
	5 Oliver Plunkett Terrace
	6 Fitzgerald Park
	7 St Patrick's Terrace (Kill O' the Grange)
	8 Dunedin Drive
	9 St Patrick's Close
	10 Highthorn Woods
	11 Aspen Park
	12 Birch Dale
	13 Willow Grove
	14 Carriglea Court
	15 Rollins Villas
59 C2	1 Hillview Cottages
	2 Whitethorn Walk
	3 Sycamore Court
	4 Hazel Lawn
	5 Eaglewood
	5a Eaglewood House
	5b Eaglewood Mews
	6 Rochestown House Apts
59 C3	1 Little Meadow
	3 Cabinteely Park
	4 O'Shea's Cottages
	5 Cabinteely Court
59 C4	1 Kilbogget Villas
60 D1	1 O'Donnell Gardens
	2 Royal Terrace North
	3 Myrtle Avenue
	4 Emmet Street (Sallynoggin)
	5 Eden Villas
	6 Laurel Hill
	7 Granite Hall
	8 Magenta Place
	9 Marlborough Park
	10 Royal Terrace Lane
	11 Beechwood Grove
	12 Rollins Court
	13 Seven Houses
	14 The Glen
	15 Glengara Close
	16 Silchester Wood
	17 Carlisle Terrace
	18 Durham Place
	19 Rus-in-Urbe Terrace
60 D2	1 Honey Park
	2 Thomastown Crescent
	3 Pearse Close

PAGE/ GRID REF	STREET NAME
60 D3	1 Auburn Road (Cabinteely)
	2 Granville Crescent
60 D4	1 Annabeg
	2 Meadow Court
	3 Oakton Green
60 E1	1 Wilmont Avenue
	2 Congress Gardens
	3 Albert Park
	4 Claremont Villas
	5 St Paul's Terrace
	6 St Peter's Terrace (Dun Laoghaire)
	7 Findlater Street (Dun Laoghaire)
	8 Devitt Villas
	9 Dixon Villas
	10 Glen Terrace
	11 Glasthule Buildings
	12 Hastings Terrace
	13 Brighton Terrace (Dun Laoghaire)
	14 Lawson Terrace
	15 Killiney Terrace
	16 Munster Terrace
	17 Neptune Terrace
	18 Cliff Terrace
	19 Beaufort
	20 Ballygihen Villas
	21 Seabank Court
	22 St Helen's
	23 Chester Square
	24 Dundela Haven
	25 Arkendale Woods
	26 Arkendale Court
	27 Adelaide Villas
	28 Adelaide Terrace (Dun Laoghaire)
	29 Atmospheric Road
	30 St Margarets Close
	31 Avondale Court
60 E2	1 Barnhill Lawn
	2 Killiney Towers
	3 Barnhill Park
	4 Kilcolman Court
	5 Edwin Court
	6 Fairlawns
	7 Urney Grove
	8 Malborough Court
60 E3	1 Hill Cottages
	2 Mount Auburn
	3 Talbot Road
	4 Talbot Lane
60 E4	1 Oakton Court
	2 Dale View Park
	3 Mountain Villa
	4 The Nurseries
	5 Mountain View Road
	6 Rainsford Lane
	7 Killiney Avenue
	8 Firgrove
60 F1	1 Carysfort Drive
	2 Ormeau Drive
	3 The Paddocks
	4 South Winds
	5 Ulverton Close
	6 Rocklands
	7 Bayswater Terrace
	8 Bullock Steps
	9 Liscanor
	10 White's Villas
	11 Mayville Terrace
	12 Castlelands Grove
	13 Ulverton Court
	14 Pilot View
	15 Bailey View
	16 Castlelands
	17 Churchill Mews
	18 Bartra Rock (Apts.)

PAGE/GRID REF			STREET NAME
60	**F2**	1	St Patrick's Avenue (Dalkey)
		2	Railway Road
		3	Anastasia Lane
		4	St Patrick's Square
		5	Cats Ladder
		6	Dalkey Grove
		7	Barnhill Grove
		8	St Patrick's Road (Dalkey)
		9	Monte Vella
		10	Summerfield Close
		11	Victoria Terrace (Dalkey)
		12	Sorrento Drive
		13	Sorrento Lawn
		14	Coliemore Villas
		15	Seafield Terrace
		16	Temple Terrace
		17	Grosvenor Terrace (Dalkey)
		18	Charlotte Terrace
		19	Meany Avenue
		20	Desmond Cottages
		21	Ardbrugh Villas
		22	Burmah Close
		23	Dalkey Court
		24	Kilbegnet Close
		25	Sorrento Close
		26	Craiglands
		27	Ullardmor
		28	Sorrento Mews
		29	Sorrento Court
		30	Sorrento Heights
		31	Ardbrugh Close
		32	Castle Cove
		33	Torca View
64	**D1**	1	The Oaks
		2	Cherry Court
		3	Cois Coillte
		4	Holly Court
64	**D2**	1	Stonebridge Lane
64	**E1**	1	Killiney Court
		2	Killiney Oaks
		3	The Sycamores
		4	The Elms
		5	St Aubyn's Court
		6	Ennel Court
		7	Sheelin Grove
		8	Glencarr Court
		9	Domville Grove
		10	Streamville Court
		11	Glen Druid
		12	Bayview Glade
		13	Sheelin Hill
		14	Sheelin Walk
		15	Sheelin Drive

PAGE/GRID REF			STREET NAME
		16	The Larches (Abberley)
		17	The Oaks (Abberley)
		18	The Rowans (Abberley)
		19	The Willows (Abberley)
		20	The Hawthorns (Abberley)
		21	The Cedars (Abberley)
		22	The Beeches (Abberley)
		23	River Close
64	**E2**	1	River Lane (Loughlinstown)
		2	Clonasleigh
		3	Beechfield Haven
		4	Athgoe Drive
		5	Maryland
		6	Station Road
		7	Windrush
		8	Shanganagh Wood
		9	Thomond
64	**E3**	1	Guilford Terrace
		2	Stonebridge Close
64	**E4**	1	Kiltuck Park
67	**B1**	1	Raverty Villas
		2	St Peter's Terrace
		3	Myrtle Grove
		4	Arbutus Grove
		5	Thornhill View
		6	Fernbrook
		7	Roseville Court
67	**B2**	1	Auburn Villas
		2	Glenburgh Terrace
		4	Ashley Heights
		5	Dargle Crescent
		6	Copper Beech Grove
		9	Sutton Road
		10	Dargan Street
		11	Fairgreen Road
		12	Pearse Road
		13	Mountpleasant Villas
		15	Diamond Terrace
		16	Parkview Terrace
		17	Sutton Villas
		18	Esmonde Terrace
		19	Old Ravenswell Row
		20	New Ravenswell Row
		21	Vale view
		22	Old Rathmore Terrace
		23	New Rathmore Terrace
		25	Gertrude Terrace
		26	Herbert View
		27	Rivervale Apts
67	**B3**	1	Ballynoe Court
		2	Rathclaren
		3	St Clair's Terrace
		4	Killarney Court
		5	Kilgrastor Court

PAGE/GRID REF			STREET NAME
		6	Glenbrook
67	**B4**	1	Ballywaltrim Cottages
		2	Ballymorris
67	**C1**	1	St Patrick's Square
		2	Martello Terrace
67	**C2**	1	Sidmonton Square
		3	Eglington Road
		4	Rosslyn Grove
		5	James Connolly Square
		6	Sidmonton Place
		7	Novara Park
		8	St Cronan's Road
		9	Cill Manntan Park
		10	Kilmantain Place
		11	Father Colohan Terrace
		12	Royal Marine Terrace
		13	Milton Terrace
		14	St Kevin's Terrace
		15	Darley Cottages
		16	Brabazon Cottages
		17	St Laurence's Terrace
		18	St Columcille's Terrace
		20	Seapoint Villas
		21	Dunbur Terrace
		22	Elmgrove Terrace
		23	St Aidan's Terrace
		24	Seapoint Terrace
		25	Goldsmith Terrace
		26	Prince of Wales Terrace
		27	Novara Terrace
		28	Waverley Terrace (Bray)
		29	Westview Terrace
		30	Augustine Villas
		31	Trafalgar Terrace
		32	Fairgreen Terrace
		33	St Brigid's Terrace
		34	Loretto Avenue
		35	Loretto Terrace
		36	Sidmonton Gardens
		37	Rosslyn
		38	Shankill View
		39	Florence Terrace
		40	Florence Villas
		41	Carlton Terrace
		42	Carlton Villas
		43	Alexander Terrace
		44	Belton Terrace
		45	Church Terrace
		46	Old Brighton Terrace
		47	New Brighton Terrace
		48	Killarney Villas
		49	Market Square
		50	Fairgreen Court
		51	Bayview
		52	Westbourne Terrace

PAGE/GRID REF			STREET NAME
		53	King Edward Court
		54	Loretto Villas
		55	Marie Villas
		56	Wellington Court
		57	Novara Mews
		58	Vevay Crescent
67	**C3**	1	Cherry Tree Drive
		2	Roselawn Park
		4	Woodview Drive
		5	Kennedy Park
		8	Newcourt Villas
		9	O'Byrne Villas
		10	Stoneylea Terrace
		11	Mountain View Apartments
		14	Putland Villas
		15	Oldcourt Terrace
		16	Lauderdale Terrace
		17	Mayfield Terrace
		18	Vevay Villas
		19	Orchard Terrace
		20	Bray Head Terrace
		21	Sugarloaf Terrace
67	**C4**	3	Bentley Avenue
		6	St Mary's Terrace
68	**D2**	1	Trosyrafon Terrace
		2	Montebello Terrace
		3	Esplanade Terrace
		4	Brennans Terrace
		5	Sidbury Court
		6	Dargan Court
		7	Warburton Terrace
		8	Sloan Terrace
		9	Belgrave Villas
		10	Belgrave Terrace
		11	Claremount Terrace
		12	Richmond Terrace
		13	Milward Terrace
		14	Brennans Parade
		15	Claddagh Terrace
		16	Marlborough Terrace
		17	Marine Terrace
		18	Jones Terrace
		19	Mount Norris Villas
		20	St Marys Terrace
		21	Fitzwilliam Terrace
		22	New Grange Park
		23	Convent View
68	**D3**	1	Eaton Court
		2	Meretimo Villas
		3	Grosvenor Avenue
		4	Brookfield Avenue
		5	Sidmonton Court
		6	Sydenham Villas